TURNER
AND THE SUBLIME

ANDREW WILTON

TURNER
AND THE SUBLIME

Published by
British Museum Publications
for
The Art Gallery of Ontario
The Yale Center for British Art
The Trustees of the British Museum

The Art Gallery of Ontario is pleased to acknowledge the generous support of the following companies in connection with this exhibition:

Allstate Foundation of Canada
Dominion Securities Limited
Wood Gundy Limited

Dates of the exhibition:
    Art Gallery of Ontario, Toronto
    1 November 1980 – 4 January 1981

    Yale Center for British Art, New Haven
    11 February – 19 April 1981

    The British Museum, London
    15 May – 20 September 1981

British Library Cataloguing in Publication Data
Wilton, Andrew
    Turner and the Sublime.
    1. Turner, Joseph Mallord William – Exhibitions
    2. Sublime, The, in art
    3. British Museum. Department of Prints and
    Drawings – Catalogs
    741'.092'4   NC242.T9
ISBN 0-7141-0778-6 (UK cased)
ISBN 0-7141-0779-4 (UK paper)
ISBN 0-930606-22-1 (CANADA paper)
ISBN 0-930606-23-X (USA paper)
ISBN 0-930606-24-8 (USA cased)

British Museum Publications Ltd
6 Bedford Square
London WC1B 3RA

Designed by Patrick Yapp

Text set in Monophoto Van Dijck 203
Printed in England by Jolly & Barber Ltd, Rugby, Warwickshire
Colour plates printed by Balding and Mansell Ltd, London and Wisbech

COVER ILLUSTRATION: J. M. W. Turner, *The Upper Fall of the Reichenbach: rainbow* (Yale Center for British Art, Paul Mellon Collection)

CONTENTS

AUTHOR'S ACKNOWLEDGMENTS

This book and the exhibition it accompanies owe their inception to the enthusiasm and energy of Katharine Jordan Lochnan, Curator of Prints and Drawings at the Art Gallery of Ontario; I am very grateful to her and to the Art Gallery's Director, William Withrow, for inviting me to organise the exhibition and for encouragement and help throughout the undertaking. The work could never have been completed in the time available without the unstinted support of my own Director, Edmund Pillsbury, who has been exceptionally indulgent in enabling me to write the text with the minimum of interruptions. John Gere, Keeper of Prints and Drawings at the British Museum, has likewise made my task as pleasant as possible by his amiable co-operation.

Several people have helped me considerably by being willing to discuss the subjects of Turner and the Sublime, and I am grateful to all of them for their ideas. David Bindman, Joan Friedman and Stephen Parks drew my attention to items which I have found particularly useful. Walter Amstutz of de Clivo Press, Zürich, has kindly made available two colour transparencies, originally made for his *Turner in Switzerland* (1976).

Where the practical details of assembling material and preparing it for the press are concerned, my debts are numerous. I should particularly like to thank Angela Bailey, Dolores Gall, Michael Marsland, Patrick Noon, Joe Szaszfai, Christopher White and Lib Woodworth for all their efforts in making and collecting photographs, typing and reading the text, and providing moral support under pressure. Stephanie Kosarin, Ursula Dreibholz and Mark Walas assembled, cleaned and mounted items at Yale, and at the British Museum Ann Forsdyke, Martyn Tillier and Reginald Williams have been constantly ready to deal with problems as they arose. Finally, I must express my gratitude to the staff of British Museum Publications for their efficient dispatch of the book itself; especially Michael Hoare, Celia Clear and Susan Leiper.

ANDREW WILTON

PREFACE

This exhibition explores one aspect of Turner's art, in watercolours, drawings and prints. The Sublime as an aesthetic concept has been discussed by numerous writers, and Turner's own interest in the theory as propounded in the eighteenth century by Edmund Burke and others has often been noted. But far from being bound by any theoretical conceptions, he used these as the starting-point for a whole series of technical and artistic innovations. Turner made many very large watercolours which emulated the grandeur and importance of oil-paintings. Several of these, together with their no less impressive full-scale preparatory studies, are included in this exhibition, some being shown for the first time. The most significant paintings in the genre of the Sublime are represented by fine impressions of prints, often engraved under the close supervision of Turner himself.

There have been many exhibitions of Turner's art in recent years, but none has attempted to define his relationship to theories of the Sublime. Andrew Wilton's introduction discusses Turner's training and early career in the light of traditional attitudes to the Sublime, and goes on to consider the mature Turner's use of them for his own ends. The selection of works is mostly drawn from the rich resources of the Turner Bequest, at present deposited in the British Museum, but also includes watercolours and a large group of prints from the Paul Mellon Collection at Yale, together with some works belonging to private owners and to the University of Toronto. We are very grateful to the Trustees of the British Museum and other lenders for their co-operation and generous support. We are also greatly indebted to Andrew Wilton, author of the excellent catalogue, and Katharine Jordan Lochnan, Curator of Prints and Drawings at the Art Gallery of Ontario, who jointly conceived the exhibition and brought it to fulfilment.

J. A. GERE,
Keeper, Department of Prints and Drawings, The British Museum

EDMUND P. PILLSBURY,
Director, Yale Center for British Art

W. J. WITHROW,
Director, Art Gallery of Toronto

The fact is, that sublimity is not a specific term – not a term descriptive of the effect of a particular class of ideas. Anything which elevates the mind is sublime, and elevation of mind is produced by the contemplation of greatness of any kind; but chiefly, of course, by the greatness of the noblest things. Sublimity is, therefore, only another word for the effect of greatness upon the feelings – greatness, whether of matter, space, power, virtue, or beauty: and there is perhaps no desirable quality of a work of art, which, in its perfection, is not, in some way or degree, sublime.

RUSKIN, *Modern Painters*, 1843, Book I, Section II, chapter 3

CHAPTER ONE

THE CLASSIC SUBLIME

All the different Degrees of Goodness in Painting may be reduc'd to these three General Classes. The Mediocre, or Indifferently Good, the Excellent, and the Sublime. The first is of a large Extent; the second much Narrower; and the Last still more so . . . I take it to consist of some few of the Highest Degrees of Excellence in those kinds, and Parts of Painting which are excellent; the Sublime therefore must be Marvellous, and Surprising. It must strike vehemently upon the Mind, and Fill, and Captivate it irresistibly.

JONATHAN RICHARDSON: *The Connoisseur*, 1719

There is, indeed, an originality of so high a class, that too few are the minds able to comprehend its excellence: I mean that which shows itself in the highest department of art, which we term the grand style. Of this style it may be asserted, that, although it appeal to us with great and commanding powers, though it convey a sentiment the most awful and impressive, yet it speaks a language so little cultivated or even rudely known, that none but minds the most highly enlightened can be made fully sensible of its essence.

JAMES NORTHCOTE: *The Artist*, 1807

In 1840, when James Fenimore Cooper was introducing his readers to one of his romances of the lakes and forests of North America, he began with this pronouncement: 'The sublimity connected with vastness is familiar to every eye.' He did not mean simply that it is pleasant to stand at a suitable vantage-point and enjoy a good view. Looking at landscape in the early nineteenth century was more complicated than that, a process accompanied by a host of mental events that took the sightseer far beyond the material circumstances of the scene – beyond, even, the confines of this world altogether: 'The most abstruse, the most far-reaching, perhaps the most chastened of the poet's thoughts,' Cooper goes on, 'crowd on the imagination as he gazes into the illimitable void. The expanse of the ocean is seldom seen by the novice with indifference; and the mind, even in the obscurity of night, finds a parallel to that grandeur, which seems inseparable from images that the senses cannot compass.'[1]

By invoking the notion of the sublime, Cooper was giving his novel a frame of reference that presupposed an almost unlimited extension of ideas by association. He was encouraging his reader to consider the story in the most serious light as a profoundly significant statement about life and the conditions of human existence. Although he begins by speaking of vastness, he quickly progresses to more general ideas, of grandeur, of illimitability, of obscurity; ideas so abstract, indeed, that we may wonder what exactly they imply.

Cooper is using the word 'sublime' in a sense very distant from its modern colloquial one, as in phrases like 'sublimely unconscious of danger' or 'sublime indifference to the feelings of others'; though these applications of the word do carry a suggestion of superiority, even if only the blissful superiority of ignorance, which retains some vestigial hint of the full meaning of the term. Not that the expression in its full sense (or senses) is entirely obsolete now; but it has probably lost much of the force that it used to possess, if only because many of its applications assume an attitude to the world, and to its creator, which is now moribund or at least dormant.

Nowadays it is usually literary historians who talk about the Sublime; and they do so very much in an archaeological spirit. But in the early nineteenth century, and for at least two centuries before that, the term was often used to express a whole range of important ideas, and was endlessly debated and redefined by scholars and critics. They were ready with long and elaborately categorised interpretations to demonstrate that in this one word all that is most significant to the human mind and consciousness is neatly packed. Not so neatly that they could not argue about details; but the main points remained settled for most of the period. Naturally the meaning of the word changed to some extent. We shall be examining some of the ways in which it did so. But one thing everyone was sure about: the sublime 'produces a sort of internal elevation and expansion; it raises the mind much above its ordinary state; and fills it with a degree of wonder and astonishment, which is certainly delightful; but it is altogether of the serious kind: a degree of awfulness and solemnity, even approaching to severity, commonly attends it when at its height; very distinguishable from the more gay and brisk emotions raised by beautiful objects.'[2]

The reference to 'beautiful objects' betrays that this quotation is of relatively late date. For by tradition the sublime had been discussed primarily in connection with literature. It was in the context of rhetoric and poetry that it was treated as early as the first century AD by an unidentified writer in Greek who is known as Longinus, and who contributed the first substantial definition of the word.

'Longinus observes,' says an eighteenth-century commentator, 'that the effect of the sublime is *to lift up the soul; to exalt it into ecstasy; so that, participating, as it were, of the splendors of the divinity, it becomes filled with joy and exultation; as if it had itself conceived the lofty sentiments which it heard.*'[3] 'All sublime feelings,' the same writer says elsewhere, 'are, according to the principles of Longinus, . . . feelings of exultation and expansion of the mind, tending to rapture and enthusiasm; and whether they be excited by sympathy with external objects, or arise from the internal speculations of the mind, they are still of the same nature. In grasping at infinity,' he continues, offering an exact philosophical parallel to the thoughts of Cooper that we have already considered, 'the mind exercises the powers . . . of multiplying without end; and, in so doing, it expands and exalts itself, by which means its feelings and sentiments become sublime.'[4]

These remarks occur in Richard Payne Knight's *Analytical Inquiry into the Principles of Taste*, published in 1805. The word 'taste' itself seems to have enjoyed a more complex use in Payne Knight's time than it does now. We should hardly include in our own discussions of taste such matters as the higher contemplations of philosophers or scientists, but these activities certainly implied, to the eighteenth century, an elevated state of the 'affections' of the mind, and therefore a superior 'taste'. Payne Knight was far from unusual in grouping the sublime with other topics under the general heading of 'taste'. Most accounts of it published in Britain occur in general essays on aesthetics, or in philosophical treatises. The topic was well suited to the new intelligentsia of eighteenth-century England, a class of educated and thoughtful people eager to get to grips with important ideas, to assemble, regulate and assess the mass of information that was becoming increasingly accessible to them about the arts and sciences, the historical past and the ever-expanding universe. It is no accident that the whole fashion for discussions of taste, including the concept of the sublime, was instigated by a popular journal – Joseph Addison's *Spectator*.

In eleven numbers of June and July 1712 Addison published a long essay *On the Pleasures of the Imagination*, a masterly example of the educational popularising of serious ideas that he excelled in. Nearly all the matter of the later expositors and quibblers can be found, in more or less complete and lucid form, in Addison's essay. The word 'sublime' itself hardly occurs – though it does so once, in a significant context, as we shall see – but all the same, Addison manages to cover most of the ground trodden by subsequent writers. These, although they borrowed extensively from Addison, modelled themselves on the more august precedent set by John Locke in his *Essay Concerning Human Understanding*, which had appeared in 1689, offering new insight into the nature of our perception of the external world. They were anxious to apply its methods, and even some of its concepts, to their own preoccupations; and they tended to set their meditations in a broad context which ranged through all the branches of knowledge.

The purpose of this book is to show not only that the sublime was a philosophical concept rigorously and repeatedly analysed by theorists, but that it was felt to have a vital relevance to the creative practice of artists as well as writers in the period immediately before and during Turner's lifetime (1775–1851). In particular, we shall, I hope, see that Turner himself, who is often thought of as a painter sublimely free (I use the phrase deliberately) of the fetters of eighteenth-century theory, was fully aware of the idea and its implications, and indeed built his art upon a foundation, and in a philosophical context, established by the theorists of the sublime.

Although Turner was able to put the theory to new and vital use, by his time it was, as we have already seen, thickly overgrown with the learned argument and dry exegesis of scholars. We must try to disentangle the principle themes from the muddle they have left. It is logical and convenient to begin with Addison. He says that pleasure proceeds 'from the sight of what is great, uncommon, or beautiful'.[5] Note that he is explicitly concerned with pleasures perceived by the *eye*. This may be why he does not use the term 'sublime', which at the period still applied more usually to works of literature than to visual things.[6] He distinguishes between the pleasures of the imagination and those of the understanding, and includes under both heads what was later to be termed the sublime. 'One of the final causes of our delight in anything that is great may be this,' he says. 'The Supreme Author of our being has so formed the soul of man, that nothing but Himself can be its last, adequate, and proper happiness. Because, therefore, a great part of our happiness must arise from the contemplation of his being, that he might give our souls a just relish for such a contemplation, he has made them naturally delight in the apprehension of what is great or unlimited. Our admiration, which is a very pleasing motion of the mind, immediately rises at the consideration of any object that takes up a great deal of room in the fancy, and, by consequence, will improve into the highest pitch of astonishment and devotion when we contemplate his nature . . .'[7]

This leads Addison into a somewhat circular argument to the effect that God has formed man in such a way that he finds pleasure in external objects which were created to be pleasurable – it is by a dispensation of God, and not through our own discrimination, that we perceive beauty in objects that are in any case beautiful. But the element of religious feeling contained in the notion of the sublime is very important. In words that recall those of some of his own hymns, Addison speaks of the pleasures of contemplating the grandeur of space:

> When we survey the whole earth at once, and the several planets that lie within its neighbourhood, we are filled with a pleasing astonishment, to see so many worlds, hanging one above another, and sliding round their axles in such an amazing pomp and solemnity. If, after this, we contemplate those wild fields of ether, that reach in height as far as from Saturn to the fixed stars, and run abroad almost to an inifinitude, our imagination finds its capacity filled with so immense a prospect, and puts itself upon the stretch to comprehend it. But if we rise yet higher, and consider the fixed stars as so many vast oceans of flame, that are each of them attended with a different set of planets, and still discover new firmaments and new lights that are sunk further into those unfathomable depths of ether, so as not to be seen by the strongest of our telescopes, we are lost in such a labyrinth of suns and worlds, and confounded with the immensity and magnificence of nature.[8]

The sublime of science and the sublime of theology here unite in a supreme ecstasy of contemplation. Later writers were to point out that the mere mathematical idea of numerical ascent carried with it sublime connotations.[9] But the impalpable 'immensity and magnificence of nature' is more commonly brought forward as the focus for ideas that are fundamentally religious.

The overt religious associations of the term 'sublime' are perhaps what differentiate its eighteenth-century usage most sharply from that of our own day. A characteristic example of its occurrence in the daily language of that period is Mr Allworthy's conception of the virtue of Charity, in *Tom Jones* (1749): 'that sublime Christian-like disposition, that vast elevation of thought, in purity approaching to angelic perfection, to be attained, expressed, and felt only by grace'.[10] The vocabulary is almost hackneyed: vastness, elevation, purity, perfection – these words recur constantly in connection with the sublime, and even when the word 'sublime' itself is not mentioned, we can infer its presence in the writer's mind as the ultimate designation of such ideas. Often a term such as 'grandeur' is substituted; but as Hugh Blair decided, 'Grandeur and Sublimity are terms synonymous, or nearly so. If there be any distinction between them, it arises from Sublimity's expressing Grandeur in the highest degree.'[11]

Whatever the exact term used, the quality we are discussing was felt to be a very positive one. The sense of elevation towards the supreme Good, towards God, is frequently to be understood. The enlargement and enrichment of the mind in contemplating the wonders of creation is thought of as a noble, uplifting experience. And the very ineffability of the ideas involved led men to attach importance to those works of literature in which great writers had succeeded in evoking the limitless splendour of God or his works. The Bible, of course, had a special advantage in this respect: not only did it contain some of the most impressive and stirring passages of human history, it was actually inspired directly by the Deity, and so the very idea of it was sublime. In addition, it was a work of venerable antiquity, dating from the period before even Greek civilisation, the period that Jacob Bryant and William Blake (1757–1827) thought of as the 'heroic age of the world' when men were nobler and altogether greater of achievement than they are now. Coleridge called the Bible 'the sublimest, and probably the oldest, book on earth'.[12]

But there was another claimant to similar distinction: Homer. It is true that Homer could not pretend to be God, but he wrote much better Greek than the authors of the New Testament, and that in itself was a favourable point. Although Milton ranked a close second to Homer as a poet of the sublime, he suffered the great disadvantage of having written his greatest work – *Paradise Lost* – in English. Conscious of this, he attempted to make his own language approximate as nearly as possible to Latin, but still, as Addison said, 'his Paradise Lost falls short of the Aeneid or the Iliad . . . rather from the fault of the language than from any defect of the author. So divine a poem in English is like a stately palace built of brick, where one may see architecture in as great a perfection as one of marble, though the materials are of a coarser nature.'[13] But then again, Milton had the edge over Homer in respect to subject-matter. The protagonists of his epic are not the imaginary gods of ancient Greece but the True God and his Angels, fallen and otherwise. People were even prepared to believe, or pretend to believe, that *Paradise Lost* was an apocryphal addition to the canonical Bible. Jonathan Richardson (1665–1745), who, though a painter by profession, was a most sophisticated connoisseur and critic, quoted lines from the poem which he claimed were 'as great as ever entered into the heart of man not supernaturally inspired, if at least this poet was not so'.[14] It will be useful to have a sample of Milton's most elevated verse for reference, and Richardson's selection is a representative one:

> On heavenly ground they stood, and from the shore
> They view'd the vast immeasurable abyss,
> Outrageous as a sea, dark, wasteful, wild,

Up from the bottom turn'd by furious winds,
And surging waves, as mountains, to assault
Heaven's height, and with the centre mix the pole.
     Silence, ye troubled waves, and thou deep, peace,
Said then th'omnific Word, your discord end.
     Nor staid; but on the wings of Cherubim
Uplifted in paternal glory rode
Far into Chaos, and the world unborn;
For Chaos heard his voice: him all his train
Follow'd in bright procession, to behold
Creation, and the wonders of his might.
Then staid the fervid wheels, and in his hand
He took the golden compasses, prepar'd
In God's eternal store, to circumscribe
The universe, and all created things:
One foot he center'd, and the other turn'd
Round through the vast profundity obscure,
And said, Thus far extend, thus far thy bounds,
This be thy just circumference, O world.[15]

The salient matter here is the image of God creating the universe out of chaos. Illustrative detail such as the 'surging waves as mountains' is minimal: Milton contrives to evoke in an extraordinarily concrete way what is essentially vague, imponderable. This was his great merit for the eighteenth century, as indeed it is perhaps still for us. Commentators made much of the fact that it was the peculiar flexibility of poetry that made such feats possible. The imagination is stimulated more fully by words which suggest vast ideas than by specific details of the appearance of things. It was for this reason, primarily, that painting could only struggle into second place against poetry in the attempt to produce art that was sublime. Artists were well aware of the problem; but they could point to some triumphant successes. The Milton passage just quoted leads us immediately to one great visual equivalent: Michelangelo's own account of the Creation on the Sistine Chapel ceiling. Everyone agreed that here was a truly sublime work of visual art. In it Michelangelo found an appropriate language in which to express the grand ideas embodied in his subject: and in a sense there is a perfectly reasonable parallel to be drawn between his style and Milton's. Both avoid superfluous detail; they deal in large terms and bold, heroic gestures. Colour is definitely subordinated to grand design – these technical terms of painting apply by natural analogy to Milton; when colour does obtrude it is to suggest the exalted status of the characters or the primitive contrasts of glorious light and brooding chaos. The rhythms of both are stately and sweeping. We might recall also the famous comparison made by Wölfflin between Michelangelo's *Expulsion of Adam and Eve from the Garden of Eden* (FIG. 1) and the music of Beethoven: he describes the compositional hiatus between the angel on the left and the fleeing couple on the right as being like 'one of Beethoven's pauses'.[16] The atmosphere of Beethoven's music is very much the atmosphere of the sublime: Berlioz, himself much concerned with the communication of grand ideas, sets this Beethovenian atmosphere firmly in its sublime context in describing the slow movement of the Fourth Symphony: 'This movement,' he says, 'seems as if it had been sadly murmured by the Archangel Michael on some day when, overcome by a feeling of melancholy, he contemplated the universe from the threshold of the Empyrean.'[17] The contemplations and tribulations of the titanic hero are a subject to which we shall have to return in due course.

To grasp the way in which Michelangelo was 'placed' by the eighteenth-century mind in its scheme of things we should turn to the thoughts of Sir Joshua Reynolds

FIG. I

Antonio Capellan *after* Michelangelo, *The Expulsion of Adam and Eve from the Garden*, Sistine Chapel ceiling, Rome, engraving. British Museum, London

(1723–92). Reynolds is the epitome of the eighteenth-century English intelligence: learned, articulate, a believer in progress by means of justly formulated rules, and in the cautious but purposeful evaluation of all knowledge so that it can be used and reused by others. He is an excellent example of the sorting, sifting mind of the eighteenth century. As the first President of the Royal Academy he was also the figurehead of the professional and educational movement which advanced the visual arts so impressively in the period. When he painted an allegorical figure of *Theory* (seated on clouds and holding a scroll inscribed with the word *Nature*) to decorate the entrance hall of the new Academy building, he nicely summed up the main bent of his own mind and those of most of his colleagues and thinking contemporaries. He himself said: 'I had something of an habit of investigation, and a disposition to reduce all that I observed and felt in my own mind, to method and system.'[18] His discourses given annually to the students of the Academy Schools are a compendium of intelligent theory and criticism which still commands the respect of artists and historians, even if most of his ideas have been out of fashion for nearly a century. For him the creation of the Royal Academy was a crucial step on the road toward a finer national art, and this of course meant an art that dealt with the highest and noblest ideas. He lost no time in stating his position; in the first Discourse, of 1769, he spoke of Raphael: 'Raffaelle, it is true, had not the advantage of studying in an Academy; but all Rome, and the works of Michael Angelo in particular, were to him an Academy. On the sight of the Capella Sistina, he immediately from a dry, Gothick, and even insipid manner, which attends to the minute accidental discriminations of particular and individual objects, assumed that grand style of painting, which improves partial representation by the general and invariable ideas of nature.'[19]

The 'sublime of Michael Angelo' became a constant referent throughout the Discourses, and, as is well known, Reynolds devoted the whole of his last Discourse to a discussion of the Master. Again, we notice a tendency to attribute supernatural powers to the great artist: Reynolds called Michelangelo 'that truly divine man'[20] and spoke of his style as 'the language of the Gods'.[21] When he sought a comparison for his achievement he was compelled to refer to Homer, and asked his audience whether the sensations excited by looking at 'the personification of the Supreme Being in the centre of the Capella Sistina, or the figures of the Sybils which surround that chapel, to which we may add the statue of Moses' are not the same as the sensations excited by 'the most sublime passages of Homer'. In fact, Reynolds argues, 'without [Michelangelo's] assistance we never could have been convinced, that Painting was capable of producing an adequate representation of the persons and actions of the heroes of the Iliad'.[22]

This 'grand style' to which Reynolds so earnestly and insistently set all the Royal Academy students was, then, essentially an art of illustration – a visual equivalent of the greatest episodes of literature or history. It was a style almost wholly concerned with the communication of exalted ideas by means of the depiction of the human figure.

The familiar dictum of Horace, that poetry should reproduce the qualities of painting – *Ut pictura poesis*[23] – was acknowledged as a solemn and essential truth, but the position was reversed: it was now the duty of painting to fulfil the conditions of poetry, which had proved itself capable of expressing the highest flights of the imagination. Even an enthusiastic and knowledgeable collector of paintings and drawings like Payne Knight felt that the visual arts laboured under a disadvantage: 'The means . . . which sculpture and painting have of expressing the energies and affections of the mind are so much more limited, than those of poetry, that their comparative influence upon the passions is small; few persons looking for anything more in a picture or a statue, than mere exactitude of imitation, or exertions of technical skill; and when more is attempted, it never approaches to that of poetry; the artist being not only confined to one point of time, but to the mere exterior expressions of feature and gesture . . .'[24]

It was taken for granted that the subject-matter of both arts was identical, even though the medium differed. And the poetry that mattered was epic, treating of gods and heroes, according to the rule laid down by Aristotle in his *Poetics*: only by choosing characters distinctive and exalted among human beings could the poet achieve universality.[25] In Dryden's opinion, 'A Heroic Poem, truly such, is undoubtedly the greatest work which the soul of man is capable to perform.'[26] So painting too should be concerned with the communication of exalted ideas by means of the depiction of the human figure in dramatic action. Henry Fuseli (1741–1825), one of the Academy's early Professors of Painting, explicitly equated the 'delineation of character' in painting with 'the drama'.[27] Even when an artist aimed at less than the heroic sublime he was well advised to take his subject-matter from the best literature. Shakespeare was considered a proper source even if he was not purely a sublime writer: the many subjects taken from his works for the ambitious 'Shakspeare Gallery' of Alderman Boydell[28] reflect Johnson's view that Shakespeare was most himself in comedy. But comedy too involved human nature and the study of psychology, concerns that the serious artist could not avoid. Johnson summed up Shakespeare's significance for the period when he spoke of him as 'the first considerable author of sublime or familiar dialogue in our language'.[29] Fuseli chose subjects of fantasy and fairyland for many of his contributions to Boydell's Gallery, but the vivid drawings that he made for his own pleasure are scenes of violence from the histories, or of horror and pathos from Hamlet and Macbeth. They alternate with Homeric subjects in his work as well as in that of his contemporaries. Other literary sources were selected with an eye to similar harvests of grand drama. One of the most popular in the 1770s was Ossian, the 'Northern Homer', whose sagas of the ancient Gaelic heroes were 'translated' and published by James Macpherson in the 1760s. Although 'Ossian' was later shown to be a hoax, his rambling, misty and violent stories of love, death and witchery in the bleak northern wilds were irresistible to artists.[30] Macpherson's peculiar staccato prose-poems are a complete catalogue of what the age understood by the sublime.

It is interesting that the genre of theatrical portraiture which became very popular in the second half of the century hardly hints at these histrionic developments.

Although they depicted actors and actresses in tragic scenes, artists like Benjamin Wilson (1721–88) and Johann Zoffany (1735–1810) rarely attempted more than to reproduce exactly the appearance of the stage set, the expressions and gestures of the performers at selected moments of famous productions. If anything, scenes from comedy were more popular than those from tragedy. But in any case no attempt was made to study atmosphere and create a fully realised pictorial mood. An exception to this is Hogarth's (1697–1764) portrait of Garrick in the role of Richard III (FIG. II), in which, with no supernatural or imaginative additions, the artist conveys, simply by the grand scale and immediacy of his rendering of the actor's deportment, a fairly impressive sense of terror. But the sublime was not Hogarth's métier, and it is precisely his failure to employ those strokes of fantasy that Fuseli turned to such advantage, which mitigates the impressiveness of his picture. It has to be admitted that, despite this, Hogarth's work is at least as interesting as Fuseli's fantastic drawing of Macbeth in a similar scene,[31] for the powerful elements of 'sublime' invention in which Fuseli specialised, and which he deployed so effectively, are nevertheless rather empty gestures.

The great misfortune of the Academy under Reynolds and his successors was that he set it on a course towards the most exalted perfection which was hardly related to the abilities or inclinations of most of its members. When Reynolds admitted that his own profession of portrait painting was 'more suited to my abilities, and to the taste of the times in which I live' (a confession which came out at the very end of his last

FIG. II
William Hogarth and C. Grignion *after* Hogarth, *Garrick in the character of Richard III*, 1746, engraving. Yale Center for British Art, Paul Mellon Collection

Discourse),[32] he seems not to have been aware of the extent to which he was condemning his whole argument as irrelevant. If he hoped to encourage a substantial number of students to follow their bent for 'history painting' to a level of real success, he was not concerned with the other ways in which artistic talent could manifest itself. In fact, although many artists tried their hands at history, few were as successful as Fuseli, whose work is convincing by its vigour and force of design rather than by any profundity of thought or human insight. Although Reynolds professed that 'were I now to begin the world again, I would tread in the steps' of Michelangelo,[33] he had prudently failed to do so in the actual circumstances in which he found himself. But he nevertheless applied many of his own lessons to his own painting, which undoubtedly betrays a more intelligent application of the principles he was inculcating than that of any other painter of the period. An ability to read between the lines of Reynolds's Discourses was essential to any young artist who was at all likely to profit from them.

The dichotomy between Academic theory and the actual abilities of the Academy's members, to say nothing of the needs of eighteenth-century English society (both of which factors Reynolds was quite aware of in his own case) was a grave, if largely suppressed, problem. No one had any doubt as to what constituted great art, just as no one doubted that the Academy, a long-awaited 'ornament suitable to' the 'greatness' of Britain,[34] ought to teach the highest and most glorious aspects of its subject. Students whose talents lay in lower fields must use their intelligence and capacity for rigorous self-discipline to produce technically accomplished work that incorporated whatever of the theory might be applicable. As Reynolds showed by his own success, portraiture, however inferior a branch of art, was of far more immediate use to the world he lived in than the grandiose theatricals which passed for 'high art'. Not that Reynolds eschewed literary or imaginative subjects altogether: he had a rather popular line in 'fancy' pictures which borrowed motifs and themes from Correggio, Guido Reni, and others among the great masters he taught his students to admire; and he finished a few large-scale historical pieces which are on the whole decidedly less successful, though, coming from his brush, they were influential.

What Reynolds demonstrated marvellously was that, even in portraiture, the grand motifs of the great masters could be reused imaginatively to endow modern sitters with dignity and heroic poise; even though the faces could not be infused with intense emotion they could be 'generalised' to suggest a universal and elevated standard of the human physiognomy, while gesture, background and colouring could all be enlisted to create a mood quite independent of the sitter or his personality. Sometimes, if the sitter is a man, the mood reflects his profession – military men are depicted in strategical cogitation before backdrops of swirling smoke and falling citadels; but ladies carried with them few connotations besides those of beauty or motherhood; they were cast as goddesses or muses or virtues, and suitable Renaissance models were wittily adapted to bring in overtones which the connoisseur might readily spot and enjoy (FIG. III).

Landscape, equally inferior to history, presented perhaps an even greater problem than portraiture. It did not deal in the human figure at all, or at least only to a very limited extent, and so was hardly amenable to the subtle jugglery that Reynolds so deftly handled. As far as the greatest masters of the past were concerned, landscape was nearly always a matter of background material. Michelangelo scarcely painted a tree in his life; Raphael did so more frequently, but always with a definitely subsidiary purpose. Raphael was, theoretically, an even greater artist than Michelangelo; but of course that last Discourse revealed Reynolds's true feelings better than the carefully weighed statements he had previously come out with. Raphael's 'Taste and Fancy' were placed against Michelangelo's 'Genius and Imagination', the 'beauty' of the one against the 'energy' of the other.

Reynolds's vocabulary with regard to the two artists is interesting, especially since we are largely concerned here with understanding eighteenth-century terminology. The words he uses to describe Raphael's work are: chaste, noble, of great conformity to their subjects; he speaks of 'the propriety, beauty, and majesty of his characters'.[35] Both 'noble' and 'majesty' are terms that fit easily into the vocabulary of the sublime. And yet he suggests that Raphael is not strictly a sublime artist: 'if, as Longinus thinks, the sublime, being the highest excellence that human composition can attain to, abundantly compensates the absence of every other beauty, and atones for all other deficiencies, then Michael Angelo demands the preference'.[36] Reynolds singled out Michelangelo's 'simplicity' as one of his most characteristically sublime attributes – the single-mindedness with which he expresses an overpowering idea, without any admixture of what Reynolds calls the 'ornamental'. Raphael, for all his grace and 'nobility' in the frescoes of the Vatican, which he produced directly under Michelangelo's influence, also painted a number of smaller works, altar pieces particularly, which are intended to create harmonious and pleasing compositions, and employ landscape to help in this. Michelangelo, of course, was first and foremost a sculptor, and landscape is almost completely irrelevant to the sculptor's art:[37] sculpture, since it was all that the eighteenth century knew of ancient art, had a particular importance as embodying in the clearest form the achievement of the Greeks. Reynolds did not have to have read Winckelmann[38] to draw a logical conclusion for himself: painting that confined itself to the human figure executed with purity of outline and dignity of conception approximated more nearly to the classical ideal than works of a more diffuse nature.

Landscape, then, was at best a dilution of history painting. It could only justify itself as an art form in its own right if it partook of the same idealisation and generalisation which elevated the depiction of the human figure above the local and particular. Claude Lorrain (1600–82) was the perfect example of an artist who did this. Claude 'was convinced, that taking nature as he found it seldom produced beauty', Reynolds said. 'His pictures are a composition of the various drafts which he had previously made from various beautiful scenes and prospects.'[39] This practice he advocated as 'there can be no doubt' that it was preferable to the mere representation of 'accidents', that is, individual places and local effects, as was the habit of the Dutch and Flemish schools. The principle was that of Apelles in painting Helen of Troy, who combined the perfections of several models in order to create an ideal heroine. Even the lowest subject-matter was the better for this quality of generality. Reynolds's position on landscape is summed up in his third Discourse: 'As for the various departments of painting, which do not presume to make such high pretensions [as Dürer, a figure painter who failed to attain the sublime because of his preoccupation with local detail], they are many. None of them are without their merit, though none enter into competition with this universal presiding idea of the Art. The painters who have applied themselves more particularly to low and vulgar characters, and who express with precision the various shades of passion, as they are exhibited by vulgar minds (such as we see in the works of Hogarth), deserve great praise; but as their genius has been employed on low and confined subjects, the praise which we give must be as limited as its object. The merry-making or quarrelling of the Boors of Teniers; the same sort of productions of Brouwer or Ostade, are excellent in their kind; and the excellence and its praise will be in proportion, as, in those limited subjects, and peculiar forms, they introduce more or less of the expression of those passions, as they appear in general and more enlarged nature. This principle may be applied to the Battle-pieces of Bourgognone, the French Gallantries of Watteau, and even beyond the exhibition of animal life, to the Landscapes of Claude Lorraine, and the Sea-Views of Vandervelde. All these painters have, in general, the same right, in different degrees, to the name of a painter, which a satirist, an

FIG. III
Joshua Reynolds, *Mrs Siddons as the Tragic Muse*, 1784, oil on canvas. Henry E. Huntington Library and Art Gallery, San Marino, California

epigrammatist, a sonneteer, a writer of pastorals or descriptive poetry, has to that of a poet.'[40]

The line of division between the 'sublime' of history or literary painting and the lower categories was as firmly drawn as that between the 'sublime' of Michelangelo and the 'beautiful' of Raphael, or, for that matter, the 'sublime' of Homer and the 'beautiful' of Virgil, as Addison classified them. The habit of categorising was deep-rooted and everyone indulged in it. Luckily for the 'department of landscape', and for my argument, there was one painter whose work was readily categorised as 'sublime' by Reynolds and the rest, but who produced a significant body of true landscapes. This was Nicolas Poussin (1594–1665), whose contemporaneity with Claude enabled the eighteenth century to pair the two off as representing the sublime and the beautiful in landscape. Poussin's eye, Reynolds declared, 'was always steadily fixed on the Sublime';[41] and yet he undoubtedly devoted much of his labour to landscape. What is the force of that 'always'? Are even Poussin's pure landscapes, after all, above the common run and truly poetical, truly elevated? His great secret was that he 'lived and conversed with the ancient statues so long, that he may be said to have been better acquainted with them, than with the people who were about him. I have often thought,' Reynolds reflects, 'that he carried his veneration of them so far as to wish to give his works the air of Ancient Paintings.'[42]

Perhaps Reynolds is referring here only to those cool, exquisitely poised figure compositions in which Poussin expatiates on Biblical and mythical themes; but in fact the same qualities of balance and dignified abstraction are to be found even in the few landscapes that he painted with no specific human motifs. Usually, his landscape is the setting for a human drama which, in itself, would be a perfectly fit subject for the history painter, though he chooses to develop it with ideas taken from the natural world. But those natural elements are refined and 'distanced' by Poussin's intellect so that they become factors in his composition of equal weight with the figures. The whole exercise is suffused with the austere though often very beautiful thought of a philosopher. Nearly always, the landscape is heavily impressed with the works of men: it is scattered with buildings to give a firm sense of the close interrelation between men and nature; sometimes the structures are clustered so densely that nature itself seems to be a work of architecture. And, as Reynolds suggests, they are based on classical models to evoke an ideal vision of an heroic world, in which any figures that appear, however unimportant their actions, are by consequence of heroic stamp themselves. Normally, though, the human event that forms the nucleus of the picture has greater relative importance. Reynolds admired Poussin particularly for welding the two disparate elements of such designs, figures and landscape, into a totally coherent, homogenous statement. It was this coherence, this unity of thought, which placed Poussin on such a high plane in Reynolds's estimation. Even his handling was at one with the central idea: '. . . the language in which some stories are told, is not the worse for preserving some relish of the old way of painting, which seemed to give a general uniformity to the whole, so that the mind was thrown back into antiquity not only by the subject, but the execution.'[43]

But how was the painter, whose calling was for landscape, to accomplish the leap from the 'local' and trivial to the grand and universal, in eighteenth-century England where the principal demand for landscape, as for portraiture, was from those who wanted flattering but recognisable delineations of their own property? In his field, Reynolds had succeeded in bridging the gulf by drawing unashamedly on the sublime language of the great masters; but in landscape such a universal language hardly existed; at any rate, it was far less articulate, having been formulated by only one or two artists for what, on the whole, were secondary purposes.

Even Claude seemed too circumscribed when judged by the highest criteria: he had concerned himself with painting 'nature's littlenesses'.[44] It is not surprising, then, that the eighteenth century produced several landscape painters whose aim was generalisation before all else. Three names are a representative sample. One is Alexander Cozens (*c.* 1717–86), whose theorising, analytical mind epitomised the contemporary concern with rules and methods. Although he published a book illustrating the *Shape, Skeleton and Foliage of thirty-two different species of Trees, for use in Landscape*,[45] he very rarely drew a recognisable species in any of his own compositions, which are predominantly executed in ink wash, on a small scale, and consist of the most generalised forms, basic landscape elements presented in endlessly varied combinations, as if Cozens were conducting an experiment, or demonstrating a mathematical proposition. This was precisely his approach, though many of his patterns do in fact achieve a harmony and even an atmosphere that is genuinely poetical. He made his living as a drawing master, and his art shows that he was temperamentally well suited for that career. He could certainly not have pursued his abstruse landscape experiments professionally and expected to live off the proceeds. In the same way, Thomas Gainsborough (1727–88) combined his pastime of landscape painting with a profitable practice as a fashionable portrait painter. His landscapes, too, especially those of his later life, are 'abstractions', compositions formed by the combination and recombination of conventional elements.[46] The third of these practitioners of the ideal is Richard Wilson (1714–82), who made the mistake of abandoning portraiture for landscape rather than maintaining it as a profitable side-line. As a result, though he probably came nearer than anyone else to the contemporary notion of 'elevated' landscape, he met with little success and was not really accorded his due meed of praise until after his death in 1782.[47] By that date the progress of the arts in England had entered a new phase – a phase in which landscape began to assert its independence.

Wilson's great contribution, it was then realised, was that he had succeeded where Claude had failed. Claude had 'painted nature's littlenesses'; Wilson, on the contrary, 'gives a breadth to nature, and adopts only those features that more eminently attract attention. His forms are grand, majestic, and well selected; and his compositions are not encumbered with a multitude of parts, a fault frequently observed in Claude . . . Wilson's compositions are grand, with a tone of colour truly Titianesque . . .'[48]

The reminiscence of Titian was perhaps more a compliment paid by the critic than any intentional allusion on Wilson's part. But there was more to Wilson's achievement than a mere simplification of the Claudean model, or the use of striking colour. Although we should now judge him principally by his pure landscapes, those in which the poetic rendering of scenery is the prime motive, he was admired first of all by his contemporaries as a painter of scenes that were historical not only in manner but also in theme. The canvases of Wilson that came to be cited as specially fine are those which take their central idea from literature, and use a number of figures, often in the context of violent action: *Cicero at his Villa, Celadon and Amelia, The Destruction of the children of Niobe*: these titles are resonant of the literary or 'poetic' preoccupations of the time, and the pictures had their due effect.

Niobe[49] was a subject from Ovid's *Metamorphoses* which had been treated as a sculptural group in classical times; Wilson borrowed the attitudes of some of his principal figures from this group, in true Reynoldsian spirit. At the same time, he invented a storm-tossed landscape to set off the action and interact with it, which is equally plainly borrowed, this time from Poussin.[50] The tragedy of the subject and the angry grandeur of the scenery are linked and combined according to Poussin's example to achieve a landscape painting that is, as nearly as such a work can be, 'sublime'. If Reynolds himself was critical of the piece, that was for incidental reasons; we shall have an opportunity to examine his comments later.

Wilson's *Celadon and Amelia* (FIG. IV),[51] on the other hand, was not taken from classical but from modern literature. It illustrates an episode from James Thomson's

FIG. IV
William Woollett *after* Richard
Wilson, *Celadon and Amelia*,
1765, engraving. Yale Center
for British Art, Paul Mellon
Collection

poem *Summer*, in which Amelia is struck dead by lightning before her lover's eyes.[52] It is an incident violent and dramatic like that of Niobe's children, but with the advantage that it occurs in the work of an English poet. Wilson's interpretation does not make any capital of the fact that it is set in English scenery: on the contrary, he deliberately suggests a more 'generalised' setting, vaguely evocative of Italy. This reflects the aim of Reynolds and his colleagues to show, not only that modern Britain had nurtured a great school of painters, but that its culture as a whole was a worthy counterpart to that of the ancient world which was taken as the ideal standard. This was an important spur to the use of motives from Milton, Shakespeare and other indigenous authors. Thomson was a particularly significant choice.

If we are to explain the rise of 'serious' landscape painting in the second half of the eighteenth century, we must look to literature for clues, just as we do in examining the fashion for history painting. *Ut pictura poesis* (in its modern, reversed form) applied, of course, in both fields. Portraiture was lucky in this respect: its palpable utility to society largely obviated formal excuses. Landscape painters might imitate Claude or borrow from Poussin as much as they pleased: they still required to show that their art could speak eloquently of the things treated by literature. Poussin and Claude, to be sure, had shown the way: but where was the modern equivalent of Milton and Shakespeare? To what contemporary source of myth and legend creditable to the patriotic ambitions of the Academy could they turn? Nature poetry was much inclined to be 'pastoral' or 'descriptive': types firmly relegated by Reynolds to inferior positions in the hierarchy. Thomson's *Seasons* burst on the artistic world (very belatedly) with something of the revelatory force with which it had affected the world of letters in the first half of the century. These four poems, published between 1726 and 1730, and progressively enlarged and rewritten, were greeted when they appeared as a new and stimulating development in the progress of English poetry, the product of an imagination 'rich, extensive, and sublime'.[53] In this century they have almost completely lost their reputation as, collectively, one of the supreme poems in the language, and it is not hard to understand why we do not take them very seriously. And yet they are probably underrated. The vividly observed detail of natural phenomena, recorded with scientific care, brought a new realism to the familiar pentameters of blank verse – a realism that made it possible for Thomson to grip and convince his audience with descriptions of a quite different kind than had previously been attempted.

> When from the pallid sky the sun descends,
> With many a spot, that o'er his glaring orb
> Uncertain wanders, stain'd – red fiery streaks
> Begin to flush around. The reeling clouds
> Stagger with dizzy poise, as doubting yet
> Which master to obey; while rising slow,
> Blank, in the leaden-colour'd east, the moon
> Wears a wan circle round her blunted horns.
> Seen through the turbid, fluctuating air,
> The stars obtuse emit a shivering ray;
> Or frequent seem to shoot athwart the gloom,
> And long behind them trail the whitening blaze.[54]

Thomson's *Seasons* are full of long descriptions of storms and other natural events, often highly dramatic, brought before the mind's eye by means of an insistent repetition of progressive detail. The rhythm and sometimes the language retain the solemnity of Milton, but the content is quite unlike that of even the most circumstantial passages of *Paradise Lost*. As Johnson remarked, *Paradise Lost* 'has this inconvenience, that it comprises neither human actions nor human manners. The man and woman who act and suffer [Adam and Eve] are in a state which no other man or woman can ever know. The reader finds no transaction in which he can be engaged; beholds no condition in which he can by any effort of imagination place himself; he has, therefore, little natural curiosity or sympathy . . . Of the ideas suggested by these awful scenes, from some we recede with reverence, . . . and from others we shrink with horror, or admit them only as salutary inflictions . . . Such images rather obstruct the career of fancy than incite it . . . poetical pleasure must be such as human imagination can at least conceive, and poetical terrors such as human strength and fortitude can combat. The good and evil of eternity are too ponderous for the wings of wit; the mind sinks under them in passive helplessness, content with calm belief and humble adoration.'

Thomson, on the other hand, 'at once comprehends the vast, and attends to the minute' (Johnson again is the commentator).[55] It was by ensuring that each separate incident, and each part of each incident, was fully realised that Thomson succeeded in evoking more elusive and indefinable effects. He also refers constantly to the human response to nature by peopling his landscapes with representative examples of common humanity, so that the criticism Johnson levelled at Milton is met. Indeed, the mainspring of Thomson's realism is the continual appeal to our experience to confirm and sympathise, to envisage pain and pleasure with equal vividness. It is no coincidence that after the success in London of Haydn's oratorio *The Creation*, based on Milton, he was asked to compose a sequel based on the *Seasons*.[56]

Johnson thought it the great weakness of these poems that they lack 'method' in the assemblage of their incidents. But the many set pieces in which Thomson describes the fortuitous conflicts between man and nature constitute a drama which no doubt Thomson himself would have defended as inevitably casual and without literary 'form'. They are rendered vivid by the exploitation of human sympathy, by placing men and women in the landscape and studying their response to it. In doing so, Thomson virtually created an important genre of the later eighteenth century: the rustic sentimental. At the same time, by attempting to treat 'great and serious subjects', as he put it, in the context of 'wild romantic country',[57] he gave the impetus to a new branch of serious art: the landscape sublime.

NOTES TO CHAPTER ONE

1. James Fenimore Cooper, *The Pathfinder* (1840), Modern Library edition, New York, 1952, p. 3.

2. Hugh Blair, *Lectures on Rhetoric and Belles Lettres*, 3rd ed., London 1787, p. 58.

3. Richard Payne Knight, *An Analytical Inquiry in the Principles of Taste*, London 1805, p. 329.

4. Payne Knight, *op. cit.*, p. 36.

5. *Spectator*, no. 412, 23 June 1712.

6. In general, Addison discusses the arts under the heading of literature, pointing out that 'most of the observations that agree with descriptions are equally applicable to painting and statuary'. (*Spectator*, no. 416, 27 June 1712.)

7. *Spectator*, no. 413, 24 June 1712.

8. *Spectator*, no. 420, 2 July 1712.

9. For instance, Lord Kames, *Elements of Criticism*, Edinburgh 1762, vol. I, p. 274.

10. Henry Fielding, *Tom Jones*, Book II, chapter v.

11. Blair, *op. cit.*, p. 58.

12. S. T. Coleridge, *Biographia Literaria*, Everyman edition, p. 112. Compare William Blake's reverence for 'The Sublime of the Bible'; *Milton*, 1804, plate 1.

13. *Spectator*, no. 417, 28 June 1712.

14. Jonathan Richardson, *Works*, 1792, p. 242.

15. *Paradise Lost*, Book VII, ll. 210–31.

16. Heinrich Wölfflin, *Classic Art*, 1899, trans. Peter and Linda Murray, London 1958, p. 56.

17. Hector Berlioz, *A Critical Study of Beethoven's Nine Symphonies*, trans. Edwin Evans, Sen., London n.d., p. 56.

18. *Discourse XV*, 1790, Wark ed., p. 268.

19. *Discourse I*, 1769, Wark ed., pp. 15–16.

20. *Discourse XV*, 1790, Wark ed., p. 282.

21. *Discourse XV*, 1790, Wark ed., p. 278.

22. *Discourse XV*, 1790, Wark ed., p. 275.

23. Horace, *Ars Poetica*, 9.

24. Payne Knight, *op. cit.*, p. 334.

25. Aristotle, *Poetics*, I, 2.

26. John Dryden, *Virgil and the Aeneid* (1697).

27. Henry Fuseli, *Lectures on Painting*, London 1801, p. 4.

28. See Winifred H. Friedman, *Boydell's Shakespeare Gallery*, New York 1976.

29. Samuel Johnson, *Proposals for Printing the Dramatick Works of William Shakespeare*, 1756, ed. Walter Raleigh, Oxford 1908, p. 2.

30. See Henry Okun, 'Ossian in Painting', *Journal of the Warburg and Courtauld Institutes*, 1967, vol. XXX, pp. 327–56; and *Ossian und die Kunst um 1800*, exhibition catalogue, Hamburg, Kunsthalle 1874.

31. Gert Schiff, *Johann Heinrich Füssli*, 2 vols, Zurich 1973, no. 458. Fuseli also drew the Richard III subject; it was engraved as an illustration by J. Neagle in 1804 (Schiff 1284).

32. *Discourse XV*, 1790, Wark ed., p. 282.

33. *Ibid.*

34. *Discourse I*, 1769, Wark ed., p. 13.

35. *Discourse V*, 1772, Wark ed., p. 83.

36. *Ibid.*, p. 84.

37. Not entirely; see for instance certain first-century AD Roman genre subjects, such as the *Farm Scene* in the Glyptothek, Munich.

38. J. J. Winckelmann (1717–68); his *Reflections on the Painting and Sculpture of the Greeks* (1755) was translated into English by Fuseli in 1765.

39. *Discourse IV*, 1771, Wark ed., pp. 69–70.

40. *Discourse III*, 1770, Wark ed., pp. 51–2.

41. *Discourse IV*, 1771, Wark ed., p. 68.

42. *Discourse V*, 1772, Wark ed., p. 87.

43. *Ibid.*, p. 88.

44. Thomas Wright, *Some Account of the Life of Richard Wilson, Esq. R. A.*, London 1824, p. 63.

45. In 1771. See A. P. Oppé, *Alexander and John Robert Cozens*, London 1952, pp. 27–8; 90.

46. See John Hayes, *The Drawings of Thomas Gainsborough*, 2 vols, London and New Haven 1971, vol. I, pp. 10–14.

47. See W. G. Constable, *Richard Wilson*, London 1953.

48. Thomas Wright, *loc. cit.*

49. Wilson treated the subject more than once. The most famous version is now in the Yale Center for British Art, Paul Mellon Collection. See Constable, pls 18–20.

50. Compare Poussin's *Landscape with a Storm* known from Louis de Chatillon's engraving (Blunt 263).

51. Constable, pl. 24b.

52. *Summer*, ll. 1191–1214. Thomson's dates are 1700–48.

53. Lord Lyttelton, *Dialogues of the Dead*, London 1760, p. 129.

54. *Winter*, ll. 118–29.

55. Johnson, *Lives of the Poets*, 'Milton'.

56. Joseph Haydn (1732–1809); *The Creation* was first performed in 1799; the *Seasons* in 1801.

57. Introduction to *Winter*, 2nd ed., 1746.

CHAPTER TWO

THE LANDSCAPE SUBLIME

Ye rocks on precipices pil'd;
Ye ragged desarts waste and wild!
Delightful horrors hail!

JOHN LANGHORNE: *Lines left with the Minister of Riponden,*
a Romantic Village in Yorkshire, 1758

. . . the tall rock,
The mountain, and the deep and gloomy wood.
Their colours and their forms were then to me
An appetite; a feeling and a love,
That had no need of a remoter charm,
By thought supplied, nor any interest
Unborrowed from the eye.

WILLIAM WORDSWORTH: *Lines composed a few miles above*
Tintern Abbey, 1798

Without the definitive success of Thomson's *Seasons* in the first half of the century, the development of landscape painting in England would have been rather different and perhaps delayed. The impact of the poem on the visual arts was not, of course, a simple one-way influence: as critics have frequently pointed out, Thomson himself derived many of his attitudes to landscape from the work of the French and Italian painters of the seventeenth century.[1] It was precisely because his literary vision was so well founded in an existing tradition of painting that it could stimulate artists as it did. To this extent, poetry was indeed, in Horace's sense, following painting. But artists, as we have seen, needed to feel themselves supported by a valid literature. Thomson supplied such a literature for the landscape painter in one comprehensive work. He also, of course, stimulated other writers and pointed to other useful sources. His grandeur and his specificity were exactly what artists were looking for; and were also what a number of poets required to set their own muses working.

The remoter aspects of nature, the 'wild romantic country' that Thomson thought so promising from a human point of view, had simply not been looked at so carefully before. Even those who were able to do so had rarely felt the urge to articulate their feelings at length. A typical early eighteenth-century example is that of a young lawyer, John Tracy Atkyns, who toured the northern counties of England in 1732, making detailed and rapturous notes[2] about the houses and gardens he visited – places such as Castle Howard, Studley Royal, or Newby – but mentioning only briefly the uncultivated landscape of Yorkshire, Northumberland and the Lakes. Here he is crossing the moors from Newcastle to Carlisle:

For fifteen miles together we travell'd through one of the most barren places in England, what they call the Fells, not a Tree, nor even a Stump to be seen, now & then a straggling sheep appears, that with the utmost difficulty keeps itself from starving, perhaps once in a Year an unthinking Crow or Two fly over it, you see a small Number of Huts scatter'd up & down in some Parts of it. The Inhabitants I believe are Aborigines or at least descended from the Ancient Picts, for no Modern would ever think of taking up his Habitation in such a Desart, you may still see great Remains of the famous Wall built by the Picts, it runs across the steepest of their Hills, and there are still standing Part of One or Two Buildings that were originally Forts . . .

It is what we might call an economic view of the landscape. One wonders whether Atkyns's interest in the wall would have been greater if he had known it to have been constructed by the Romans. He was not inaccessible to stronger feelings, but on the whole he preferred to find grandeur in more familiar places. Just as he enjoyed a well laid out garden for its judicious variety of effect, so he responded to nature most warmly when she provided contrast and what was soon to be known as 'Picturesque' diversity. A natural waterfall, for instance, gives him pleasure rather as an artificial one would do, though there is a hint that he finds an added *frisson* in the element of surprise and danger:

> . . . the river is exceeding Rapid, and just at the Bridge is one of the most Beautiful natural Cascades that I ever saw. The Water falling down a steep among some huge Rocks, makes a very notable Roar, and dashing against 'em throws it to such a Height, that Wheat [Atkyns's companion] affirms the Water very often wash'd your face as you ride over the Bridge . . .

But his response to wild nature is more emphatic when it is closely associated with human achievement. Atkyns warms decidedly to the combination of ruggedness and venerable antiquity at Tynemouth:

> I landed among the Rocks in a Place call'd the Prior's Haven, the most monstrous ones I ever saw, a horrid, yet a pleasing look at the same Time, over 'em is a Light House . . . here are very fine Ruins, of an ancient Monastery one of the first Religious Foundations in England, the most beautiful Gothic Building that can be seen . . .

Once again, it is the 'economic' connotations which help Atkyns to respond. But that tug-o'-war between the 'horrid' and the 'pleasing' is exactly the state of mind that was to crystallise in the ensuing decades as the appropriate response to uncultivated nature. There grew up a love-hate relationship assiduously nursed, a source of frictions that were to provide many sparks for the Muses' fire.

Atkyns's is a rare case of an articulate account surviving from the early decades of the century. It antedates even the famous letters of Thomas Gray describing his visit to the Grande Chartreuse in 1739. These, however familiar, must be quoted again here as a *locus classicus* of the emergence of the landscape sublime.

> It is six miles to the top; the road runs winding up it, commonly not six feet broad; on one hand is the rock, with woods of pine-trees hanging overhead; on the other, a monstrous precipice, almost perpendicular, at the bottom of which rolls a torrent, that sometimes tumbling among the fragments of stone that have fallen from on high, and sometimes precipitating itself down vast descents with a noise like thunder, which is still made greater by the echo from the mountains on each side, concurs to form one of the most solemn, the most romantic, and the most astonishing scenes I ever beheld: add to this the strange views made by the craggs and cliffs on the other hand; the cascades that in many places throw themselves from the very summit down into the vale, and the river below; and many other particulars impossible to describe; you will conclude we had no occasion to repent our pains.[3]

The last comment is revealing: the letter is to Gray's mother, and we are left in no doubt that she would have understood the kinds of feelings he describes. He was not, therefore, alone in his heightened response to the Alps. But it is likely that he brought to them a capacity for wider association than most travellers:

> I do not remember to have gone ten paces without an exclamation, that there was no restraining: not a precipice, not a torrent, not a cliff, but is pregnant with religion and

poetry. There are certain scenes that would awe an atheist into belief, without the help of other argument. One need not have a very fantastic imagination to see spirits there at noon-day: you have Death perpetually before your eyes, only so far removed, as to compose the mind without frighting it . . . I have Livy in the chaise with me, and beheld his 'Nives coelo prope immistae, tecta informia imposita rupibus, pecora jumentaque torrida frigore, homines intonsi et inculti, animalia inanimamque omnia rigentia gelu; omnia confragosa, praeruptaque' . . . Mont Cenis, I confess, carries the permission mountains have to be frightful rather too far; and its horrors were accompanied with too much danger to give one time to reflect upon their beauties.[4]

This passage illustrates the intimate connection between the landscape sublime and the religious feeling we have already found to be strongly present in sublime ideas. The characteristic patterns of sublime association are much in evidence. Gray can comfort himself with the reflection that such scenes were known to the Ancients; Livy was to prove a useful source for historical painters in future.[5] But the line drawn between the horrid and the pleasing is still present, as we see from his comments on the Mont Cenis. Gray's appreciation is still a matter of degree. And there now begins to creep in a new note, a note of which we hear overtones in Gray's judgement that 'too much danger' prevents us enjoying the 'beauties' of grand scenery. I have had occasion elsewhere to compare Gray's experience with a considerably earlier one, that of the Yorkshire antiquarian and topographer, Ralph Thoresby. I think it is worth bringing them together again here. Thoresby wrote of a journey made in 1681:

> . . . the precipice grew to that height and narrowness, and withal so exceedingly narrow, that we had not one inch of ground to set a foot upon to alight from the horse. Our danger here was most dreadful, and, I think, inconceivable to any that were not present: we were upon the side of a most terrible high hill . . . We had above us a hill, so desperately steep, that our aching hearts durst not attempt the scaling of it it being much steeper than the roofs of many houses; but the hill below was still more ghastly, as steep for a long way as the walls of a house . . . To add to our torments there was a river run all along (which added to the dizziness of our heads) close to the foot of the precipice, which we expected every moment to be plunged into, and into eternity.[6]

Thoresby does not indulge in the complex associational meditations of Gray, and his apprehension of the impressiveness of nature here resolves itself crudely into one of fear; but his relish in telling the story, his insistence on the danger, indicate that he was responding at a level rather higher than that of simple brute terror. His account does not realise the possibilities of the landscape sublime, but it implies them.

The ingredient of *fear* in fact plays an important part in this new development of the theme. It is present, of course, in the classic theory of the sublime, but bears only obliquely on the mental patterns discussed by that theory. It is a sub-category, as it were, of the religious awe that is central to the idea. 'Awe' comprehends both the exalted state of mind appropriate to the contemplation of God, and the 'fear and trembling' also associated with that state. As Kant observed 'the virtuous man fears God without being afraid of him' – it is largely a question of one's relative position; does the object of our contemplation threaten us or are we protected (by virtue or some more material barrier) from its power? On this ambiguity pivots the change of stress that came over the eighteenth-century definition of the sublime. Some writers argued that the emotion of fear was too base and contemptible to be associated with it. '. . . the word *sublime*, both according to its use and etymology,[8] must signify *high* or *exalted*; and, if an individual chooses that, in his writings, it should signify *terrible*, he only involves his meaning in a confusion of terms, which naturally leads to a confusion of ideas.'[9] Others felt that it was a special *kind* of fear which was present in the sublime experience. 'The combination of passions in the sublime, render the idea of it obscure. No doubt the sensation of fear is very distinct in it; but it is equally obvious, that there is something in the sublime more than this abject passion. In all other terrors the soul loses its dignity, and as it were shrinks below its usual size: but at the presence of the sublime, although it be always awful, the soul of man seems to be raised out of a trance . . .'[10]

There was excellent authority for the idea that fear is central to the experience of sublime art, for Aristotle had laid it down that tragedy depends for its effect on the two emotions, fear (or terror) and pity.[11] This rule was usually agreed to without question but its application to the drama raised a philosophical problem. As Payne Knight put it, 'how any man, in his senses, can feel either fear or danger, which he knows to be fictitious, I am at a loss to discover; . . . I sympathise, indeed, with the expressions of passion, and mental energy, which those fictitious events recite; because the expressions are real; . . . but the acute Stagirite [that is, Aristotle] appears to have been lead into an error, on this point, by imagining that stage exhibitions were really meant to be deceptions . . .'[12]

The question is, do we attribute 'sublimity' to objects or events, or do we use the term to describe our emotions on experiencing those objects or events? In the case of a play, we cannot experience any *real* emotion in response to what is enacted; and yet it is true that 'the expressions are real', and they embody the sublimity of great poetry. Payne Knight refuses to admit that he can even temporarily 'believe' what the actors tell him, 'never having found any such pliability in my own feelings'. But in general, we adopt quite involuntarily the strategem that Coleridge described in his famous phrase, 'that willing suspension of disbelief for the moment, which constitutes poetic faith'.[13] Poetic faith is necessary to the business of enjoying a great deal of art; with art that operates on the 'highest' emotional level, demanding our complete involvement, it is essential. The sublime in nature is, perhaps, as Ralph Thoresby shows, and as even Gray hints, not conductive to human pleasure since, at its most intense, it involves dangers that obliterate delight. In art, conversely, conviction has to be won, since the medium itself cannot be either awe-inspiring or terrifying. The processes by which this conviction is attained will occupy us considerably later on.

An indication of the extent to which the concept of fear as a pleasurable experience had attached itself to eighteenth-century aesthetic thinking is the place given to it by Edmund Burke in his *Philosophical Enquiry into the Origin of our Ideas of the Sublime and Beautiful*, which appeared in 1757. Here the Sublime is not simply one of many moral and aesthetic categories. It is treated as a phenomenon in its own right, paired with the beautiful and so by implication a matter of aesthetics, but in fact tackled by Burke (as his title encourages us to notice) in a thorough-going scientific way as a universal philosophical question. Burke couches his argument in the language of the moral philosophers, going back, of course, to Locke, but relying too on the more recent work of David Hume, whose dour Scottish logic and rational doubt was not perhaps very congenial to Burke, but whose clear reasoning set a dialectical standard for his age. Hume, discussing Beauty and Deformity in his *Treatise of Human Nature*, put the point very plainly that 'Beauty of all kinds gives us a peculiar delight and satisfaction; as deformity produces pain . . . Pleasure and pain, therefore, are not only necessary attendants of beauty and deformity, but constitute their very essence.'[14] Accordingly, Burke traces our sense of the beautiful and the sublime to sources in our notions of pleasure and pain. Obviously what is beautiful produces pleasure. But it is more basic even than that: the principal source of human gratification or pleasure is that associated with what Burke calls 'generation', or what we would now more bluntly refer to as 'sex'. This was a point Addison had made when he observed that the beautiful markings of birds performed the function of attracting mates.[15] Female beauty in humans is likewise the central and definitive source of our notion of beauty. A similar physiological cause lies behind the concept of the sublime: 'Whatever is fitted in any sort to excite the ideas of pain and danger, that is to say, whatever is in any sort terrible, or is conversant about terrible objects, or operates in a manner analogous to terror, is a source of the *sublime*; that is, it is productive of the strongest emotion which the mind is capable of feeling.'[16] We are therefore to understand that the sublime is an emotion perceived in ourselves as a result of certain experiences. It is not strictly to be used in describing the objects that give rise to those experiences. But Burke and several other writers make all too little distinction here. 'Grandeur and sublimity have a double signification', Lord Kames explained. 'They generally signify the quality or circumstance in the objects by which the emotions are produced; sometimes the emotions themselves.'[17] Often we are told, in effect, that a sublime object occasions sublime sensations in the observer – the word covers the whole range of ideas from the external phenomenon through the gamut of intermediary events and sensations to the felt emotion.

Kant, who admired Burke's analysis of the sublime, clarified matters somewhat by suggesting that the sublime was characterised primarily by boundlessness while the beautiful, dependent on form, naturally resulted from the presence of boundaries. The boundlessness of the sublime, which reflects or implies all the central significance of the classic conception that we have discussed, entails its practical inconceivability. Something that is inconceivable cannot be conceived as sublime or as anything else – but the act of imagining it, even though it is beyond the power of imagination to envisage it, is itself a strenuous exalted mental or emotional state which we may describe as 'sublime'. Hence Kant says that the sublime is a dynamic state of mind while the beautiful is contemplated by the mind at rest. And he justifies Burke's association of pain with the sublime by arguing that there is a 'painful' discrepancy between the capacity of the reason to estimate the magnitude of an external phenomenon, and the capacity of the imagination to represent it. Hence the contemplation of, say, mountain peaks, chasms, vast solitudes or high waterfalls does not engender real fear, 'but only an attempt to feel fear by the aid of the imagination'.[18] These objects 'raise the energies of the soul above their accustomed height, and discover in us a faculty of resistance of a quite different kind, which gives us courage to measure ourselves against the apparent almightiness of nature.'[19] Thus Kant united the two aspects of the sublime in a specifically mental state centering on a moral capacity of human beings to transcend danger.

There is an important idea to be gleaned from this awkward controversy: despite the elevated and idealising tendencies that the idea carries with it in its classic definition, it also contains an appeal to, even a demand for, what we nowadays call a 'gut reaction'. There is no difficulty in demonstrating this. Most of the phenomena which, thanks to Thomson and later to Burke and the 'terror' school of sublime theorists, the eighteenth century came to associate with the sublime were events of the type that can also be described, in another modern term, as 'sensational'. The common fascination with death (especially violent death), human tragedies and natural disasters, the love of grandiose spectacle and everything grotesquely out of the ordinary (like the giants and dwarfs, the fat men and thin women who appear in works of reference like the *Guinness Book of Records*, a world best-seller), all this is a popular and perverted manifestation of the power of the sublime. A little book of 1683 entitled *The Surprizing Miracles of Nature and Art* illustrates how universal and perennial the interest is. Its sub-title is: 'The Miracles of Nature, or the Strange Signs and Prodigious Aspects and Appearances in the Heavens, the Earth, and the Waters . . .' and it lists, at great length, not only innumerable miracles of the saints (a fascination with miracles, real or imagined, is one of the few surviving vestiges of the religious sublime in the popular mind), but earthquakes, volcanic eruptions, storms, shipwrecks, fires, wars, and all the hideous brutality ensuing on war: rapine and torture, described in careful detail; together with monsters and prodigies of every sort – elephants, whales and so on. The atmosphere of the book is close to that of a modern popular newspaper. Dugald Stewart, one of the most thoughtful commentators on the sublime, remarked that 'according to the phraseology of Longinus . . . the opposite to the *sublime* is not the *profound*, but the *humble*, the *low*, or the *puerile*.'[20] Sometimes a sublime event elicits a response at the opposite end of the scale.

Before we turn away from this apparent digression let us remember that it is owing to the close connection between the sublime and the vividly shocking that the subject concerns us at all. In order to 'work', art must demonstrate its relevance to us as human beings in whatever age we happen to live. It was the most ambitious art which most required complete conviction. When painters attempted the 'grand style' advocated by Reynolds they tended to fail of conviction. When they attempted it in the landscape mode, they had, on the whole, much better success. But landscape, it will be said, can hardly be shocking. Nor does it in itself express heroic virtues, as the eighteenth century saw. That was why it was an inferior branch of art. But because of the growing confusion between the sublime in external objects and events, and the sublime in human perceptions and emotions, the power of landscape to move came to be seen as relatively greater. In addition to this, from a fairly early date there was felt to be some sort of correspondence between landscape types and poetic types. We have seen Reynolds drawing a parallel between epigrammatist, sonneteer and so on and the minor branches of painting. Likewise, the pigeonholing instinct of the time could pair off categories of landscape with different poets. Addison gives a key example: 'Reading the Iliad, is like travelling through a country uninhabited, where the fancy is entertained with a thousand savage prospects of vast deserts, wide uncultivated marshes, huge forests, misshapen rocks and precipices. On the contrary the Aeneid is like a well-ordered garden . . . But when we are in the Metamorphoses, we are on enchanted ground, and see nothing but scenes of magic lying around us.'[21]

Now Homer is the one writer of whom Addison speaks explicitly as 'sublime';[22] 'Homer,' he says, 'fills his readers with sublime ideas.' His epithets 'mark out what is great', 'his persons are most of them godlike and terrible'.[23] The landscape that is evoked as symbolic of these qualities is 'uninhabited', 'vast', 'uncultivated', 'huge', 'savage'. All these terms are to be found over and over again in later descriptions of sublime landscape. Lack of cultivation, for instance, was essential to the sublime when Archibald Alison discussed it: 'The sublimest situations are often disfigured by objects that we feel unworthy of them – by the traces of cultivation, or attempts towards improvement . . .'[24] A tract of land with no inhabitants would automatically suggest the hostility of the place to human life, and so evoke fear. A few inhabitants, if sufficiently 'savage', could however enhance the sense of isolation and remoteness, as in the case of John Tracy Atkyns and the 'aborigines' of the northern wilds. Alternatively the absence of human life might leave the fancy free to invent some on appropriate lines: 'Observe this mountain which rises so high on the left, if we had been farther removed from it, you might see behind it other mountains rising in strange confusion, the furthest off almost lost in the distance, yet great in the obscurity; your imagination labours to travel over them, and the inhabitants seem to reside in a superior world.'[25]

The vast, the remote, the obscure, qualities that give rein to the imagination, can be enumerated in respect to landscape more easily and precisely than in connection with religious, mental or abstract ideas. The greatness of a Greek hero is an abstract conception; the greatness of a mountain is very palpable. In fact, once the idea had caught on, it became much easier to talk about the sublime in terms of landscape than in the context of Aristotelian heroics. Hence, although Burke's treatise is a general philosophical discussion, the clear-cut categories into which he divided sublime experience – obscurity, privation, vastness, succession, uniformity, magnificence, loudness, suddenness and so on – came to be affixed enthusiastically to aspects of nature which were beginning to be appreciated not only by poets like Gray but by the rank and file of cultured English folk. The desire to put these ideas into words remained the first response; but that was bound, in the end, to produce paintings, since artists were, in a sense, only waiting for the literary stimulus in order to begin. As the wish to travel became more widespread, so the publication of 'Tours' became a fashion. By the 1770s it was a regular craze:

> As every one who has either traversed a steep mountain, or crossed a small channel, must write his Tour, it would be almost unpardonable in Me to be totally silent, who have visited the most uninhabited regions of North Wales – who have seen lakes, rivers, seas, rocks, and precipices, at unmeasurable distances, and who from observation and experience can inform the world, that high hills are very difficult of access, and the tops of them generally very cold.[26]

So wrote Joseph Cradock in 1777, introducing his *Account of some of the most Romantic Parts of North Wales*, a production typical of its time in everything but its author's ironic consciousness of the voguishness of his activity. Most people were more pompous, and many saw fit to enshrine their experiences in blank verse. Some used them to advance private aesthetic theories of their own; notably the Rev. William Gilpin, Prebendary of Salisbury, who, having conceived the notion of 'the Picturesque' while visiting Lord Cobham's new house, Stowe, in the 1740s,[27] applied the rules governing Cobham's careful design of his gardens as a sequence of changing vistas and rustic tableaux to the whole of nature. It was Gilpin who promulgated the fully-fledged 'Picturesque Tour' in which aesthetic theory and topographical observation are combined in one supremely didactic exercise. His authoritative statements on such matters as the correct disposition of hills in a view, or the number of cows permissible in a painting, were exactly attuned to the eighteenth-century longing for clear distinctions and definitions and enabled countless sightseers to appreciate actively the natural scenery which was of culturally legitimate interest for the first time. Some of Gilpin's rules were genuinely helpful: when he pronounced, for instance, that a ruin is bound to be more pleasing in a landscape than a newly built house he did not merely reflect a whim of contemporary taste; he reinforced a perennial truth about our perception of the environment. His basic premise, that when looking at nature we try to find combinations of elements that correspond to what we have already experienced in art, is equally valid. He became tendentious only when he asserted his own talent for discriminating desirable arrangements from undesirable ones as superior to nature's. At Gilpin's starting-point, the landscape garden, this was a valid position. It had, indeed, been held by Addison: 'we find the works of nature still more pleasant, the more they resemble those of art'. Much of the essence of Gilpin's message is to be found in the *Spectator* essay: 'We take delight in a prospect which is well laid out, and diversified with fields and meadows, woods and rivers; in those accidental landscapes of trees, clouds, and cities, that are sometimes found in the veins of marble; in the curious fret-work of rocks and grottos; and, in a word, in any thing that hath such a variety or regularity as may seem the effect of design in what we call the works of chance.'[28]

Variety was the core of Gilpin's Picturesque, and his survey of the works of nature as potential subject-matter for the aesthetician of course included wild, mountainous and 'terrific' scenery as well as the more homely diversity of cultivated land. But precisely because he was mainly concerned with 'that particular quality, which makes objects chiefly pleasing in painting',[29] Gilpin was inclined to shy away from the unpaintable immensities of the sublime. He recognised that sublime elements could enormously heighten our response to scenery; but like Gray he was prepared to go only so far. He would have found James Fenimore Cooper's North America too much altogether:

> In America the lakes are seas; and the country on their banks, being removed of course to a great distance, can add no accompaniments [to the view].

Among the *smaller* lakes of Italy and Switzerland, no doubt, there are many delightful scenes: but the *larger* lakes, like those of America, are disproportioned to their accompaniments: the water occupies too large a space, and throws the scenery too much into the distance.

The mountains of Sweden, Norway, and other northern regions, are probably rather masses of hideous rudeness, than scenes of grandeur and proportion. Proportion, indeed, in all scenery is indispensably necessary; and unless the lake, and its correspondent mountains have this just relation to each other, they want the first principle of beauty.[30]

For Gilpin's was a theory of beauty quite explicitly: he sought those aspects of nature that he found in the works of Claude and Poussin. But there was another seventeenth-century painter of landscape who had evolved a pictorial language of the 'horrid': Salvator Rosa (1615–73). The popularity of Salvator's paintings in England from his lifetime onward should contradict the idea that the more hostile aspects of nature were not enjoyed in England before the mid-eighteenth century; at least so long as they were confined to works of art. And in so far as Gilpin could find the rugged rocks, stark tree-stumps and stormy skies that were for Salvator what full-leaved chestnuts, verdant valleys and classical temples were to Claude, he included such scenes in his category of the Picturesque. There was no doubt, either, that this subject-matter was not strictly beautiful: wild and savage, decidedly uncultivated, often suggestive of desert, Salvator's was clearly the landscape sublime.[31] As such it epitomised that brand of the sublime which derives, *à la* Burke, from fear rather than from elevation or grandeur. So the theory of the Picturesque, while not directly bearing on the sublime proper, played an important role in the establishment of the accepted language of the landscape sublime. Thomson made the distinction in his often-quoted couplet in the *Castle of Indolence* (which came out in 1748 and so predates almost all Gilpin's writings):

> Whate'er Lorraine light-touch'd with softening hue,
> Or savage Rosa dash'd, or learned Poussin drew.[32]

We might speak of the two sublimes as the 'savage' and the 'learned' but I shall adhere to my chosen nomenclature, asking the reader to bear in mind the ambiguous place held by Poussin in this set of correspondences.

In spite of the prescribed limits of his interest, or rather because of them, Gilpin was of some use to artists in their exploitation of the new field of sensibility. His recipes and regulations gave guidance for the digestion of somewhat daunting raw material into acceptable pictorial fare; he writes, for instance, of the North of England:

> . . . it cannot be supposed that every scene, which these countries present, is *correctly picturesque*. In such immense bodies of rough-hewn matter, many irregularities, many deformities, must exist, which a practised eye would wish to correct. Mountains are sometimes crouded – their sides are often bare, when contrast requires them to be wooded – promontories form the water-boundary into acute angles – and bays are contracted into narrow points, instead of swelling into ample basons.
>
> In all these cases, the imagination is apt to whisper, What glorious scenes might here be made, if these stubborn materials could yield to the judicious hand of art! – And, to say the truth, we are sometimes tempted to let the imagination loose among them.
>
> By the force of this creative power an intervening hill may be turned aside; and a distance produced. – This ill-shaped mountain may be pared, and formed into a better line . . .[33]

It need not be supposed that landscape artists earnestly studied the Rev. William Gilpin and solemnly acted on his advice: this was largely directed at the layman. But we may assume that his attitudes coincide more or less with the mental processes of artists engaged in the problems presented by landscape composition. He spoke for his period, even if he was not a leader in it. But his ideas could have direct influence upon painters: we know, for instance, that the youthful Turner copied some of Gilpin's illustrations, and did so very much in Gilpin's spirit, altering them according to his own ideas of picturesque composition as he went along.[34] His approach was certainly not that of an amateur: we have evidence in plenty of Turner's dedicated professionalism from his early years. But, dedicated as he was, and ambitious as he was, he was never afraid to learn from others. Gilpin was not, perhaps, the kind of model that Reynolds would have recommended, but as he matured Turner quickly found more rewarding masters. The lessons of Gilpin remained with him, however, and he was to put them to good use during the first decade or so of his career.

In addition to copying plates from Gilpin's books, he made his own studies of the kinds of scenery that Gilpin drew, and which were also recorded in the verse of the Picturesque tourists. When Turner, on his tour of South Wales in 1795, went to Melincourt to draw the waterfall there (FIG. V), he may have known that in the

FIG. V
J. M. W. Turner, *Melincourt Waterfall*, 1775, pencil and watercolour. British Museum, London

previous year a *Tour through parts of Wales* in blank verse pentameters had been published by William Sotheby, containing these effusions on the same spot:

> . . . lured by the fall
> Of the far flood through pathless glens I roam,
> Where Melincourt's loud echoing crags resound.
> Not bolder views Salvator's pencil dashed
> In Alpine wilds romantic. Far descried
> Through the deep windings of the gloomy way,
> The hoar Cledaugh, swoln by autumnal storms,
> Down the o'erhanging rock's declivity
> Curves the broad cataract, and on the stones
> Rent from the shattered mass prone rushing, spreads
> The foamy spray around . . .

The subject was also illustrated (FIG. VI) by one of the leading picturesque watercolourists of the time – John 'Warwick' Smith (1749–1831).[35] Unlike Turner's concentrated sketch of the fall of water itself, the rocks and shrubs round it only outlined in pencil, Smith's view presents the wall of rock extending from one side of the composition to the other, in a formal design which Turner himself was later to make use of in his views of Hardraw Force and Malham Cove.[36] For the moment, however, the waterfall is studied as an isolated picturesque phenomenon.[37]

A few of the oil paintings that Turner submitted for exhibition at the Academy in the 1790s belong to the class that has come to be known as the 'Picturesque Sublime' – a term that indicates the origin of this type of landscape in ideas promulgated by Gilpin, or akin to his theories. For the most part, it is not sublime in any of the full

FIG. VI
S. Alken *after* John 'Warwick' Smith, *Melincourt Cascade*, aquatint. Yale Center for British Art, Paul Mellon Collection

senses we now have terms for: it is a diluted sublime, in which the rather circum-scribed imagination of the good Prebendary can be felt to operate.

Typically these pictures choose subjects from the mountains of the North Country, such as Gilpin had drawn to people's attention, but they do not seek to *frighten* us. One of them, exhibited under the title *Buttermere Lake with part of Cromackwater, Cumberland, a shower* (FIG. VII),[38] contains many of the elements of this type of landscape in a very mature form. The dark sides of the mountains rise into turbulent vapours around the faintly gleaming lake, which partially reflects light from the obscured sky and the arc of a brilliant rainbow that spans half the composition. Beneath its arch lies a flat alluvial valley dotted with buildings, also reflecting light. Beyond, a sombre mountain heaves itself up into the clouds. The stillness of the lake in the foreground is emphasised by a small boat containing two figures, which creates slight ripples as it moves. The evocation of climate and space is assured, and the picture is remarkable for the simplicity of its design, the stately dignity of its rhythms. Only a few branches of trees in the left lower corner betray a self-conscious need on the part of the artist to 'balance' his composition. The ingredients of the Picturesque Sublime are handled with confidence and conviction; the view that the picture presents to us is impressive – grand in a sense that Gilpin could fully have understood and approved. Even so, at least one of his contemporaries thought Turner's effort 'timid'.[39] This may reflect the fact that Turner has carefully elaborated the detail of his subject rather than suppressing it in favour of generalised grandeur: we feel that his intention was to persuade by the accuracy of his statement rather than by aiming at stark grandeur. Why indeed did he so carefully inform the viewer that he was painting 'a shower' – which in itself is far from being a sublime phenomenon?

FIG. VII
J. M. W. Turner, *Buttermere Lake*, 1798, oil on canvas. Tate Gallery, London

The picture was not, however, merely a visual statement. Turner printed with the title in the catalogue a few verses taken from Thomson's *Spring*, which are clearly meant to underline this quality of specific description:

> Till in the western sky the downward sun
> Looks out effulgent – The rapid radiance instantaneous strikes
> The illumin'd mountains – in a yellow mist
> Bestriding earth – the grand ethereal bow
> Shoots up immense, and every hue unfolds.[40]

These lines, chosen deliberately by Turner to accompany his painting during its exhibition, confirm that his aim was to create an image conveying a sublime natural effect – an effect involving 'effulgence', 'grandeur' and 'immensity', among other ideas mentioned in Thomson's lines. But it was an honest attempt to copy these incidents direct from nature; a young man's homage, as it were, to the self-sufficiency of his raw material. The coloured sketch that he made of the subject in one of his notebooks is evidence that he painted what he saw, and embellished only just sufficiently to round out his design.[41]

If it is a picture painted in homage to the natural world that must supply the landscape artist's subject-matter, *Buttermere Lake* is also a homage to Thomson. It was not the only one of Turner's paintings to be linked with his poetry: in the same exhibition another north-country subject, *Dunstanburgh Castle*,[42] was also accompanied by lines from the *Seasons*. Numerous similar parallels, drawn by Turner himself between his paintings and Thomson's poetry, occur in the Academy's exhibition catalogues. They are evidence of a lifelong regard for the poet which is apparent in Turner's own attempts to write verse. For he inherited in full measure the traditional view of the alliance between painting and poetry, and demonstrated that alliance throughout his career. He did this not only by printing verse with the titles of his pictures in exhibition catalogues from the first year that the Academy rules allowed the practice (1798), but also by composing poetry himself. One of the primary influences on his own verse was undoubtedly that of Thomson. For instance, these lines, which appeared with *Hannibal crossing the Alps*[43] in the catalogue of 1812, are Turner's own:

> . . . still their chief advanced,
> Looked on the sun with hope; – low, broad, and wan;
> While the fierce archer of the downward year
> Stains Italy's blanch'd barrier with storms . . .

They evidently derive from memories of a passage from *Winter*:

> Now when the cheerless empire of the sky
> To Capricorn and Centaur-Archer yields,
> And fierce Aquarius stains the inverted year –
> Hung o'er the farthest verge of Heaven, the sun
> Scarce spreads o'er ether the dejected day.
> Faint are his gleams, and ineffectual shoot
> His struggling rays, in horizontal lines,
> Through the thick air; as cloth'd in cloudy storm,
> Weak, wan, and broad, he skirts the southern sky . . .[44]

And the longest of all Turner's contributions to the catalogues consists of no less than thirty-two lines composed specially by him to commemorate Thomson. They accompany his picture of 1811, *Thomson's Aeolian harp*,[45] and are, of course, an imitation of his style. The picture reminds us that Thomson was buried at Richmond, close to Turner's own house at Twickenham, and we know that the painter liked to see the landscape of that area through Thomson's eyes from the quotation from *Summer* appended to his picture of *Richmond Hill*[46] in 1819:

> Which way, Amanda, shall we bend our course?
> The choice perplexes. Wherefore should we chuse?
> All is the same with thee. Say, shall we wind
> Along the streams? or walk the smiling mead?
> Or court the forest-glades? or wander wild
> Among the waving harvests? or ascend,
> While radiant Summer opens all its pride,
> Thy Hill, delightful Shene?

We know from Turner's lecture notes, made in preparation for the courses he gave at the Academy in his capacity as Professor of Perspective, that he was in the habit of referring to Thomson for verbalisations of his own response to landscape, as well as for models of poetic excellence. Looking for an example of the poetic description of a river, he chooses Thomson's account of the Nile,[47] 'as poetic, metaphorical, Historical and with geographical truth'.

That last criterion, of 'truth', is important. The word is ambiguous in the context of eighteenth-century criticism, for it could be applied to artists when they were 'generalising' in Reynolds's sense: for instance, one writer observes that Richard Wilson's 'taste was so exquisite, and his eye so chaste, that whatever came from his easel bore the stamp of elegance and truth'.[48] Here the word refers to that truth to what we conceive as the ideal in nature which Reynolds advocated. The 'truth' that Turner found in Thomson no doubt partook of this sense, but it also and more clearly refers to Thomson's factual accuracy, the love of precision that prompted the poet to revise his *Seasons* periodically to bring them up to date with the latest scientific knowledge. Turner's sketchbooks testify to his own lifelong attention to the literal truth of nature as the foundation of his art. Just as Thomson saw that he could only bring the full grandeur of natural events to bear on his readers' imaginations by vivid exactness, so Turner believed that close observation of the real world was vital to his purpose in landscape painting. Hence the precise adherence of *Buttermere Lake* to its study, and the careful delineation of detail that seemed 'timid'.

In his first exhibited pictures the desire to achieve a clear, unambiguous image is even more marked than in *Buttermere Lake*. In 1796 he made his début as a painter in oil with *Fishermen at Sea* (FIG. VIII).[49] This was a night-piece – in itself evidence that he was in search of 'effect': although he had cast himself as a landscape painter, he intended from the outset to use landscape as a vehicle for statements appealing to the emotions at a more intense level than that of gentle pastoral subjects viewed in full unimpeded daylight. Even compared with *Buttermere Lake*, *Fishermen at Sea* is a work of very careful and precise execution. Its subject is not one of violent drama, but what it sets out to convey it conveys with the utmost nicety. The brooding darkness, the windy sky, the heaving surface of the sea, are not made the excuses for a flurry of expressive brushwork. This is an exercise in classic purity of technique, a purity that Turner was soon to find at odds with his intentions. Here, in his first publicly shown painting, he demonstrates that he can handle the oil medium as chastely as any academician. In particular he seems to have been thinking of the night-pieces of Joseph Wright of Derby (1734–97), which are themselves of unusual crispness and refinement of finish, reminiscent not of the work of his English contemporaries but of continental artists like Philippe Jacques de Loutherbourg.[50] De Loutherbourg (1740–1812) was a virtuoso of the sharply defined manner of presentation that he brought to England from France, and his essays in the landscape sublime were to have considerable influence on Turner, who owned a number of his drawings. But all these artists looked back to the acknowledged master of contemporary landscape, Claude-

Joseph Vernet (1714–89), who specialised in romantic sea-pieces (FIG. IX), and whose work Turner is known to have copied.[51] Vernet's supremacy in his field was universally recognised. His Mediterranean harbours suffused with the golden light of sunset, peopled with elegantly grouped fisherfolk or fashionable ladies and gentlemen, were considered the direct descendants of Claude. But they marked an advance on Claude: 'Vernet', wrote Diderot, 'balance le Claude Lorrain dans l'art d'élever des vapeurs sur la toile; et il lui est infiniment supérieur dans l'invention des scènes, le dessin des figures, la variété des incidents, et le reste. Le premier n'est qu'un grand paysagiste tout court; l'autre est un peintre d'histoire, selon mon sens . . .'[52] Vernet showed how landscape could be raised to a more serious level of communication, and we shall see Turner later concerning himself with just these questions of 'the invention of scenes', 'the variety of incidents' and so on, which Diderot mentions. It was Vernet who in the 1750s had encouraged Wilson to take up landscape painting, and his mixture of landscape and history (in a sense that Diderot understood and approved) was what Wilson himself attempted. There can be no doubt that Diderot considered Vernet an artist of the sublime. 'Ce n'est donc plus de la Nature, c'est de l'art; ce n'est plus de Dieu, c'est de Vernet que je vais vous parler.'[53] Of a *Moonlight* shown at the Salon of 1763 Diderot remarks 'Il a rendu en couleur les ténèbres visibles et palpables de Milton.'[54] Again: 'C'est comme le Créateur pour la célérité, c'est comme la nature pour la vérité.'[55] Notice that, as with Wilson, the idea of grandeur alternates in the critic's mind with the idea of 'truth'; and Diderot does not mean truth to an ideal only: in 1767 he said of a Vernet canvas at the Salon: 'Tout est vrai. On le sent . . . J'ai oui dire à des personnes qui avaient fréquenté longtemps les bords de la mer, qu'elles reconnaissaient sur cette toile, ce ciel, ces nuées, ce temps, toute cette composition.'[56]

The landscape painter must astonish his audience by the immediacy of his effects, and that immediacy is produced by a truth both of general conception and of detail in the rendering of light, air, climate, space and atmosphere. It is a truth that forces the viewer to say: 'I recognise this from my own experience', which is the first premise in the argument by which he is to be convinced of the grandeur of the artist's intention. Whatever that intention may be, the landscape painter is confronted willy-nilly by the necessity for accurate imitation. This involves the spanning of a particularly wide gap: the gap between infinite space and the constricted two-dimensionality of the canvas.

Turner tried Vernet's method partly because it had such remarkable results in Vernet's hands, and partly to impress his colleagues with his technical proficiency. But he did not regard it as the only answer to his own problems. Few other pictures of his are executed in the tight, smooth manner of *Fishermen at Sea*, though at different times in his career he returned to the technique for special reasons: to reproduce the immaculate realism of Dutch seventeenth-century landscape in the *Dort* of 1818, for instance,[57] or to explore again in later life the complex lighting system of contrasted flame and moonlight that he had used in *Fishermen at Sea* when he painted his *Keelmen heaving in Coals by night* of 1835.[58] Already in the 1798 *Morning amongst the Coniston Fells, Cumberland*[59] a more broken touch is noticeable, the paint applied more richly and the lights scumbled warmly across darker glazes of sensuously laid in colour. This upright composition, soaring from a gloomy ravine towards the mist-wreathed peaks of mountains lit by the pale radiance of dawn, is at a far remove from Vernet. It owes something to the Welsh subjects of Wilson, whose sonorous colouring it approaches. Wilson also employed his brush in broad, loose strokes somewhat like the handling here. But Turner is still concerned to render the particular even if, as in *Fishermen at Sea*, he deploys a bold scheme of lighting to unify the design. We are made to feel familiar with every fold of these obscurely-seen hills, even with the convolutions of the slowly unwinding veil of mist that hides them. Again the artist's intention is pointed by a quotation, this time from Milton himself: lines which Turner remembered when he was preparing his lecture on Reflections in about 1810:

> Ye mists and exhalations that now rise,
> From hill or streaming lake, dusky or gray,
> Till the sun paints your fleecy skirts with gold,
> In honour to the world's great Author, rise.[60]

At the time he was exploring the north of England, Turner also became acquainted with north Wales, where he went in search simultaneously of grand subject-matter and the birthplace of Wilson.[61] Wilson's influence on his method of painting increased during the late 1790s, and he produced several pictures of Welsh subjects at that time. They culminated in the canvas that he submitted to the Academy as his Diploma picture on his election as full Academician in 1802 – a moment of great importance in his career. This picture (FIG. X), exhibited in 1800, shows *Dolbadern Castle, North Wales*,[62] and exemplifies the progress of his style towards the greater generalisation which the Academy approved. It bears witness to an awareness not only of Wilson, but of the even more sublime Salvator Rosa. The rather delicate colouring of *Coniston Fells* has given way to broad and powerful masses articulated by sharper and more dramatic tonal contrasts. Instead of presenting an intricate pattern of interrelating natural phenomena, Turner gives a single bold idea: the lonely stump of the castle's ruined tower presides over a beetling cliff, at the base of which two figures are dwarfed by the high rocks. Restless clouds press down on the design from a fitfully lit sky. Technically, the picture could hardly be further removed from the suave finish and sharp detail of *Fishermen at Sea*, although the two works are linked by their mood of uneasy, threatening repose. There is another difference, too: whereas the canvas of 1796 is allowed to speak for itself, the *Dolbadern* has the lines of verse that were now permitted to appear in the catalogue. Incidentally, it is noteworthy that during these years, when a citation of verse is almost *de rigeur* for Turner, the sea-pieces are always without them. This is perhaps a reflection on the state of nautical poetry at the time; though Turner was later to borrow from Thomson and others in connection with certain of his marines. The lines quoted with the title of *Dolbadern* are as follows:

> How awful is the silence of the waste,
> Where nature lifts her mountains to the sky.
> Majestic solitude, behold the tower
> Where hopeless OWEN, long imprison'd, pin'd,
> And wrung his hands for Liberty, in vain.

It is thought that these are the first lines of Turner's own poetry to be used by him in an Academy catalogue. Once again, they bring together the group of ideas that 'belong' to the subject and leave us in no doubt as to the effect that Turner seeks. The 'awful silence' is a typical element of the sublime – an element that the artist could not incorporate visually – and had been noted by Burke as a type of 'Privation', along with Vacuity, Darkness, and Solitude.[63] 'Majestic solitude' is evoked two lines later. 'Darkness, vacuity, silence, and all other absolute privations of the same kind,' says Payne Knight, 'may also be sublime by partaking of infinity: which is equally a privation or negative existence: for infinity is that which is without bounds, as darkness is that which is without light, vacuity that which is without substance, and silence that which is without sound. In contemplating each, the mind expands itself in the same manner; and, in expanding itself, will of course conceive grand and sublime ideas, if the imagination be in any degree susceptible of grandeur and sublimity.'[64] All the qualities of the natural scene at Dolbadern are given additional force by being related to the experience of a specific human being – 'hopeless Owen' – with whom

FIG. X
J. M. W. Turner, *Dolbadern Castle*, 1800, oil on canvas. Royal Academy of Arts, London

we can identify, and who, though unseen, takes the part of protagonist in the natural drama. This is Thomson's principle of human reference reapplied in a visual context, and of course the idea of historical association leading to the contemplation of heroic virtue and suffering is essential to the full sublime experience. The idea had been stated as a principle of Taste by John Gilbert Cooper in 1755:

> . . . even the Ruins of an old Castle properly dispos'd, or the Simplicity of a rough-hewn Hermitage in a Rock, enliven a Prospect, by recalling the Moral Images of *Valor* and *Wisdom* . . . amiable Images, belonging to the Divine Family of Truth . . .[65]

In *Dolbadern Castle* the specific 'Moral Image' is Liberty, a subject dealt with at length by Thomson in his poem of that title,[66] and treated by Turner in some later canvases.[67] The simultaneous suggestion of a hero and a universal ideal in the context of the gloomy Welsh mountains creates a complex play of ideas visual, moral and political which Turner may well have considered worthy of the attention of his fellow academicians.

With rather similar intentions, he worked on another north Welsh subject,[68] showing the army of Edward I marching through the foothills of Snowdon, on its mission of subduing the country and extirpating Welsh culture in the persons of its bardic priests. This act of suppression had been the theme of Gray's poem *The Bard* of 1757, a work which immediately entered the canon of sublime literature, and which lent itself with peculiar aptness to the use of painters specialising in the landscape sublime, more particularly since they could easily visit and study the scenery in which the story is set. Reynolds set the imprimatur of his approval on the poem in his fifteenth Discourse, when he referred to 'our great lyric poet, when he conceived his sublime idea of the indignant Welsh Bard . . .'[69] and several artists took inspiration from the subject.

> Ruin seize thee, ruthless king!
> Confusion on thy banners wait,
> Though fann'd by conquest's crimson wing
> They mock the air with idle state.
> Helm, nor hauberk's twisted mail,
> Nor e'en thy virtues, tyrant, shall avail
> To save thy secret soul from nightly fears,
> From Cambria's curse, from Cambria's tears!
> Such were the sounds, that o'er the crested pride
> Of the first Edward scatter'd wild dismay,
> As down the steep of Snowdon's shaggy side
> He wound with toilsome march his long array.[70]

It is the last two lines of this stanza that Turner illustrates. The work was never finished, and all that we have of it are a few studies, one or two of which are in watercolour on very large sheets of paper. For the finished picture was planned as a watercolour, not as an oil painting. Watercolour was a further means by which Turner could approach the problem of achieving serious art. It was a medium in which, at the time, limitless possibilities of technical advance were opening up. The experiments that Turner himself had been making during the 1790s were paralleled by developments in the work of contemporaries as dissimilar as Thomas Girtin (1775–1802), Richard Westall (1765–1836) and William Blake (1757–1827). The last two both attempted to give watercolour the density and power necessary for grand statements of 'historical' subjects, Westall trying with rich resonant colours reinforced by gum arabic to reproduce as exactly as he could the effect of his (much larger) oil paintings; Blake experimenting with his 'fresco' (tempera) and colour printing techniques to broaden the basis of watercolour. Girtin, who worked closely with Turner in the mid-1790s, confined himself almost exclusively to landscape, and hardly modified his watercolour medium at all, but achieved a breadth and warmth in his use of it that contemporaries found impressive. He rarely needed to work on a large scale, having solved the problem of relative scale by his own subtly refined system of composition and colouring, which seems to have influenced Turner to some extent. But since both artists were pursuing a similar objective, the infusion of emotional force into the landscape watercolour, some of their solutions were likely to coincide in any case. In practice, their work turned out very different. Turner, for instance, was willing to paint his watercolours on enormous sheets of paper. In doing so, he was perhaps obeying a 'rule' of the sublime – that great size is conducive to grandeur.[71] Several of the watercolours that he submitted to the Academy exhibitions in the late 1790s and early 1800s follow this rule. There were other reasons, of course: in a public display of mixed works, watercolours needed to attract attention away from the paintings which all too easily monopolised the interest of visitors. Turner, unlike Girtin, had a mastery of oil which made it strictly unnecessary for him to paint in watercolour; but, as I have suggested, the technical potential of watercolour seemed immense. The studies for the *Bard* picture indicate the wonderful evocative power with which he could infuse the medium, and there are finished works of the same period which confirm this impression. For instance, another treatment of the theme of the Bard appeared as a finished watercolour on the Academy's walls in 1800 (the year of *Dolbadern Castle*). It is a much less dramatic subject, in which mountain grandeur plays no part:[72] Turner's model is Claude, and the Bard is seated beneath a graceful tree, singing to a small group of listeners. Beyond, a sunlit landscape of great beauty stretches away to the towers of Caernarvon Castle in the distance. Only the verses, probably by Turner, which appear in the catalogue, hint at the gruesome fate that the Bard will suffer:

> And now on Arvon's haughty tow'rs
> The Bard the song of pity pours,
> For oft on Mona's distant hills he sighs,
> Where jealous of the minstrel band,
> The tyrant drench'd with blood the land,
> And charm'd with horror, triumph'd in their cries.
> The swains of Arvon round him throng,
> And join the sorrows of his song.

Another watercolour view of Caernarvon Castle had been shown at the Academy in the previous year.[73] This too is a reminiscence of Claude, though the mood is greatly heightened by a sunset which suffuses the scene with golden light. No figures supply a 'historical' connotation; but the picture is nevertheless a translation into visual terms of a typical 'sublime' subject. One of the many tourists who visited the region had provided what might almost be the literary source for Turner's watercolour:

The solemn turrets of Caernarvon Castle, contrasted with the gay scenery of ships and villas in its neighbourhood, formed the foreground; to the left appeared the dark precipices of the Rivals, three mountains of great bulk, and immense height, which were now in the shade; and beyond them, the ocean, glittering with the rays of the departing sun, stretched as far as the vision extended. Nothing could exceed the glory of his setting; as he approached the waves, his radiance became more tolerable, and his form more distinct, exhibiting the appearance of an immense ball of fire. When he reached the ocean, he seemed to rest upon a throne, for a moment, and then buried his splendid rotundity in its waters; reminding us of that beautiful apostrophe to the orb of light, and sublime description, in the father of Erse poetry:

Hast thou left thy blue course in heaven, golden-haired son of the sky! The west has opened its gates; the bed of thy repose is there. The waves come to behold thy beauty.

They lift their trembling heads. They see thee lovely in thy sleep; they shrink away with fear. Rest in thy shadowy cave, O sun! Let thy return be with joy.

This must be our sole sample of the 'poetry' of Ossian, who, as the passage indicates, had considerably influenced people's way of looking at the mountainous regions of Britain. Turner himself produced only one work directly inspired by Ossian – a picture now lost which appeared at the Academy in 1802 with the title: *Ben Lomond Mountain, Scotland: The Traveller, vide Ossian's War of Caros*.[74] The traveller of our quotation is the Rev. Richard Warner, whose *Walk through Wales* came out in 1798,[75] and was followed a year later by *A Second Walk through Wales*. Warner's excited descriptions marvellously suggest the landscape of Snowdonia, and, in particular, convey the *scale* of the scenery, which was the element that caused artists most problems. He thus recounts his descent of Snowdon:

We accordingly proceeded through the gloom, following the steps of our conductor, who walked immediately before us, as we literally could not see the distance of a dozen feet. The situation was new to us, and brought to our recollection the noble passage with which a prophecy of Joel magnificently begins: 'A day of darkness and gloominess, a day of clouds and of thick darkness, as the morning spread upon the mountains'; it produced however, an effect that was very sublime. Occasional gusts of wind, which now roared around us, swept away for a moment, the pitchy cloud that involved particular spots of the mountain, and discovered immediately below us, hugh rocks, abrupt precipices, and profound hollows, exciting emotions of astonishment and awe in the mind, which the eye, darting from an immense descent of vacuity and horror, conveyed to it under the dreadful image of inevitable destruction.[76]

Once again we have a literary parallel, this time from the Bible; and note the ritual succession of predictable adjectives and nouns: Gray's spontaneous awe, Thoresby's equally spontaneous terror, are now elements in a prescribed response; though it is not for that reason necessarily insincere, simply that the language for articulating the response is now fully forged. For Turner, the forging of a suitable language was still in progress. How, within the dimensions of even the largest sheet of paper, to present with forcible conviction the immensity of space which is the vehicle by which landscape operates upon our feelings? It was not, as Turner knew, simply a matter of drawing mountains and valleys and colouring them with suitably sumptuous tints. The whole composition had to embody that physical vastness which takes the breath away when we are confronted with it. This could be achieved partly by adjustments of scale; the tiny figures of the soldiers straggling along the valley in the view of Snowdon, humanity dwarfed by nature: that is one way to suggest vastness. But the vastness of Turner's landscapes had to be more palpable than that, much more a quality inherent in the way they were painted. He had seen that it could be done in the watercolour views of John Robert Cozens (1752–97), Alexander Cozens's more inspired son, many of whose compositions Turner copied (as did Girtin). He would have been able to see how Cozens, choosing subjects whose principal interest was the immensity of their scale, refined on the traditional techniques of watercolour to create a fully realised spatial dimension – vistas that recede into infinity, skies that are immeasurably deep, mountains that soar to immense heights, defining valleys of wonderful grandeur. To attain this remarkable power of atmospheric evocation, Cozens first of all restricted his colour range to a few greys, greens and blues, and secondly developed the natural distinction in watercolour between small, densely hatched strokes and broad washes. By deploying these to construct, respectively, solidly formed masses and ethereal spaces he translated, as it were, the opposing qualities of mass and space which he found in nature, into a literal equivalent in pigment on paper. Simple though this process sounds, it is tremendously effective. Turner understood it thoroughly, even if he never used it quite as Cozens did. He exploited the delicacy of finely hatched touches to build up the concrete detail of a view, while flooding the sheet at the same time with bold sweeps of coloured wash to suggest space and light. A landscape is always constructed out of two elements: the physical forms of which it is composed, and the space between those forms. Before Cozens, landscape artists had generally left the space to look after itself – a wash of blue for a sky, a few formalised clouds, and a neat suggestion of sunlight falling on particular objects, were all that was required. It was a revised understanding of the reality of natural phenomena which prompted this change of approach: far from being more fantastic, Cozens and Turner aimed at a more comprehensive realism in conveying the grandeur of nature. After all, that grandeur was *there*; it did not need to be invented – it only had to be imitated adequately. This is what Diderot meant when he commended the 'terrible' Vernet for his 'truth'.

Vernet, however, was limited in what he could perform by the academic restrictions of his technique. By 1800 Turner had liberated himself from technical restrictions, as we have seen, by greatly expanding the capacity of watercolour, and by teaching himself to paint in a manner expressively consistent with his subject-matter. It was no doubt Reynolds who gave him the hint as to the advantages of a flexible oil technique: in his Discourses he had pointed to the consistency of style and content in Poussin and Salvator,[77] and Turner must have been alive to the value of this idea. And although he seems to have set himself to make watercolour do exactly what he required of it without recourse to extraneous media – gum, or bodycolour (gouache),[78] for instance – he did some experiments with more elaborate materials. His view of Gordale Scar (no. 30) is an instance of this experimentation: on a huge sheet of paper, it is a drawing in pencil over which Turner seems to have used watercolour, bodycolour and gum to create a texture close to that of oil paint.[79] This is only a study, once again, but it has all the force of an oil sketch. Gordale Scar was a phenomenon absolutely typical of the landscape sublime. It was a place where 'The rocks dart their bold and rugged fronts to the heavens, and impending fearfully over the head of the spectator, seem to threaten his immediate destruction.'[80] It was subsequently recorded unforgettably by James Ward in his enormous canvas[81] of the identical view, where the 'threat' is conveyed almost literally. Ward's choice of such a vast scale for his picture illustrates the compulsion exerted on artists by the landscape sublime to approximate to the actual scale of nature in their views. Needless to say, it was rarely attempted, though it was typical of Ward that he tried.

The impressive size of Turner's Gordale study is alone enough to indicate that in making it he was pursuing ends rather different from those he had in mind while drawing Melincourt waterfall in 1795. Picturesqueness is no longer a consideration; it is the sheer power of the scene that is the overriding factor. This is a new manifestation of the landscape sublime – the 'terrific': a category that comes into existence when the element of human danger is introduced. The historical themes of the works connected with the Bards or with 'hopeless Owen' thus directly contribute to the change of mood from one of agreeable, mainly aesthetic contemplation, to one of active involvement giving rise to a state of awe or fear. In the *Gordale Scar* historical figures are dispensed with, and even the representation of contemporary ones is superfluous – the spectator is the protagonist. Similarly in Switzerland, to which the sublime compulsion irresistibly led Turner along with many other artists, overwhelmingly grand statements are constructed out of individual features of the scene. The great fall of the Reichenbach, for example, inspired a large watercolour which is a revision of the composition of *Coniston Fells*.[82] It is upright, with the river falling down a cleft in the centre of the design. But instead of the assiduously suggested mist and obscurity of the earlier essay in the Picturesque Sublime, this drawing presents its subject with remarkable clarity. The details of dead trees, tumbled rocks, and blown spray are shown with scrupulous regard for vivid exactness. The grandeur of the subject lies in the sheer size of the waterfall, in the scale that Turner creates on his sheet of paper, and in its immediacy. His technique enables him to render with fidelity a wide range of natural effects, forms and textures, a multitude of incidents compiled into a monumental image of great simplicity and directness. The human figure is absent, as so often in these early Alpine watercolours: this is the stark and inhospitable reality of the mountains brought vividly before us so that we can enjoy the *frisson* of horror that they give us. But the force of these Swiss views is more the result of confident directness than of an elaborately created atmosphere. Turner acknowledges the power of literal truth in the workings of the sublime.

'What are the scenes of nature that elevate the mind in the highest degree, and produce the sublime sensation? Not the gay landscape, the flowery field, or the flourishing city; but the hoary mountain, and the solitary lake, the aged forest, and the torrent falling over the rock. Hence, too, night-scenes are commonly the most sublime.' Hugh Blair's crisp definitions[83] of sublimity in landscape describe very accurately the preoccupations apparent in Turner's early work. But there is a further class of subjects that is prominent among his exhibited pictures, and which we have as yet barely touched upon: the marines. 'The idea of *literal sublimity*,' Dugald Stewart asserts, is 'inseparably combined with that of the sea, from the stupendous spectacle it exhibits when agitated by a storm.'[84] 'The excessive Grandeur . . . of the Ocean', says Blair, arises 'not from its extent alone, but from the perpetual motion and irresistible force of that mass of Waters.'[85]

Scholars of the sublime pointed out that there was an immediate connection between our responses to the ocean and to mountains: we speak quite naturally of 'mountain billows', Stewart observes, and conversely we talk of 'a tempestuous sea of mountains'.[86] It was therefore appropriate that Turner should study both these 'immensities' of nature together, and choose his subjects alternately from each. His first exhibited painting, as we know, was a sea-piece, and a night-scene into the bargain. But, as with his landscapes, he did not broach the most high-flown sublimities immediately. By a series of essays, progressively more ambitious, he explored gradually the technical problem of representing the sea, and the in-terrelationship between the sea and human beings. It is significant that many of the criticisms levelled against his early marines attacked his unrealistic depiction of water; this must have distressed him, since he attached such importance to literal truth in establishing the language of his dramas. Unfortunately, the criticism was to follow him throughout his career, although he modified his procedures considerably, as we shall see. The point that the critics were making was nevertheless important: they asserted (and Turner would have agreed with the premise) that if a picture of the sea is to impress us with awe, horror, or sympathy with its victims, then the painter must convince us that it is the sea we are looking at. The struggle to attain this conviction is evident in the sequence of his paintings: not all the subjects are dramas of human survival, but those which are show a steady intensification of dramatic excitement not only in handling and incident but also in broad conception. The progression from *Dutch Boats in a gale: fishermen endeavouring to put their fish on board* of 1801, to the *Shipwreck* of 1805, to the *Wreck of a Transport Ship* of about 1810[87] is one of gradually increasing involvement of the spectator in the scenes depicted. In the first a minor incident at sea is presented objectively as an external event; in the second a more serious incident is shown, the composition catching us up in a swirl of water and rocking vessels. The third is no longer an external event at all: the spectator is wholly absorbed into what is happening, actually in the water which reels and towers about him, a victim of the catastrophe that he witnesses. A visitor to Turner's studio thought it 'one of the most sublime and awful pictures that ever came from mortal hand . . . the dread reality seems before us'.[88] The old dilemma of the known artificiality of what we are supposed to respond to as if it were real is resolved by masterly design and vivid realism of presentation. Gray might well have felt that in this picture the reality of the terror militated against the pleasure of beholding it. The dictum of Lucretius that defines this brand of enjoyment no longer applies:

Suave mari magno turbantibus aequora ventis,
E terra magnum alterius spectare laborem.[89]

This detachment, the detachment that makes it possible to distinguish between what other people experience and what we experience ourselves, while aesthetically pleasurable, is in a sense a fallacious basis for serious art. The landscape sublime relied on the contrary pulls of dread and enjoyment, the titillation of a fear that we cannot really feel. To evoke that sensation was no doubt agreeable enough; but it could have little to do with an art which set itself seriously and profoundly to treat of the eternal verities of human existence. This was merely playing with 'truth', and shirking the consequences. Turner, who saw more deeply into Reynolds's reasons for admiring Michelangelo than a simple effects-monger could, wanted to use his chosen medium of landscape for more important purposes.

NOTES TO CHAPTER TWO

1. As early as 1789 it was concluded that 'the Greeks had no Thomsons because they had no Claudes'. See Lindsay, op. cit., p. 62; also Jean H. Hagstrum, The Sister Arts, Chicago 1958, pp. 251–2.

2. J. T. Atkyns, Iter Boreale, Yale Center for British Art, MS 1732.

3. William Mason, ed., The Poems and Letters of Thomas Gray, London 1820, p. 62.

4. Ibid., p. 70, The passage from Livy translates: 'the mountain snows almost touching the sky, wretched huts placed on cliff-tops, cattle and animals shivering with cold, squalid and brutal people; everything animate and inanimate stiff with frost . . .'

5. See below, p.72.

6. D. H. Atkinson, Ralph Thoresby, The Topographer, his Town and Times, 2 vols, 1885–7, Vol. I, p. 129.

7. Immanuel Kant, Critique of Judgement (Kritik der Urteilskraft, Berlin 1790), trans. J. H. Bernard, London 1931, p. 124.

8. The etymology of the word has been hotly debated. The OED gives: Lat. sub + limen = lintel. 'Sub' has the force of 'over' or 'above' rather than 'below'; See Stewart, op. cit., Appendix, p. 606–15.

9. Payne Knight, op. cit., p. 332.

10. I. U. [Usher], Clio; or Discourse on Taste, Addressed to a Young Lady, 2nd ed., London 1769; p. 103.

11. Aristotle, Poetics, II, 13.

12. Payne Knight, op. cit., pp. 328–9.

13. Coleridge, Biographia Literaria, ed. cit., p. 169.

14. David Hume, Treatise of Human Nature, 1739, ed. L. A. Selby-Bigge, 1888, Bk II, p. 298–9.

15. Spectator, No. 412, 23 June 1712.

16. Burke, Philosophical Enquiry . . ., London 1757, p. 13.

17. Kames, op. cit., p. 264.

18. Kant, op. cit., p. 136.

19. Kant, op. cit., p. 125.

20. Stewart, op. cit., p. 390.

21. Spectator, No. 417, 28 June 1712.

22. In his Essay on the Pleasures of the Imagination Elsewhere he discusses the sublime of Milton at length. See Spectator, Nos 267 (Saturday, 5 January 1712) etc.; an essay on Paradise Lost.

23. Spectator, No. 417, 28 June 1712.

24. Archibald Alison, Essays on the Nature and Principles of Taste, 4th ed., Edinburgh 1815, Vol. I, p. 121.

25. I. U., Clio . . . pp. 107–8.

26. Joseph Cradock, An Account . . ., London 1777, p. 1.

27. Gilpin's 'picturesque' was not strictly his own invention. The Abbé du Bos, in his Reflexions Critiques sur la Poésie et sur la Peinture, 1719, had already summarised many of the ideas Gilpin was to explore: J'appelle composition pittoresque, l'arrangement des objets qui doivent entrer dans un tableau par rapport à l'effet général du tableau. Une bonne composition pittoresque est celle dont le coup d'oeil fait un grand effet . . . Il faut pour cela que le tableau me soit point embarassé par les figures quoi qu'il y en ait assez pour remplir la toile. Il faut que les objets s'y démêlent facilement . . . que les groupes soient bien composés, . . .' etc.

28. Spectator, No. 414, 25 June 1712.

29. William Gilpin, Three Essays: On Picturesque Beauty; On Picturesque Travel; and On Sketching Landscape . . . 2nd ed., London 1794, p. 6.

30. Gilpin, Observations relative chiefly to Picturesque Beauty, made in the year 1772, on Several Parts of England, Particularly the Mountains, and Lakes of Cumberland, and Westmoreland, 2 vols, London 1786, vol. I, p. 3.

31. Horace Walpole's response to the Alps which he visited in the same year as Gray, 1739, is well known: 'Precipices, mountains, torrents, wolves, rumblings, Salvator Rosa –' (letter to Richard West, 28 September 1739).

32. Thomson, The Castle of Indolence; Canto I, xxxviii, ll. 8–9.

33. Gilpin, 1786, pp. 119–20.

34. TB I, D, H.

35. William Sotheby, A Tour through Parts of Wales, Sonnets, Odes and other Poems, London 1794, p. 16, and plate facing p. 17. Smith's dates are 1749–1831.

36. See nos 35 and 28.

37. See John Gage, 'Turner and the Picturesque', Burlington Magazine, CVII, January 1965, pp. 16–26 and February, pp. 75–81.

38. Butlin & Joll 7.

39. Farington, Diary, 5 January 1798. The critic was John Hoppner, RA, who said the picture showed 'a timid man afraid to venture'.

40. Thomson, Spring, ll. 88–9, 191–2, 193, 203–4.

41. TB XXXV, f. 84.

42. Butlin & Joll 6.

43. Butlin & Joll 126.

44. Winter, ll. 41–9. For comment on Turner's admiration for Thomson see Jack Lindsay, JMW Turner, 1966, pp. 58–62.

45. Butlin & Joll 86.

46. Butlin & Joll 140. The quotation is from Summer, ll. 1401–8.

47. Ms N, f. 8 verso. The lines Turner quotes are from Summer, ll. 804–21.

48. See T. Wright, op. cit., p. 62.

49. Butlin & Joll 1.

50. For example, Wright's Lighthouse in the Mediterranean, Nicolson, pl. 312.

51. TB XXXVII, 104–5. rep. Wilton 1979, pl. 32.

52. Diderot, Oeuvres Esthétiques, Paris 1959, p. 574.

53. Diderot, op. cit., p. 574.

54. Diderot, op. cit., p. 564.

55. Diderot, op. cit., p. 568.

56. Diderot, *op. cit.*, p. 575.

57. Butlin & Joll 137.

58. Butlin & Joll 360, see no. 73.

59. Butlin & Joll 5.

60. *Paradise Lost*, Bk v, ll. 185–8. ('Streaming' is a misprint for 'steaming'.) See Turner's MS Perspective Lecture, British Library Add. Ms 46151, H, f. 45.

61. See a letter of 27 December 1847, quoted by Finberg, *Life*, p. 419.

62. Butlin & Joll 12.

63. Burke, *op. cit.*, pp. 50–1.

64. Payne Knight, *op cit.*, p. 363.

65. John Gilbert Cooper, *Letters concerning Taste*, London 1755, p. 13.

66. Published in 1735–6.

67. See Butlin & Joll 374, 375.

68. No. 41.

69. *Discourses*, Wark ed., p. 271.

70. Thomas Gray, *The Bard*, 1757, stanza 1.

71. Burke, *op. cit.*, p. 51: 'Greatness of dimension is a powerful cause of the sublime.' Sir George Stewart MacKenzie was of the opinion that 'Sheer size is not conducive to sublimity.' (*An Essay on Some Subjects connected with Taste*, Edinburgh 1817, p. 90.) In attempting to 'reproduce' on paper the scale of the mountains, Turner seems already to understand something broader by the sublime than the Burkean school of theorists.

72. Wilton 263, pl. 52.

73. Wilton 254, pl. 47.

74. Thought to have been a watercolour: see Wilton 346.

75. The quotation is from pp. 133–4.

76. Warner, *op. cit.*, p. 128.

77. See *Discourse v*, Wark ed., pp. 85, 87.

78. Turner is reported to have despised bodycolour: 'If you fellows continue to use that beastly stuff you will destroy the art of watercolour painting in our country.' See J. C. Horsley, *Recollections of a Royal Academician*, London 1903, p. 241.

79. Finberg considered that the medium is oil paint. He is possibly right.

80. *The Works of the late Edward Dayes*, London 1805, p. 62.

81. In the Tate Gallery, no. 1043.

82. Wilton 367; repr. in colour in *Turner in Switzerland*, p. 64.

83. Blair, *op. cit.*, p. 62.

84. Stewart, *op. cit.*, p. 422.

85. Blair, *op. cit.*, p. 58.

86. Stewart, *loc. cit.*

87. Butlin & Joll 14, 54, 210.

88. *Selections from the Literary and Artistic Remains of Pauline Lady Trevelyan*, ed. D. Wooster, London 1879, p. 117–18.

89. Lucretius, *De Rerum Natura*, II, ll. 1,2. The lines can be translated: 'It is sweet when on the great sea the winds trouble the waters, to behold from land another's deep distress.'

1 Llanthony Abbey, 1794 (no. 1)

2 *Evening Landscape with Castle and Bridge*, 1798–9 (no. 2)
3 *Norham Castle: Study*, c. 1798 (no. 3)

4 *A view in North Wales,* c. 1799 (no. 4)

5 *Dolbadern and the pass of Llanberis, c.* 1799 (no. 5)

6 River with cattle and mountains beyond, c. 1799 (no. 6)

7 *Pembroke-castle: Clearing up of a thunder-storm*, 1806 (no. 8)

8 *Illustration to a lecture on Perspective:*
Interior of a Prison, c. 1810 (no. 15)

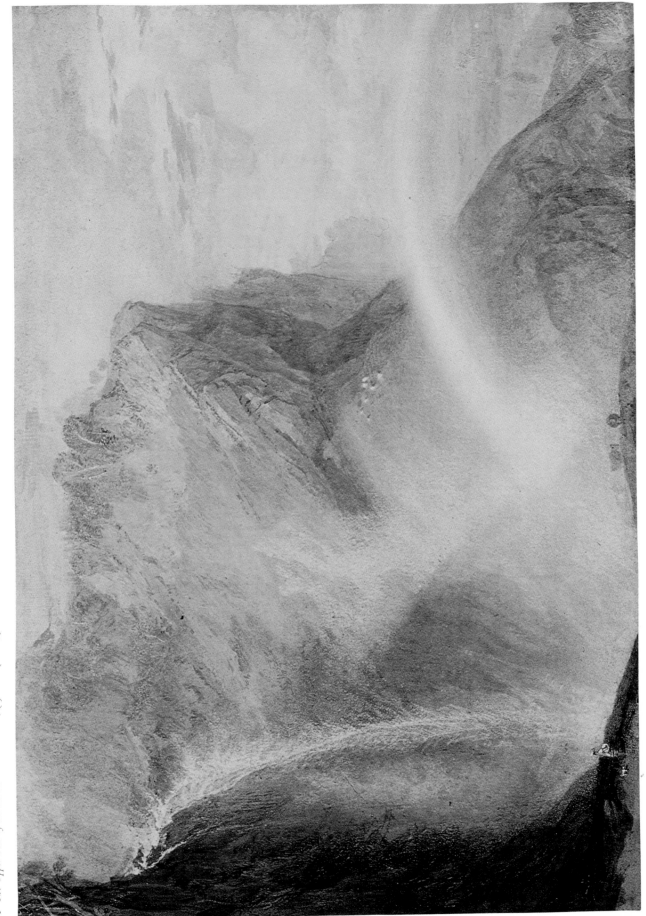

11 *The Upper Fall of the Reichenbach: rainbow*, (?) 1810 (no. 27)

12 *Malham Cove, c. 1810 (no. 28)*

14 *Scene in the Welsh Mountains with an army on the march*, c. 1800 (no. 41)

15 The Battle of Fort Rock, Val d'Aouste, Piedmont, 1815 (no. 51)

16 *The Whale, c.* 1845 (no. 69)

CHAPTER THREE

THE TURNERIAN SUBLIME

Distinguish with exactness, if you mean to know yourself and others, what is so often mistaken – the SINGULAR, the ORIGINAL, the EXTRAORDINARY, the GREAT, and the SUBLIME man: the SUBLIME alone unites the singular, original, extraordinary, and great, with his own uniformity and simplicity: the GREAT, with many powers, and uniformity of ends, is destitute of that superior calmness and inward harmony which soars above the atmosphere of praise . . .

JOHANN CASPAR LAVATER, *Aphorisms on Man*, (Aphorism 600), 1787

Tis not the giant of unwieldy size,
Piling up hills on hills to scale the skies,
That gives an image of the true sublime,
Or the best subject for the lofty rhyme;
But nature's common works, by genius dress'd,
With art selected, and with taste express'd;
Where sympathy with terror is combin'd,
To move, to melt, and elevate the mind.

RICHARD PAYNE KNIGHT: *Landscape. A Poem*, 1794

The branch of art to which Turner was initially trained was not of the most elevated, even in the field of landscape: from childhood until the age of about twenty he was a topographical draughtsman, making views of antiquarian interest for the popular magazines, in which they were rather inadequately engraved, or on commission for private clients. He also showed his watercolours regularly at the Academy, and, as we have noted, he attended the Academy's Schools where, in 1790, he listened to Reynolds's last Discourse.

That event must have impressed itself vividly on his memory, and the injunctions of the President been borne home to him in good earnest, for he frequently referred to Reynolds when he himself came to give lectures to the students in his capacity as Professor of Perspective. The assiduity with which he tried to discharge this office, and the pride with which he often signed his works 'R.A.P.P.' (for Royal Academician and Professor of Perspective) indicate his great dedication to the Academy and its function as preceptor to young artists. At the outset of his first lecture he reminded his listeners of Reynolds, 'whose Discourses must be yet warm in many a recollection'; and he devoted some space to a panegyric of the late President:

His worth as a man and his abilities as an artist were of the most conspicuous kind, whose constant attention to the interest of this establishment deserves all our thanks: whose whole life did prove by deeds 'the hardest lesson which his precepts taught' and which all prove unquestionably the greatness of his mind; and who, so far from vindicating the line of pursuit he had adopted (but which his works irrefrangibly prove exclusively to be his own), yet boldly stept forth, and recommended with his last words in this seat the study of Michael Angelo, to regard the energetic conceptions of his thoughts, the dignified manner of his expressing and embodying these thoughts; and to attend unto the lofty workings of his mind through all his works.[1]

It may well be that Turner felt the parallel between himself and Sir Joshua: both of them were there to teach disciplines to which in their professional capacities they had not entirely adhered. Like Reynolds, Turner tried to inculcate the elevated notion of the 'grand style' founded as much on a careful study of the great masters as on the observation of nature. He may have proposed methods from which he exempted himself on the ground that his own field was perforce an inferior one; but just as we nonetheless attribute to Reynolds himself the ideas he promulgated in his Discourses, so we may fairly assume that Turner believed wholeheartedly in what he told his audiences. Besides, he, like Reynolds, did not confine his activities to the one field in which he excelled: with even greater pertinacity than Reynolds he produced works in other genres. But unlike Reynolds, he never really considered his own an inferior field, and modified it to embrace an altogether broader concept of art.

With such ideas, it is not surprising that the genre of topographical view-painting, in which he began his career, should have provided Turner with a basis for a much more sophisticated form of communication. Buildings, which he learnt at an early age to draw with accuracy, were in fact repositories of a good deal of inherent sublimity. Often it was for this very quality that they were drawn; but topographers did not traditionally attempt to convert their antiquarian records into works of art – that is, they were not concerned with interpreting what they saw, or with creating atmosphere in their drawings. As a natural consequence of the vogue for the landscape sublime, architecture was accorded more weight in this context. Any building might be the focus of serious ideas if it was sufficiently ancient; castles, like Dolbadern or Caernarvon, were inherently grand because of their size and age; often they connoted particular historical events involving military prowess or the drama and terror of war. A cathedral connoted ideas of the grandeur of human achievements: 'In looking up to the vaulted roof of a Gothic Cathedral, our feelings differ, in one remarkable circumstance, from those excited by torrents and cataracts; that whereas, in the latter instances, we see the *momentum* of falling masses actually exhibited to our senses; in the former, we see the triumph of human art, in rendering the law of gravitation subservient to the suspension of its own ordinary effects.'[2]

But over and above these considerations, a cathedral embodied the religious sublime, and was the most impressive of all buildings by virtue of its direct connotations of the Deity. Addison did not much approve of the Gothic style, but he acknowledged the force of religious awe:

> We are obliged to devotion for the noblest buildings that have adorned the several countries of the world. It is this which has set men at work on temples and public places of worship, not only that they might, by the magnificence of the building, invite the Deity to reside within it, but that such stupendous works might, at the same time, open the mind to vast conceptions, and fit it to converse with the divinity of the place. For every thing that is majestic imprints an awfulness and reverence on the mind of the beholder, and strikes it with the natural greatness of the soul.[3]

In his great works in the mode of the 'architectural sublime' Turner strove not merely to inform the viewer of the appearance of the edifice he portrayed; he sought to imbue him with the same awe that he would experience in the building itself. Hence it was appropriate to make these watercolours on a large scale, as he did his landscapes of the same period. The views of Ely and Salisbury[4] that he produced in the decade around 1800 convey the grandeur of these great cathedrals by sheer scale, rather as the large Swiss watercolours of a little later present us starkly with the natural grandeur of the mountains. The use of sombre colour to suggest age-old interiors of dimly-lit stone is the equivalent of the palette employed to convey the rugged barrenness of the Alps, or the sullen storms of the Welsh mountains. All conform to the rule laid down by Burke:

Among colours, such as are soft or cheerful (except perhaps a strong red which is cheerful) are unfit to produce a grand image. An immense mountain covered with a shining green turf is nothing, in this respect, to one dark and gloomy; the cloudy sky is more grand than the blue; and night more sublime and solemn than day. Therefore, in historical painting, a gay or gaudy drapery can never have a happy effect; and in buildings, when the highest degree of the sublime is intended, the materials and ornaments ought neither to be white, nor green, nor yellow, nor blue, nor of a pale red, nor violet, nor spotted, but of sad and fuscous colours, as black, or brown, or deep purple, and the like . . .[5]

Colour is indeed a key element in these early watercolours, for it alone renders them quite separate in intention from the architectural or topographical tradition from which they spring. It proclaims the artist's wish to sway the emotions rather than to inform the mind: a radical change of role for the traditional topographical watercolour.

But studies of individual structures remarkable for their architectural and associational grandeur did not by any means comprehend all that Turner performed in the way of topography. In his view of the *Cathedral Church at Lincoln* of 1795 (FIG. XI) the

FIG. XI
J. M. W. Turner, *Lincoln Cathedral*, 1795, pencil and watercolour, British Museum, London

soaring towers and spires of the cathedral itself are not permitted to engross our interest; the foreground street scene with its backdrop of picturesque houses and walls is just as important to his purpose. The art of inventing appropriate figures to occupy the foreground of a view was one in which every topographer of any merit was skilled. Turner, in the years when such work occupied him almost exclusively – that is, until about 1795 – proved himself exceptionally adept in this. As the *Lincoln Cathedral* drawing shows, the foreground was not merely a space to be suitably filled with 'staffage': it was the stage on which much of the action of his design took place. For his view is not simply a cold statement of certain architectural facts. It is a picture of Lincoln, where architecture is only one element in a complex of interrelated facts about the city and its inhabitants. There is no large romantic 'message', only a full, lively and sympathetic account of the world Turner finds around him – the traditional 'economic' approach. Other topographical works of the 1790s carry the possibilities of that approach still further. The brilliant, bustling fair at *Wolverhampton*[6] of 1796 incorporates a wealth of human character, surveying the occupations of a wide variety of men and women in a provincial market town with something of a novelist's love of detail. A view of the west front of *Llandaff Cathedral*[7] drawn in the same year, at first glance a purely architectural study, contains a group of two girls dancing to a fiddler on a tombstone, touchingly suggestive of the larger issues that are raised by the subject. Imaginative human colour of this kind raises Turner's topography to a level of thought that is already considerably more sophisticated than that of the commonplace view.

What we are witnessing in these watercolours is the application of Thomson's principle of the interaction of human life and its environment. As we have seen, Turner was as ready to pair his watercolours with verses as he was his oils. Executed in the richer, more full-bodied palette Turner had evolved by this date, the drawings of the late 1790s convey far more of a sense of atmosphere than their predecessors of mid-decade, and there is a tendency for Turner deliberately to suppress the human element, for, as we know, he was pursuing the ideal of the landscape sublime, in which the brooding hostility of nature to man is a dominant note. The verses that he selected to accompany the 1799 *Warkworth Castle, Northumberland,*[8] from *Summer*, typify the mood:

> Behold slow settling o'er the lurid grove
> Unusual darkness broods; and growing, gains
> The full possession of the sky; and yon baleful cloud
> A redd'ning gloom, a magazine of fate,
> Ferment.[9]

But we have also noticed that the human element could be reintroduced, as it were, by oblique allusion: by bringing forward the latent associations of the spot recorded, as in *Dolbadern Castle*. Another of the watercolours shown in 1799, now unfortunately lost, does so in a particularly interesting way. It was entitled *Morning, from Dr Langhorne's Visions of Fancy*, and the catalogue supplied these verses from John Langhorne's *Elegy IV*:

> Life's morning landscape gilt with orient light,
> Where Hope and Joy, and Fancy hold their reign,
> The grove's green wave, the blue stream sparkling bright,
> The blythe hours dancing round Hyperion's wain.
>
> In radiant colours Youth's free hand pourtrays,
> Then holds the flattering tablet to his eye;
> Nor thinks how soon the vernal grove decays,
> Nor sees the dark cloud gathering o'er the sky.
> Mirror of life, thy glories thus depart.[10]

As in the *Dolbadern Castle* (FIG. X), the verses introduce a 'Moral Idea' which expands the sense of the picture and builds a group of connotations round it. Langhorne's poem is of special interest since it treats of a theme that Turner was to make his own: the Fallacy of Hope.

> Oh! yet, ye dear, deluding visions stay!
> Fond Hopes, of Innocence and Fancy born!
> For you I'll cast these waking thoughts away,
> For one wild dream of Life's romantic morn:
>
> Ah! no: the sunshine o'er each object spread
> By flattering Hope, the flowers that blew so fair;
> Like the gay gardens of Armida fled,
> And vanish'd from the powerful rod of care.[11]

When Turner began regularly to affix his own verses to his exhibited pictures, in 1812, it was a fragmentary 'Manuscript Poem' called *Fallacies of Hope* which provided the quotations. He continued to use this 'source' until the end of his life, and by its means gave literary interpretations to many pictures which seem to us to stand perfectly satisfactorily without them. His adherence to the eighteenth-century notion of *Ut pictura poesis* was staunch and lasting.

An amusing illustration of this is the pair of drawings that he made in his early thirties, satirically comparing an unsuccessful poet and an amateur painter.[12] The first is seen at his lucubrations in a garret scattered with 'Hints on an epic poem' and other papers, and beseeching his muse to 'finish well my long-sought line'. The other (no. 50) pores gloatingly over a newly completed canvas; the sheet is cluttered with notes on 'sublime' effects, and lists of historical subjects. Both aspire to the highest branch of their art, and while one is 'sublimely unaware' of his shortcomings, the other struggles against them, enlisting the aid of his muse. Turner's own struggles to write poetry are reflected in the *Garreteer's Petition*; his sense of the dangers of an inflated notion of one's own abilities as a painter emerges from the other drawing. Perhaps he asks us to draw the moral that we must adapt our notions of the sublime to suit our own capacities and abilities, rather than forcing ourselves into an ill-fitting mould.

But if he was diffident about his literary talents, he was not really in any doubt as to his powers as an artist, and the first decade of the new century saw him vying as earnestly as any student of Reynolds with the great masters of the past: Titian, Poussin, Backhuisen, Rembrandt, Salvator, Claude — all were used as models for pictures which explicitly set out to do what they had done. Even before he visited the Louvre he experimented with a grandiose history piece, exhibited in 1800, which he called the *Fifth Plague of Egypt* (see no. 43).[13] This embraces a much wider range of influences and associations than the *Dolbadern Castle* (FIG. X) of the same year, borrowing its combination of classical architecture and tempestuous landscape from Poussin, its wild paintwork and emotionally charged detail from Salvator, and its figures from Wilson. Later, influences are explored in a more disciplined way — the *Tenth Plague of Egypt* (see no. 44) aims at the unified tragic mood of Poussin, while *Jason* (see no. 42) imitates Salvator and *Macon* Claude.[14]

These subjects were to provide material for the early issues of Turner's *Liber Studiorum* which began to appear in 1807, and which in publishing his major pictures quite explicitly allocates them to their proper 'departments' of art: The *Plagues of Egypt* and *Jason* are, of course, 'Historical'; *Macon* was not used for the publication, but we know how Turner would have classified it, for his system is a typically eighteenth-century scheme for ordering and categorising, and the whole of the *Liber Studiorum* is, apart from being a means of disseminating his work, a sort of check-list of the various kinds of art at which he had tried his hand. He discriminates between the

'Historical' and the 'Mountainous Sublime' of course, and gives separate classifications to Architecture and Marine subjects; but he also makes distinctions between
the 'Pastoral' and the 'Elevated Pastoral', drawing attention to a most interesting
application of his system: most of the plates that are labelled 'P' for Pastoral treat of
informal, homely subjects – farmyards, children's games (the 'Puerile'?) and so on;
while 'E.P.' clearly denotes a more stately and splendid type of subject-matter; a
subject-matter that, in its own calm and expansive way, belongs as much to the
regions of the sublime as do rough seas and mountains. This is a matter about which
we shall have more to say later. Turner's use of the term 'Elevated Pastoral' (and
although it is not certain, there is every reason, including his own fondness for the
word 'elevated' in association with landscape, to believe that the 'E.P.' does mean
that)[15] affords important evidence of the development by this early date of his
personal interpretation of the 'hierarchy' of his own paintings.

This great series of mezzotints after his pictures perfectly illustrates Turner's
concern for the values that the eighteenth century had instilled in him. They reflect
the spirit of healthy rivalry with the greatest of his predecessors which Reynolds had
tried to inculcate, and a characteristically didactic attitude to his relations with the
public at large. He approached the old masters with Reynoldsian eagerness to learn,
but was equally eager to convey their teachings to others. The notebook that he filled
with observations on the paintings he saw in the Louvre on his continental visit of
1802,[16] and the jottings that he made in preparation for his lectures, contain many
thoughtful analyses and reflections on techniques, styles and idioms, which he
absorbed into his own practice and tried to pass on to his students.

His teaching of perspective was unorthodox, for he combined it with lectures on
the history of landscape painting and general observations on technical problems. He
was accused of talking off the point, but for him all these things were of central
importance, and to isolate the theory of perspective and teach it dryly as a 'pure'
discipline would have been absurd. He went so far as to admit that in itself the study
of perspective was boring: 'however arduous, however depressing the subject may
prove; however trite, complex or indefinite . . . however trammeled with the turgid
and too often repelling recourace of mechanical rules, yet those duties must be
pursued and altho they have not the charms or wear the same flattering habiliments of
taste as Painting, Sculpture or Architecture, yet they are to the full as usefull and
perhaps more so for without the aid of Perspective Art totters on its very foundation.'[17] He reiterated with almost platitudinous firmness the importance of rules:
'True rules are the means, nature the end,' he said.[18]

As a landscape painter he was perhaps not the obvious choice for a teacher of the
Rules of Perspective as propounded by Malton, Kirby, Brook Taylor and the rest.
But as a trained architectural topographer he was well qualified for the task and he
thoroughly acquainted himself with the technical literature in preparing his course.[19]
He recognised that the laws of perspective are essential to the achievement of that
verisimilitude which the painter needs to attain in order to make any effect
emotionally valid. 'Parallel lines carry with them no idea of height,' he explained in
his first lecture, 'while the oblique line may rise to infinity. Consequently Perspective
and not geometrical drawings can produce an appearance [of] altitude, elevation or
size of form, which must be the feelings of the mind; the association of Ideas upon
viewing a fragment only of the Athenian Temples, a grain, a part of a whole, or before
the massy remnant of the Temple of Jupiter Stator without being impressed into ideas
of Grandeur by the mere recurrence of thought, the accompanying power of man's
intellectual capacity in supporting its extent of front or elevated entablature, but can
he, however colossal in intellect, for a moment think he is so in the scale of form or of
height equal to the fragments; how can it then be possible that a representation
Geometrically considered as to lines can give by any indulgence of effect the least idea

of the extent, the impression of height, dignity and towering majesty of architecture . . .'[20] The basic laws of perspective bear directly on our ability to communicate the grandest ideas. The point was fully borne out by the comments of a critic on Turner's *Decline of Carthage*[21] when it appeared in 1817: 'It is impossible to pass over the execution of the architectural parts of this picture: they are drawn with purity and correctness; the Grecian orders are carefully preserved, and the arrangement of the buildings in perspective is formed with so much adherence to geometrical rule, that the eye is carried through the immense range of magnificent edifices with such rapidity, that we entirely forget the artist, and merely dwell on the historic vision.'[22] Turner had already demonstrated the principle in his studies in the 'architectural sublime'; and he believed that no aspect of his art was so far outside the pale that it could not be elevated likewise:

> To select, combine and concentrate what is beautiful in nature and admirable in art is as much the business of the Landscape painter in his Line as in the other departments of art; and from the early drawings of nature in the work [of] Pietro Perugino can be traced the value of attending to method which each Master established for himself . . . by combining what was to them remarkable in nature . . . with the highest qualities of the Historic school.[23]

This states the principle on which Wilson constructed his landscapes in the grand manner – *Niobe, Celadon and Amelia, Solitude*, or *Cicero at his Villa*. When he came to discuss 'the immortal Wilson' in his lecture on Landscape, Turner cited these works as examples of his achievement. He pointed to the display of 'contending elements' in the *Celadon and Amelia*, and commended the 'dignified or more than solemn *Solitude*'.[24] It is no accident that the pictures that attracted Turner most, and which prompted the longest and most effusive of his commentaries, were two which achieved in a pre-eminent degree the combination of the 'remarkable in nature' with the 'highest qualities of the Historic school': Titian's *Death of St Peter Martyr* and Poussin's *Deluge*.[25] The first of these he called 'the standard of his [Titian's] powers of Landscape'. 'The high honour that Landscape Painting receives from the hands of Titian proves how highly he considered its value not only in employing the varieties of contrast, color and dignity in most of his Historical Pictures, but the triumph even of Landscape may be safely said to exist in his divine picture of St Peter Martyr. Even over History he felt not those puerile thoughts of making it subservient . . .'[26] The picture inspired Turner to ecstasies of poetic description: '. . . the sublimity of the arrangement of lines by its unshackled obliquity obtains the associated feelings of free continuity that rushes like the ignited spark struggling as the ascending Rocket with the Elements from Earth towards Heaven; and when no more propelled by the force it scatters around its falling glories, ignited embers, seeking again its Earthly bourne, while diffusing around its mellow radiance in the descending cherub with the palm of Beatitude sheds the mellow glow of Gold through the dark embrowned foliage to the dying Martyr.'[27] In his *Louvre* sketchbook he noted: 'This picture is an instance of his great power as to conception and sublimity of intellect – the characters are finely contrasted, the composition is beyond all system, the landscape tho natural is heroic, the figure wonderfully expressive of surprise and its concomitant fear . . . Surely the sublimity of the whole lies in the simplicity of its parts and not in the historical color . . .'[28]

On the other hand, it was the colour of Poussin's *Deluge* which Turner found 'sublime'. He thought it 'natural – it is what a creative mind must be imprest with by sympathy and horror'.[29] Turner follows Sir Joshua closely in using the word 'sublime' in connection with Poussin almost as a matter of course – endorsing the eighteenth-century judgment that the greatest sublimities are those associated with the mind. Once more he attempts to marshal words to form a literary parallel to the picture: 'let us consider [a picture] where she [Nature] has ceased to place a barrier to the overwhelming waters of the Deluge swamping and bearing only one tone[,] the residue of Earthy matter . . . For its color it is admirable, impressive, awfully appropriate, just fitted to every imaginative conjecture of such an event . . . Deficient in every requisite of line so ably displayed in his other work, inconsistent in the coloring of the figures, for they are positively red, blue and yellow, while the sick and wan sun is not allowed to shed one ray but Tears.'[30] Another picture of Poussin's, *Landscape with Pyramus and Thisbe* (FIG. XII), called forth an equally rapt response: 'To the proofs of his abilities of Grandeur and pastoral subjects we possess another truly sublime in the Picture at Ashburnham House of Pyramus and Thisbe. Whether we look upon the dark dark sky illumined at the right hand corner by lightning rushing behind the bending trees and at last awfully gleaming its dying efforts upon some antique buildings on the left, while all beneath amid scattered foliage and broken tombs lies the dying figure of Pyramus; and [in] the depth of darkness all is lost but returning Thisbe.'[31]

This is to interpret painting as drama in the fullest sense: the man capable of these intense, involved responses to Titian, Poussin or Wilson was himself advocating an art to which such responses were appropriate, and there can be little doubt that he expected the public to view his own pictures in the same spirit.

Accordingly, he chose subjects that contained in themselves moving human incidents, and invented landscape settings in which those incidents found a sympathetic place. From the overt imitations of old masters that he produced in the first decade of the century he moved on to a more personal style of historical landscape, in which the lessons he had learned were amalgamated into a new unity. In 1811 he could still paint a more or less direct pastiche of Salvator, the *Apollo and Python*,[32] which is perhaps the last of his paintings to be couched unequivocally in the mode of the landscape sublime. It shows a rocky gully among the mountains, in which torn trees contribute to an atmosphere of desolation: the god, though he irradiates the bright beams of his solar responsibility, cannot illuminate the black cavern in which Python lurks. Apollo is conceived as a classical hero contending against the powers of darkness in a traditional opposition of light and shade, good and evil.

This is a simplistic view of the world that the mature Turner increasingly rejected. His next historical work is utterly different in conception. It treats of a hero, certainly; but the hero is a man, whose relationship with his surroundings is real and palpable – he does not float, like Apollo, in a circle of his own light, magically protected from reality. Hannibal crosses the Alps (FIG. XIII) in a blinding tumult of snow and storm that makes his perilous passage the more arduous. The literary source is precisely that passage from Livy quoted by Gray in his letter of 1739.[33] Gray once suggested that the subject should have been treated by Salvator Rosa: 'Hannibal passing the Alps; the mountaineers rolling down rocks upon his army; elephants tumbling down the precipices.'[34] But such an interpretation is no longer adequate to Turner's purpose. The crisp precision of his earlier delineations of the Alps is replaced by a vast blur of involved and battered fragments of the air in which the landscape is disintegrated. Does he thereby sacrifice that crucial 'truth' which he has all along recognised as the key to meaning? On the contrary. The conditions that he needs to describe are more vividly and accurately rendered like this than by any nice attention to minutiae. Here indistinctness is the essence of the sublime, the essence indeed of realism. 'Many images,' Gilpin had declared, 'owe their sublimity to their *indistinctness*; and frequently what we call sublime is the effect of that heat and fermentation, which ensues in the imagination from its ineffectual efforts to conceive some dark, obtuse idea beyond its grasp. Bring the same within the compass of its comprehension, and it may continue *great*; but it will cease to be *sublime* . . . In general,

FIG. XII
Nicolas Poussin, *Landscape with Pyramus and Thisbe*, c. 1651, oil on canvas. Städelsches Kunstinstitut, Frankfurt am Main

FIG. XIII
J. M. W. Turner, *Snow storm: Hannibal and his army crossing the Alps*, 1812, oil on canvas. Tate Gallery, London

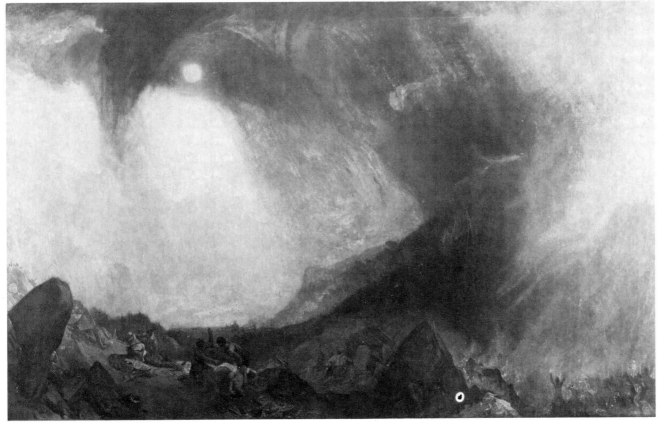

the poet has great advantages over the painter, in the process of *Sublimication*, if the term may be allowed. The business of the former is only to *excite ideas*; that of the latter, to *represent* them.'[35]

The contrast which critics had so often made between the expressive flexibility of poetry and the representational precision of painting had for generations inhibited painters from grasping the sublime bull by the horns. Reynolds had pointed in the right direction; but the generalisation he looked for was closely allied to the depiction of the human figure and the manipulation of facial expression in order to show emotion, and so could not help the landscape painter with his rather different problems. The dilemma reveals itself in the criticism of Wilson's *Niobe* which he made in his fourteenth Discourse (1788):

> Our late ingenious academician, Wilson, has, I fear, been guilty, like many of his predecessors, of introducing gods and goddesses, ideal beings, into scenes which were by no means prepared to receive such personages. His landskips were in reality too near common nature to admit supernatural objects. In consequence of this mistake, in a very admirable picture of a storm, which I have seen of his hand, many figures are introduced in the fore-ground, some in apparent distress, and some struck dead, as a spectator would naturally suppose, by the lightning; had not the painter injudiciously (as I think) rather chosen that their death should be imputed to a little Apollo, who appears in the sky, with his bent bow, and that those figures should be considered as the children of Niobe.[36]

This seems to destroy at a blow the whole argument of the 'Historical Landscape' school. If a convincing presentation of natural phenomena could not be combined with a heroic subject, what *could* one paint? But Reynolds had already pointed to Poussin as the model and stated categorically that his success derived from his self-consistency. Wilson had attempted two different sorts of 'truth' simultaneously and had failed to marry them. He needed to have a 'mind thrown back two thousand years, and, as it were, naturalised in antiquity'[37] to succeed. Turner's answer, after some years of thought and experiment, was an astonishing compromise. He chose natural phenomena of such grandeur or splendour that they were inherently 'universal' on account of their rare power and scale; and he proceeded to paint them as grandly and splendidly as his medium would allow. In a sense, he painted 'realistically'; but he had perceived, as we know, that realism does not necessarily reside in tightness and fine finish: it would be absurd to paint a snowstorm or a sunset like that. As Blair put it: 'it is one thing to make an idea clear, and another to make it affecting to the imagination; and the imagination may be strongly affected, and, in fact, often is too, by objects of which we have no clear conception.'[38] The absurdity of misapplied definition was to be demonstrated a very few years after the appearance of *Hannibal*, for Turner's picture inspired many of John Martin's apocalyptic subjects (FIG. XIV), in which cataclysms are rendered on huge canvases with painstaking attention to the details of rending granite and screaming women.[39] The effect is nearly always closer to the sensational or even the ridiculous than to the sublime.

Martin's crisply delineated multitudes of agonised human beings have their precursors in the blindly struggling armies of Hannibal. Turner does not attempt, like a club bore, to recount endless little incidents in detail. He invents figures just sufficient to convey the horror of the situation he describes. Ambush, rape, looting and murder are dimly suggested; the grim battles of men with each other and with the storm that envelopes them are evoked by mere indications: agitated mobs of half-lit figures shrouded in haze. The hero himself is nowhere to be seen. Turner tells his grand story of classical strength and human weakness in terms of the nameless men who composed Hannibal's forces. He rarely envisaged a hero without summoning to mind the effect of his actions on the human condition generally. Perhaps he saw a parallel with himself, heroic as a creative artist, materially altering the world in which

his fellow men lived.[40] So he was inclined not to place his protagonists at the centre of the stage, but to immerse them in the multitudinous crowds whose fate they controlled. This is in itself an extension of the sublime concept of the great man – a compelling restatement of his greatness in terms not of his appearance but of his power over men. It is a universality far more real and vital than the imagined features or gestures of an individual.

The identification of the actions of leaders and heroes with those of the men they led or controlled was an important development in his art which, as we shall see, was a necessary step in the integration of the two principal fields of his practice: the historical and the topographical. A striking example of the process in watercolour is his revision in 1815 of an earlier view of *Mont Blanc from Fort Rock in the Val d'Aosta*. The first version of the subject is a magnificent specimen of the landscape sublime,[41] in which the *frisson* created by a deep gorge among towering mountains is beautifully conveyed in the expressions and gestures of three girls who stand at a parapet. Their astonishment is apparent, their delighted terror embodies what we all feel before such a view. In the later version (*colour 15*) the girls are replaced by a woman holding a baby, who tends a wounded man lying on a bare shoulder of rock beneath the narrow mountain road on which a fierce battle is in progress. Napoleon's army is invading Italy, and, like Hannibal's, involved in a bloody skirmish among the mountains. The most conspicuous figures represent not the grand designs of Napoleon himself, but the remote effects of those designs on the common man.

In the same way, the paintings of *Dido building Carthage* and the *Decline of the Carthaginian Empire*[42] tell the tale of a whole society rather than recounting the exploits of one person. It is typical of Turner's progressing thought that the first subject focuses on a single character and purports to illustrate an epic poem, the *Aeneid*, while the second brings the story from mythology into history, supposes the triumphs and disasters of Hannibal's campaigns over, and presents a leaderless people 'enervated', as the catalogue title says, in their anxiety for peace, consenting 'to give up even their arms and their children'.

The two episodes of Carthaginian history are set in golden harbours of the type that Turner deliberately borrowed from Claude. But the scale of these harbours is grander than anything conceived by Claude: Turner uses his chosen model as the springboard for a communication that is unequivocally sublime. The drama of human affairs that he narrates is itself a powerful one, and his setting is calculated to enhance it. The splendour of Dido's city is a reflection of the nobility of her accomplishment, and all the more tragic a loss when it sinks into decay. The glorious sunrise in which it dawns, the 'ensanguin'd sun' that 'sets portentous'[43] over its decline – these are reinforcements of the theme at the level of direct symbolism. But they carry with them their own expressive force, as described by Dugald Stewart:

> There is a fourth [circumstance] which conspires, in no inconsiderable degree, in imparting an allegorical or typical character to literal *sublimity*. I allude to the Rising, Culminating, and Setting of the heavenly bodies; more particularly to the Rising, Culminating, and Setting of the Sun; accompanied with a corresponding increase and decrease in the heat and splendour of its rays. It is impossible to enumerate all the various analogies which these familiar appearances suggest to the fancy. I shall mention their obvious analogy to the Morning, Noon, and Evening of life; and to the short interval of Meridian Glory, which, after a gradual advance to the summit, has so often presaged the approaching decline of human greatness.[44]

Turner used this symbolism again very literally in his painting of 1842, *War. The exile and the rock limpet* (FIG. XV), which shows Napoleon in exile on St Helena. The sky

FIG. XV
J. M. W. Turner, *War. The Exile and the Rock Limpet*, 1842, oil on canvas. Tate Gallery, London

behind the solitary figure is of a deep and unmistakably bloody red, taking up an image that had been used by Byron in his *Ode to Napoleon*:

> – who would soar the solar height,
> To set in such a starless night?[45]

The opposition of night to day which sunset naturally implies greatly increases its emotional effect. And the symbol has a double meaning since it refers not only to the fallen hero, but to his sanguinary career. Although we see him alone, the lives and fates of his armies and all those who were sacrificed to his ambition are remembered. Turner's verses, in which Napoleon apostrophises the limpet, poignantly contrast his loneliness with the relative happiness of the humble soldier who can enjoy the company of his fellows:

> Ah! Thy tent-formed shell is like
> The soldier's nightly bivouac, alone
> Amidst a sea of blood –
> – but you can join your comrades.

This bitter opposition of fame and power to loneliness and decline was much on Turner's mind, and on the mind of the romantic generation that witnessed the fall of Napoleon. Beethoven had of course already celebrated the optimism that he inspired during his rise to power. His career gave him a rare historical status, coloured with a grandeur that seemed to involve the whole gamut of the sublime. A younger contemporary of Turner's brought many of these strands together in an essay *Sur la Mort de Napoléon* composed in 1843:

> Napoléon naquit en Corse et mourut à St. Hélène. Entre ces deux îles rien qu'un vaste et brûlant désert et l'océan immense. Il naquit fils d'un simple gentilhomme, et mourut empereur, mais sans couronne et dans les fers. . . . Sa vie, c'est l'arc en ciel; les deux points touchent la terre; la comble lumineuse mesure les cieux . . . sur son lit de mort Napoléon est seul; plus de mère, ni de frère, ni de soeur, ni de femme, ni d'enfant! . . . Il est là, exilé et captif, enchaîné sur un écueil. Nouveau Prométhée il subit le châtiment de son orgueil! Prométhée avait voulu être Dieu et Créateur; il déroba le feu du ciel pour animer le corps qu'il avait formé. Et lui, Bonaparte, il a voulu créer, non pas un homme, mais un empire . . . Jupiter indigné de l'impiété de Prométhée le riva vivant à la cime du Caucase. Ainsi, pour punir l'ambition rapace de Bonaparte, la Providence l'a enchaîné jusqu'à ce que la mort s'ensuivit, sur un roc isolé de l'Atlantique. . . . Sans doute d'autres conquérants ont hésité dans leur carrière de gloire . . . lui, jamais! Il n'eut pas besoin, comme Ulysse, de se lier au mât du navire, ni de se boucher les oreilles avec de la cire; il ne redoutait pas le chant des Sirènes – il le dédaignait; il se fit marbre et fer pour exécuter ses grands projets.[46]

In this piece of prose, almost contemporary with Turner's picture of Napoleon, a wealth of sublime imagery is clustered round the central figure of the fallen hero. Burning deserts, immense oceans, rainbows, Prometheus, Ulysses, marble, iron – all are suggested, not so much by the actual circumstances of Napoleon's death, but by the mere fact of his heroic stature in the history of the world. Turner's choice of subject implied for his audience just such an infrastructure of sublime reference; what is surprising is his insistence, which we see to be consistent with his other pictures about heroes, on the reverse, as it were, of the coin: the unremembered and not very sublime human beings whose suffering makes heroism possible.

Turner had already commemorated the men who died at Waterloo in his painting of that battle exhibited in 1818 (see no. 71), to which he appended a stanza of Byron's *Childe Harold* that dwells on the humanity and individuality of those who are killed. Waterloo was itself a subject eminently suited to the sublime: 'Nothing,' says Blair, 'is more sublime than mighty power and strength . . . the engagement of two great armies, as it is the highest exertion of human might, combines a variety of sources of the Sublime . . .'[47] We have noticed that war is a subject that easily loses its sublimity and becomes merely sensational; Turner, following the literary lead given him by Byron, reformulates the message to emphasise neither the heroics nor the horror of the subject, but its broad human significance. While Napoleon broods in exile under a blood-red sunset, his soldiers at Waterloo lie – 'Rider and horse, – friend, foe, – in one red burial blent!' – already entombed in the darkness of night.

An earlier example of this process of transferring the actions of a hero to the swarming ranks in his command is the illustration to Gray's *Bard* which we have discussed. Here neither Bard nor 'ruthless king' appears, but only the army which is the instrument of tyranny, itself dominated almost to annihilation by the vastness of the mountains. It may be that to transfer historical significance from the leader to his people, his armies or his subjects, was something that had been suggested to Turner by his work as a topographer. That profession had taught him to embody the meaning of any landscape subject in the figures that belonged to it. As Archibald Alison observed, 'the occupations of men' are 'so important in determining, or in heightening the characters of Nature . . . and afford [the painter] the means of producing both greater strength, and greater unity of expression, than is to be found either in the rude, or in the embellished state of real scenery.'[48] Art can concentrate and intensify by judicious selection what is often apparent only by implication in nature itself. Turner evolved his mature topographical style on this principle. For he certainly did not abandon his practice in that field when he acquired fame and wealth. But he could not help infusing it with ideas he had developed as a painter of 'heroic landscape'.

He gradually diverged, for instance, from the strict and literal recording of facts that characterised his earliest views. His successful essays in the architectural sublime of the late 1790s showed that there was a new public for expressive and atmospheric topography designed to stimulate a romantic mood rather than gratify curiosity about scientific facts. So although the nineteenth century began with a continuation of the demand for views, it witnessed a change in the nature of topography, for which Turner was largely responsible. Thanks to his highly sophisticated watercolour technique, developed by his repeated exercises in depicting the mountains first of Wales, then of Scotland and Switzerland, he was able to present, even on the modest scale of a small sheet of paper, a vividly convincing likeness of immense spaces, panoramic views and infinitely receding vistas seen in all kinds of atmospheric conditions. He could afford to choose for his subject-matter scenery and natural effects that had previously been beyond the range of even the most proficient technicians. If the place to be depicted did not admit of such theatrical treatment, he would nevertheless endow it with those qualities of light, air and space which all scenery possesses in reality, thereby rendering the most commonplace spots grand: simply as representations of the plain truth of the hitherto inexpressible elements of nature his watercolour drawings were breathtaking. And he would not hesitate to add drama to a view by breaking a violent storm over it, or arching a rainbow in the air above it. Air, sunshine, shadow, storm, clouds, the wind itself, he could render; not, as we should expect, by the free use of a wet brush, spreading broad washes across the paper, but by carefully building up the very substance of these insubstantialities with minute touches of a fine brush. He still employed the alternative of a free wash as Cozens had suggested to him, but now the wash and the fine hatched strokes were so intricately interwoven that the old clear opposition of the one technique to the other no longer appeared. By a strange contrariety of matter, in order to obtain effects on a small sheet of paper which on canvas he would get by means of breadth, he needed to apply a miniature touch to every separate part of the composition.

By doing so, he could simultaneously increase the relative scale of his paper (crowding many thousands of tiny strokes onto a sheet that would take only a few dozen broad ones), and control his effects from millimetre to millimetre of the surface of the design. He could also say far more in a confined space, as indeed he had to. For these reasons, he was able to abandon large sheets of paper: grandeur of effect was a matter of relative scale and not of absolute size. At the same time he raised the colour key of his drawings – rather as he was doing with his oil paintings over the same period. These technical developments were intimately related to the heightened perception of natural phenomena that demanded other variations on the traditional language of landscape. It may have been the influence of Burke's theory of the 'terrific' sublime that initially encouraged Turner to distort the geographical details of what he saw to express more forcibly such ideas as height, depth and distance. These modifications of reality to achieve a more significant and essential reality in landscape quickly became a crucial element in Turner's heroic pictorial language. An example is his artificial treatment of recession in 'subsidiary perspectives', a common feature of his compositions, particularly those with a classical basis. Views through arcades, avenues of trees, tunnels of rock, even vortices of dust or storm, create an arrow-like retreat through the picture-space that is often at odds with the calmer perspective of the principal view.[49] These distortions are devised to increase the dynamic of landscape, not simply to reconstruct as vividly as possible in two dimensions the spatial complexities of the actual scene, but to impose a dramatic mode of vision upon the viewer, who is compelled to enact with the eye leaps and plunges, ascents, penetrations and progressions that plot for him the three-dimensional presence of the perceived landscape. The 'unnaturalness' of these devices is evident, and they are largely responsible for our sense that Turner is a theatrical, and not a naturalistic painter; yet they are employed primarily in order to convey certain fundamental truths about the physical world and as such are the artist's literal equivalents to what he experiences. And such distortions were entirely permissible to the theorists of the sublime. They were indeed inevitable in the processes of heightened communication: 'Longinus maintains,' as an eighteenth-century commentator noted, 'that a high degree of sublimity is utterly inconsistent with accuracy of imagination; and that Authors of the most elevated Genius, at the same time that they are capable of rising to the greatest excellencies, are likewise most apt to commit trivial faults.'[50] By the early 1820s, though we are conscious of these sometimes extreme exaggerations of space and form in Turner's work, we rarely feel that our susceptibility to fear is being played upon. It is far more often a sense of the overwhelming splendour of the world that emerges from the watercolours of this central period in his career.

Their impressiveness is not simply a consequence of their depicting grand scenery. His old fascination with the human life of the places he drew developed alongside the other aspects of his art to become a vital element in the heightened topography of his maturity. He began to conceive his views, not as a topographer, but as the great master of romantic landscape that he had become. And just as nature itself was imbued with new power, so the human 'staffage' gained in weight and significance, to become the same heroic multitudes that embody the moral purpose of his epic canvases. There is no need in the watercolours of the *Picturesque Views in England and Wales* (1825–37) to look for a named hero: man himself, the ordinary inhabitant of the scenes depicted, is the protagonist of these splendid dramas. And, as we have seen in the operation of the sublime elsewhere, a certain degree of detailed precision gives the verisimilitude that brings us into immediate contact with the experience that Turner is trying to communicate: the horror of a sea storm is the more appalling when we watch men vomiting up salt water as they drown, or slipping on wet sand as they try to salvage wreckage from the surf (nos 62, 64). The magic of a summer evening is palpable if we can identify with people who have stripped off their clothes to plunge into the warm still water of a quiet pool.[51] The bleakness of Penmaenmawr (no. 38) is appreciable more readily if we can see a stage-coach drawn at top speed across it by frightened horses galloping through a ferocious downpour of rain. The individual effects of these watercolours may well (and frequently do) partake of the sublime fear we have discussed; the *Penmaenmawr* last mentioned clearly does so; though not in the crude, archaic way that emerges from, say, a travel guide account of 1757, which records that Penmaenmawr 'hangs perpendicularly over the Sea, at so vast a Height, that it makes most spectators giddy who venture to look down the dreadful Steep; and in the narrow passage to the other Side, the ventrous Traveller is threatened, every Moment to be crushed to Atoms, with the Fall of impending Rocks.'[52] Turner is not afraid to use devices that evoke this kind of horror, when his subject merits such treatment; but his overriding object in these watercolours is to impress us first with the grandeur of nature, and second with the reality of that grandeur as experienced by human beings like ourselves, who live out their lives in the conditions he presents. This is the point that Ruskin makes when, in discussing the great watercolour of *The Pass of Faido* of 1843 (*colour 24*), he concentrates not so much on the wild confusion of the scene as on the postchaise that Turner introduces on the road that winds through the pass. Blair observed that disorder 'is very compatible with grandeur; nay, frequently heightens it . . . A great mass of rocks, thrown together by the hand of nature with wildness and confusion, strike the mind with more grandeur, than if they had been adjusted to one another with the most accurate symmetry.'[53] And certainly the scene that Turner recreates in the *Faido* is sublime in this sense; it is one of his most grandiose evocations of the rugged and hostile scenery of the Alps, achieved on a small scale by means of an extraordinarily flexible and varied technique. As Ruskin observes, many people might be content with this, enjoying the primitive horrors of the landscape sublime, and feeling that to introduce even the most insignificant element of human life is to dilute 'the majesty of its desolation'. But Ruskin realised that for Turner it was not the emptiness of the scene alone, nor its hostility to human life, that needed to be stressed: the pass of Faido was one of the great natural events of the traveller's journey through the Alps to Italy, and could only be approached and understood in that context, in the traveller's state of mind, and through the medium of the road: 'in no other wise could we have come than by the coach road. One of the great elements of sensation, all the day long, has been that extraordinary road, and its goings on, and gettings about . . . so smoothly and safely, that it is not merely great diligences, going in a caravannish manner, with whole teams of horses, that can traverse it, but little postchaises with small postboys, and a pair of ponies . . .'[54] By the same token, the two panoramic views of Zurich that also came from Turner's brush in the 1840s take full cognisance of the fact that Zurich is a thriving city: however expansive and ecstatic the broad vision of the rising sun, the town is incomplete without its thronging inhabitants going about their affairs, or gathering for a day of civic revelry (see no. 93).

These watercolours proclaim what had long been evident in Turner's output, that the urban view is as capable of embodying grandeur as the wildest natural landscape. It is true that Blair had expressed the opinion that 'the flourishing city' was not conducive to elevation of the mind; but there are recurrent passages in the Tours of the period in which a panorama filled with varied evidence of human activity is described as sublime. Sometimes cities take only a subordinate place in a more general vista, as in Richard Warner's account of the view from Cader Idris: '. . . the vast unbounded prospect lay before us, unobscured by cloud, vapour or any other interruption to the astonished and delighted eye; which threw its glance over a varied scene, including a circumference of at least five hundred miles . . . Numberless mountains, of different forms, appearances, and elevation, rise in all directions around us; which, with the various harbours, lakes and rivers, towns, villages, and seats, scattered over the extensive prospect, combine to form a scene inexpressibly august, diversified, and impressive.'[55]

18 *Luxembourg, c.* 1825–34 (no. 88)
19 *Lausanne, Sunset,* (?) 1841 (no. 90)

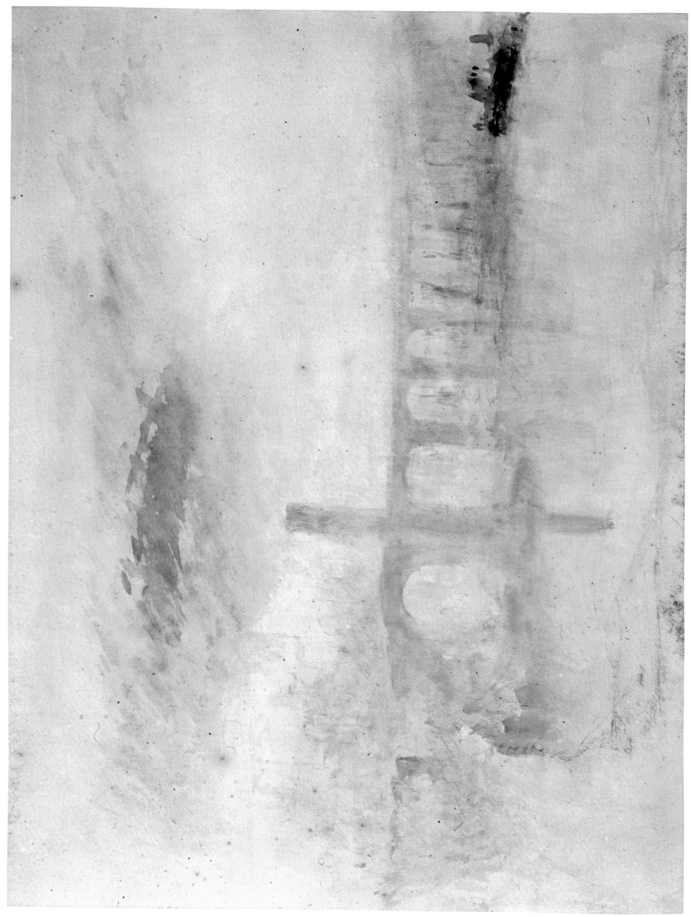

20 *The Moselle Bridge, Coblenz, c.* 1842 (no. 91)

21 *Heidelberg: looking west with a low sun*, 1844 (no. 92)

22 *Among the mountains*, (?) *c.* 1835 (no. 97)

23 *The Glacier des Bossons*, (?) 1836 (no. 99)

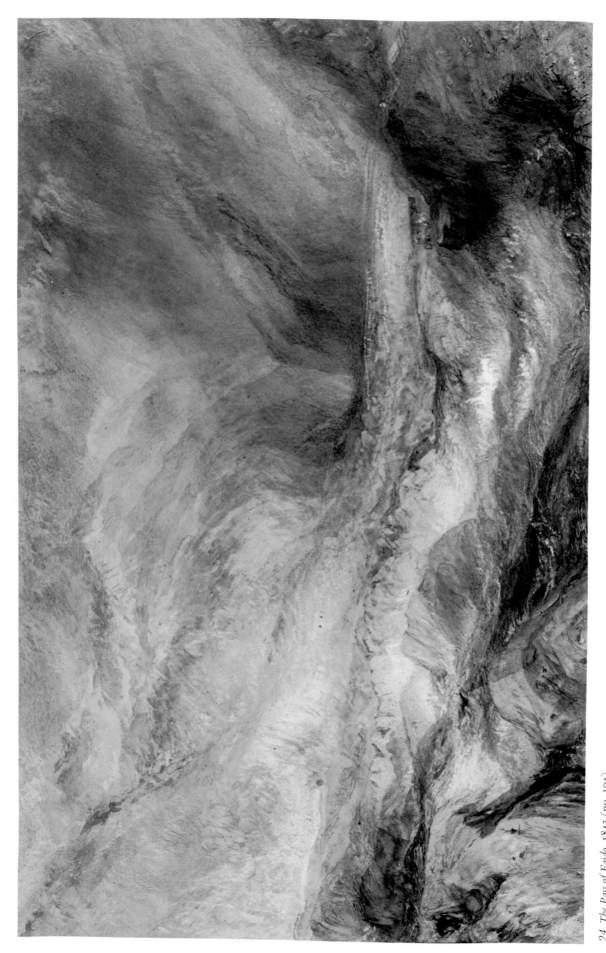

24 *The Pass of Faido*, 1843 (no. 104)
25 *Goldau with the Lake of Zug in the distance*,
1841–2 (no. 105)

26 *Goldau*, 1843 (no. 106)

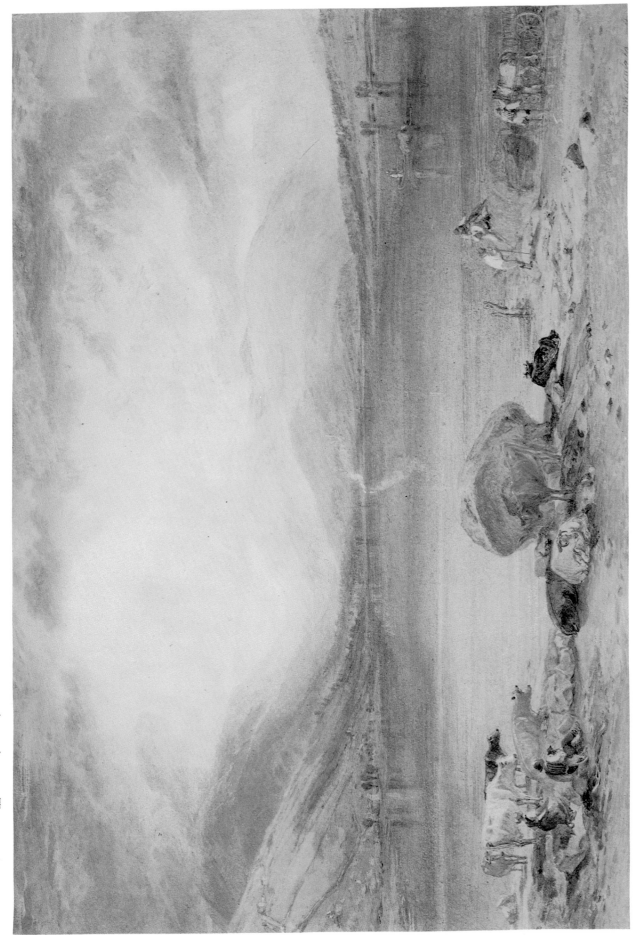

27 *Simmer Lake, near Askrigg,* c. 1818 (no. 109)

28 *The Bay of Uri from Brunnen, c. 1841* (no. 115)
29 *Lake Lucerne: the Bay of Uri from above Brunnen,*
1842 (no. 116)

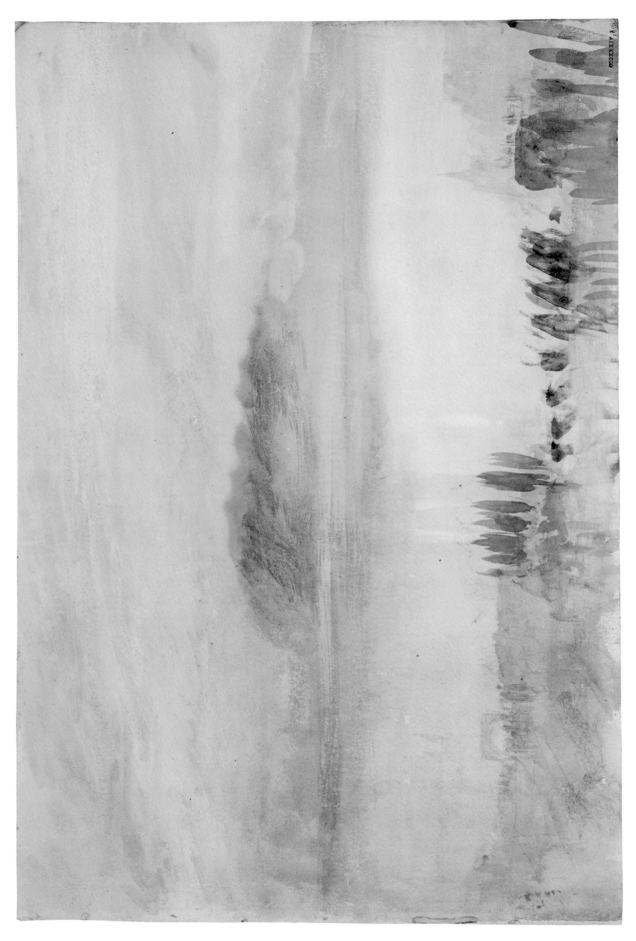

30 *The Lake of Geneva with the Dent d'Oche,
from Lausanne: a funeral*, 1841 (no. 117)

31 *The Lake of Geneva with the Dent d'Oche, from Lausanne*, 1841 (no. 119)

Turner's views of cities are usually more compressed than this. They are topographical in the sense that they present the appearance of a single defined place, with more or less of its neighbouring countryside. But even the most factual of them provide such a broad sweep of informative matter that they transcend the prosaic boundaries of ordinary topography. Climate, architecture, trades, entertainments, everything that modifies or colours the local life, play a part in his comprehensive 'economic' vision. On occasion these 'town portraits' reflect that excitement with the progress of the industrial revolution which many artists and writers felt at the time. It was not only Blake who compared the factory towns with Milton's inferno, though the 'dark satanic mills' of his account[56] seem less attractive than the grandiose and atmospheric scenes that some people found in them.[57] Turner's all-embracing fascination with the conditions in which men live, his sense of the intrinsic grandeur of man and his affairs, enabled him to infuse the sublime as readily into his city views as into his historical canvases.

The sweeping comprehensiveness of the Zurich subjects, for all their expressive splendour, is still rooted in the topographer's concern for the richness and multiplicity of human activity which enlivened even Turner's earliest watercolours. It is not only the rarefied products of wild nature but mankind itself in its endless and often humdrum patterns of existence which is truly impressive: Wordsworth's 'sense sublime of something far more deeply interfused' apprehended 'a motion and a spirit that impels All thinking things, all objects of all thought.'[58] There is no boundary beyond which things animate and inanimate no longer qualify as sublime: sublimity is the elevated thought and inspired perception that resides in the mind of the beholder, and suffuses everything it touches with grandeur.

The 'topographical sublime' with its strong overtones of the 'economic' view of landscape is not confined to the watercolours, however. There are numerous examples of similar themes treated as oil paintings; some with specific topographical reference[59], such as the two views of the *Burning of the Houses of Parliament* exhibited in 1835, which exploit a popular 'sensation' – a big conflagration – with the grandest results; or the canvas shown in the same year, *The Bright Stone of Honour (Ehrenbreitstein) and the Tomb of Marceau, from Byron's 'Childe Harold'*,[60] where a purely topographical subject is provided with sublime overtones by its association with a great general – a military hero[61] – and with Byron's poem, which, superseding Thomson, provided Turner with a new literary source almost from the moment that it was published.[62] Other pictures are less precise as to location, but equally firmly yoke a sublime phenomenon with the lives of men. The late paintings of whalers are characteristic: whales had always been recognised as 'sublime' on account of their enormous size and their association with the dangers of the sea.[63] They form a very appropriate theme for the last of Turner's sea pictures (*colour 16*). The sketches he made[64] are in themselves evocative of the grandeur of the animal as it flounders in water rendered perilous by its lashing movements. The paintings, however, lay a strong emphasis on the activities of whalers themselves, on the hardships and dangers they undergo, as well as on the pleasures of the chase. Even if the canvases are little more than vivid presentations of the arctic conditions in which these men work, their titles betray Turner's interest: *Hurrah for the Whaler Erebus! Another Fish!, Whalers (boiling blubber) entangled in flaw ice, endeavouring to extricate themselves*[65] and suggest that the painter had joined a whaling ship in order to understand its activities and the lives of its men; but he acquired his knowledge only from books. Nevertheless, his interest was deep, his sympathy far-reaching, and his imaginative perception of the whaler's existence dependent on no mere generalisations.

In some of the greatest of his late paintings, then, Turner is to be found still balancing the demands of topography as he had learnt it in his youth with the requirements of High Art. The relationship between men and their surroundings that

Thomson illustrated is now explored on an altogether wider front; but the basic preoccupation is much the same. There is even one important late painting that seems to be based directly on a passage from the *Seasons*, showing that Turner kept Thomson in mind to the end: the *Slavers throwing overboard the dead and dying – Typhoon coming on* (FIG. XVI), is now recognised as being a sumptuous visual equivalent to a long passage in *Summer* describing the 'mighty tempest' that 'musters its force' while 'the direful shark' surges round a slave ship:

> . . . he rushing cuts the briny flood
> Swift as the gale can bear the ship along;
> And from the partners of that cruel trade
> Which spoils unhappy Guinea of her sons,
> Demands his share of prey – demands themselves.[66]

There can be no doubt here of the human significance of the subject. But no protagonist of the drama appears in the picture: the direct presentation of life is reduced to an expressive minimum, the overpowering atmosphere achieved by the most emphatic statement of the natural effects of sunset and brooding stormcloud. Turner aims unambiguously at the sublime, reproducing with all his skill a stupendous natural phenomenon in order to impress us with the larger argument of his picture.

The process is even more pronounced in one of the greatest of the late Swiss watercolours – that of *Goldau (colour 26)*, a work of 1843 which commemorates the disastrous fall of the Rossberg on the village of Goldau in 1806. Turner had already treated the subject of an avalanche in his painting of the *Fall of an Avalanche in the Grisons* of 1810, which, like the *Slavers*, relies on a passage from Thomson's *Seasons* for its literary basis.[67] The basis of Goldau is an actual historical event. As in the *Slavers* and the *Fall of an Avalanche*, the tragic idea is concentrated in a single immense image of natural power: a vast sunset floods the whole sheet with its scarlet light. Of figures there are practically none; only a few boys fishing from the huge rocks that crushed the village a generation earlier. This is the reduction of landscape to that universal and compelling simplicity that Reynolds demanded for the true sublime.

How do these images of natural grandeur differ from the 'terrific' landscape

FIG. XVI
J. M. W. Turner, *Slavers throwing overboard the dead and dying – Typhoon coming on*, 1841, oil on canvas. Museum of Fine Arts, Boston

sublime of Turner's youth? Many of the same elements are present. The *Fall of an Avalanche* (really quite an early work) is, on one level, a fairly conventional evocation of the physical terror we expect from such subjects. But it seeks to go beyond the local and individual both technically and conceptually. Unlike say, de Loutherbourg's picture of an Avalanche painted in 1803,[68] which Turner knew well, this avoids depicting a specific event, by the elimination of figures (de Loutherbourg's are conspicuously theatrical and unreal as well as being all too elegantly delineated), and at the same time achieves stunning conviction by the mixture of two opposed styles of painting – the vividly precise, in the details of the cottage and falling rock; and the expressionistically indistinct, in the surrounding blur of violent movement. By this means the eye is both engaged and confused in a way analogous to the visual effect of the event itself, and thus accepts the essential truth of what it is told.

Turner thereby avoids the merely theatrical, which few artists of the landscape sublime managed to do, and yet attains the realism essential to his purpose. The result of this virtuoso balancing act is a universalised presentation of an event that can only be appreciated as a specific one, though its real meaning is general. In the other works we have discussed the same balance is maintained, though by rather different means, depending on the nature of the subject-matter. As we have said, the only way to make a sunset emotionally effective is to make it convincingly real; and yet sunsets by their very nature allow the artist a good deal of expressive freedom in inventing and developing the language of reality. What distinguishes Turner's sunsets from any others is his constant reference to the human experience which is our only means of approaching them. Even in his most 'abstract' studies of natural phenomena we feel the vital response of the human mind and emotions. By his sheer technique in painting, say, a wave, Turner informs us of the subtlety and depth of his own feelings about the sea. As Archibald Alison put it, speaking of the new school of landscape painters generally: 'It is not the art, but the Genius of the Painter, which now gives value to his compositions; and the language he employs is found not only to speak to the eye, but to affect the imagination and the heart. It is not now a simple copy which we see, nor is our Emotion limited to the cold pleasure which arises from the perception of accurate Imitation. It is a creation of Fancy with which the artist presents us, in which only the greater expressions of Nature are retained, and where more interesting emotions are awakened, than those which we experience from the usual tameness of common scenery.'[69] So the very force of Turner's brush strokes enables us to identify with the imagination that has contemplated the sea, and to understand its significance in the lives of men. So Turner's great *Snow storm: steam boat off a harbour's mouth* of 1842 is the supreme example in all his art of that sublime realism which accurately records a natural event as perceived by a profoundly receptive mind. In lashing himself to the mast of the steamship *Ariel*[70] in order to observe this storm, as Turner said he had done, he was following the example of the great masters still: both Vernet and Backhuisen had made similar experiments in the interest of infusing greater realism into their art. But whereas these two men succeeded only in conveying an approximation in paint, limited by their narrow conception of realism and their restrictive technique, Turner was able, as he claimed, to 'show what such a scene was like'. He did not, as he irritably told an enquirer, 'paint it to be understood',[71] because his meaning was in the experience itself, and his object was to present the experience as totally and overwhelmingly as his art would allow. He proclaims clearly that the sublime is accessible to us all, that it is indeed a common property of the human mind, given the wonders with which nature surrounds us. A later artist, Gustave Courbet (1819–77), would paint the expanse of open sea, unencumbered with storms or other climatic effects, unvaried by figures or shipping, and call his picture *L'immensité*.[72] Turner eschews this kind of abstraction, retaining in all but his roughest studies a firmly perceived framework of human reference. He appreciates and communicates what Stewart calls 'the sympathetic dread associated with the perilous fortunes of those who trust themselves to that inconstant and treacherous element [the ocean]'. Stewart goes on: 'It is owing to this, that, in its most placid form, its temporary effect in soothing or composing the spirits is blended with feelings somewhat analogous to what are excited by the sleep of a lion; the calmness of its surface pleasing chiefly, from the contrast it exhibits to the terrors which it naturally inspires.' And Stewart adds, in a footnote, that 'Gray had manifestly this analogy in his view when he wrote the following lines':

> Unmindful of the sweeping whirlwind's sway
> That hush'd in grim repose expects its evening prey.[73]

This very quotation from the *Bard* was used by Turner to make the same point about the sea in his painting of 1843, *The Sun of Venice going to Sea*. He did not acknowledge Gray as its author, but redrafted the passage and ascribed the verses to his own *Fallacies of Hope*. Gray had written:

> Fair laughs the morn, and soft the zephyr blows,
> While proudly riding o'er the azure realm
> In gallant trim the gilded vessel goes;
> Youth on the prow, and Pleasure at the helm;
> Regardless of the sweeping whirlwind's sway,
> That, hush'd in grim repose, expects his evening prey.[74]

Turner printed in the Academy catalogue:

> Fair shines the morn, and soft the zephyrs blow,
> Venetia's fisher spreads her painted sail so gay,
> Nor heeds the demon that in grim repose
> Expects his evening prey.

Gray's lines were so well known that Turner cannot have imagined that his thin disguise would deceive anyone. He deliberately invoked the 'sublime idea' of Gray's *Bard*, and a passage of the poem that had been cited as particularly expressive of a certain type of sublimity, in order to underscore the point of his otherwise light-hearted and joyful picture. It was, of course, the purpose of the *Fallacies of Hope* to tell us that joy is transient: after the calm comes the storm.

But Turner was not practising an art which could at best only illustrate literature. His intention was to raise landscape painting to a level of seriousness and universality that had previously been thought impossible. He did this both by bringing his profound contemplations to bear on the works of nature and on man's condition, and by developing his technical skills to a pitch at which they could, for the first time in the history of art, overcome the barriers of space and light, of immensity and obscurity and darkness, to describe with breathtaking realism the particular incidents by which these great themes manifest themselves.

Hence it was possible for him to paint landscapes from which violence, agitation and danger are totally absent, but which yet convey the most exalted sense of sublimity. And if Switzerland could yield subjects like the 'wildness and confusion' of Faido, or the tragic reminiscence of Goldau, it was also a source of scenery that was grand without any connotations beyond its own serenity and splendour. When Turner drew his long series of views of Lake Lucerne and Lake Geneva (see nos 114–23) he focused his meditations on the sheer amplitude of their vistas and the infinite calm of their waters at dawn or sunset. He did not lose sight of the surrounding world: in one of his most ecstatic views of the Rigi at sunrise the vast silence is broken by a small dog barking as it jumps off a boat into the water.[75] There are no heroic associations; even the views of the Bay of Uri do not invoke the shade of William Tell, though they do show the daily work of the steam ferry that takes passengers from one end of the lake to the other. The mood in these late Swiss lake scenes is a return to the sanctified calm of John Robert Cozens, a faintly elegiac absorption of the mind and spirit in the grandeur of creation. The Rigi subjects are a far cry indeed from an earlier view of a mountain across water, *Vesuvius in eruption* of 1817 (no. 33), in which the crisp precision of the landscape sublime vividly conveys a violent natural upheaval, prompting a reaction of astonishment and terror. Even the relatively late painting of *Snowstorm, Avalanche and Inundation – a scene in the upper part of the Val d'Aosta* (1837)[76] seems overburdened with incident by comparison, and piles catastrophes one upon another so that its purpose is almost defeated. On the Swiss lakes Turner could dispense altogether with the trappings of 'horror' to distil the essence of the true sublime from his own soul in harmony with those spaces whose vastness Gilpin had dismissed as both unpaintable and uninteresting. In them land and sky, earth, air and water, are wrought into a fluid medium of colour and light: the space that intervenes between the eye and the object now becomes the real subject of the work. At the same time, the old symbolisms of sunrise and sunset take on a fresh and personal meaning, a significance which relates neither to a hero nor to the common man, but to the artist himself, who is both.

Turner knew that the phenomenon of sunset exercises a powerful influence over us. It elicits a vigorous response by virtue of its stupendous grandeur, and because it is one of the most immediately impressive of our glimpses of the vast realms of space. Theorists of the sublime attached much importance to the associational significance of the sky, and usually placed the night sky full of stars at the head of their list of its sublimities; but the sun is the heavenly body most intimately associated with our livelihood, the star capable of the most immediate grandeur. Burke actually preferred darkness to light for sublime power – he quoted Milton's description of Death in Book II of *Paradise Lost*, where, he says, 'all is dark, uncertain, confused, terrible, and sublime to the last degree';[77] and he listed Darkness among the 'privations' which, as we have seen, are specially conducive to the sublime. 'Darkness is more productive of sublime ideas than light.' 'Mere light,' he says, 'is too common a thing to make a strong impression on the mind, and without a strong impression nothing can be sublime. But such a light as the sun, immediately exerted on the eye as it overpowers the sense, is a very great idea.'[78] Burke's preference for darkness is typical of his whole understanding of the sublime as an emotion dependent on fear: 'Terror is, in all cases whatsoever, either more openly or latently, the ruling principle of the sublime.'[79] Other writers, as we have seen, attributed the sublime principle to grandeur, to energy, or to the Deity Himself. If some of Turner's works, in particular the earlier ones, adopt the language of Burke and the landscape sublime, it is clear that in his maturity he took a broader view. There are examples, of course, in which darkness is made the dominant theme; sometimes a whole suite of works, such as the 'Sequel to the Liber Studiorum' or 'Little Liber' (see nos 74–8), pursues the motif of darkness deliberately; in this case, the medium of mezzotint seems to have dictated the choice of theme, and prompted some of the most intensely felt night-scenes in Turner's art or anyone else's. But in general, he preferred to invest his pictures with the sublimity of brilliant sunlight 'immediately exerted on the eye'. A painting like the *Regulus* (see no. 54) is a vortex that revolves round a central hub, the sun at its most irradiantly dazzling. Some critics have thought it to be no coincidence that Regulus was a hero who suffered the punishment of having his eyelids cut off so that he was actually blinded by the sun. This is a conception that presents the idea of brilliant light and total darkness as necessary and complementary opposites. In works such as this, as much as in the late Swiss watercolours, Turner transcends the technical problems that traditionally beset the painter of grand effects. For him the complaint of a later artist was irrelevant: 'It is the "material" difficulty that forever vexes the soul of the painter. Is not white lead the only material we have with which to express the divine light of heaven?'[80]

Turner's famous remark, supposedly the last words he spoke, to the effect that 'the sun is god'[81] may or may not be authentic, but it sums up very well the impression that is overwhelmingly given by much of his output: sunlight, in its power to illuminate the world we live in, and in the inherent grandeur of its effects, is a supremely moving force, a force that is often felt in his paintings and watercolours to have a divine strength and beauty. Turner is generally considered to have been a pessimist, and to have had no religion – Ruskin, who knew him well in later life, and Thornbury, his first biographer, seem agreed on the point.[82] But the symbolism of his views of *Salisbury* and *Stonehenge*, made in the 1820s (see no. 83), if it is correctly interpreted by Ruskin,[83] strongly suggests that he shared with most of his contemporaries certain deep-seated assumptions about the validity of Christianity in contrast to other religions. It is quite possible that, with no very strong intellectual commitment, he subscribed to a vaguely deistic version of Christianity such as was common enough in England in the late eighteenth century. In any case, that he painted with no sense of religion is denied by his works. The numinous power of nature is repeatedly celebrated in them, and the omnipotent energy and saving grace of the sun constantly hymned. This was for Turner the religious sublime – far from being pessimistic his work often ecstatically exults in the consciousness of a superhuman force working in and through the natural world to the good of men.

Turner succeeded in breaking through the barrier of reality by pursuing many of the principles of realism in the painting of nature to their logical conclusion. Perhaps the idea that his latest works were in any sense 'realist' will be scouted as absurd. The confusion and irritation that his critics experienced in front of his pictures is surely an indication that he had gone beyond mere reality? Of course, in a sense he had. But their notion of realism in painting was still bounded by what Vernet understood by the term. Turner, as we have discovered, saw the need for a new and broader realism that would accurately describe phenomena of greater emotional power than any that had been painted in the past: a realism that would open up the imagination to deeper insights into the real world. If he had no followers in this it was because only a genius of his stature could master such a potent language. But there were contemporaries for whom it was, apparently, axiomatic that Turner, even the late Turner, was a realist. In 1849, two years before Turner's death, Charles Kingsley wrote in his novel *Yeast*: '. . . follow in the steps of your Turners, and Landseers, and Stanfields, and Creswicks, and add your contribution to the present noble school of naturalist painters . . . These men's patient, reverent faith in nature as they see her, their knowledge that the ideal is neither to be invented nor abstracted, but found and left where God has put it, and where alone it can be represented, in actual and individual phenomena – in these lies an honest development of the true idea of Protestantism . . .'[84]

It was of course Ruskin who, in *Modern Painters*, had promulgated the idea that Turner was a realist, whose power rests on truth to nature. He did not link him so glibly with Stanfield[85] and the rest of the successful and superficial generation that followed Turner, but he would have wholeheartedly endorsed Kingsley's view that Turner did not invent or abstract. It is a question of degree: Stanfield could adequately describe the 'littlenesses' of nature – the shape of clouds and the colour of the sea. But he could not begin to depict with convincing accuracy the height and breadth and depth of the sky, or the incalculable movement of the ocean. He could draw a mountain, but not convey its true height and its distance from the eye in terms that the heart could feel as well as the mind could understand. He could delineate the achievements of men, but not impress us with their grandeur. Above all, though he could scatter groups of well-posed figures across his landscapes, he could not make them, as Turner did, the focus of his subject, the heroic protagonists of the eternal drama of life.

NOTES TO CHAPTER THREE

1. Ms. C, ff. 3–4.
Quotations from Turner's lecture notes (British Museum, Add Ms. 46151, A–88) are transcribed directly from the Mss, but irregularities of spelling, punctuation, and occasionally phrasing, have been amended to make for clarity and ease of reading. An exact rendering of what Turner actually wrote is, in any case, not always possible on account of the illegibility and fragmentary nature of many of his jottings.

2. Stewart, *op. cit.*, p. 411.

3. *Spectator*, no. 415, 26 June 1712.

4. See Wilton 193–203.

5. Burke, *op. cit.*, p. 64.

6. Wilton 139 and pl. 23.

7. Wilton 143 and pl. 24.

8. Wilton 256, the full title is: *Warkworth Castle, Northumberland – thunder storm approaching at sun-set.*

9. *Summer*, ll. 1103–5; 1111–13.

10. Stanzas 6 and 7. The final line seems to have been added by Turner himself.

11. Langhorne, *Elegy IV*, stanzas 1 and 2.

12. See no. 50.

13. Butlin & Joll 13.

14. Butlin & Joll 17, 19, 47.

15. There is a long discussion of the precise meaning of the letters 'E. P.' in J. L. Roget and J. Pye, *Notes and Memoranda respecting the Liber Studiorum by J.M.W. Turner*, London 1879, pp. 26, ff. Roget and Pye concluded that they stood for 'Epic Pastoral'; the significance is almost identical. 'Elegant Pastoral' is a less satisfactory alternative proposal.

16. TB LXXII.

17. Ms. C, f. 2.

18. Ms. E, f. 19.

19. See Gage, 1969, chapter 6.

20. Ms. K, f. 11 verso.

21. Butlin & Joll 135.

22. *Repository of Arts*, June 1817, quoted in Butlin & Joll.

23. Ms. I, f. 1 verso.

24. Ms. I, f. 21. Turner's admiration for subjects engraved after Wilson by William Woollett, including *Niobe* and *Celadon and Amelia*, is recorded in a letter from him to the print publishers Hurst and Robinson, 28 June 1822 (printed in Thornbury, p. 342).

25. Both were works that he had seen in the Louvre in 1802. The Titian was destroyed by fire in 1867, but is reproduced in several copies and in an engraving by M. Rota (repr. Wilton, 1979, pl. 78); the Poussin *Deluge* is Blunt, pl. 245.

26. Ms. I, f. 4 verso.

27. Ms. G, f. 27.

28. TB LXXII, pp. 28 verso, 28 recto.

29. TB LXXII, p. 42.

30. Ms I, ff. 16 verso, 17.

31. Ms I, f. 16.

32. Butlin & Joll 115.

33. Livy, *History of Rome*, XXI, 31.

34. Mason ed., *Gray*, p. 302.

35. Gilpin, *Remarks on Forest Scenery*, 1791, vol. I, p. 252. Compare the theory of Kant summarised on p. 29. Burke had stressed the importance of obscurity for the sublime, *op. cit.*, pp. 43–49.

36. *Discourse XIV*, 1788, Wark ed., p. 255.

37. *Ibid.*, p. 256.

38. Blair, *op. cit.*, p. 62. See note 35.

39. No doubt earlier works by Turner, such as the *Destruction of Sodom* of 1805 (Butlin & Joll 56) were influential on Martin, who may also have known *The Army of the Medes destroyed in the Desert by a Whirlwind*, now lost, but exhibited at the R.A in 1801 (Butlin & Joll 15).

40. He may also have noticed that the theorists recognised sublimity in individuals as a function of their character and achievements, not of their stature; Lord Kames noted (*op. cit.*, p. 280) that 'the Scythians, impressed with the fame of Alexander, were astonished when they found him a little man.' To one of Turner's unprepossessing appearance, such ideas would have been important.

41. Wilton 369, repr. pl. 104.

42. Butlin & Joll 131, 135.

43. See the verses by Turner appended to the R.A. catalogue entry for the *Decline of Carthage*.

44. Stewart, *op. cit.*, p. 384.

45. Byron, *Ode to Napoleon*, stanza II, ll. 8, 9.

46. Charlotte Brontë, quoted by Mrs. Gaskell, *The Life of Charlotte Brontë* (1857), Everyman ed., p. 173.

47. Blair, *op. cit.*, p. 59.

48. Alison, *op. cit.*, vol. I, p. 126.

49. Examples of this dynamic perspective are to be found in *Calais Pier* of 1803, *Frosty Morning* of 1813, *Rome from the Vatican* of 1820, and *Hero and Leander* of 1831 (Butlin & Joll 48, 127, 228, 370) among the paintings, and in numerous watercolours of all periods.

50. William Duff, *An Essay on Original Genius, and its varied modes of exertion in Philosophy and the Fine Arts, particularly in Poetry*, London 1767, p. 166, note.

51. See *Caernarvon Castle*, Wilton 857; Shanes 65.

52. *The Beauties of England: or, a Comprehensive View of the Public Structures, the Seats of the Nobility and Gentry, the two Universities, the Cities, Market Towns, Antiquities and Curiosities, natural and artificial, for which this Island is remarkable*, London 1757, p. 339.

53. Blair, *op. cit.*, p. 65.

54. John Ruskin, *Modern Painters*, Pt V; *Works*, VI, pp. 38–9.

55. Warner, *op. cit.*, p. 97.

56. Blake, *Milton*, 1804, pl. 1.

57. See the often-quoted description of Coalbrookdale by Arthur Young, 1771: 'the noise of the forges, mills, etc., with all their vast machinery, the flames bursting from the furnaces with the burning of the coal and the smoak of the lime kilns, are altogether sublime, and would unite very well with craggy and bare rocks . . .' Quoted in Francis D. Klingender, *Art and the Industrial Revolution* (1947) revised ed., 1968, p. 89; and see pp. 88–103.

58. See Albert O. Wlecke, *Wordsworth and the Sublime*, Berkeley 1973, *passim*, and especially pp. 47 ff.

59. Butlin & Joll 359, 364.

60. Butlin & Joll 361.

61. Turner depicts the monumental pyramid under which Marceau's ashes were placed; it was designed by his colleague General Kléber, who is thus both military hero and artist.

62. The first two Cantos of *Childe Harold* appeared in 1812, the third in 1816 and the fourth in 1818.

63. *The Surprizing Miracles of Nature and Art* (see above, p. 29) includes whales among the astonishing phenomena it lists (e.g. p. 162: 'In 1658, a great Whale came up to Greenwich near London, a thing seldom known before.')

64. TB CCCLVII–6, and Wilton 1141 and 1142.

65. Butlin & Joll 423, 426.

66. The whole passage is ll. 980–1025. See T. S. R. Boase, 'Shipwrecks in English Romantic Painting', *Journal of the Warburg and Courtauld Institutes*, 1959, pp. 332–46.

67. *Winter*, ll. 414–423. See Jack Lindsay, *J.M.W. Turner*, 1966, p. 107.

68. The two Avalanche pictures are reproduced side by side in Wilton, 1979, pls 101, 102. De Loutherbourg's version hung in the collection of Sir John Fleming Leicester, at Tabley House, which Turner visited in 1808, two years before the exhibition of his own avalanche subject.

69. Alison, *op. cit.*, vol. II, p. 128.

70. Is Turner's choice of name for the ship itself a kind of 'historical' allusion? The *Ariel* was the vessel in which Prince Albert of Saxe-Coburg came to England to marry Queen Victoria in 1840.

71. Ruskin, *Works*, VII, p. 445, note.

72. Courbet's *L'Immensité* (c. 1865) is in the Victoria and Albert Museum, Ionides Collection.

73. Stewart, *op. cit.*, p. 422.

74. *The Bard*, pt II, stanza 2, ll. 9–14.

75. Wilton 1524.

76. Butlin & Joll 371.

77. Burke, *op. cit.*, p. 45. The passage of Milton's *Paradise Lost*, Book II, ll. 666–673.

78. Burke, *op. cit.*, p. 62.

79. Burke, *op. cit.*, 2nd ed., 1759, II, 2.

80. J. C. Horsley, *op. cit.*, p. 168.

81. Ruskin, *Works*, XXVIII, p. 147.

82. Thornbury, p. 303.

83. Ruskin, *Works*, VII, pp. 190–1.

84. Charles Kingsley, *Yeast*, Everyman ed., p. 228.

85. Clarkson Stanfield, 1793–1867.

CONCLUSION

I love all waste
And solitary places; where we taste
The pleasure of believing what we see
Is boundless, as we wish our souls to be.

P. B. SHELLEY: *Julian and Maddalo*, 1824

Landscape photography which successfully captures the scale of nature can often make the creations of man seem insignificant. But even when people and their dwellings are dwarfed by the scenery or excluded from the picture altogether, it would be a mistake to think that human interest is lacking. What gives a good landscape picture its appeal is its ability to reflect human emotions and to express ideas about the relationship between man and nature. If a view of a mountain or an area of countryside is sufficiently spectacular, you may be content simply to record it, but you are likely to be disappointed with the results unless the photograph succeeds in capturing not only what you saw but also what you felt.

JOHN HEDGECOE, *Introductory Photography Course*, 1979

When Turner was an old man he visited the American photographer J. J. E. Mayall in London and spent many hours questioning him about his procedures and the physical laws governing photography. 'He came again and again, always with some new notion about light', Mayall recalled for the benefit of Thornbury. 'He wished me to copy my views of Niagara – then a novelty in London – and enquired of me about the effect of the rainbow spanning the great falls. I was fortunate in having seized one of these fleeting shadows when I was there, and I showed it to him. He wished to buy the plate . . . He told me he should like to see Niagara, as it was the greatest wonder in Nature; he was never tired of my descriptions of it.'[1]

It was no accident that the school which took up Turner's ideas with the greatest enthusiasm and conviction was that of the American 'Hudson River' painters, who responded to the immensity and grandeur of the North American continent by producing pictures of great size and exploiting the most grandiose effects of storm, sunlight and vast space. In such a landscape as theirs it was hardly possible to avoid the sublime. James Fenimore Cooper's remarks at the beginning of *The Pathfinder* were both necessary and inevitable. It is touching that Turner himself, at the end of his life, was able to glimpse something of the sublime possibilities of America, and appropriate that he should have done so through the eminently 'realistic' medium of photography.

The Hudson River school took the New World as they found it and instinctively created works of art on a grand scale. They were far enough from Europe to be unconcerned about the more elevated aspirations of Academic landscape artists, and were content to inspire and uplift by the faithful rendering of nature in all her splendour. They introduced into American culture a love of the vast, the magnificent and the overpowering that has been an essential part of it ever since. It is largely through the medium of the American imagination that we still savour the sublime today. For in spite of a perhaps inevitable debasement of its significance, sublimity remains a potent element in our consciousness, whether we use the word itself or not. We continue to be awed by the enormous, the very high, the immensely vast, the imponderably great, and we may still feel that these qualities in natural phenomena suggest the presence of a power that cannot be expressed in material terms. North America is peculiarly rich in such phenomena both natural and man-made. Hollywood's 'epic' movies are the 'sensational' art of our age, the natural successors of John Martin's cataclysms. The Empire State Building, the World Trade Center, the CN Tower at Toronto, are tourist attractions for no other reason than that they are 'productive of the sublime' – even if we should hesitate to say that they are sublime in themselves. They are the modern counterparts of the Temple of Jupiter Belus at Babylon, which was a mile high, and, as Addison says, for that reason alone sublime. Addison also refers to 'the huge rock that was cut into the figure of Semiramis, with the smaller rocks that lay by it in the shape of tributary kings',[2] which was surely only an earlier version of Mount Rushmore. The illimitable deserts and boundless forests so much beloved by the theorists of the sublime are a visitable reality in the United States and Canada. Even the achievement of taking men to the moon is strictly classifiable as a sublime attainment of the human mind, of human energy and heroism. And it has been possible for one of the leaders of the modern American school of abstraction to speak of its work as embodying 'a modern Stonehenge, with a sense of the sublime and the tragic that had not existed since Goya and Turner'.[3]

As human beings we cannot avoid being responsive to the sublime in nature and in the works of man. We must still be responsive to it in works of art. This instinctive human response is what prompts much of our admiration for Turner. He did not, of course, paint only in the sublime mode. He has moods of lyric tenderness, of pastoral calm and domestic jollity; he is as much a recorder of the quiet ordinariness of daily life as of its storms and passions. But there can be no doubt that he gauged his own most serious and powerful works by the notion of the sublime as it had been so fully and elaborately formulated by the theorists of the period. Just because that formulation is not so readily available to us now, or because we have other, perhaps more sophisticated reasons for appreciating him, we should not fail to respond to his art as he certainly intended us to.

NOTES

1. Thornbury, *op. cit.*, p. 349.
2. *Spectator*, no. 915, 26 June 1712.
3. Robert Motherwell, 1965, quoted in Frances Carey and Anthony Griffiths, *American Prints 1879–1979*, London 1980, p. 18.

Notes to the catalogue

The catalogue is divided into nine sections. These are not intended to include every aspect of the sublime, which lends itself to categorisations of many kinds. They are to suggest, rather, some of the principal ways in which theories of the sublime make themselves apparent in various types of works. For instance, 'Darkness' is only one of several 'abstract' categories (such as infinity, vastness, emptiness, etc.), and there are included in it examples which might also be catalogued as, say, 'Historical' (no. 71) or 'Industrial Sublime' (no. 73). These inclusions illustrate how an abstraction associated with the sublime could be applied to subjects with other characteristics, sublime or not. The Industrial Sublime itself, really a derivative of the Picturesque Sublime, has been incorporated into the section of 'Cities', a broader category that comprehends Turner's developments of other themes – the 'Topographical Sublime' or even the sublime of brilliant sunlight.

The arrangement of the sections is somewhat arbitrary, but it is hoped that a sense of development will be conveyed, and that the individual catalogue entries will be read against the general background of argument provided by the main text. The 'Picturesque Sublime', for instance, played a role of diminishing importance in Turner's paintings after about 1800, but continued to shape his approach to many watercolour subjects as late as the 1830s. The 'Terrific' was a mode that he radically modified for his own purposes so that his later views of mountain scenery have a very different mood. Hence they appear in a separate section. Whatever the disadvantages of the arrangement, Turner would perhaps have sympathised with the wish to order and categorise his works, since he was so much inclined to do so himself.

Items are catalogued in roughly chronological order within sections, and dimensions are given in inches and millimetres, height preceding width. The support is assumed to be white wove paper unless otherwise stated.

The following abbreviations are used in the catalogue entries:

BM 1975	Wilton, Andrew, *Turner in the British Museum*, London 1975
Butlin & Joll	Butlin, Martin and Joll, Evelyn, *The Paintings of J. M. W. Turner*, 2 vols, London 1977
Finberg	Finberg, A. J., *Life of J. M. W. Turner*, 2nd ed., 1961
R.	*either* Rawlinson, W. G. *The engraved work of J. M. W. Turner*, London 1908
	or Rawlinson, W. G., *Turner's Liber Studiorum*, 2nd ed., London 1906
RA 1974	Royal Academy, Turner Bicentenary Exhibition
Ruskin, *Works*	Cook, E. T. and Wedderburn, A. (eds), *The Works of John Ruskin*, 39 vols, London 1903–12
Shanes	Shanes, Eric, *Turner's Picturesque Views in England and Wales*, London 1979
TB	Turner Bequest (numbers in A. J. Finberg, *Inventory of the Drawings in the Turner Bequest . . .*)
Thornbury	Thornbury, Walter, *Life and Correspondence of J. M. W. Turner* revised ed., 1877
Turner in Switzerland	Russell, John and Wilton, Andrew, *Turner in Switzerland*, Zurich 1976
Wilton	Wilton, Andrew, *The Life and Work of J. M. W. Turner*, London 1979

CATALOGUE

THE PICTURESQUE SUBLIME

1 Llanthony Abbey 1794

Pencil and watercolour, $12\frac{7}{8} \times 16\frac{11}{16}$ (327 × 424)
Inscr: lower left *1794 W Turner*
TB XXVII – R, RA 1964 (11), Wilton 65
Colour plate 1

This is the grandest of the subjects that Turner gleaned from his trip to South Wales in 1792,[1] combining the fascination of a venerable ruin with the drama of the Black Mountains and an approaching rainstorm: a concatenation of historical, natural and climatic ideas that Turner was to use repeatedly all his life, especially in topographical work but also in many paintings of broader intention. The reinterpretation of the subject that makes its appearance in the *England and Wales* series (see no. 11) shows how flexible the formula could become in his hands. This first version of the theme achieves atmospheric unity by means of a restricted palette of greys and blue-greens which Turner found in the work of other artists of the Picturesque – Edward Dayes (1763–1804) and Thomas Hearne (1744–1806) in particular. He also had in mind, no doubt, the more impressive performances of John Robert Cozens, who specialised in wild mountainous subjects that attain to a misty grandeur which Turner seems to be emulating here.

1. It is based on a pencil drawing, TB XII–F.

2 Evening Landscape with Castle and Bridge *c*. 1798–9

Watercolour, $7\frac{7}{16} \times 10\frac{1}{2}$ (189 × 226)
Yale Center for British Art, Paul Mellon Collection, B1977.14.5380,
Wilton 250
Colour plate 2

Nothing marks Turner's development from the early 1790s to the later years of the decade more distinctively than the change that came over his colouring. His work in oil no doubt had much to do with this, but his experiments in both media were inspired by the same wish to create more powerful and impressive statements than before. It was in the course of these experiments that he developed the habit of making colour sketches for his watercolour compositions, rather as he might lay in a canvas for a subject in oil. This sheet is a rather unusual example, being smaller than the expansive 'colour-beginnings' he often made around 1800 (see no. 3). It probably comes from a sketchbook, but was evidently not drawn in front of the subject: it concentrates certain aspects of Turner's idea in an intense, brooding image which is the generalised basis for a finished work – though no known watercolour relates to it directly.

3 Norham Castle: Study *c*. 1798

Pencil and watercolour, $26\frac{1}{8} \times 33\frac{1}{16}$ (663 × 840)
TB L–B, RA 1974 (639)
Colour plate 3

Turner exhibited a powerful, sombre watercolour view of Norham at the RA in 1798 (no. 353), and repeated the subject shortly afterwards.[1] Both versions are based on a pencil sketch made on the spot in 1797,[2] and may have made use of this colour-beginning and another similar one,[3] which exploit Turner's new technical skills to create an atmosphere of great intensity. Watercolour is laid on in broad washes which are then partially blotted away, to reveal either a different wash beneath, or the white of the paper. Some-

times the resulting effects are similar to those achieved by oil paint, but the fluidity and integrity of the watercolour medium is maintained in the bold and free handling of these elaborate devices. This view of Norham was one of the subjects which at the end of his career Turner reinterpreted to express his conception of the sublimity of sunlight as opposed to that of gloom (see no. 9).[4]

1. Wilton 225, 226.
2. TB XXXIV–57.
3. TB L–C.
4. Butlin & Joll 512. Others in the series are generally taken from *Liber Studiorum* subjects. (See Butlin & Joll 509–21.)

4 A View in North Wales *c*. 1799

Watercolour, $21\frac{3}{4} \times 30\frac{3}{8}$ (553 × 772)
TB LX(a)–A, BM 1975(19)
Colour plate 4

5 Dolbadern and the pass of Llanberis *c*. 1799

Watercolour and stopping-out, $21\frac{7}{8} \times 29\frac{7}{8}$ (555 × 758)
TB LXX–Z
Colour plate 5

6 River with cattle and mountains beyond *c*. 1799

Watercolour and stopping-out with some bodycolour, $21 \times 30\frac{11}{16}$ (533 × 780)
TB LXX–b
Colour plate 6

These three studies form part of a group of large drawings that resulted from Turner's tour of north Wales in 1799.[1] In scale and mood they are similar to some finished watercolours of about that time,[2] although they are not in themselves exhibitable works. They are a close visual equivalent of the descriptions published in the fashionable tours of the period – that of Richard Warner, for instance (see pp. 43–4). In them the notion of the sublime as emotionally charged, gloomy and grandiose reaches full maturity; but already we sense Turner's desire to expand the terms of reference of the sublime, to comprehend a wider range of feeling than the merely 'astonishing'.

1. These are all in the Turner Bequest: TB LX(a) was originally catalogued by Finberg as a series of scenes in the Lake District, done in about 1801; he later (*Life*, pp. 159–60) redated them to 1809. They must in fact belong to the earlier period, and are all, apparently, scenes in north Wales.
2. E.g. Wilton 252–4, 259.

7 A Mountain Torrent 1801

Pencil, watercolour and white bodycolour on a buff prepared ground, $19 \times 13\frac{9}{16}$ (483 × 344)
TB LVIII–34

One of the series of sixty large studies made during Turner's Scottish tour of 1801.[1] He worked on a ground tone mixed from 'india ink and tobacco water',[2] using the pencil with a force and experimental freedom new in his work. The expansive landscapes of the Highlands seem to have acted as a stimulus, almost as a challenge: how is the artist to persuade his audience of the scale of such scenery with the aid of one monochrome implement? The deliberate restriction of means, the penetrating search for significance, are reminiscent of John Robert Cozens's understated yet passionate accounts of the Alps. These Scottish drawings give the first hint that Turner was beginning to understand what Cozens had to teach the painter of mountain grandeur. They constitute an exercise, a discipline that was to stand Turner in good stead when he went to Switzerland in the following year.

1. TB LVIII: they were christened by Ruskin 'Scottish Pencils'.
2. Joseph Farington, *Diary*, 6 February 1802.

8 Pembroke-castle: Clearing up of a thunder-storm
1806

> Watercolour and bodycolour over pencil, with some scraping-out, $26\frac{3}{8} \times 41\frac{1}{8}$ (670 × 1045)
> Art Gallery of Ontario, Toronto (on loan from the Governing Council of the University of Toronto), Wilton 281
> *Colour plate 7*

This watercolour is one of two showing Pembroke Castle seen from a similar angle and in stormy conditions. The other was exhibited at the Royal Academy in 1801 as *Pembroke Castle, South Wales: thunder storm approaching*.[1] This one was shown in 1806 with the title given here. Until recently the titles had been allocated to the wrong subjects, as it had not been noticed how carefully Turner distinguishes the meteorological effects that he specifies. Whereas in the other work only a fitful gleam of sunlight penetrates thick clouds, here there is a real 'clearing up' of the sky to the right, while boats which had previously huddled inshore for shelter now strike out across the sound once more. Such careful observations always underlie the general dramatic statements made by Turner's pictures. Even so, it is odd that he should have shown two such similar works at the Academy. He had done the same thing a few years before when, in 1796 and 1797, he exhibited almost identical views of the interior of Ely cathedral,[2] differing only in the direction of the sunlight that falls through the windows: a subtle reflection on the power of light to alter our experience of things, even when we are indoors and least conscious of it. So in the *Pembroke Castle* pair Turner seems to be saying that nothing is ever the same on different occasions, for time and climate constantly alter our perception, and indeed the reality itself, of what we see.

1. Wilton 280.
2. Wilton 194, 195.

J. M. W. Turner and Charles Turner (1773–1857), after J. M. W. Turner

9 Falls of the Clyde (*Liber Studiorum*) 1809

> Etching and mezzotint, printed in brown ink, first published state (R. 18), subject: $7\frac{3}{16} \times 10\frac{3}{8}$ (182 × 264); plate: $8\frac{1}{4} \times 11\frac{7}{16}$ (209 × 291)
> Inscr. above: *E. P.*; below: *Drawing of the CLYDE. In the possession of J. M. W. Turner.* with measurements (3ft 4in. × 2ft 3in.); and: *Drawn & Etched by J. M. W. Turner Esq? R.A.P.P.* and: *Engraved by C. Turner*; bottom: *London, Published March 29. 1809. by C. Turner, N.º 50, Warren Street, Fitzroy Square.*
> Yale Center for British Art, Paul Mellon Collection, B1977.14.8120

Turner made several studies of the fall of Cora Linn on the Clyde during his tour to Scotland in 1801;[1] from these he worked up a large watercolour of the fall[2] which he exhibited at the Royal Academy in the following year, with a reference in the catalogue to Mark Akenside's *Hymn to the Naiads* of 1746. Akenside explained[3] that his poem was about the 'Nymphs who preside over springs

and rivulets' giving 'motion to the air, and exciting summer breezes; . . . nourishing and beautifying the vegetable creation.' The *Liber Studiorum* subject is a considerably modified version of the original design, giving greater prominence to the depth of the fall, which is caught in a slanting beam of light that also spills across the scene through the trees at the left. This creates a sustained diagonal that lends a breadth to the scale of the plate in keeping with its 'Elevated Pastoral' status. When Turner returned to the subject for one of his last paintings,[4] these formal devices were abandoned in favour of an altogether more experimental use of diffused and iridescent light, perhaps, as has been suggested,[5] a further gloss on Akenside's theme, in which the personification of 'the elemental forces of nature' as nymphs, which the early versions share with the eighteenth-century poem, is replaced by a more direct expression of the inner meaning of the landscape.

1. Wilton 322–4.
2. Wilton 343; and see James Holloway and Lindsay Errington, *The Discovery of Scotland*, Edinburgh 1978, pp. 47–55.
3. In the 'Argument' which prefaces the poem.
4. *The Fall of the Clyde*, Butlin & Joll 510.
5. By John Gage, *Colour in Turner*, 1969, p. 143.

J. M. W. Turner and Robert Dunkarton (1744–c. 1811), after J. M. W. Turner

10 Hind Head Hill On the Portsmouth Road (*Liber Studiorum*) 1811

> Etching and mezzotint, printed in brown ink, first published state (R. 25), subject: $7 \times 10\frac{3}{16}$ (177 × 259); plate: $8\frac{1}{8} \times 11\frac{3}{8}$ (207 × 289)
> Inscr. above: *M*; below: with title and: *Drawn & Etched by J. M. W. Turner, R.A.P.P.*, and: *Engraved by R. Dunkarton*, and: *Published Jan? 1. 1811, by M.r Turner, Queen Ann Street West.*
> Yale Center for British Art, Paul Mellon Collection, B1977.14.8131

This plate reminds us that the countryside of southwest Surrey is among the most dramatic in England, possessing many of the attributes of the landscape sublime. It is overlooked nowadays as being too close, probably, to London to be of interest, and Turner's categorisation of 'Mountainous' would seem surprising. He passed this way on his route to make drawings at Portsmouth and Spithead in October, 1807, and sketched the hill in a book that also contains some verses scribbled by him on the subject of 'Hindhead the cloud-capt',[1] a demonstration of the way that sublime scenery of all sorts roused his responses not only visual but literary. The hill shown by Turner is now known as Gibbet Hill, and is 894 feet high; the gibbet was removed early in the nineteenth century and, as Rawlinson records, was replaced by a stone cross inscribed *Post Tenebras Lux*, which is, in a sense, the theme of this survey of Turner's work. The original drawing for this plate is TB CXVII–C.

1. The *Spithead* sketchbook, TB C. The verses are on the inside cover; drawings of Hindhead Hill are on ff. 20–3 and 70 verso. The sketch for the *Liber* subject is on f. 49 verso.

James Tibbitts Willmore (1800–63), after J. M. W. Turner

11 Llanthony Abbey, Monmouthshire (*England and Wales*) 1836

> Engraving, progress proof(b), touched by Turner with pencil and white bodycolour (R. 287), subject: $6\frac{5}{8} \times 9\frac{7}{16}$ (168 × 240); plate: $9\frac{1}{2} \times 12\frac{1}{8}$ (242 × 309)
> Yale Center for British Art, Paul Mellon Collection, B1977.14.7086

13△ ▽ 14

ture that Turner brings before us here. It is remarkable that he should have pursued his interest in large-scale watercolours to the extreme of actually making a full-size drawing on the spot, and still more remarkable that in this drawing he anticipates his practice of making such gigantic watercolours by about two years. It is a matter of some importance to determine whether Turner had a large-scale watercolour in mind when the drawing was made. He had certainly never produced anything on such a scale at that date, though one or two other topographers had set a precedent for work of this kind – Edward Dayes, for instance, had drawn the exterior of Ely in 1792 on a sheet measuring 680 × 925.[1] In Turner's own output, this is the first firm evidence we have for the interest in large works that was to preoccupy him for a decade or more.

1. In the Victoria and Albert Museum (FA 674) repr. Andrew Wilton, *British Watercolours, 1750–1850*, Oxford 1977, pl. 26.

14 Interior of Christ Church Cathedral, Oxford, c. 1799

Pencil, watercolour and stopping-out, touched with bodycolour, 26¾ × 19¾ (680 × 501)
TB L–G

It was Sir Richard Colt Hoare of Stourhead in Wiltshire who first gave Turner commissions to make watercolour drawings of architectural interiors – in particular, the interior of Salisbury Cathedral, of which Turner made several large finished watercolours between 1796 and about 1802. In addition, there are two views of the interior of Ely cathedral, and one of Westminster Abbey, all belonging to the same years.[1] No. 13 is a pencil study of one of these subjects. Colt Hoare's own collection of watercolours included works by the French artist Abraham-Louis-Rodolphe Ducros (1748–1810), which exhibited a range of effects unknown to English artists in the mid-1790s;[2] in his work for Colt Hoare, then, Turner set himself to vie with the strength and dramatic immediacy of Ducros's views, and it is in the Salisbury interiors especially that he achieves the grandeur and power that he aimed for. This study of another interior, that of Christ Church cathedral, is perhaps an indication of how these highly wrought drawings looked when half finished. The system of stopping-out colour that Turner had developed by this date is in evidence (compare the study of Norham Castle of about the same time, *Colour 3*). The atmosphere of the old church is rendered in a rich chiaroscuro, shafts of light reinforcing the compositional thrust of the steep perspective.

1. Wilton 138; 194–203.
2. For an account of Turner's relations with Colt Hoare, and reproductions of Hoare's drawings by Ducros, see Kenneth Woodbridge, *Landscape and Antiquity*, 1970, pt II, chap. 14.

15 Illustration to a lecture on Perspective: Interior of a Prison c. 1810

Pencil, watercolour and bodycolour, 19⅛ × 27 (486 × 686)
Inscr. upper left: 65
TB CXCV–120, RA 1974(B54)
Colour plate 8

Turner's course of lectures on Perspective was first delivered in January, 1811, after more than three years' delay: he had been appointed Professor of Perspective at the Royal Academy in 1807.

12 View through the columns of St Peter's Piazza,
    Rome *c.* 1795

Pencil and grey wash, $15\frac{3}{4} \times 17\frac{1}{16}$ (400 × 433)
TB CCCLXXV–7

This drawing has been thought to be by some other hand than
Turner's,[1] for it is executed in a style which he shared, briefly, with
other artists in the mid-1790s. It is perhaps the work of his
colleague Thomas Girtin; but on balance seems more likely to be by
Turner himself, and reflects his bold sense of scale. It no doubt
derives from a study made in Italy by another artist – many
drawings by J. R. Cozens were adapted by Turner and Girtin in
this way – but shows signs of having been thought out afresh, with
its small figures in historic costume, which suggest that Bernini's
columns belong to some colossal temple of antiquity, much vaster
than they are in reality. A piece of direct topographical recording is

converted by these simple means into a classical fantasy in the
spirit of artists like Pannini and Piranesi.

1. See Finberg, *Inventory*, vol. II, p. 1234.

13 The Octagon, Ely Cathedral 1794

Pencil, $30\frac{3}{8} \times 23\frac{1}{8}$ (772 × 588)
TB XXII–P, RA 1974(12)

This study, made on the spot during a tour of 1794, was used by
Turner as the basis for two watercolours shown at the Royal
Academy (see no. 8). It is typical of the careful and accurate
architectural record-taking in which Turner became so proficient
during the early 1790s. But it betrays in its sheer size an intention
far beyond the usual topographical exercise. We hardly need the
addition of colour to be impressed by the huge and soaring struc-

12

11

A return to the subject of a watercolour of 1794 (no. 1), in which
the unstable, tumbling diagonal of the mountainside is reinforced
by new diagonals in the very air itself: shafts of light that beat
across the scene, binding its various elements together in an
exhilarating 'downpour' that is both topographical and climatic.
Similar uses of light and shadow to create compositional structures
that reinforce, but are independent of, the geography of the landscape, can be found in nos 39 and 110. Ruskin, who spoke of the
drawing[1] as a 'noble work', confirmed the accuracy with which it
portrays weather conditions: 'The shower is here half exhausted,
half passed by, the last drops are rattling faintly through the
glimmering hazel boughs, the white torrent, swelled by the sudden
storm, flings up its hasty jets of springing spray to meet the
returning light; and these, as if the heaven regretted what it had
given, and were taking it back, pass as they leap, into vapour, and
fall not again, but vanish in the shafts of the sunlight; hurrying,
fitful, wind-woven sunlight, which glides through the thick leaves,
and paces along the pale rocks like rain; half conquering, half
quenched by the very mists which it summons itself from the
lighted pastures as it passes, and gathers out of the drooping
herbage and from the steaming crags; sending them with messages
of peace to the far summits of the yet unveiled mountains, whose
silence is still broken by the sound of the rushing rain.'[2]

1. Wilton 863; Shanes 71.
2. Ruskin, *Works*, III, p. 402.

9

10

passionate accounts of the Alps. These Scottish drawings give the first hint that Turner was beginning to understand what Cozens had to teach the painter of mountain grandeur. They constitute an exercise, a discipline that was to stand Turner in good stead when he went to Switzerland in the following year.

1. TB LVIII: they were christened by Ruskin 'Scottish Pencils'.
2. Joseph Farington, *Diary*, 6 February 1802.

8 Pembroke-castle: Clearing up of a thunder-storm
1806

> Watercolour and bodycolour over pencil, with some scraping-out, $26\frac{3}{8} \times 41\frac{1}{8}$ (670 × 1045)
> Art Gallery of Ontario, Toronto (on loan from the Governing Council of the University of Toronto), Wilton 281
> *Colour plate 7*

This watercolour is one of two showing Pembroke Castle seen from a similar angle and in stormy conditions. The other was exhibited at the Royal Academy in 1801 as *Pembroke Castle, South Wales: thunder storm approaching*.[1] This one was shown in 1806 with the title given here. Until recently the titles had been allocated to the wrong subjects, as it had not been noticed how carefully Turner distinguishes the meteorological effects that he specifies. Whereas in the other work only a fitful gleam of sunlight penetrates thick clouds, here there is a real 'clearing up' of the sky to the right, while boats which had previously huddled inshore for shelter now strike out across the sound once more. Such careful observations always underlie the general dramatic statements made by Turner's pictures. Even so, it is odd that he should have shown two such similar works at the Academy. He had done the same thing a few years before when, in 1796 and 1797, he exhibited almost identical views of the interior of Ely cathedral,[2] differing only in the direction of the sunlight that falls through the windows: a subtle reflection on the power of light to alter our experience of things, even when we are indoors and least conscious of it. So in the *Pembroke Castle* pair Turner seems to be saying that nothing is ever the same on different occasions, for time and climate constantly alter our perception, and indeed the reality itself, of what we see.

1. Wilton 280.
2. Wilton 194, 195.

J. M. W. Turner and Charles Turner (1773–1857), after J. M. W. Turner

9 Falls of the Clyde (*Liber Studiorum*) 1809

> Etching and mezzotint, printed in brown ink, first published state (R. 18), subject: $7\frac{3}{16} \times 10\frac{3}{8}$ (182 × 264); plate: $8\frac{1}{4} \times 11\frac{7}{16}$ (209 × 291)
> Inscr. above: *E. P.*; below: *Drawing of the CLYDE. In the possession of J. M. W. Turner.* with measurements (3ft 4in. × 2ft 3in.); and: *Drawn & Etched by J. M. W. Turner Esq! R.A.P.P.* and: *Engraved by C. Turner*; bottom: *London, Published March 29. 1809. by C. Turner, N.º 50, Warren Street, Fitzroy Square.*
> Yale Center for British Art, Paul Mellon Collection, B1977.14.8120

Turner made several studies of the fall of Cora Linn on the Clyde during his tour to Scotland in 1801;[1] from these he worked up a large watercolour of the fall[2] which he exhibited at the Royal Academy in the following year, with a reference in the catalogue to Mark Akenside's *Hymn to the Naiads* of 1746. Akenside explained[3] that his poem was about the 'Nymphs who preside over springs

and rivulets' giving 'motion to the air, and exciting summer breezes; . . . nourishing and beautifying the vegetable creation.' The *Liber Studiorum* subject is a considerably modified version of the original design, giving greater prominence to the depth of the fall, which is caught in a slanting beam of light that also spills across the scene through the trees at the left. This creates a sustained diagonal that lends a breadth to the scale of the plate in keeping with its 'Elevated Pastoral' status. When Turner returned to the subject for one of his last paintings,[4] these formal devices were abandoned in favour of an altogether more experimental use of diffused and iridescent light, perhaps, as has been suggested,[5] a further gloss on Akenside's theme, in which the personification of 'the elemental forces of nature' as nymphs, which the early versions share with the eighteenth-century poem, is replaced by a more direct expression of the inner meaning of the landscape.

1. Wilton 322–4.
2. Wilton 343; and see James Holloway and Lindsay Errington, *The Discovery of Scotland*, Edinburgh 1978, pp. 47–55.
3. In the 'Argument' which prefaces the poem.
4. *The Fall of the Clyde*, Butlin & Joll 510.
5. By John Gage, *Colour in Turner*, 1969, p. 143.

J. M. W. Turner and Robert Dunkarton (1744–c. 1811), after J. M. W. Turner

10 Hind Head Hill On the Portsmouth Road
(*Liber Studiorum*) 1811

> Etching and mezzotint, printed in brown ink, first published state (R. 25), subject: $7 \times 10\frac{3}{16}$ (177 × 259); plate: $8\frac{1}{8} \times 11\frac{3}{8}$ (207 × 289)
> Inscr. above: *M*; below: with title and: *Drawn & Etched by J. M. W. Turner, R.A.P.P.*, and: *Engraved by R. Dunkarton*, and: *Published Jan! 1. 1811, by M.r Turner, Queen Ann Street West.*
> Yale Center for British Art, Paul Mellon Collection, B1977.14.8131

This plate reminds us that the countryside of southwest Surrey is among the most dramatic in England, possessing many of the attributes of the landscape sublime. It is overlooked nowadays as being too close, probably, to London to be of interest, and Turner's categorisation of 'Mountainous' would seem surprising. He passed this way on his route to make drawings at Portsmouth and Spithead in October, 1807, and sketched the hill in a book that also contains some verses scribbled by him on the subject of 'Hindhead the cloud-capt',[1] a demonstration of the way that sublime scenery of all sorts roused his responses not only visual but literary. The hill shown by Turner is now known as Gibbet Hill, and is 894 feet high; the gibbet was removed early in the nineteenth century and, as Rawlinson records, was replaced by a stone cross inscribed *Post Tenebras Lux*, which is, in a sense, the theme of this survey of Turner's work. The original drawing for this plate is TB CXVII–C.

1. The *Spithead* sketchbook, TB C. The verses are on the inside cover; drawings of Hindhead Hill are on ff. 20–3 and 70 verso. The sketch for the *Liber* subject is on f. 49 verso.

James Tibbitts Willmore (1800–63), after J. M. W. Turner

11 Llanthony Abbey, Monmouthshire (*England and Wales*) 1836

> Engraving, progress proof(b), touched by Turner with pencil and white bodycolour (R. 287), subject: $6\frac{5}{8} \times 9\frac{7}{16}$ (168 × 240); plate: $9\frac{1}{2} \times 12\frac{1}{8}$ (242 × 309)
> Yale Center for British Art, Paul Mellon Collection, B1977.14.7086

THE PICTURESQUE SUBLIME

1 Llanthony Abbey 1794

Pencil and watercolour, $12\frac{7}{8} \times 16\frac{11}{16}$ (327 × 424)
Inscr: lower left *1794 W Turner*
TB XXVII – R, RA 1964 (11), Wilton 65
Colour plate 1

This is the grandest of the subjects that Turner gleaned from his trip to South Wales in 1792,[1] combining the fascination of a venerable ruin with the drama of the Black Mountains and an approaching rainstorm: a concatenation of historical, natural and climatic ideas that Turner was to use repeatedly all his life, especially in topographical work but also in many paintings of broader intention. The reinterpretation of the subject that makes its appearance in the *England and Wales* series (see no. 11) shows how flexible the formula could become in his hands. This first version of the theme achieves atmospheric unity by means of a restricted palette of greys and blue-greens which Turner found in the work of other artists of the Picturesque – Edward Dayes (1763–1804) and Thomas Hearne (1744–1806) in particular. He also had in mind, no doubt, the more impressive performances of John Robert Cozens, who specialised in wild mountainous subjects that attain to a misty grandeur which Turner seems to be emulating here.

1. It is based on a pencil drawing, TB XII–F.

2 Evening Landscape with Castle and Bridge *c.* 1798–9

Watercolour, $7\frac{7}{16} \times 10\frac{1}{2}$ (189 × 226)
Yale Center for British Art, Paul Mellon Collection, B1977.14.5380,
Wilton 250
Colour plate 2

Nothing marks Turner's development from the early 1790s to the later years of the decade more distinctively than the change that came over his colouring. His work in oil no doubt had much to do with this, but his experiments in both media were inspired by the same wish to create more powerful and impressive statements than before. It was in the course of these experiments that he developed the habit of making colour sketches for his watercolour compositions, rather he might lay in a canvas for a subject in oil. This sheet is a rather unusual example, being smaller than the expansive 'colour-beginnings' he often made around 1800 (see no. 3). It probably comes from a sketchbook, but was evidently not drawn in front of the subject: it concentrates certain aspects of Turner's idea in an intense, brooding image which is the generalised basis for a finished work – though no known watercolour relates to it directly.

3 Norham Castle: Study *c.* 1798

Pencil and watercolour, $26\frac{1}{8} \times 33\frac{1}{16}$ (663 × 840)
TB L–B, RA 1974 (639)
Colour plate 3

Turner exhibited a powerful, sombre watercolour view of Norham at the RA in 1798 (no. 353), and repeated the subject shortly afterwards.[1] Both versions are based on a pencil sketch made on the spot in 1797,[2] and may have made use of this colour-beginning and another similar one,[3] which exploit Turner's new technical skills to create an atmosphere of great intensity. Watercolour is laid on in broad washes which are then partially blotted away, to reveal either a different wash beneath, or the white of the paper. Some-

times the resulting effects are similar to those achieved by oil paint, but the fluidity and integrity of the watercolour medium is maintained in the bold and free handling of these elaborate devices. This view of Norham was one of the subjects which at the end of his career Turner reinterpreted to express his conception of the sublimity of sunlight as opposed to that of gloom (see no. 9).[4]

1. Wilton 225, 226.
2. TB XXXIV – 57.
3. TB L – C.
4. Butlin & Joll 512. Others in the series are generally taken from *Liber Studiorum* subjects. (See Butlin & Joll 509–21.)

4 A View in North Wales *c.* 1799

Watercolour, $21\frac{3}{4} \times 30\frac{3}{8}$ (553 × 772)
TB LX(a)–A, BM 1975(19)
Colour plate 4

5 Dolbadern and the pass of Llanberis *c.* 1799

Watercolour and stopping-out, $21\frac{7}{8} \times 29\frac{7}{8}$ (555 × 758)
TB LXX–Z
Colour plate 5

6 River with cattle and mountains beyond *c.* 1799

Watercolour and stopping-out with some bodycolour, $21 \times 30\frac{11}{16}$ (533 × 780)
TB LXX–b
Colour plate 6

These three studies form part of a group of large drawings that resulted from Turner's tour of north Wales in 1799.[1] In scale and mood they are similar to some finished watercolours of about that time,[2] although they are not in themselves exhibitable works. They are a close visual equivalent of the descriptions published in the fashionable tours of the period – that of Richard Warner, for instance (see pp. 43–4). In them the notion of the sublime as emotionally charged, gloomy and grandiose reaches full maturity; but already we sense Turner's desire to expand the terms of reference of the sublime, to comprehend a wider range of feeling than the merely 'astonishing'.

1. These are all in the Turner Bequest: TB LX(a) was originally catalogued by Finberg as a series of scenes in the Lake District, done in about 1801; he later (*Life*, pp. 159–60) redated them to 1809. They must in fact belong to the earlier period, and are all, apparently, scenes in north Wales.
2. E.g. Wilton 252–4, 259.

7 A Mountain Torrent 1801

Pencil, watercolour and white bodycolour on a buff prepared ground, $19 \times 13\frac{9}{16}$ (483 × 344)
TB LVIII–34

One of the series of sixty large studies made during Turner's Scottish tour of 1801.[1] He worked on a ground tone mixed from 'india ink and tobacco water',[2] using the pencil with a force and experimental freedom new in his work. The expansive landscapes of the Highlands seem to have acted as a stimulus, almost as a challenge: how is the artist to persuade his audience of the scale of such scenery with the aid of one monochrome implement? The deliberate restriction of means, the penetrating search for significance, are reminiscent of John Robert Cozens's understated yet

He illustrated his talks with drawings carefully prepared by himself, often, like this one, of great beauty and brought to a high degree of finish. This sheet is one of a small group of studies[1] based on an etching of Giovanni Battista Piranesi (1720–78), plate 2 of the *Prima Parte di Architettura e Prospettive* which appeared in 1743. Piranesi was another master whose work Turner had been able to study in the collection of Sir Richard Colt Hoare (see no. 14), and his magnificent architectural fantasies played a large part in forming Turner's style as an artist of the architectural sublime.[2] Here the rigid demonstration of a perspective system in no way hinders him from producing a grand effect of tenebrous and slightly sinister gloom. His interest in architecture is well documented, and we know that he himself was responsible for more than one building scheme, including the design of his own picture gallery and a small house in Twickenham.[3] He was also a friend of Sir John Soane (1753–1837), whose neo-classical designs may have had some influence on the appearance of this drawing. It is possible that some of Turner's later, more ambiguous paintings of architectural interiors draw inspiration from Soane's work.[4]

1. Others are TB CXCV–121, 128.
2. See Woodbridge, *op. cit.*
3. Another of Turner's architectural projects was a gate lodge at Farnley; his own drawing of this is Wilton 589.
4. See Wilton, 1979, p. 210, and Butlin & Joll, pp. 445–50.

16 Rome: The Portico of St Peter's with the Entrance to the Via Sagrestia 1819

Pencil and watercolour with bodycolour on white paper prepared with a grey wash, $14\frac{3}{8} \times 9\frac{1}{8}$ (369 × 232)
TB CLXXXIX–6, BM 1975(68)

Just as, in drawings of 1819 like nos 17 and 82, Turner seems to have been reminded by his experiences in Rome of the art of Ducros whom he had admired in the 1790s, this study recalls another of the great influences of those years – Piranesi (see no. 15). It was indeed difficult not to see Rome through the eyes of artists, and it is surprising that, in general, Turner's view of it was so fresh, uncluttered by the prepossessions that he certainly took with him to Italy. Here, despite a Piranesian sense of scale, the vision is entirely original and direct, a masterly and personal response to the architecture of St Peter's, the scale of which is greatly exaggerated by the tiny figure beside it. He was to pursue the theme further in a finished watercolour of 1821 showing the interior of the basilica,[1] a brilliant Renaissance variant on the shadowy gothic interiors of Ely and Salisbury of the 1790s.

1. Wilton 724, pl. 159.

17 Rome: The Interior of the Colosseum: Moonlight 1819

Pencil, watercolour and bodycolour on white paper prepared with a grey wash, $9\frac{1}{16} \times 14\frac{9}{16}$ (231 × 369)
TB CLXXXIX–13, BM 1975(70)
Colour plate 9

Apart from the sweeping panoramas of Rome with which Turner filled many pages of his Italian sketchbooks, there are a number of studies of individual buildings, usually monuments of great size and historical significance like the Colosseum or the Vatican (see no. 16), which are presented in close-up, crowding in on the

16

spectator as gigantic and awe-inspiring piles of masonry.[1] In this sense, they continue the tradition of the architectural sublime that Turner had established in the 1790s. The drawings of 1819, however, do not make use of large sheets of paper, and achieve their effect by understatement. This sheet and no. 82 are exceptional among the many colour studies that Turner made during his first visit to Rome, in that they subordinate the grandeur of ancient buildings to climatic or atmospheric effects. It was usual, for instance, to show the interior of the Colosseum peopled with the contemporary inhabitants of Rome, listening to monks preaching or taking part in religious processions. Turner dispenses with these formalities of 'grand tour' topography, substituting his own associations, which perhaps hark back to the imagery of Ducros that he had seen at Stourhead (see no. 14). This drawing might be a design for the setting of the climax to Henry James's tale of *Daisy Miller* (1879).

1. A finished watercolour of the exterior of the Colosseum, in which the height of the structure is deliberately increased to tower off the edge of the paper, is in the British Museum, Lloyd Bequest (Wilton 723).

18 Ben Arthur 1801

Pencil and white bodycolour on a buff ground, $11\frac{1}{2} \times 16\frac{7}{8}$
(293 × 428)
TB LVIII–5

One of the 'Scottish Pencils' of Turner's tour of 1801 (see no. 7), this spare, brooding study exemplifies the economy of means by which Turner taught himself to note accurately the essentials of mountain scenery. Concentrating as it does on the forms of the rocks alone, the composition already contains something of the writhing energy of Turner's last masterpiece of the mountainous sublime – the *Faido* of 1843 (no. 104). Ben Arthur was to be used as the subject-matter for one of the latest of the published *Liber Studiorum* plates (no. 32). Rapid pencil studies of Ben Arthur occur in the *Tummel Bridge* sketchbook, and this sheet seems to have been worked up subsequently from one of them.[1]

1. TB LVII, 13 verso, 14.

19 The Devil's Bridge, Pass of St Gothard 1802

Pencil, watercolour and bodycolour with scraping-out on white paper prepared with a grey wash, $18\frac{9}{16} \times 12\frac{1}{2}$ (471 × 318)
TB LXXV–34, BM 1975(32)

The St Gothard pass, from Lucerne and Altdorf to Bellinzona, was one of the chief routes over the Alps for travellers of Turner's day,

and the Devil's Bridge was its most celebrated *Sehenswürdigkeit*. It was frequently drawn, though rarely by English artists before Turner. One exception was William Pars (1742–82), who made a watercolour of it for his patron Lord Palmerston in 1770.[1] Pars brought to the subject an eighteenth-century desire for accuracy that almost completely overrides any sense of excitement in the grandeur of the spot; careful delineation of form, allied to an insistent horizontal stress, make for stability and reassurance, whereas Turner's loose washes and powerful vertical, where both the cliff tops and the bottom of the chasm are out of sight, create a mood of dizzying instability. The theme was one that he was to repeat often, bringing it to a peak of expressive force in the *Battle of Fort Rock* (colour *15*). Another study of the gorge, taken from the bridge itself,[2] was used for a large finished watercolour of 1804.[3] A similar watercolour based on this view of the bridge is recorded, but untraced.[4] Turner executed oil paintings of both subjects,[5] and used this one for a 'Mountainous' plate in the *Liber Studiorum* (no. 26).

1. In the British Museum, 1870–5–14–1221. See Andrew Wilton, *William Pars: Journey through the Alps*, Zurich 1979, p. 45. Pars's drawing was engraved by William Woollett in 1773 (Fagan LXXVII).
2. TB LXXV–33. The two studies are reproduced side by side in *Turner in Switzerland*, pp. 62–3.
3. Wilton 366.
4. Wilton 368, repr. Frederick Wedmore, *Turner and Ruskin*, 2 vols, London 1900, vol. II, p. 256.
5. Butlin & Joll 146, 147.

18

20

20 A ravine on the pass of St Gothard 1802

Pencil and watercolour with bodycolour and scraping-out on white
paper prepared with a grey wash, $12\frac{1}{2} \times 18\frac{11}{16}$ (318×475)
TB LXXV–35, BM 1975(30)

An elaborately worked up study from the *St Gothard and Mont Blanc*
sketchbook of 1802, which embodies many of the salient ideas
associated with the landscape sublime: brooding shadow, tree-
grown crags and steep cliffs dropping into chasms. It is perhaps
surprising that no finished watercolour was developed from this;
but the sequence of drawings of Fort Rock in the Val d'Aosta
contain many of the same elements (see *colour 15*).

21 The Mer de Glace, Chamonix 1802

Pencil, watercolour and bodycolour on white paper prepared with a
grey wash, $12\frac{3}{8} \times 18\frac{5}{16}$ (314×468)
TB LXXV–23, BM 1975(31)

Turner made this drawing on a leaf of his *St Gothard and Mont Blanc*
sketchbook, and although he did not use it as the basis for any of
the finished watercolours that resulted from his Swiss tour of 1802,
he adapted it for a plate of the *Liber Studiorum* published in 1812, in
the 'Mountainous' category.[1] The monochrome greys of the ice
and rock create the impression of a rough sea frozen into immo-
bility; a perfect demonstration of the contention of the theorists of
the sublime that mountain peaks and rough seas are closely related
visually.[2] The bleakness of the subject perhaps discouraged Turner
from developing it into a finished work: in a sense, this direct and
spontaneous study needs no elaboration. Life is alien in such a
setting, and to add figures and other details for the sake of a

complete composition would have been inconsistent with the
mood and meaning of the place represented. The 'privation' of the
scene is expressed as much in the limited means used to convey it as
in any formal design of Turner's.

1. R. 50.
2. See p. 46; and *Turner in Switzerland*, p. 48.

22 The Hospice of the Great St Bernard 1802

Black and white chalks on grey paper, $8\frac{7}{16} \times 11\frac{3}{16}$ (215×284)
TB LXXIV–55

Turner's technique in this drawing owes much to the exercises he
had accomplished in Scotland in the previous year (nos 7 and 18),
and like those, the sheet may not be a record made on the spot, but
a more carefully wrought development of a slight out-of-doors
sketch, for the purpose of concentrating and refining an idea that
might subsequently be used for a picture. We have evidence that
Turner did indeed intend to make a finished watercolour of the
scene, for there is a study that explores the composition in broad
masses of colour (*colour 10*). No finished work is known, however.
The dramatic possibilities of the Great St Bernard with its famous
Hospice (which appears in Dickens's *Little Dorrit*)[1] were explored
by Turner in two vignette designs that he made for Samuel Rogers
in the late 1820s. In these, dogs prowl through the snow, and
cowled men carry the body of a victim of the mountain on a
stretcher.[2]

1. 1857; Bk II, Chapter I.
2. The vignettes were published in Roger's *Italy*, 1830 (R. 351, 352); Wilton 1155,
   1156.

21

22

23
24
25 ▷

23 The Hospice of the Great St Bernard: colour study
(?)*c.* 1806

Watercolour over traces of pencil, 13⅜ × 16¾ (340 × 425)
TB CCLXIII–195, BM 1975(71)
Colour plate 10

A meditation in pure colour on the subject of a drawing from
Turner's *Grenoble* sketchbook (no. 22), this study is evidently a
preliminary 'structure' for a fully worked out watercolour which
was never completed. It affords an opportunity to examine, un-
alloyed by local detail, the broad scheme of a work of the early
sublime type, in which Burke's 'sad and fuscous' colours play a
dominant part (see p. 67).

24 Glacier and Source of the Arveiron, going up to the
Mer de Glace 1803

Watercolour, 27 × 40 (685 × 1015)
Yale Center for British Art, Paul Mellon Collection, B1977.14.4650,
Wilton 365

Of all the subjects that Turner gathered during his tour of Switzerland in 1802, the views along the Valley of Chamonix from near the
Mer de Glace were among the most fruitful. Apart from the austere
drawing of the glacier and its surrounding peaks (no. 21), he made
several other studies in the same area, including a rough chalk
drawing[1] of the view which was used as the basis for this large
watercolour. No less than three other finished drawings make use
of a similar motif:[2] the sharp diagonal, which Turner had first
experimented with in his *Llanthony Abbey* of 1794 (no. 1), now
embodies all the mobility and contrast of full-scale mountain

scenery. The sharply slanting line is more than a mere equivalent
on paper of the side of a mountain. It is the 'oblique line' that 'may
rise to infinity', which Turner discussed in his lectures.[3] It links
the placid tranquillity of the valley with the harsh energy of the
cloudy peaks, and imbues the whole design with the unsteady
rhythm of the rocky, unsure goat-paths and the avalanche-invaded
forest. Human influences on this wild landscape are few: a solitary
goatherd is dwarfed by his surroundings, and a snake coiled on a
rock suggests that man is not welcome here. Watercolour technique is stretched to its utmost to describe the great variety of
forms and effects in this comprehensive survey of the grandeur and
ugliness of Alpine scenery. A final version of the subject appeared in
the form of a plate for Part XII of the *Liber Studiorum* in 1816,
categorised as 'Mountainous'.[4]

1. TB LXXIX–L.
2. Wilton 383, 387, 389.
3. See p. 70.
4. R. 60.

J. M. W. Turner and Charles Turner (1773–1857),
after J. M. W. Turner

25 Mount St Gothard (*Liber Studiorum*) 1808

Etching and mezzotint, printed in black-brown ink, first published
state (R.9), subject: 7 × 10³⁄₁₆ (178 × 259); plate: 8⅛ × 11⅜
(207 × 289)
Inscr. above: *M. S*; below: *M! S! Gothard.* and *Drawn & Etch'd by
J.M.W. Turner Esq! R. A. P. P.* and *Engraved by Cha! Turner* and
bottom: *London Published Feb! 20, 1808, by C. Turner № 50, Warren
Street Fitzroy Square.*
Yale Center for British Art, Paul Mellon Collection, B1977.14.8106

Turner's use of initial letters to denote the various categories of landscape included in the *Liber Studiorum* is sometimes erratic. Apart from the well-known uncertainty attached to the letters 'E.P.' which he sometimes uses instead of 'P' for Pastoral, there is some ambiguity attending the heading to this plate. Rawlinson notes[1] that Turner occasionally gives 'Ms' rather than simply 'M' for Mountainous, to distinguish the category from Marine, which is also denoted by 'M.' In this plate the dot between the two capital letters 'M.S' suggests that they stand, like 'E.P' for two separate words. Presumably the category is the 'Mountainous Sublime'. This is in fact the first 'mountainous' plate of the series, and Turner did not use the form again;[2] perhaps because he felt that the phrase was tautologous: mountainous scenery is by its nature sublime. Pastoral scenery is not; hence his need to emphasise the 'elevated' nature of many of the more serene subjects by adding the letter 'E' to the plain 'P'.[3]

1. Rawlinson, *Liber Studiorum*, 1878, p. v.
2. The next 'mountainous' plate is the *Lake of Thun*, R. 15 (see no. 108), designated as 'M.'. All subsequent examples of the category are 'M' except the *Little Devil's Bridge* of 1809, R. 19 (see no. 26) which is headed 'Ms.'.
3. See p. 70.

J. M. W. Turner and Charles Turner (1773–1857), after J. M. W. Turner

26 Little Devil's Bridge over the Reuss above Altdorf (*Liber Studiorum*) 1809

Etching and mezzotint, printed in brown ink, engraver's proof(f) (R. 19), subject: $7 \times 10\frac{3}{16}$ (177 × 258); plate: $8\frac{3}{16} \times 11\frac{3}{8}$ (208 × 289)

Inscr. below: *Little Devils Bridge over the Russ above Alldorft Swiss.*[d] and: *Drawn & Etched by J. M. W. Turner Esq.*[r] *R.A.P.P.* and: *Engraved by Cha.*[s] *Turner.* bottom: *London Published March 29. 1809. by C. Turner, N*[o] *50. Warren Street Fitzroy Square.*
Yale Center for British Art, Paul Mellon Collection, B1977.14.8123

The subject is derived from a drawing in the *St Gothard and Mont Blanc* sketchbook (no. 19). Turner remodels the emphatically vertical composition of that study in the horizontal format of the *Liber* plate, deliberately giving prominence to the horizontal formed by the parapet of the bridge, and substituting for the vertical depth of the original a new depth of recession through the arch, with strong contrasts of tone giving a sense of great space beyond what we glimpse of the river gorge. The inhospitable landscape is made bleaker by the presence of bleaching bones near the blasted tree in the foreground. No. 25 is another *Liber* plate showing the same route; and the *Faido* of 1843 (*colour 24*) is Turner's final statement on the theme of this difficult mountain road.[1]

1. Ruskin insisted that it was the road, a vital link for travellers between north and south (more specifically between England and Italy), which gave the place its peculiar attraction for Turner. See *Works*, VII, p. 435, note.

27 The Upper Fall of the Reichenbach: rainbow
(?) 1810

Watercolour and bodycolour with scraping-out over pencil, $10\frac{7}{8} \times 15\frac{1}{2}$ (276 × 394)
Yale Center for British Art, Paul Mellon Collection, B1977.14.4702, Wilton 396
Colour plate 11

26

The fall of the Reichenbach, near Meiringen in Haslital, was a sublime phenomenon that had been consecrated by John Robert Cozens, who made several drawings of it in 1776.[1] Two impressive studies of it occur in Turner's *St Gothard and Mont Blanc* sketchbook of 1802,[2] and these were used as sources for two finished works, the large *Great Fall of the Reichenbach* now at Bedford[3] and this smaller view of the cascade seen from the side. The most famous literary association of this spot is with Conan Doyle's Sherlock Holmes, who plunged over the fall with Moriarty to his death.[4] Even though that 'event' occurred many decades later, it underlines the suggestive force of the subject as one lending itself naturally to drama – or melodrama. As in the *Glacier and Source of the Arveiron* (no. 24), and the other early Swiss subjects, there is an overriding concern with technical precision in this drawing: effects of mist, spray, rainbow or hazy distance are rendered not by impressionistic washes but by minutely calculated adjustments of colour and tone from one stroke to the next. Turner's virtuosity in scraping the surface of his drawings is realised to the full: the windblown spray of the fall, in which much of its majestic effect lies, is entirely achieved by scratching and rubbing away the painted surface.

1. C. F. Bell and T. Girtin, 'The Drawings and Sketches of John Robert Cozens', Walpole Society vol. XXIII, 1934–5, nos 20–6.
2. Wilton 361, 362.
3. Wilton 367, repr. in colour, *Turner in Switzerland*, p. 64.
4. A. Conan Doyle, *The Memoirs of Sherlock Holmes*, 1894.

28 Malham Cove *c.* 1810

Watercolour and scraping-out, $11 \times 15\frac{5}{8}$ (279 × 396)
Inscr. lower right: *I M W Turner RA*
British Museum, Salting Bequest, 1910–2–12–277, Wilton 533
Colour plate 12

Malham, says a writer of the 1820s, is a village 'situate in a deep and verdant dale' and 'chiefly remarkable on account of an immense cragg of limestone, called Malham Cove. It is 286 feet high, stretching in the shape of the segment of a large circle across the whole valley, and forming a termination at once so august and tremendous, that the imagination can scarcely figure any form or scale of rock within the bounds of probability that shall go beyond it.'[1]

The similarity of both the size and the handling of this sheet with *Patterdale Old Church* (colour *13*) strongly suggests that they were executed as a pair, if not as members of a longer series of related views in the north of England. They bear some resemblance to a group of watercolours executed for Sir Henry Pilkington in about 1813–15,[2] and were perhaps done for him, but there is no record of his having owned them. Turner made a pencil study of Malham Cove, which he used for this watercolour, in a sketchbook of about 1808.[3] As in the view of Patterdale, he presents a quiet scene of rustic life among grand scenery, which becomes the backdrop for a sudden change from sunshine to storm. Both are restatements of his old interest in the picturesque sublime in the light of his experience of Switzerland and in terms of his increasingly flexible technique. Although this is not one of Turner's best-known subjects, and was never engraved, it has been traditionally associated with him, at least in Yorkshire, just as Gordale Scar is associated with James Ward (1769–1859).[4]

1. Thomas Allen, *A New and Complete History of the County of York*, 3 vols, London 1828 31, vol. III, p. 354.
2. Wilton 534–6, 538, and possibly others of the Yorkshire views of the period.
3. The *Tabley No. 1* sketchbook, TB CIII–10.
4. See William Rothenstein, *Men and Memories*, London 1931, pp. 14–15.

29 Patterdale Old Church *c.* 1810

Watercolour and scraping-out, $11\frac{3}{8} \times 15\frac{9}{16}$ (279 × 395)
Inscr. lower left: *J M W Turner RA PP*
Yale Center for British Art, Paul Mellon Collection, B1975.4.1618, Wilton 547
Colour plate 13

After his return from Switzerland, Turner was well equipped with sublime material on which to work; he sought contrast in the more pastoral aspects of English scenery, and many of his watercolours of the first decade of the century are gentler in mood than the grandiose Swiss subjects he was producing. But after his first stay at Farnley in Yorkshire, which probably took place in 1810, he approached the wilder landscapes of England with a new interest, a vision modified by what he had seen abroad. As Ruskin noticed (see no. 70), he recorded a greater warmth of understanding in the face of British wildnesses than he could yet muster for continental ones, and there is a tenderness and grace about even such violent subjects as this one, which allies them to the picturesque tradition which had formulated so effective a language for the interpretation of English scenery. Even so, the breadth of his handling of the electric storm that suddenly drenches these Westmorland mountains is superb. The sharp gusts of driving wind and rain are suggested by bold diagonal strokes of the brush in the sky and in objects near at hand – the wind-tossed tree to the left of the church, for instance. While it is not known whether Turner had any particular patron in mind when he made this drawing, it is possible that he intended it to form one of a series of north-country subjects, of which another is perhaps the *Malham Cove* (colour *12*). An earlier drawing of Patterdale, showing the new church,[1] was engraved in 1805 for Mawman's *Excursion to the Highlands and English Lakes*;[2] it is now lost, but the engraving is a staid affair with none of the brooding drama of this later watercolour.

1. Wilton 229. It is referred to in a list of watercolours jotted by Turner on a leaf of the album into which the 'Scottish Pencils' were pasted; see Finberg, *Inventory*, vol. I, p. 153.
2. R. 75.

30 Gordale Scar *c.* 1816

Pencil, watercolour, bodycolour and gum, $21\frac{5}{8} \times 29\frac{7}{8}$ (550 × 760)
TB CLIV – O

Gordale Scar is 'one of the most stupendous scenes in Yorkshire, immensity and horror being its inseparable companions uniting together to form subjects of the most awful cast. The rocks are of extraordinary height, being not less than 300 feet, and in some places projecting more than ten yards over their base. An opening was formed in this limestone rock by a great body of water, which collected in a sudden thunderstorm in about 1730, and now forms a highly romantic cascade of twenty or thirty yards in height.'[1]

The medium in which this study is executed has been thought to be oil colour, applied thinly over pencil underdrawing. There is no reason, however, why Turner should have worked in oil on such a sketch, since the projected picture was almost certainly to have been in watercolour. A note of the title appears with the names of other watercolours that Turner was preparing for his patron Walter Fawkes, listed in the *Greenwich* sketchbook.[2] His pencil study on the spot for this subject occurs in one of the Yorkshire sketchbooks of about 1816.[3] No finished work is known. A number of the Yorkshire studies of this period are on large sheets like this, but few exploit the size of the paper in quite this way to achieve a physical sense of awe and terror. This is in fact a rather late

30

specimen of Turner's use of the large scale for such purposes, and the study is closer in mood to his Welsh mountain views of about 1799 (*colour 4, 5, 6*) than to his characteristic work of the 1810s. Nevertheless, it succeeds in its intention of conveying the rugged grandeur of the Scar, paralleling James Ward's attempt to achieve the same end on an enormous canvas.[4]

for two hundred years: Turner 'painted the mill in the valley. Precipices overhanging it, and wildness of dark forests round; blind rage and strength of mountain torrent rolled beneath it, – calm sunset above, but fading from the glen, leaving it to its roar of passionate waters and sighing pine-branches in the night.'[3]

1. Thomas Allen, *op. cit.*, Vol. III, p. 355.
2. TB CII, inside front cover and p. 52.
3. TB CXLV, 167–8.
4. Tate Gallery, no. 1043.

1. R. 54.
2. Richard Colebrand, *Journal*, 12 September 1659, Yale University Library, Osborne Collection, MS b266.
3. Ruskin, *Works* VII, p. 433.

31 Mill near the Grande Chartreuse, Dauphiny *c.* 1815

Pen and brown ink and wash, $9\frac{1}{6} \times 9\frac{1}{2}$ (230 × 241)
TB CXVIII–B

This is the drawing of a *Liber Studiorum* plate engraved by Henry Dawe and issued in 1816. It has been supposed that Turner himself took some hand in applying the mezzotint.[1] He categorised the subject as 'mountainous'. The Grand Chartreuse occupied a central place in the consciousness of early searchers for the sublime among the Alps. Long before Gray passed that way in 1739, travellers had visited it and been struck with 'that strange solitude where the grand Chartreuse is scituated', and with 'such precipices as would affright any eye to look downe upon them'.[2] Turner confines himself to expressing the primitive power of the spot by simple means; Ruskin, who admired the *Liber Studiorum* print enormously, sums up its import in terms of basic elements that had been cited

J. M. W. Turner and Thomas Goff Lupton (1791–1873), after J. M. W. Turner

32 Ben Arthur, Scotland (*Liber Studiorum*) 1819

Etching and mezzotint, printed in brown ink, first published state (R. 69), subject: $7\frac{3}{16} \times 10\frac{9}{16}$ (183 × 268); plate: $8\frac{1}{4} \times 11\frac{7}{16}$ (209 × 291)
Inscr. above: *M*; below: with title, and *Drawn and Etched by J. M. W. Turner Esq. R.A.P.P.* and *Engraved by T. Lutton.* [sic]; and: *London, Pub. Jan 1. 1819. by I. M. W. Turner Queen Ann Str West.*
Yale Center for British Art, Paul Mellon Collection, B1977.14.8189

Turner made sketches of Ben Arthur on the spot, and worked up some of these into more elaborate drawings in the 'Scottish Pencils' series (see no. 18). He returned to the subject much later when looking for motifs for a late issue of the *Liber Studiorum*. The impressive curving line that dominates the design is reminiscent of

31△   ▽32

33

the movement of breakers in a high swell at sea; compare the less fluid rhythms of the 'waves' created by the aiguilles at Chamonix (no. 21). Turner reverted to the same wave-like rhythms, though they take a more violent form, in his small drawing of *Loch Coriskin* for the *Poetical Works* of Scott of about 1832.[1] Rawlinson considered this *Liber* plate exceptionally impressive, maintaining even that 'were all Turner's other works lost, upon the strength of it alone, his pre-eminent fame as a landscape draughtsman might safely rest. Whose hand but his could have so drawn those sweeping mountain curves, could have so wedged in the loose array of stones at their base, could have given that grand gloom to the storm at the head of the ravine, or the grace to the fleecy clouds which cling about the hill-tops?'

1. Wilton 1088.

33   Eruption of Vesuvius 1817

Watercolour and scraping-out, $11\frac{1}{4} \times 15\frac{5}{8}$ (286 × 397)
Inscr. verso: *Mount Vesuvius in Eruption JMW Turner RA 1817*
Yale Center for British Art, Paul Mellon Collection, B1975.4.1857,
Wilton 697

The sublimities of Italy were not all engrossed by the achievements of man: Vesuvius was perhaps the most celebrated of volcanoes, and one whose activities had been recorded in the writings of a classical author, the younger Pliny, whose account of the destruction of Pompeii and Herculaneum[1] had comparatively re-

cently acquired new interest and importance from the discovery of the remains of those towns on the southern slopes of the mountain.[2] The sensational appeal of volcanic eruptions was perennial; Vesuvius had provided matter for innumerable modern accounts as well as that of Pliny. The early masters of the landscape sublime had revelled in depictions of it: Joseph Wright painted its performances often.[3] Turner made three views of the volcano before his first visit to Italy in 1819; two show an eruption.[4] They must have been based on drawings by some other artist, perhaps John Robert Cozens,[5] or perhaps James Hakewill, who supplied pencil outlines from which Turner worked up eighteen watercolours for Hakewill's *Picturesque Tour in Italy* published in 1818–20.[6] He had shown a painting of a volcano in eruption at the Academy in 1815:[7] *The eruption of the Souffrier Mountains, in the Island of St Vincent, at midnight, on the 30th of April, 1812* (a title characteristically circumstantial and concrete; see no. 57). This too was dependent upon the sketch of an amateur. He wrote these lines to accompany the picture in the catalogue:

> Then in stupendous horror grew
> The red volcano to the view
> And shook in thunders of its own,
> While the blaz'd hill in lightnings shone,
> Scattering their arrows round.
> As down its sides of liquid flame
> The devastating cataract came,
> With melting rocks, and crackling woods,
> And mingled roar of boiling floods,
> And roll'd along the ground!

34

In realising for himself the eruption of Vesuvius, Turner gave full reign to his technical inventiveness, creating one of his most exuberant and exciting watercolours, a fantasy of fire and night, in which fear is replaced by a more positive emotion – one of wondering delight in the extravagant beauty of a natural cataclysm.

1. Pliny the younger, *Letters*, VI, 16 (to Cornelius Tacitus).
2. Excavations at Herculaneum had begun in 1711, and at Pompeii in 1733.
3. Nicholson, *Wright*, pls 163, 165, 167–70.
4. Wilton 697–9.
5. No drawing by Cozens of Vesuvius from this viewpoint is known, however.
6. Wilton 700–17.
7. Butlin & Joll 132.

Samuel Middiman (1750–1831), after J. M. W. Turner

34 Moss Dale Fall (*History of Richmondshire*) 1822

Engraving, progress proof (b), printed on india paper (R. 181), subject: $7\frac{1}{2} \times 11$ (190 × 268); plate: $11\frac{3}{8} \times 16\frac{5}{8}$ (290 × 422)
Inscr. below, right: *Eng.d by S. Middiman 1822*
Yale Center for British Art, Paul Mellon Collection, B1977.14.6814

John Pye (1782–1874), after J. M. W. Turner

35 Hardraw Fall (*History of Richmondshire*) 1818

Engraving, printed on india paper, first published state (R. 182), subject: $7\frac{1}{2} \times 10\frac{3}{4}$ (190 × 273); plate: $11\frac{1}{4} \times 17\frac{1}{2}$ (285 × 445)

Inscr. below: with names of artist and engraver; centre: *Etched by S. Middiman.* and with title, and: *Published by Longman, Hurst, Rees, Orme & Browne, London, and Robinson, Son & Holdsworth, Leeds Oct.r 1. 1818*[1]
Yale Center for British Art, Paul Mellon Collection, B1977.14.13282

John Landseer (1769–1852), after J. M. W. Turner

36 High Force or Fall of Tees (*History of Richmondshire*) 1822

Engraving, printed on india paper, first published state (R. 173), subject: $7\frac{5}{8} \times 10\frac{5}{8}$ (194 × 270); plate: $11\frac{9}{16} \times 17\frac{7}{16}$ (293 × 442)
Inscr. below: with names of artist and engraver, and with title; lower right: *Printed by H. Triggs*; bottom: *Published by Longman & C.o Paternoster Row, and Hurst, Robinson, & C.o Cheapside, London. Sept.r 12. 1821.*
Yale Center for British Art, Paul Mellon Collection, B1977.14.1329

T. D. Whitaker's *History of Richmondshire* afforded Turner an opportunity to design an extensive series of views in the north of England,[2] including many views of the grand natural scenery for which the region is famous, and which he had already drawn on for subject-matter (as in nos 28 and 30). These three plates are typical of the sublime topography required for Whitaker's sumptuous volumes. They are accompanied by descriptive text:
'From Meerbeck [in Wensleydale] upwards the appearances of fertility and verdure gradually diminish: there is little alluvial land; long and sweeping surfaces of mountain pasture range from the

35

36

immediate vicinity of the Ure to the foot of the highest fells; the river diminishes to a beck, and the beck to a sike. The collateral features shrink in proportion, and the traveller finds himself on a level peatmoss, suddenly appalled by a dreadful and perpendicular disruption in the rock, where a stream is heard to murmur at a vast depth beneath. This is Hellgill, the Stygian rivulet of Camden, which forms a striking natural boundry to the counties of York and Westmorland. Yet is this not like some of the Lancashire forests, a mere unfeatured scene of desolation. The junction of the Ure with Mossdale Beck exhibits two waterfalls, one in each stream, seen from the same point, and enclosed within noble boundaries of dell and rock, happily uniting at an oblique angle to the eye.' Turner has taken his drawing of Mossdale Fall from the position described by Whitaker.

'At Hardraw is another waterfall of a character almost peculiar to itself. It is a grand column of water projected from the edge of a rock, so as to detach itself completely from the strata beneath, and to plunge without dispersion or interruption into a black and boiling cauldron below. This singular and happy effect has been produced by two causes: first, the bed of the torrent above is a stratum of rock, broken off at the point from which the projection takes place, so hard that the perpetual attrition of a violently agitated current has made little impression upon its edge. And secondly, the strata beneath are schistus, perpetually decompounding by the action of the air, and widening the interval between the face of the rock and this vast column of liquid crystal, which may easily be surrounded and viewed in its ever varying refractions on every side.'[3] This kind of description, partly lyrical, partly scien-

tific, anticipates the spirit of Ruskin's analyses in *Modern Painters*, where Turner's watercolours themselves are submitted to the same scrutiny, and found to yield the same satisfaction both to the geologist and to the poet. Ruskin seems to have learned some of his characteristic methods from Whitaker: his love of categorising natural phenomena, for instance (whether the old eighteenth-century philosophical categorisation, or a newer scientific type it would perhaps be hard to say), is foreshadowed in this discussion of the *Fall of the Tees*; which 'is one of the finest cataracts in the island, whose roar is audible long before it is perceptible to the eye. Its character is that of the falls of Aysgarth [of which Turner also made a drawing],[4] but the scale is beyond comparison more magnificent, the projection much deeper, the mass of water more entire, and equally precipitous. Cataracts in this country may be divided into two classes, first, the falls of considerable rivers, of which the expanse is necessarily grand, while the depth is seldom very great, because their course has ceased to be very precipitous before they acquire so great a bulk of water. The second consists of mountain torrents of no ample dimensions, but precipitated down the abrupt and often perpendicular chasms of glens and gullies, with a force and to a depth which amply compensates for their narrowness. Of the former kind the falls of Aysgarth and Tees stand perhaps unrivalled in Britain.'[5]

1. Rawlinson prints 1815 in error.
2. Wilton 559–81.
3. T. D. Whitaker, *History of Richmondshire*, vol. I, p. 413.
4. Wilton 570.
5. Whitaker, *op. cit.*, vol. I, p. 142.

37

Edward Goodall (1795–1870), after J. M. W. Turner

37 Fall of the Tees, Yorkshire (*England and Wales*)
1827

Engraving, third state (R. 214), subject: $6\frac{7}{16} \times 8\frac{13}{16}$ (163 × 224);
plate: $9\frac{11}{16} \times 11\frac{15}{16}$ (246 × 303)
Inscr. below: with names of artist and engraver with title: lower
right: *Printed by Mc Queen*; bottom: *Published June 1. 1827, for the
Proprietor, by Robert Jennings, Poultry*.
Yale Center for British Art, Paul Mellon Collection, B1977.14.13311

A comparison of this subject with the view of the *Fall of the Tees*
made for Whitaker's *Richmondshire* less than a decade earlier (no. 36)
indicates the extent to which Turner's conception of the landscape
sublime had moved away from sheer physical terror to a more
expansive sense of the vastness and variety of natural phenomena.
He contemplates mountains and hills in infinite recession rather as
Addison ponders the interminable and incalculable occurrence of
planet after planet in the universe. In doing so, he gives emphasis to
the great spaces between objects – or between objects and the eye,
rather than on the magnitude of the objects themselves. As a result,
this view of the fall, though less 'stunning', is ultimately grander.

James Tibbitts Willmore (1800–63) after J. M. W. Turner

38 Penmaen Mawr, Caernarvonshire (*England and
Wales*) 1832

Engraving, india proof before all letters (R. 276), subject: $6\frac{1}{2} \times 8\frac{15}{16}$
(164 × 228); plate: $10 \times 12\frac{1}{2}$ (255 × 318)
Yale Center for British Art, Paul Mellon Collection, B1977.14.7061

Henry Wigstead, in his *Remarks on a Tour to North and South Wales, in
the year 1799*, records: 'From *Conway* to *Caernarvon* is twenty-four
miles. The road is at first uninteresting; but, at about four miles,
the scenery becomes really terrific. *Penman Ross*, on the right hand,
awfully raises its aspiring head, and intercepts the beams of the sun
in his highest elevation; while *Penman-maur*, on the left, seems, from
its desolated and rocky summit, to threaten the traveller with
instant annihilation. The road runs round near the base of the
mountain one hundred yards above the sea: the whole height of this
terrific and barren elevation is 1545 feet. This road . . . is flanked by
a stone wall on the side towards the sea. This is about three feet
high, over which the water and the distant isle of *Anglesea* are seen.
On the other side, the surface of the mountain, which is very steep,
is covered with tremendous masses of stone, which seem ready to
slide from their slippery base, and overwhelm the passenger in
inevitable destruction. – From the almost incessant rain we had
experienced for some time before, and the rapidity of the land-
springs, which poured down on every side from the very summit,
we were very much alarmed in our passage, lest one of these masses
should arrest us; particularly as the wall had been driven in several
parts down the precipice into the sea by similar accident . . .'[1] It is
the vivid experiences of the traveller that Turner makes the focus
of his drawing: he recasts the 'terrific' sublime in terms of the
human response which makes it terrific.[2] As so often in his scenes of
mountain and storm for the *England and Wales* series he binds his
composition together with an emphatic diagonal stress.[3] Compare
nos 11 and 39.

1. Wigstead, *op. cit.*, London 1800, pp. 26–7.
2. Compare comments on *Faido*, no. 104.
3. The original watercolour is in the British Museum, Lloyd Bequest; Wilton 852;
Shanes 61.

W. R. Smith (fl. *c.* 1832–51), after J. M. W. Turner

39 Chain Bridge over the River Tees (*England and
Wales*) 1838

Engraving, second state printed on india paper (R. 302), subject:
$6\frac{1}{2} \times 9\frac{7}{8}$ (165 × 251); plate: $9\frac{1}{2} \times 12\frac{7}{8}$ (242 × 327)
Inscr. below: with title and names of artist and engraver; lower
right: *Printed by Mc Queen*; bottom: *London, Published 1838 for the
Proprietor, by Longman & Co Paternoster Row*.
Yale Center for British Art, Paul Mellon Collection, B1977.14.13415

In his work on the *Picturesque Views in England and Wales* Turner
attempted a variety almost as studied as that of the *Liber Studiorum*;[1] but he rarely included a subject as 'mountainous' as this.
The sheer vertiginous excitement of this close-up view of a waterfall reverts to the mood and methods of the 'terrific'; but its
vigorous rhythms look forward to the great *Faido* of 1843, (*colour
24*). It is worth noting how Turner has unobtrusively pointed up
the impassability of the torrent by placing the sportsman on one
side of it and his quarry, a nest of grouse, on the other.[2]

1. See Shanes, p. 16, and Wilton 1979, p. 178.
2. The original watercolour is Wilton 878; Shanes 84.

38

39

40

42

40 A wild Landscape, with Figures, at Sunset

c. 1799–1800

Oil with some pen and ink on paper, $10\frac{1}{4} \times 15\frac{1}{4}$ (261 × 388)
TB XCV(a)–G, Butlin & Joll 35

Although he made small oil sketches for various purposes at all stages of his career, Turner rarely planned a formal composition for an oil painting, in oil on a sheet of paper like this. The precise nature of the subject here is a little obscure, but there seems to be no doubt that the scene is a contrived one such as Turner would have used for a painting, and not a record of a particular spot. The two figures in the foreground have every appearance of being a group of the Good Samaritan, for one, clothed, tends the other, who lies naked on the ground. This is therefore in all probability one of Turner's first exercises in painting a Biblical subject. It did not result in a finished picture, but some of its ideas may have been used in the untraced picture of *Ben Lomond Mountains, Scotland: The Traveller*, exhibited in 1802. This has been thought to be an oil painting but seems more probably to have been a watercolour.[1]

1. Wilton 346.

41 Scene in the Welsh Mountains with an army on the march *c.* 1800

Watercolour with stopping-out, $27\frac{1}{16} \times 39\frac{1}{4}$ (687 × 996)
TB LXX–Q
Colour plate 14

This enormous sheet is either an elaborate preliminary study for one of the large watercolours that Turner was exhibiting about 1800, or is actually an unfinished work of that type. The view up a long valley towards snowy peaks anticipates the composition of *The Battle of Fort Rock (colour 15)*, with which it shares a similar theme: an army presses its way through bleakly hostile mountains to carry out its work of murder and devastation. Just as Napoleon's troops were to submit 'fair Italy' to ravage and plunder, so this army is bent on subduing a civilisation by force. Various other drawings in the Turner Bequest inform us that Turner was interested at this date in the story of the Welsh bards who were exterminated by Edward I,[1] and in 1800 he exhibited at the Royal Academy a finished watercolour[2] depicting a bard in his rightful place, singing to a peaceful audience in a sunny landscape. The verses he composed to accompany that work speak more of the 'tyrant' who 'drench'd with blood the land' than of the happier aspects of the subject, and it is possible that Turner intended this to be a companion picture, giving the other side of the story. Such a pairing would have been especially poignant if, as seems to be the case, Turner planned deliberately to omit the figure of a bard from this wild landscape: the resulting contrast between the searching army and the innocent, unprotected singer and his followers would have been vividly reinforced by the different landscape of the two works.[3]

1. e.g. LXX–N.
2. Wilton 263; repr. in colour in RA 1974, p. 17.
3. For further comment on the place of this work in Turner's development, and especially as it relates to *Hannibal*, see Lynn Matteson, 'The Poetics and Politics of Alpine Passage: Turner's Snowstorm: Hannibal and his army crossing the Alps,' *The Art Bulletin*, September 1980.

J. M. W. Turner and Charles Turner, after J. M. W. Turner

42 Jason (*Liber Studiorum*) 1807

Etching and mezzotint, printed in brown ink, first published state (R. 6), subject: $7\frac{1}{4} \times 10\frac{1}{8}$ (184 × 257); plate: $8\frac{3}{16} \times 11\frac{3}{8}$ (207 × 289)
Inscr. above: *H*; below: with title and: *Drawn & Etched by J.M.W. Turner R.A.* and *Engraved by C. Turner.*; bottom: *Published as the Act directs by J.M.W. Turner Harley Street.*
Yale Center for British Art, Paul Mellon Collection, B1977.14.8101

Turner's painting of this subject was shown at the Academy in 1802, with the title *Jason, from Ovid's Metamorphosis*.[1] It is one of his most conscious imitations of Salvator Rosa, though de Loutherbourg's *Jason enchanting the Dragon* may also have been in his mind.[2] The subject belongs to a series of mythological works executed in the first few years of the century, including *The Goddess of discord choosing the apple of contention in the garden of the Hesperides*,[3] exhibited in 1806, and *Apollo and Python*[4] of 1811. All these works seem to treat of the opposition of good and evil; in each case a heroic or idealised state is contrasted with the baseness of corrupt forms of life – dragons and snakes representing the flaw in the created world as the serpent does in *Genesis*. Turner frequently used the snake in his non-historical works to intimate the hostility of nature to man; see for example no. 24.[5]

1. Butlin & Joll 19.
2. Not exhibited at the R.A., but easily accessible in the London collection of Michael Bryan (author of the *Biographical Dictionary of Painters and Engravers*) until it was sold in 1798.
3. Butlin & Joll 57.
4. Butlin & Joll 115; for further comment on *Apollo and Python* see p. 72.
5. For a discussion of these paintings, see Gage, 1969, pp. 137–40.

J. M. W. Turner and Charles Turner, after J. M. W. Turner

43 The Fifth Plague of Egypt (*Liber Studiorum*) 1808

Etching and mezzotint, printed in brown ink, first published state (R. 16), subject: $7\frac{1}{6} \times 10\frac{1}{8}$ (179 × 257); plate: $8\frac{1}{4} \times 11\frac{3}{8}$ (209 × 289)
Inscr. above: *H*; below: *Drawn & Etched by J.M.W. Turner Esq.r R.A.P.*; *Engraved by C. Turner* and with title: *The 5th Plague of Egypt the Picture late in the possession of W. Beckford Esq.r*; lower left: *Proof*; bottom: *London Published June 10, 1808. by C. Turner N.o 50, Warren Street, Fitzroy Square.*
Yale Center for British Art, Paul Mellon Collection, B1977.14.8118

Although Turner gave his picture[1] the title that appears on his *Liber Studiorum* print when it was originally exhibited at the Academy in 1800, he published in the catalogue a quotation which shows that his subject is really the seventh plague: 'And Moses stretched forth his hands toward heaven, and the Lord sent thunder and hail, and the fire ran along the ground. Exodus, chapter ix verse 23.' This was the first full-scale historical work to come from Turner's brush, and announced him clearly as a major subject-painter, drawing his inspiration from Poussin among the old masters, and from Wilson among the moderns. By subduing the light that falls, in the painting, on the central group of blasted trees, and in other ways modifying the composition, the print gives greater emphasis to the horizontal stress of the landscape – a surprising feature in so dramatic a work. It draws attention to the fact that the dynamic turbulence of the picture is derived almost entirely from the handling of chiaroscuro and the suggestion of atmospheric disturbance that fills the scene with intense but intangible unease.

43

44

The print, on the other hand, exploits mezzotint to present powerful contrasts of tone across a flat landscape that looks forward to some of the industrial subjects of a later period.[2]

1. Butlin & Joll 13.
2. Ruskin disapprovingly likened the pyramids to 'brick kilns' (*Works*, III, p 240); surely not an inappropriate connotation given the occupation of the Israelites in Egypt – making bricks.

J. M. W. Turner and William Say (1768–1834),
after J. M. W. Turner

44   Tenth Plague of Egypt (*Liber Studiorum*) 1816

Etching and mezzotint, printed in reddish-brown ink, first published state (R. 61), subject: $7\frac{1}{6} \times 10\frac{3}{16}$ (179 × 259); plate: $8\frac{3}{16} \times 11\frac{5}{16}$ (208 × 288)
Inscr. above: *H*; below: with title and *Drawn & etched by I.M.W. Turner Esq RA* and *Engraved by W Say Engraver to H R H the Duke of Gloucester*; and *Published Jan 1. 1816 by I M W Turner, Queen Ann Street West*.
Yale Center for British Art, Paul Mellon Collection, B1977.14.8178

The painting from which this subject derives was exhibited at the Royal Academy in 1802.[1] It was therefore completed before Turner's continental journey of that year, but it evidently makes use of ideas gleaned from works by Poussin which he had seen in England – including, perhaps, the *Landscape with Pyramus and Thisbe* in Lord Ashburnham's collection on which he commented in his Perspective Lecture on Landscape.[2] In its bleak grandeur it is one of the most thoroughgoing of all Turner's attempts to reconstruct the language of Poussin, which, as he said (echoing Reynolds), depends on a deep sympathy with ancient art: 'his love for the antique prompted his exertion and that love emanates thro all his works: it clothes his figures rears his Buildings disposes his materials arrainges his landscapes and gives a color that removes his works from truth'.[3] The print that Turner published in the *Liber Studiorum* manages to convey much of the gloomy weight of the canvas itself. Rawlinson could say of it: 'In early and fine impressions . . . there seems to me a striking sense of horror and terror, giving it much more impressiveness than the *Fifth Plague of Egypt* . . . you cannot doubt but that the painter has meant you to feel that there is here something beyond any mere physical cause of terror and awe. This, but this alone, prevents its being a melodramatic and wholly inadequate rendering of one of the most sublimely-told tragedies of any literature . . .'

1. Butlin & Joll 17.
2. See p. 70.
3. Add. ms. 46151 I, f. 13.

45

45 Study for a Historical Composition: the Egyptian Host in the Red Sea(?) *c.* 1800

Pen and brown ink and wash with white bodycolour on rough grey paper, $10\frac{13}{16} \times 13\frac{1}{4}$ (275 × 336), irregular
TB CXIX–R

When Turner first launched into History painting proper, he noted down a mass of ideas for subjects, many of which were never used. At first the Bible seems to have been a prime inspiration, though it was later superseded by Homer, Virgil and other sources. The *Fifth* and *Tenth Plagues of Egypt* (see nos 43 and 44) and the *Destruction of Sodom*,[1] together with a possible treatment of the Good Samaritan subject,[2] are all recorded. *The army of the Medes destroyed in the desert by a whirlwind*, illustrating a prophecy of Jeremiah, was shown at the Academy in 1801, though the picture is now lost.[3] This scrap may belong to the same series of ideas. It is, at any rate, a variant on the Deluge theme that Turner found so fascinating (see nos 46–49). Whether the men floundering in the waves here are indeed Pharoah's host is uncertain. Possibly we can read in Turner's hasty pen marks the prows of Roman galleys – some classical sea-fight may be in train. The basic theme, however, is clear: with a few strong washes Turner suggests the depth and power of the sea, and the helplessness of men against it.

1. Butlin & Joll 56.
2. See no. 40.
3. Butlin & Joll 15.

46 Study for 'The Deluge' *c.* 1804

Pen and brown ink with pencil on grey paper, $16\frac{1}{8} \times 23$ (410 × 585)
Verso: another study for the same subject
TB CXX–X

The two sketches on this sheet are characteristic of the elaborate studies Turner made in preparation for the large historical pictures that he exhibited in the first decade of the century. They are concerned principally with the organisation of figures in the picture-space, often with complex groups of interwoven bodies – an aspect of pictorial design that he had not had to tackle previously. *The Deluge* is thought to have been shown at Turner's own gallery in 1805 (see no. 49), and is among the most elaborate of these exercises in the deployment of the human form in the whole of his art. These studies, therefore, are important documents of his response to the central problems posed by the historical sublime; problems that had been solved by Raphael, and resolved by Poussin, but which still dominated the conception of great art, and its execution, throughout Turner's life. In this drawing there are indications of a background of classical architecture like that of the *Tenth Plague of Egypt* (no. 44), but almost all traces of this are suppressed in the final painting, where the other elements of the sketch are also almost entirely reorganised. Another study is in the *Calais Pier* sketchbook.[1]

1. TB LXXXI, 120–121.

46

47 The Deluge *c.* 1815

Pen and brown ink and wash with scraping-out over pencil,
$7\frac{7}{16} \times 10\frac{9}{16}$ (188 × 268)
TB CXVIII–X, Vaughan Bequest

A design for the *Liber Studiorum* which was never published, though
Turner himself worked on a mezzotint plate of it (no. 48). The
subject is scarcely recognisable as an adaptation of the large *Deluge*
picture of about 1805 (see no. 49), but elements such as the
windblown tree and the cliffs at the right, together with the general
surge of water from right to left, are common to both. In this
economical drawing a mood of desolation worthy of Poussin[1] is
evoked by fragmented yet rhythmic lines and sombre washes; the
figures, only schematically suggested, nevertheless embody the
hopelessness of the whole subject.

1. See Turner's comments on Poussin's painting of the Deluge, p. 71.

48 The Deluge (*Liber Studiorum*, unpublished)
c. 1815–20

Mezzotint, printed in dark brown ink (R. 88), impression taken in
the 1870s, subject: $7\frac{15}{16} \times 10\frac{7}{8}$ (201 × 276); plate: $8\frac{13}{16} \times 11\frac{13}{16}$
(224 × 300)
Yale Center for British Art, Paul Mellon Collection, B1977.14.13967

Turner's drawing for this subject (no. 47) only hints at the
grandeur of the mezzotint itself, in which the subject of the
painting (see no. 49) has been further modified and simplified so
that a single powerful statement is made. As Rawlinson observed,
'The "fountains of the great deep" are indeed "broken up", and the
"windows of heaven opened"' (*Genesis*, vi, 11).

J. P. Quilley (fl. 1812–42), after J. M. W. Turner

49 The Deluge 1828

Mezzotint, printed in black ink, proof (R. 794), subject:
$14\frac{15}{16} \times 22\frac{11}{16}$ (380 × 576); plate: $18\frac{1}{16} \times 24\frac{3}{4}$ (459 × 629)
Inscr. below: *To the Right Honorable (the late) Earl of Carysfort,*
K.P./This Plate of THE DELUGE, in grateful remembrance/Is most
Respectfully Inscribed by J. M. W. Turner R.A.; with the names of
painter and engraver, and lower right: *Printed by J. Lahee*; lower
left: *Proof/Picture 4ft 6 by 7ft 10*; bottom centre: *London, Published*
June 24, 1828, by Moon, Boys & Graves, Printsellers to the King,
6, Pall Mall.
Yale Center for British Art, Paul Mellon Collection, B1977.14.8338

Although Rawlinson lists this as the published state of the plate, he
records uncertainty as to whether the print was ever actually
published, but see *Field of Waterloo* (no. 71). The picture itself[1] had
been painted several years earlier, and was probably shown in
Turner's gallery in 1805.
Exhibited again at the RA in 1813, it was accompanied in the
catalogue by these lines from *Paradise Lost*:[2]

> Meanwhile the south wind rose, and with black wings
> Wide hovering, all the clouds together drove

47

48

49

From under heaven –
– the thicken'd sky
Like a dark ceiling stood, down rush'd the rain
Impetuous, and continual, till the earth
No more was seen.

This is, then, an illustration to Milton, and not to the Bible – an English equivalent of the canvas by Poussin which had so stirred Turner when he saw it in the Louvre in 1802. Another of his early Poussin-inspired canvases, *The Garden of the Hesperides* of 1806[3] was engraved by Quilley at about the same time.[4] It is interesting that he should have wished to exhibit it again in 1813, especially after the showing of his own *Hannibal* in the previous year; but it was in 1812 that John Martin first entered the Academic lists as a painter of the sublime (with his *Sadak in search of the Waters of Oblivion*)[5] and Turner may have felt a need to assert his supremacy in this department. A similar reason may lie behind the production of this print at an even later date: it was in the mid-1820s that an 'apocalyptic' painter rather akin to Martin, Francis Danby (1793–1861), began to show his Biblical subjects at the Academy – *The delivery of Israel out of Egypt* appeared there in 1825; and his *Sunset at Sea after a storm* shown in 1824 may have inspired Turner to work on his 'Little Liber' prints at about the same time (see nos 72, 74, 78). Turner's subject of the *Deluge* foreshadows much of what Danby had to say in the 1820s, and Turner perhaps wanted to remind the public that he had been the first in the field. The print includes much crisply wrought detail that is absent from the original painting, and, again, Turner may have wished to demonstrate that he could invent with the same crisp immediacy as Danby. The free application of paint in the picture itself, however, is more exciting, and anticipates the emancipated handling of the *Fall of an Avalanche in the Grisons* of 1810. Turner was to explore the subject again in his great pair of 1843 *Shade and Darkness – The Evening of the Deluge* and *Light and Colour (Goethe's Theory) – The Morning after the Deluge*.[6]

There is a certain mystery surrounding the dedication of the plate. John James Proby, 1st Baron Carysfort, had died just before it was published, on 7 April 1828. It was therefore quite appropriate that he should be commemorated in this way, and Turner may have had a particular respect for him – he was an outspoken abolitionist and reformist, and his political views would have chimed in with Turner's own, if, as some have done, we interpret the pictures of the *Slavers* (FIG. XVI) and the *Burning of the Houses of Parliament* as liberal political statements.[7] But Turner often dedicated his prints to patrons with whom he was on especially good terms – Sir John Swinburne, for instance, received the dedication of Cousen's plate of *Mercury and Herse*[8] for he was the picture's first owner; and for the same reason B. G. Windus was the dedicatee of Willmore's plate of *Oberwesel*;[9] see also the *Lake of Lucerne* (no. 123). Lord Carysfort did not own a picture of Turner's, but just at the time when Turner was working on the *Deluge*, in about 1804, he entered Lord Carysfort's name in a list of patrons jotted in the *Academies* sketchbook.[10] There, his lordship is down as having commissioned a 'Historical' work – that one word is the only indication of the type of picture concerned, except that a figure of '300' (pounds?) is written beside the name. It is possible that the *Deluge* was intended for Lord Carysfort, but that for some reason it never entered his possession.

1. Butlin & Joll 55.
2. Book XI, ll. 738–40; 742–5.
3. Butlin & Joll 57.
4. R. 793.
5. Repr. Christopher Johnstone, *John Martin*, London 1974, p. 41.
6. Butlin & Joll 404, 405.
7. By e.g. Prof. John McCoubrey in an unpublished lecture on the *Houses of Parliament* paintings; and by Jack Lindsay, *op. cit.*, pp. 189–90.
8. R. 655; Butlin & Joll 114.
9. R. 660; Wilton 1380.
10. TB LXXXIV, 67 verso.

50

50 The Amateur Artist *c.* 1808

Pen and brown ink and wash with some watercolour and scraping-out, $7\frac{1}{4} \times 11\frac{7}{8}$ (185 × 302)

Inscr. recto: Pictures either { *Judgment of Paris* / *Forbidden Fruit* }
Old Masters scattered over y[e] floor
Stolen hints from celebrated Pictures Phials/Crucibles retorts.
label'd bottles . . . [illegible] varnish quiz

verso: *Please [d] with his Work he views it o'er and o'er*
And finds fresh Beauties never seen before
The Tyro mind another feast controuls
. . . [several lines of draft]
The Master loves his art, the Tyro butter'd rolls

TB CXXI–B, RA 1974(121)

This is one of a pair of drawings which Turner probably executed under the influence of David Wilkie (1785–1841) and Hogarth in the first decade of the century. The other subject[1] corresponds to that of a painting exhibited at the Academy in 1809 with the title *The garreteer's petition*;[2] it deals explicitly with the problems of the unsuccessful poet – a character with whom Turner may have identified. His notes on the sketch for it mention Vida's *Art of Poetry* and *Hints on an Epic Poem*, indicating the high-flying ambitions of the garreteer. This drawing seems to make a similar point about a 'tyro' artist, who seeks inspiration in 'Old Masters', using 'Stolen hints from celebrated Pictures'. The lesson is that of Reynolds, but it is misapplied: no amount of self-satisfaction can turn a feeble work into an inspired one. Turner's comment on the nature of inspiration is a wry one, for he was aware that, if a 'master' of painting, he himself was a 'tyro' in poetry.

1. TB CXXI–A.
2. Butlin & Joll 100.

51 The Battle of Fort Rock, Val d'Aouste, Piedmont 1796 1815

Watercolour with scraping-out, $27\frac{3}{8} \times 39\frac{3}{4}$ (695 × 1010)
Inscr. lower left: *I M W Turner 1815*
TB LXXX–G, BM 1975(43), Wilton 399
Colour plate 15

The landscape setting for this subject was recorded by Turner in a monochrome study of 1802;[1] he later produced a large finished watercolour of *Mont Blanc, from Fort Rock, in the Val d'Aosta*, with figures expressive of awe and astonishment in the spirit of the picturesque or terrific sublime.[2] This version followed in 1815, in which year Turner showed it at the Royal Academy with verses composed by himself in the catalogue:

The snow-capt mountain, and huge towers of ice,
Thrust forth their dreary barriers in vain;
Onward the van progressive forc'd its way,
Propelled; as the wild Reuss, by native glaciers fed,
Rolls on impetuous, with ev'ry check gains force
By the constraint uprais'd; till, to its gathering powers
All yielding, down the pass wide devastation pours
Her own destructive course. Thus rapine stalked
Triumphant; and plundering hordes, exulting, strew'd,
Fair Italy, thy plains with woe.

These lines, which Turner stated were taken from his poem *Fallacies of Hope*, are written in a strongly Thomsonian vein; they comprise what is perhaps the most complete statement in the verse that he published of his sense of the destructive force of war. The hostile progress of the invading army is linked by a direct simile

with the devastating onset of the winter floods, as the swollen river pushes its way down the gorge. This is a development of the theme of the *Bard* drawing (*colour 14*) and of *Hannibal and his army crossing the Alps* (FIG. XIII). Man and nature are allied in savagery; and yet nature is also the enemy of man, halting his plans, barring his progress, separating people from people by vast barriers of mountains. And nature is greater than man: beyond the petty, vicious and futile struggles of ambitious men the serene Alps remain immutable; the empty cliffs and crags that occupy the right-hand half of this strangely bisected composition are totally unaffected by the bloody events of the battle. When Turner came back to this scenery in later life, he was concerned not with impermanence and transition, but with the enduring and eternal; men play a different and more sympathetic role. See nos 98 and 100.

1. In the Fitzwilliam Museum; Cormack 10.
2. In a private Scottish collection; Wilton 369. The three versions of the view are reproduced together in Wilton, 1979, pp. 102–3.

Edward Goodall (1795–1870), after J. M. W. Turner

52 The Fall of the Rebel Angels (*Milton's Poetical Works*) 1835

Engraving, proof (R. 599), subject (vignette): $4\frac{1}{2} \times 3\frac{3}{8}$ (115 × 85); plate: $8\frac{1}{2} \times 5\frac{7}{8}$ (215 × 149)
Inscr. below: with names of artist and engraver, and: *Printed by J. Yates*, and: *London, John Macrone, 3, St. James's Square, MDCCCXXXV*
Yale Center for British Art, Paul Mellon Collection, B1977.14.7926

Turner's drawing for this vignette is untraced.[1] The subject is taken from Book VI of *Paradise Lost*, and is one of Turner's very rare essays in the depiction of the Deity. For comment on this see no. 53. Rawlinson records that the engraver's son informed him that 'when his father was engraving this plate, Turner wrote across the upper part of the proof, "put me in innumerable figures here". These the engraver himself had to draw.' The idea that crowds of figures beyond computation conduce to a sublime effect is strongly present in many of Turner's late landscape subjects; here, the intention is directly related to the religious and Miltonic sublime that he illustrates. The swarming figures, as well as the oval shape of the design, recall Baroque ceiling decoration, which Turner was to make use of again in one of the great 'circular' paintings of the 1840s, *Light and Colour . . . The morning after the deluge*.[2]

1. Wilton 1265.
2. Butlin & Joll 405; and see Wilton 1979, p. 216.

Robert Wallis (1794–1878), after J. M. W. Turner

53 Sinai's Thunder (*Campbell's Poetical Works*) 1837

Engraving, India proof (R. 616), subject (vignette): $4\frac{1}{8} \times 2\frac{5}{16}$ (104 × 75); plate: $11\frac{9}{16} \times 6$ (294 × 153)
Inscr. below: *Turner, R. A.* and *Wallis Proof*
Yale Center for British Art, Paul Mellon Collection, B1977.14.7947

Turner indicated on his drawing for this subject[1] the lines from Campbell's *Pleasures of Hope* that are illustrated here: 'Like Sinai's Thunder, pealing from the cloud'. The figure of God appearing to Moses on Mount Sinai is more circumstantially drawn than the faint shadow in a burst of radiance that appears in *The Fall of the Rebel Angels* (no. 52). The convention of religious painters in representing the Deity amid clouds, accompanied by symbols of

52

eternity and the Trinity and sending out thunderbolts, is followed, but it is combined with Turner's more naturalistic (though still elaborately distorted) landscape. The combination of imagery in this illustration foreshadows the pair of paintings of 1843, *The evening of the deluge* and *The morning after the deluge*:[2] the former shows the ark, which appears in the left-hand distance in the Campbell illustration; the latter deals with 'Moses writing the book of Genesis' and depicts him seated in glory rather as God is shown here. That Turner chose to give so detailed an interpretation of the manifestation of God to men in this vignette is perhaps explained by the fact that Campbell's poem deals with a subject that engrossed Turner's interest: Hope. Campbell, however, lays firm emphasis on the blessings provided by Hope, and not on its 'fallacies'.[3] Another rendering of the Israelites in the desert of Sinai was made for Finden's Bible a few years earlier than the Campbell illustrations.[4]

1. Wilton 1274.
2. Butlin & Joll 404, 405.
3. In particular, he speaks of the comforts of Hope at the approach of death: 'Unfading Hope! when life's last embers burn,/When soul to soul, and dust to dust return', etc.
4. Wilton 1238. The Campbell designs are Wilton 1271–90.

53

Daniel Wilson (fl. *c.* 1840), after J. M. W. Turner

54 Ancient Carthage – the Embarcation of Regulus
1840

Line engraving, india proof (R. 649), subject: $15\frac{7}{16} \times 22\frac{9}{16}$
(392×573); plate: $18\frac{1}{2} \times 26\frac{3}{8}$ (470×670)
Inscr. with names of artist and engraver, and with date
Yale Center for British Art, Paul Mellon Collection, B1977.14.8032

Turner exhibited his painting of this subject in Rome in 1828, and
reworked it for showing in London at the British Institution in
1837, when it appeared with the simple title *Regulus*.[1] When this
print was published, however, three years later, it had the longer
and more explicit title given here. As one of the most powerful of all

Turner's attempts to render the physical effect of brilliant sunlight
it made a great impression when it was first shown. More recently,
the effect has been given justification by reference to Regulus's
punishment for failing to betray Rome to the Carthaginians, whose
prisoner he was: his eyelids were cut off so that he was blinded by
the sun. The whole picture can thus be interpreted as an evocation
of the sun's most sublime attribute – its ability actually to deprive
us of sight by its own strength. If we identify with Regulus in this
way, Kant's definition of the sublime is stretched to its utmost,
further even than in *The Wreck of a Transport Ship* (no. 57). No one in
Turner's time seems to have read the picture like this – probably
because it is a most unorthodox way of handling the relationship
between viewer and canvas; so unorthodox indeed that Turner
himself may not have intended it. The deliberate statement of the

title published with the print suggests that he had a more traditional programme in mind, and it appears that Regulus, who
has been thought to be absent altogether, is depicted in the scene,
descending the stairs to a waiting boat in the right middle-distance.
Turner summed up the essence of the story in some verses of his
own:

> Oh! powerful beings, hail! whose stubborn soul
> Even o'er itself to urge [?even] self-control.
> Thus Regulus, whom every torture did await,
> Denied himself admittance at the gate
> Because a captive to proud Carthage power,
> But his [fierce?] soul would not the Romans lower.
> Not wife or children dear, or self, could hold
> A moment's parley, – love made him bold,
> Love of his country; for not aught beside
> He loved, – but for that love he died.[2]

These lines suggest that Turner's ultimate source is Horace, who
tells the story of Regulus in one of his Odes:[3]

> He on the Senate doubting long
> Unwearied press'd his Reasons strong;
> He gain'd at length their joint Consent
> To Counsel giv'n before by none;
> And thro' his weeping Friends he went
> A matchless Exile from the Town.
>
> He knew ev'n then the barb'rous kind
> Of Torture by the Foes design'd
> Yet through his kindred that enclos'd
> He bravely press'd without Delay;

> Remov'd the People that oppos'd,
> And back to Carthage urg'd his way.
> To horrid Racks severely great
> He pass'd, as to his Country Seat;
> As when, his Clients causes try'd,
> The *Forum*'s tedious Hurry o'er,
> He sought Venatrum's peaceful side
> Or fair Tarentum's pleasing shore.

Despite the title of the engraving, therefore, the picture must show
the moment of Regulus's departure from Rome to certain punishment at Carthage. It exactly parallels another, equally splendid
harbour scene of the same period, *Ancient Italy – Ovid banished from
Rome*,[1] exhibited at the Academy in 1838. Although the reason for
Ovid's banishment is obscure – it was traditionally ascribed to his
publication of the *Ars Amatoria* – the parallel with *Regulus* is made
plain by the similarity of the treatment, and even a complementary
compositional layout. Turner was to explore the parallelism between the fate of artists and the fate of military heroes in his pair of
1841, *Peace – burial at sea* (the burial of David Wilkie) and *War. The
exile and the rock limpet*.[5] In both cases, he celebrates the creative
genius – the 'powerful being' – who can change the course of
civilisation either physically or morally – the Aristotelian hero
whose actions are significant for all mankind.

1. Butlin & Joll 294.
2. Thornbury, *Life*, rev. ed., p. 217.
3. Horace, III, od. 5, stanzas 11–14. T. Hare, *A Translation of the Odes and Epodes of Horace into English Verse*, London 1737.
4. Butlin & Joll 375.
5. Butlin & Joll 399, 400.

54

55

56

55 A Storm off Dover c. 1793

Pencil and watercolour, $10\frac{1}{16} \times 14\frac{1}{4}$ (256×362)
TB XVI–G, BM1975(2)

Turner's earliest experience of the grandeur and terror of the sea must have been on the coast of Kent, which he visited as a boy, and again in 1792 and 1793. It was a coast that was to attract him all his life, not only for the scenes of toil and danger in the daily lives of fishermen which he repeatedly painted, but for the sunsets to be seen from Margate, the most spectacular in the world, Turner thought.[1] In this early study the picturesque confusion of the weathered timbers of the pier (which he drew in another sketch without the stormy background)[2] seems about to be engulfed by the heaped waves and inky clouds. The ship too appears to be swamped. It is a precocious statement of the overwhelming and disintegrating force of elemental nature both in the context of men's lives and as a power that was to take Turner's art far beyond the niggling 'charm' of picturesqueness: the contrast of the pencil work in the foreground and the broad effects achieved by water-colour wash embodies the change that was to revolutionise his work within the decade.

1. Ruskin, *Works*, XXVII, p. 164.
2. TB XVI–D; other studies of the pier are XVI–E, F.

Charles Turner, after J. M. W. Turner

56 A Shipwreck 1806

Mezzotint, printed in dark brown ink, engraver's proof, touched in pencil by the artist (R. 751), plate: $22\frac{1}{16} \times 32\frac{13}{16}$ (560×833)
Inscr. bottom centre: *London Pub.d July 1st 1806. by C.Turner N.o 50, Warren Str.t Fitzroy Square.*
Yale Center for British Art, Paul Mellon Collection, B1977.14.8254

This print was undertaken by the engraver Charles Turner (no relation of the artist but a colleague of his from student days at the Academy Schools) as his own financial speculation. He advertised it in 1805 and it was completed, as in this impression, by the middle of 1806; but publication was delayed, and the final publication line reads *Jan.y 1, 1807*. The appearance of the print marked an epoch in Turner's career. It was the first engraving to be made from one of his paintings,[1] and reflected not merely the interest of the en-graver, but the enthusiasm of the general public: numerous in-fluential members of the nobility as well as artists young and old subscribed to the plate.[2] This was also the first time that Turner had been able to see his work translated into mezzotint, and by 1807 Charles Turner was fully involved in the production of the mezzotint plates of the *Liber Studiorum*,[3] a project that was to continue until 1819, though after 1811 the artist replaced Charles Turner by other engravers, and executed more and more of the mezzotint work himself, completing several plates entirely un-assisted before the series was discontinued. These experiments led him naturally into the 'Little Liber' prints of the 1820s, as well as to collaboration with Thomas Lupton and others over the *Rivers and Ports of England*.[4] The medium attracted him particularly for its atmospheric expressiveness, its ability to suggest vastness, un-certainty, night, obscurity and so on – all elements of the sublime for which he urgently needed an equivalent in one of the repro-ductive media. John Martin's adoption of mezzotint for his own visionary ideas must also have stimulated his interest in the method, and two of his most explicitly historical prints were produced by this means in the late 1820s (see nos 49 and 71). Among the many superlative qualities of this early plate, it should be noticed that great care is given to the differentiation of in-dividual figures in the three foreground vessels: this is no general-ised evocation of suffering, but a vividly presented and fully documented incident (though it is presumably entirely imaginary). Compare the still more compelling immediacy of no. 57, a painting of about five years later. It has been thought that Turner's 'in-spiration' for choosing this subject was the republication in 1804 of William Falconer's poem *The Shipwreck*, which originally appeared in 1762, and enjoyed a considerable reputation as a marine epic of Thomsonian power.

1. Butlin & Joll 54. The picture was exhibited at Turner's gallery in 1805.
2. For an account of the production of the print, see Finberg, *Life*, pp. 118–19.
3. See pp. 69–70.
4. R. 752–68; 778–90; see no. 73.

Thomas Oldham Barlow (1824–89), after J. M. W. Turner

57 The Wreck of a Transport Ship c. 1856

Mezzotint, printed in brownish-black ink, on india paper, published state (R. 811), subject: $23\frac{1}{8} \times 32\frac{5}{16}$ (587×821);
plate: $26\frac{15}{16} \times 34\frac{7}{16}$ (684×875)
Inscr. below: with the arms of the Earl of Yarborough (the owner of the picture), and *Artist's copy from the plate presented by the Right Hon.ble the Earl of Yarborough to the Artists General Benevolent Institution*; and signed by the engraver, lower right.
Yale Center for British Art, Paul Mellon Collection, B1977.14.8364

This is one of two large plates mezzotinted by Barlow after subjects by Turner; the other is *The Vintage at Macon*, from the painting of 1803;[1] impressions are dated 1856, which may be the approximate date of this print as well. *Macon* was also a picture in Lord Yarborough's collection. This subject of a shipwreck[2] was exhib-ited in 1851 with the title *The Wreck of Minotaur*, by which name it has frequently been known, though it was shown in London in 1849 as *The Wreck of a Transport Ship*. Since the date of execution of the picture is uncertain, it is difficult to refer it to any specific historical event, but current opinion tends to doubt the accuracy of the association with the sinking of the Minotaur. This took place, as the 1851 catalogue states, on '22nd December 1810', and since Turner appears to have used sketches made before that year it seems unlikely that there can be a connection between the picture and the event. But the painting itself was probably not executed until about 1810, and although Turner's conception is largely imaginary, there is no reason why he should not have wanted to give his subject greater point and immediacy by identifying it with a specific wreck. This would be wholly in keeping with the overwhelming immediacy and conviction of the whole work. It is also characteristic of Turner to make such direct associations between his pictures and real occurrences, even if he sometimes suppressed the factual information when giving his works titles. The matter is of no great importance, but the mere fact that this powerfully documentary work should have attracted a title (whether given it by Turner or not) as precise as 'The Wreck of Minotaur, Seventy-four, on the Haak Sands, 22nd December 1810' is itself a tribute to the success of the piece as sheer realism.

1. Butlin & Joll 47.
2. Butlin & Joll 210.

57

58

59

J. M. W. Turner and William Say (1768–1834),
after J. M. W. Turner

58 Coast of Yorkshire near Whitby (*Liber Studiorum*)
1811

Etching and mezzotint, printed in brown ink, first published state
(R. 24), subject: $7\frac{1}{16} \times 10\frac{5}{16}$ (180 × 262); plate: $8\frac{3}{16} \times 11\frac{3}{8}$
(208 × 290)
Inscr. above: *M*; below: *Drawn & Etched by J. M. W. Turner. R.A.*
and *Engraved by W Say Engraver to H.R.H. the Duke of Gloucester.*; and
with title, and *Published Jan.ʳ 1 1811, by Mʳ. Turner, Queen Ann Street
West*
Yale Center for British Art, Paul Mellon Collection, B1977.14.8130

A graphic early account of the violence with which sea meets land,
and of the dangers men face on rocky coasts. Compare later
treatments of the theme such as nos 62–65. The drawing for this
subject is in the Turner Bequest.[1]

1. TB CXVII–B

most interesting experiments, for it concentrates on the plight of
the ship's crew almost to the exclusion of the sea itself. In another
marine subject of the same year, the *First-Rate taking in stores*,[2]
Turner is known to have attempted 'a drawing of the ordinary
dimensions that will give some idea of the size of a man of war'.
There, he contrasts the huge warship with the smaller shipping
around it, from a viewpoint low down in a small boat alongside.
Here, he seems to tackle the same theme, but quite differently: the
ship's size is appreciable from the minuteness of the figures on its
deck, and the proportion of it in relation to the whole sheet – but
despite its bulk the vessel is overwhelmed by the fury of the sea:
a vivid statement of a familiar sublime topic, influenced perhaps
by some famous painting of wrecks, like Northcote's *Loss of the
Halsewell*,[3] showing the sufferings of men and women crowded
onto a ship's deck which occupies most of the canvas.

1. Wilton 500.
2. Wilton 499.
3. Exhibited at the RA, 1786(240).

59 Study for the Loss of a Man o' War *c.* 1818

Watercolour, $12\frac{3}{16} \times 18\frac{1}{8}$ (310 × 460), watermark 1816
Inscr. lower left: *Begun for Dear Fawkes of (? or at) Farnley*
TB CXCVI–N, RA 1974(187)

The finished watercolour for which this is a study is in an English
private collection.[1] It shows many figures clinging to the ship's
sharply canted deck, which occupies the whole picture space. As an
essay in portraying the horror of a sea storm it is one of Turner's

60 Storm over a rocky Coast *c.* 1815–20

Watercolour with some pencil, $14\frac{9}{16} \times 21\frac{9}{16}$ (370 × 547)
Inscr. lower right: *Stranded Vessel (?); Willow Paper*
TB CCLXIII–32, BM 1975(52)

The note of a *Stranded Vessel* on this sheet may refer to a particular
sight witnessed by Turner, but is perhaps a memorandum of an
idea for inclusion in a finished watercolour for which this sheet is a
preliminary study. Another sheet in the Turner Bequest, similarly

60

61

inscribed *Willow Paper* (he was evidently experimenting with a new surface) is annotated *Durham* so it is likely that both are the products of a tour in the north of England in the 1810s.

61 Ship in a Storm *c.* 1825

> Pencil and watercolour, $8\frac{1}{2} \times 11\frac{3}{8}$ (216 × 290)
> Inscr.: in various parts of the sheet: *1, 2, 3, 4, 5*
> TB CCLXIII–309(a), Wilton 772

Although he made elaborate pen and wash drawings for the *Liber Studiorum* plates that were to be mezzotinted by other artists, and even for those, like the *Stonehenge*, that he alone worked on, Turner adopted a different procedure when he was creating the series of 'sequels' to the *Liber*, in which the potential of mezzotint for rich effects of chiaroscuro is exploited more fully and dramatically than ever. For these subjects the merest hint was sometimes enough to provide a guide so that Turner could work directly onto the mezzotint plate. Here, for example, the two elements of the subject, ship and stormy sea, are indicated briefly in opposing media – pencil and watercolour – with a minimum of detail. This is an interesting development from the presentation of Dover pier in no. 55, which makes use of a similar opposition of techniques to suggest the antagonism of man and the sea. The numerals scattered about the design are difficult to interpret, though they may indicate the principal tonal blocks into which the design divides itself. If they do, it is not clear what purpose they served, though we know that at this period – the early and mid-1820s – Turner was perfecting his method of watercolour composition by constructing his subjects from broad segments or patches of colour, over which specific detail was added. The loose washes of this sketch create a vivid sense of the fury of the sea, anticipating the motif and even the technique of the *Snow storm: steam boat off a harbour's mouth* of 1842. In the 'Little Liber' mezzotint[1] the tonality is darker and the mood one of greater horror.

1. R. 803.

W. R. Smith, after J. M. W. Turner

62 The Entrance to Fowey Harbour, Cornwall (*England and Wales*) 1829

> Engraving, printed on india paper, first published state (R. 225), subject: $6\frac{7}{16} \times 9\frac{1}{16}$ (163 × 230); plate: $10\frac{3}{16} \times 12\frac{1}{2}$ (258 × 318)
> Yale Center for British Art, Paul Mellon Collection, B1977.14.6919

62

63

W. R. Smith, after J. M. W. Turner

63   Long-ships Light House, Lands End (*England and Wales*) 1836

Engraving, printed on india paper, first published state (names of artist and engraver only, partially erased), (R. 288), subject: $6\frac{7}{16} \times 9\frac{15}{16}$ (164 × 252); plate: 10 × $12\frac{15}{16}$ (253 × 328)
Yale Center for British Art, Paul Mellon Collection, B1977.14.7090

Thomas Jeavons (1816–67), after J. M. W. Turner

64   Lyme Regis, Dorset (*England and Wales*) 1836

Engraving, printed on india paper, first published state (R. 290), subject: $6\frac{1}{2} \times 10\frac{1}{16}$ (165 × 256); plate: $9\frac{7}{8} \times 12\frac{5}{8}$ (250 × 320)
Yale Center for British Art, Paul Mellon Collection, B1977.14.7094

W. R. Smith, after J. M. W. Turner

65   Lowestoffe, Suffolk (*England and Wales*) 1837

Engraving, third state (R. 293), subject: $6\frac{5}{16} \times 9\frac{3}{4}$ (160 × 248); plate: $9\frac{7}{8} \times 13$ (250 × 330)
Yale Center for British Art, Paul Mellon Collection, B1977.14.13442

All four of these plates from the *Picturesque Views in England and Wales*[1] are, like others in the series, concerned with the re-lationship of the sea to the land, and in particular with those aspects of that relationship which make life in such places hazardous to men. They vary in the degree of explicitness with which this theme is treated. The *Long-ships Light House* makes an indirect statement, using fragments of wreckage to present the effects of the destructive fury of the sea, which is so vividly shown in the subject;[2] while the *Lowestoffe* and *Lyme Regis* depict various aspects of the toil associated with a seafaring or coastal life. The latter was published with the mistaken title of 'Lyme Regis Norfolk', perhaps confusing the Dorset port with Yarmouth, the setting for some of Turner's grandest scenes of wreck and salvage (see no. 67). The most graphic of all these accounts, however, is the *Fowey Harbour*, which presents the horrors of the sea with brutal realism. This design is based on that showing the same view in the *Picturesque Views on the Southern Coast of England*, engraved by W. B. Cooke in 1820,[3] which also shows stormy weather, but does not suggest danger and death. Here these elements of the subject are given prominence, and the spectator witnesses a human tragedy as ferocious, in its less sensational way, as the wreck of the transport ship (no. 57).

1. The original drawings are Wilton 801, 864, 866, 869; Shanes 63, 73, 74, 76.
2. It seems to derive from the composition of *Ilfracombe* for the *Picturesque Views on the Southern Coast of England* (Wilton 462).
3. Wilton 466.

64△　▽65

66△ ▽67

66 Stormy Sea *c.* 1830–35

Watercolour, $14\frac{3}{4} \times 21\frac{3}{4}$ (375 × 554)
TB CCCLXV–36

Colour studies like this one are difficult to place in Turner's output: were they, like many colour-beginnings, preliminary sketches for finished works, or have they a more independent existence as essays, experiments in portraying particular effects? If they belong to the former category, we must suppose that Turner saw them as only partial statements, which his eye filled out with the abundant detail and complex significance of a fully realised subject. If they are of the latter type, it is likely that they belong to a late period in his career – certainly after 1830 and perhaps after 1840. The washes of colour would then indicate, not the foundation on which a particular effect was to be built up, but a solution to the problem of conveying an effect – and not a unique or even a successful solution: late studies of this kind almost always exist in series, in which Turner returns again and again, rapidly, to one idea, without necessarily having a finished work in mind. Characteristics of both types of study may be present in this sheet, which does not, it seems, belong to a long series of similar sketches, but does not, either, relate to a finished watercolour. Stylistically it appears to be a study for the *England and Wales* series, and there are parallels between the treatment of the waves here and that in finished subjects like *Lowestoffe* (no. 65) or *Lyme Regis* (no. 64).

67 Yarmouth Sands (?)*c.* 1840

Watercolour with scraping-out, $9\frac{3}{4} \times 14\frac{1}{4}$ (248 × 362)
Yale Center for British Art, Paul Mellon Collection, B1975.4.1417, Wilton 1406

One of a series of scenes on the shore, or just out at sea off Yarmouth, which Turner perhaps made about 1840,[1] and which relate to the subject-matter of his painting *Rockets and blue lights (close at hand) to warn steam-boats of shoal water*,[2] exhibited at the Academy in that year. Turner had been interested in the seashore at Yarmouth earlier than this, however: his *Life-boat and Manby apparatus going off to a stranded vessel making signals (blue lights) of distress*[3] is also set at Yarmouth, and was exhibited in 1831. The great freedom with which these watercolour studies are executed argues in favour of the later date. They precede by only a few years Dickens's famous description of the wreck of Steerforth's ship off Yarmouth in *David Copperfield*.[4]

1. Wilton 1405–10. Another drawing from the series is in the Tate Gallery, no. 5239.
2. Butlin & Joll 387.
3. Butlin & Joll 336.
4. Chapter 55. The novel first appeared in 1850.

68 Lost to all Hope . . . *c.* 1845–50

Pencil and watercolour, $8\frac{5}{8} \times 12\frac{3}{4}$ (220 × 324)
Inscr. at bottom: *Lost to all Hope she lies/each sea breaks over a derelict* [?]*/on an unknown shore the sea folk* [?]*/only sharing* [?] *the triumph*
Yale Center for British Art, Paul Mellon Collection, B1977.14.5378, Wilton 1425

One of a group of bleak late watercolour studies to which Turner has appended tentative drafts of verses. Another sheet seems to have further lines from the same poem: *And Dolphins* [?] *play around the wreck* [?] *The man's hope holding all that hoped/Admits the work* [*?mark*] *of the almighty's hand failing* [?] *hope for sail.*[1] That drawing is also inscribed *Wreck on the Goodwin Sands*, and we may suppose that Turner made these studies at Margate, from which the Goodwin Sands are visible, on one of his visits there in the last years of his life. Some of the late oil studies of breakers and wrecks near the coast appear to be concerned with the same theme.[2] These rough sketches – for most of them are little more – give expression to a private mood of lonely despair, the introspective depression of old age, and are an extension of some of the themes that run through much of Turner's marine painting. But their message is not one that comes to the surface in his public utterances – the finished paintings and drawings. Broad moral points are made in his exhibited works, as, for instance, in *The Sun of Venice going to sea*,[3] which have been interpreted as personal reflections by Turner on his own condition.[4] But their mood is always very different from that of these studies. It is usually buoyant, if not exultant, at least as far as visual qualities are concerned, and pessimism is only apparent in the verses appended to them in the catalogues; just as these watercolour sketches derive most of their poignancy from the inscriptions. Is this the opposition of the painter, the confident master of his medium, to the anxious 'tyro' poet? (See no. 50.)[5]

1. Wilton 1426.
2. E.g. Butlin & Joll 459.
3. Butlin & Joll 402.
4. E.g. by Louis Hawes, 'Turner's Fighting Temeraire', *Art Quarterly*, Vol. XXXV, 1972, pp. 22–48.
5. And see Wilton, 1979, pp. 14–15.

69 The Whale *c.* 1845

Pencil and watercolour, $9\frac{5}{16} \times 13\frac{3}{16}$ (237 × 335)
Inscr. lower left: *I shall use this*
TB CCCLVII–6
Colour plate 16

This is a sheet from Turner's *Ambleteuse and Wimereux* sketchbook, used on his final visit to the continent in 1845. It is supposed that he saw the whale while crossing the Channel, but if so it is surprising that he did not make a more precise study of the creature's appearance. There is an atmosphere of fantasy about this sketch, in which the whale seems to materialise out of the waves as if conjured up by an effort of Turner's imagination. If he had been reading Beale's *Natural History of the Sperm Whale* and other works on whaling, as we know he did at this time, he may well have invented this subject rather than having relied on direct experience for it. The oil paintings that he produced in 1845 and 1846[1] are certainly works of the imagination, and Turner's titles refer specifically to Beale's book. It is of particular interest in this context that Turner should have taken up one of the archetypal motifs of the sublime – the vast, strange and elusive monster of the deep, Leviathan – as a final theme in his life-long exploration of the sea as a subject for his art.

1. Butlin & Joll 414, 415, 423, 426.

68

70

J. M. W. Turner and George Clint (1770–1859),
after J. M. W. Turner

70 Peat Bog, Scotland (*Liber Studiorum*) 1812

Etching and mezzotint, printed in brown ink, fifth state (R. 45);
subject: $7\frac{1}{16} \times 10\frac{1}{4}$ (180 × 260); plate: $8\frac{1}{4} \times 11\frac{1}{2}$ (210 × 292)
Inscr. above: *M*; below: with title and names of artist and engraver;
bottom: *Published April 23, 1812, by J.M.W. Turner, Queen Ann
Street West.*
Yale Center for British Art, Paul Mellon Collection, B1977.14.13996

This plate is recorded by Rawlinson as having deteriorated in later
stages, but this impression of the fifth state is of great richness and
strength, fully conveying the power of Turner's design, which
Ruskin referred to as 'the darkest' of his views of Scotland. He goes
on to suggest that it was the rugged scenery of Scotland that taught
Turner 'to despise the affections of Italian landscape and the
comforts of Dutch'.[1] More plausibly, perhaps, it was the Picturesque that Turner finally abandoned as a consequence of his Scottish
tour of 1801. This subject is similar to some of his north country
scenes of the picturesque sublime – *Buttermere Lake* (FIG. VII), for
instance – but its mood is heightened, its drama more intense, and
there is no longer any wish on the artist's part to charm his
audience with the polite formalities of picture-making.

1. Ruskin, *Works*, XXI, p. 219.

Frederick Christian Lewis (1779–1856),
after J. M. W. Turner

71 Field of Waterloo 1830

Mezzotint, printed in black ink, second published state (R. 795),
subject: $13\frac{15}{16} \times 23$ (354 × 584); plate: $18\frac{1}{8} \times 25\frac{1}{2}$ (464 × 647)
Inscr. below: with title and: "-----*heapd and pent/Rider and horse in one
red burial blent"/Byron's Childe Harold*; and with the names of painter
and engraver; lower right: *Proof*; bottom centre: *London, Published
May 1830, by J.M.W. Turner, R.A. 47, Queen Ann Street, West.*
Yale Center for British Art, Paul Mellon Collection, B1977.14.8339

Rawlinson doubted whether this, like the plate of the *Deluge* (no.
49), was ever actually published; but an earlier state with publication line and the date, July 1st 1829, is recorded, which suggests
that the print was issued. The lines from Byron that appear on the
plate are condensed from the verses that Turner quoted in the RA
exhibition catalogue when the painting[1] was shown there in 1818:

Last noon behold them full of lusty life;
Last eve in Beauty's circle proudly gay;
The midnight brought the signal – sound of strife;
The morn the marshalling of arms – the day,
Battle's magnificently stern array!
The thunder clouds close o'er it, which when rent
The earth is covered thick with other clay
Which her own clay shall cover, heaped and pent,
Rider and horse – friend, foe, in one red burial blent!

71

The subject, issued in a format similar to that of the *Deluge* of a year before, might be seen as a companion to that work – a modern historical piece in which Turner exploits even more dramatically the theme of darkness and firelight. Although it was painted several years before Danby's *Delivery of Israel out of Egypt* (1825), this work again seems to presage it, especially in the column of light in the air, which resembles Danby's pillar of fire. Turner made a watercolour showing the carnage at Waterloo at about the time he was working on the painting;[2] and he was to return to the subject for illustrations to Scott and Byron in the 1830s. None of these exploits the effect of darkness that is so unexpected a feature of this work. Night has overtaken the dead; time passes, the battle is lost and won, yet they remain impotent to affect the course of history or even their own existence any longer: 'Roll'd round in earth's diurnal course, With rocks, and stones, and trees';[4] these are ideas powerfully conveyed by the lighting which also lends the whole subject an apocalyptic quality entirely appropriate to its mood of hopeless loss and emptiness. It is thus also an entirely apt counterpart to the *Deluge* picture with which Turner seems to be comparing it.

1. Butlin & Joll 138.
2. Wilton 494.
3. Wilton 1097, 1116, 1229.
4. Wordsworth, *Lucy*, v, ll. 7, 8.

72 Stonehenge at daybreak (*Liber Studiorum, unpublished*) *c.* 1820

Mezzotint, printed in brown ink, late 19th-century impression from Turner's unfinished plate (R. 81), subject: 7⅝ × 10⅜ (193 × 263); plate: 8¾ × 11¾ (222 × 288)
Yale Center for British Art, Paul Mellon Collection, B1977.14.13969

Although associated by Rawlinson with the *Liber Studiorum*, this plate, entirely worked by Turner himself, belongs to a group of prints which lie between the *Liber* itself and the 'sequels' that he apparently made about 1825 (see no. 74).[1] In subject-matter and mood it is considerably closer to the works of the later series, and the drawing on which it is based[2] also seems to have moved technically towards the loose washes of those used in that project. The distinctive penwork of the *Liber Studiorum* drawings, which Turner translated into etched outline in the plates, has vanished, and the whole subject is expressed in tones of sepia ink – the equivalent of the mezzotint work of the print. Stonehenge was of course a monument of antiquity whose mystery and great age rendered it sublime (see also no. 79).

1. This group of plates in pure mezzotint by Turner himself are R. 81, 82, 84, 85, 86, 87, and 88.
2. In the Museum of Fine Arts, Boston, gift of Ellen T. Bullard, 59.795. It was formerly in the collection of J. E. Taylor and measures 7⅝ × 10 9/16 (194 × 268).

Charles Turner, after J. M. W. Turner

73 Shields, on the River Tyne (*Rivers of England*) 1823

Mezzotint, printed in black ink, second state (R. 752), subject: 6⅛ × 8⅝ (156 × 219); plate: 7 11/16 × 10¼ (195 × 260)
Inscr. below: with title and names of artist and engraver; bottom: *Rivers of England. Plate 1. Published June 2ᵈ 1823. by W. B. Cooke 9. Soho Square.*
Yale Center for British Art, Paul Mellon Collection, B1977.14.8257

The *Rivers of England* series on which Turner worked in the early 1820s was conceived as a series of small-scale views with a re-markably wide range of landscape types and emotional moods.[1]

72

73

74

While some of the subjects are gently pastoral, there are also hilly panoramas, squally marines, and impressive cityscapes. One subject is actually taken directly from a large watercolour of Turner's early sublime period – a brooding view of Warkworth Castle.[2] This scene on the Tyne is the only night-piece, and it anticipates the beautiful nocturnes of the 'Little Liber' executed, probably, only a year or two later (see nos 74–8). It also provided the basis for an oil painting of 1835, *Keelmen heaving in coals by night*,[3] in which the 'industrial sublime' is elevated into a statement as serenely beautiful as a Claude.

1. The watercolour designs for the series are TB XCVI (Wilton, nos 732–48).
2. Wilton 256.
3. Butlin & Joll 360.

74 Paestum ('Little Liber') *c.* 1825

Mezzotint, printed in black ink, early trial proof, trimmed to the edge of the subject (R. 799), 6 × 8½ (152 × 216)
Yale Center for British Art, Paul Mellon Collection, B1977.14.8348

This and nos 75–8 are plates from the series of twelve mezzotints scraped by Turner himself at some point after the conclusion of the

Liber Studiorum in 1819. A date around 1825 is considered likely; they cannot date from before the 1820s for stylistic reasons and because some are on steel plates, not introduced until about 1820. There seem to be connections between these designs and some of those for the *Rivers* and *Ports of England* on which Turner was engaged between about 1823 and 1828 (see no. 73). Although they form a distinct group, they were not published and their purpose remains obscure. Rawlinson attempted to prove that they were 'originally intended as studies of moonlight under various conditions' but abandoned this idea.[1] They are all linked, however, by a common preoccupation with exploiting the dramatic possibilities of mezzotint; hence their concentration on night scenes and scenes of strongly contrasted tones. Their importance in Turner's development as a colourist in the 1820s seems to be significant, though it has not been precisely defined.[2] The design of this subject is sketched in a sheet in the Turner Bequest (no. 75). Later impressions of the plate show a second temple to the right of the one visible in this proof, and a buffalo skeleton in the foreground. Compare the motif with that of the dead shepherd with his flock in the *Stonehenge* of the *England and Wales* series (no. 79).

1. Rawlinson, *Engravings*, Vol. 1, pp. xliv, 385.
2. See White, 1977, p. 79, and Wilton, 1979, pp. 168–70.

75

75 Paestum in a thunderstorm *c.* 1825

Watercolour with pencil, 8⅜ × 12 (213 × 305)
TB CCCLXIV–224, Wilton 769

Like the towns of Herculaneum and Pompeii, the Greek temples at Paestum (Pesto) south of Naples were 'discovered' in the eighteenth century and contributed largely to the progress of Neoclassicism in Europe. They were magnificently engraved by Piranesi.[1] Turner visited them in 1819, making several drawings.[2] In 1824 Lady Blessington recorded her response to the temples as follows: '. . . the first view . . . must strike every beholder with admiration. Nor is this sentiment diminished on approaching them; for the beauty of their proportions, and the rich and warm hues stamped on them by time, as they stand out in bold relief against the blue sky, . . . render the spot, even independent of the classical associations with which it is fraught, one of the most sublime and interesting imaginable. The solitude and desolation of the country around, where naught but a wretched hovel, a short distance from the temples . . . breaks on the silent grandeur of the scene, adds to the sublime effect of it.'[3] This study appears to have been made with the intention that it should be translated into mezzotint, for it belongs to a group of stylistically similar drawings which all relate to the 'Little Liber' series which Turner scraped in the mid-1820s. The resulting print is no. 74. According to Ruskin, Turner commonly associated lightning with the monuments of dead religions; compare the view of *Stonehenge* (no. 79).[4]

1. Piranesi, *Différentes Vues de quelques Restes de trois grands Edifices de L'ancienne Ville de Pesto*, 1778–9.
2. In the *Naples, Paestum and Rome* sketchbook, TB CLXXXVI.
3. Edith Clay, ed., *Lady Blessington at Naples*, London 1979, p. 88.
4. Ruskin, *Works*, XXI, p. 223.

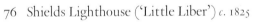

76

76 Shields Lighthouse ('Little Liber') *c.* 1825

Mezzotint, printed in black ink, trial proof(a) (R. 801), subject:
5$\frac{15}{16}$ × 8$\frac{3}{8}$ (151 × 212) trimmed inside plate-mark
Yale Center for British Art, Paul Mellon Collection, B1977.14.8351

A wash drawing related to this subject is in the Turner Bequest.[1]
Turner modified his design considerably as he proceeded with it; a
second proof at Yale[2] has the moonlight diffused in a haze of
radiance over the whole scene; later, the moon was reduced in size.
In this plate Turner completely dispels any association of darkness
with fear, while reaffirming that it is truly sublime. The stillness of
this moonlit night is one of his profoundest conceptions, executed
with great breadth and with a simplicity of touch that denotes the
mastery that Turner had acquired over this medium, which of all
the reproductive methods he made most his own.

1. TB CCLXIII—308.
2. Reproduced in Christopher White, *English Landscape 1630–1850*, Yale 1977, pl. CXXIX.

77a Catania, Sicily ('Little Liber') *c.* 1825

Mezzotint, printed in black-brown ink, touched by Turner in
pencil and (?) white chalk, trial proof(b), (R. 805), subject:

6 × 8$\frac{7}{16}$ (153 × 215); plate: 7$\frac{5}{8}$ × 9$\frac{15}{16}$ (193 × 252)
Yale Center for British Art, Paul Mellon Collection, B1977.14.8355

77b Catania, Sicily ('Little Liber')

Mezzotint, printed in black (R. 805); impression taken by
Seymour Haden, 1872
Yale Center for British Art, Paul Mellon Collection, B1977.14.8356

Turner's drawing of this subject is in the Boston Museum of Fine
Arts.[1] It was presumably made from a sketch by another artist,
since Turner never visited Sicily himself. In the trial proof, Turner
has indicated with touches of chalk the reflections from the water
which are realised in the final state. The felucca at the left is
pencilled in, and there is a smudge of white in the darkest part of
the thundercloud. This does not seem to have been incorporated
into the mezzotint, but the boat is added in the later state, as is the
distant outline of Mt Etna, with its plume of smoke. This is one of
the grandest of all Turner's lightning storms.

1. Wilton 774.

77a

77b

78

79

78 The Evening Gun ('Little Liber') *c.* 1825

Mezzotint, printed in black ink, trial proof(c), touched by Turner (R. 800), subject: $5\frac{15}{16} \times 8\frac{3}{8}$ (151 × 212); plate: $7\frac{1}{2} \times 9\frac{3}{16}$ (190 × 233)
Yale Center for British Art, Paul Mellon Collection, B1977.14.8349

Turner's alterations to this proof consist of scraping-out of the mezzotint tone with a sharp point in the upper sky, the rays of the sun, and the foreground ripples.[1] If Turner had the work of Francis Danby in mind when he made the 'Little Liber' plates, this subject approaches closest to the spirit of Danby's paintings. Danby in fact produced a picture with the same title which he exhibited in 1848.[2]

1. See S. Colvin, 'Turner's Evening Gun', *The Portfolio*, 1872, pp. 75–6.
2. At the Royal Academy, no. 595. Its full title was *The Evening Gun – a calm on the shore of England.*

Robert Wallis, after J. M. W. Turner

79 Stone Henge (*England and Wales*) 1829

Engraving, second state, on india paper (R. 235), subject: $6\frac{1}{2} \times 9\frac{1}{4}$ (165 × 234); plate: $9\frac{15}{16} \times 9\frac{1}{4}$ (252 × 310)
Inscr. below: with title and names of artist and engraver; lower right: *Printed by Mr Queen.*; bottom: *London, Published 1829, for the Proprietor, by R. Jennings, Poultry, & by Giraldon Bovinet, Gallerie, Vivienne, Paris.*
Yale Center for British Art, Paul Mellon Collection, B1977.14.13346

The neolithic circle of Stonehenge has always been recognised as an object specially evocative of the sublime.[1] Even an antiquary preoccupied with scientific description could write in 1740 that 'the yawning ruins' provoke 'an ecstatic *reverie*, which none can describe';[2] and subsequently poets and tourists found inspiration in its antiquity, mystery and desolate situation. As William Gilpin said, 'Standing on so vast an area as Salisbury Plain, it was lost in the immensity around it. As we approached, it gained more respect . . . But when we arrived on the spot, it appeared astonishing beyond conception. A train of wondering ideas immediately crowded into the mind. Who brought these huge masses of rock together? Whence were they brought? For what purpose? . . .'[3] Burke considered that 'Stonehenge, neither for disposition nor ornament, has anything admirable; but those huge rude masses of stone, set on end, and piled each on other, turn the mind on the immense force necessary for such a work. Nay the rudeness of the work increases this cause of grandeur, as it precludes the idea of art, and contrivance . . .'[4] Turner made a number of pencil studies of the structure[5] and used it as the subject of a mezzotint (no. 72), which suggests the bleakness of its setting. Here, by contrast, he makes the monument a backdrop to a drama reminiscent of Thomson, in which a shepherd is struck dead by lightning in the middle of the deserted plain. The sky is worked up into one of Turner's most violent electric storms. Rawlinson relates that the President of the Royal Meteorological Society was impressed by the artist's rendering of the lightning. It is interesting to note that he was determined on absolute accuracy here, while the actual positions of the stones have been modified to suit his purposes in the design.[6]

1. For a survey of the place of Stonehenge in British romantic art see Louis Hawes, *Constable's Stonehenge*, Victoria and Albert Museum, London 1975.
2. William Stukeley, *Stonehenge, a Temple restor'd to the Druids*, 1740, p. 12.
3. William Gilpin, *Observations on the Western Parts of England, relative chiefly to Picturesque Beauty*, London 1798, p. 77.
4. Burke, *op. cit.*, p. 60.
5. e.g. TB LXIX 79, 80; TB CXXIII–211, 212.
6. The original watercolour is Wilton 811; Shanes 25.

80

80 A Mountain Pass: night (?)c. 1830

Watercolour, 13¾ × 19⁵⁄₁₆ (305 × 490)
TB CCLXIII–91

This enigmatic colour study may be connected with one of
Turner's watercolours showing incidents during his travels across
Europe in winter. The large scene of a diligence overturned in a
snowdrift which he exhibited in 1829 as *Messieurs les Voyageurs ... in
a snowdrift upon Mount Tarrar*[1] is the most likely, though the
finished composition differs from this in most respects. The
contrast between the tunnel of darkness on the left and the area of
light at the right is typical of Turner's compositional organisation
in the 1830s, but it is impossible to be sure precisely what is
intended here: are we among the wilds of a bleak mountain pass, or
is the scene a more familiar one, with streets and houses, and
perhaps a torchlight procession? It would be appropriate to link the
study with the *England and Wales* subjects of the early 1830s, but no
obvious connection suggests itself. Compare, however, the tunnel-
like cutting at the right of Turner's view of *St Catharine's Hill,
Guildford*,[2] which has compositional analogies, though the design is
in reverse.

1. Wilton 405.
2. In the Yale Center for British Art, Wilton 837; Shanes 48.

81 Leeds 1816

Watercolour, $11\frac{3}{8} \times 16\frac{3}{4}$ (290 $\times$ 425)
Inscr. lower left: *J M W Turner RA 1816*
Engr. by J. D. Harding (lithograph), 1823
Yale Center for British Art, Paul Mellon Collection, Wilton 544

Although not a work in the sublime mode, this view of Leeds marks the point at which Turner's progress as a topographer began to reflect the breadth of reference and coherence of handling that he had achieved in meeting the technical challenges of the sea and the mountains. This sheet is dated to the year after Turner had painted *The Battle of Fort Rock (colour 15)*, and no topographical view could ever be the same after that experience.[1] Here, there is no sense of technical strain – perhaps precisely because so much effort had gone into the earlier work – and a wealth of information is incorporated into a lucidly organised and stably composed panorama. The inherent grandeur of the youthful industrial cities is celebrated in quiet enjoyment of the new atmospheric effects created by innumerable chimneys pouring their smoke into the broad sky. The proximity of country to town is presented even while we are made conscious of the long lines of new houses that straggle up the hills, the insidious outcrops of building that are just beginning to alter the landscape irrevocably. Turner does not, however, draw any tragic conclusions: he records objectively, but with fascination, the work of masons building a wall, the morning errands of butchers and farmers. Two men appear to be erecting a stall, for a fair or market, in a field where people are gathering mushrooms. Later, in the *England and Wales* series (compare especially no. 84), Turner was to invest such views with much greater drama; here he allows the sheer diversity of life to make its

own impression, and by doing so evokes almost unawares the spirit of the sublime.

1. Compare the breathtaking, but equally 'topographical' view of *Raby Castle*, an oil painting of 1818 now in the Walters Art Gallery, Baltimore (Butlin & Joll 136).

82 Rome: The Forum with a Rainbow 1819

Pencil, watercolour and bodycolour on white paper prepared with a grey wash, $9 \times 14\frac{5}{16}$ (229 $\times$ 367)
TB CLXXXIX–46, BM 1975 (67)

Turner's responses to Rome, 'the Eternal City', were inevitably coloured by the host of associations historical, literary and artistic, with which all Englishmen were equipped when they set out on the tour of Italy. His studies of it can be divided into two types: small pencil sketches recording details of architecture, and larger compositions, often in colour and usually executed on a prepared grey ground, which evoke aspects of the character of the city, and which have much of the expressive force of finished watercolours. This sheet is an unusually elaborate study, a page from the same sketchbook as no. 16, in which a sublime natural phenomenon is superimposed on the various antiquities of the Roman Forum. Buildings that appear in this somewhat rearranged view of the heart of the ancient empire include the Temple of Antoninus and Faustina, the three columns of the Temple of Castor and Pollux, the mass of the Basilica of Constantine, and above it, the church of S. Francesca Romana. Turner exhibited a large painting of the *Forum Romanum* at the Academy in 1826. It presents the various edifices of the site among a jumble of fragments of classical masonry

81

82

that give it something of the atmosphere of the architectural fantasies of Sir John Soane and his draughtsman Joseph Michael Gandy (1771–1843). It was perhaps Gandy's highly imaginative projections of buildings ancient and modern that Turner had in mind when he painted the picture, as its subtitle says, 'for Mr Soane's Museum'. The canvas never in fact entered Soane's collection.[1]

1. Butlin & Joll 233.

William Radclyffe (1780–1855), after J. M. W. Turner

83 Salisbury, Wiltshire (*England and Wales*) 1830

Engraving, first published state, printed on india paper (R. 260), subject: $6\frac{5}{8} \times 9\frac{1}{2}$ (169 × 242); plate: $9\frac{1}{2} \times 13\frac{13}{16}$ (242 × 351)
Inscr. below: with names of artist and engraver
Yale Center for British Art, Paul Mellon Collection, B1977.14.13382

While his view of Leeds (no. 81) is dominated by the chimneys of new industry and the smoke they generate, Turner's Salisbury is still, in the 1820s,[1] the city dominated by its great cathedral which he drew in the 1790s. The structure loses nothing of its majesty from being placed in the centre of a panorama instead of being isolated as a monument of the architectural sublime; just as Turner can stand back from the fall of the Tees (no. 37) and in doing so enlarge our sense of its grandeur, so in placing Salisbury cathedral in its context, he enhances its value as a cultural monument and religious symbol. As Ruskin noticed, that symbolism is carried out in the foreground group of shepherd with his flock, a parallel, couched in Biblical language, to the pastoral significance of the church. He compared this idea with the central motif of the *Stone Henge* (no. 79) in which 'the shepherd lies dead, his flock scattered'.[2]

1. Like most of the *England and Wales* drawings, the original watercolour probably dates from a year or two earlier than the print; about 1828 (Wilton 836; Shanes 24).
2. Ruskin, *Works* VII, pp. 190–1, see also *Works* XXI, p. 223.

S. Fisher (fl. 1831–44), after J. M. W. Turner

84 Coventry, Warwickshire (*England and Wales*) 1833

Engraving, printed on india paper, second published state (R. 273), subject: $6\frac{7}{16} \times 9\frac{5}{8}$ (164 × 245); plate: $9\frac{13}{16} \times 12\frac{9}{16}$ (250 × 319)
Inscr. below: with title and names of artist and engraver; lower right: *Printed by Mᶜ Queen*; bottom: *London, Published 1833, for the Proprietor, by Moon, Boys & Graves, 6, Pall Mall.*
Yale Center for British Art, Paul Mellon Collection, B1977.14.13394

A comparison of this subject with the *Leeds* of 1816 (no. 81) tells us much about the way in which Turner's topography had become imbued with the lessons of his more 'serious' painting. Both are expansive views of cities, seen from the rising country immediately outside them, and both communicate many details about the way of life of their inhabitants. But while the information given in the *Leeds* is allowed to accumulate unobtrusively until a complete picture is formed, Coventry bursts upon the eye as a revelation – an Elysian colony with its clustered houses and soaring spires brilliant in a burst of stormy light. The composition is not a gentle assemblage of parts, but a rapid and vivid *coup de théâtre*, dependent on a few salient stresses and tonal divisions. This is the rhetoric of 'high art', not the learned conversation of topography. And yet the elements are much the same as before: there is no sacrifice of immediacy or of truth. Indeed, the truth is now given to us with much greater immediacy than before, and we are conscious that it is a superior brand of truth – the rhetoric is perhaps couched in heroic couplets. The original watercolour is in the British Museum.[1]

1. Lloyd Bequest, 1958–7–12–434 (Wilton 849; Shanes 58).

83

84

86

85 Study of an Industrial Town at Sunset *c.* 1830

Watercolour, 9⅝ × 19 (244 × 483)
TB CCLXIII–128
Colour plate 17

This colour-beginning is apparently one of the numerous studies
that Turner made for the series of *Picturesque Views in England and
Wales*, and probably shows one of the industrial Midlands towns
that he visited on a tour of 1830. A finished subject of this type is
the view of *Dudley* (no. 86). This is not the same town, it seems, but
the study presents many of the same ideas: obscurity and smoke
hazily illuminated by the fires of industry; a spacious landscape
crowded with the activity of men, obliterated by an atmosphere
quite different from the mists and storms of the mountains, and lit
by a sun diffused through an artificial fog. In spite of Ruskin's
opinion that Turner felt the tragedy of the industrial revolution
and its ravages of the English landscape, this drawing is unequivocally a poem of almost lyric enchantment with the new conditions
in which the world assumed such grand forms – even if, perhaps,
there is a hint of Milton's Hell in the combination of fire and
darkness.

R. Wallis (1794–1848), after J. M. W. Turner

86 Dudley, Worcestershire (*England and Wales*) 1835

Engraving, third state (R. 282), subject: 6⁷⁄₁₆ × 9⁷⁄₁₆ (163 × 240);
plate: 9⅞ × 11¹⁵⁄₁₆ (251 × 304)

Inscr. below: with title and names of artist and engraver; lower
right: *Printed by M*ͬ *Queen*; bottom: *London, Published 1835, for the
Proprietor, by Longman & C*ͦ *Paternoster Row*.
Yale Center for British Art, Paul Mellon Collection, B1977.14.13436

The history of criticism of this design provides interesting evidence
of the influence of Ruskin's personal interpretation of Turner's art.
Ruskin, distressed to the point of despair by the effects of in-
dustrialisation on English life and scenery, and moving towards a
philosophical position close to that of his contemporary, Karl
Marx, was unable to see the phenomena of the industrial revolution
with the eyes of the earlier generation to which Turner belonged.
He spoke of the watercolour of this subject[1] as 'One of Turner's
first expressions of his full understanding of what England was to
become,' and drew attention to the ruined castle and the church
spires as 'emblems of the passing away of the baron and the monk'.[2]
Rawlinson also calls attention to this contrast between past and
present, 'so profoundly felt, so impressively rendered. The quiet,
pathetic beauty of the once dominant, but now ruined feudal castle,
is strikingly brought out by the forges and the busy life of the
nineteenth century below.'[3] This just observation has been combined with Ruskin's in a recent comment to the effect that 'Gloom
and ceaseless industry abound . . . the only romantic feature is that
of the sun's last rays [*sic*: it is of course moonlight, as usual in
Turner's oppositions of industrial to natural light; cf. no. 73]
illuminating the ruined castle and Cluniac priory in regretful
farewell.'[4] The 'regret' here is undoubtedly Ruskin's, transmitted
unenfeebled through several generations. Turner's view of Dudley

itself does not convey any such mood. It is a work alive with activity, a fully-realised transcript of the life of industrial man as seen by the generation of artists for whom these scenes were novel and immensely stimulating experiences. Turner chooses night-time because it was by night that the industrial glare was most vivid, as Joseph Wright and others had done before him in the late eighteenth century.[5] The contrast of old and new is certainly here; as it is, for instance, in Turner's nocturnal view of *Stonehenge* (no. 72), where the ancient structure is passed by a modern stage coach.[6] Turner's fascination with the changes that society inevitably undergoes was by no means necessarily accompanied by dismay. On the contrary, as an artist, there is little doubt that he hailed the new with delight.[7] In fact, *Dudley* is one of the most complete of Turner's essays in the 'Industrial Sublime' which was quintessentially a department of the eighteenth-century 'Picturesque Sublime'.

1. Wilton 858.
2. Ruskin, *Works*, XIII, p. 435.
3. Rawlinson, vol. I, p. 158.
4. Shanes, p. 43, no. 66; and see p. 21.
5. e.g. Nicolson, *Wright*, cat. 198, pl. 104, or de Loutherbourg's *Coalbrookdale by night* (1801) in the Science Museum, London; and compare Turner's own *Limekiln at Coalbrookdale* in the Yale Center for British Art (Butlin & Joll 22).
6. See Rawlinson's comments on this subject, *Liber Studiorum*, no. 81.
7. See comments on Ruskin's opinion of the railways, no. 122.

87 Carlisle *c*. 1832

Watercolour, $3\frac{1}{4} \times 5\frac{5}{8}$ (83 × 142)
Engr. by E. Goodall for Scott's *Poetical Works*, 1833 (R. 493)
Yale Center for British Art, Paul Mellon Collection, B1975.4.966, Wilton 1070

Turner's activities as an illustrator, which occupied him extensively in the late 1820s and the 1830s, have been found puzzling by some commentators: granted that he was eager to find a wider public for his work, and recognised the advantages of disseminating it by means of engravings, why, in addition to creating magnificent landscape designs for picturesque series like the *England and Wales*, or superintending the reproduction of his paintings (see nos 49, 56, 71), did he laboriously execute such quantities of small-scale plates and vignettes for books? The answer is to be found in the very names of the authors to whose works he paid this dedicated tribute. They are Scott, Byron, Campbell and Milton (as well as his friend Samuel Rogers, who is the only writer of the group who cannot be said to occupy a significant place in the literary hierarchy of Turner's day).[1] Milton's standing is clear; Scott and Byron were unquestionably the most celebrated figures in romantic literature – Scott, a writer who had given literary value to the whole of Scotland as well as to many parts of England, immortalising many places by giving them new 'historical' and dramatic associations. In making 'topographical' views of such spots, Turner was actually creating landscapes with a direct literary reference and with, often, connotations of romantic and passionate events. This view of Carlisle does not illustrate any specific episode, but, in its concentrated elaboration, conveys the range and variety of ideas that Turner wished to present in connection with the city. In such a drawing, the sheer virtuosity by which the artist controls his material to evoke so much in so little space is itself a manifestation of the sublime, an aspect of man's achievement comparable to the gravity-defying technology of a Gothic cathedral.

1. Though some contemporary critics thought highly of him, e.g. Sir James Mackintosh.

87

88 Luxembourg *c.* 1825–34

Bodycolour with some pen and chalk on buff paper, $5\frac{3}{8} \times 7\frac{7}{16}$
(135×189)
Yale Center for British Art, Paul Mellon Collection, B1975.4.963,
Wilton 1019
Colour plate 18

A study connected with Turner's ambitious project of views along
the 'Rivers of Europe', of which only the Loire and Seine series
were published (in 1833–5).[1] Here Turner sees the fortified city as
an extension of the rocky structure of the earth itself: a view of
man's achievements in building that corresponds to Turner's
frequent treatment of human beings themselves, as an integral part
of the ancient organic fabric of nature. Notice that he does introduce figures even into this visionary sketch: a city is not a
desert, and is inseparable in conception from the idea of man and his
doings. Technically, this drawing is at the opposite pole from the
view of Carlisle (no. 87), a city view of quite a different type,
though executed on an equally small scale, and at about the same
date.

1. See Wilton 930–1051.

89 Fribourg 1841

Pencil, watercolour and some pen, $9\frac{3}{16} \times 13\frac{3}{16}$ (233 × 334)
TB CCCXXXV–12

Turner was strongly attracted to Fribourg, and made numerous
studies of it on a visit there in 1841.[1] He never made a finished
picture, either in oil or in watercolour, however, and his ideas
about the place are enshrined in drawings like this one. At Fribourg, an ancient city is surrounded by high cliffs; small buildings
clustered together seem about to be engulfed by towering waves of
rock: the picturesqueness and historical interest of man's work is
always to be found in direct confrontation with the stark force of
nature. Many of the Fribourg studies express this opposition in
their very technique: delicate outlines in pencil and pen contrast
with broad washes of colour that convey the mass of the precipitous cliffs and their scale, as the light moves intangibly over
their surfaces. Compare the study of an *Alpine Gorge* (no. 100).

1. In various sketchbooks, e.g. the *Fribourg* sketchbook, TB CCCXXXV, from which
this sheet comes. Turner made pencil sketches of the city in the *Lucerne and
Berne* sketchbook, TB CCCXXVIII, especially f. 17, a panoramic view identified by
Finberg as showing Lucerne, but undoubtedly a study at Fribourg.

89

90 Lausanne, Sunset (?)1841

Pencil and watercolour, $9\frac{7}{8} \times 14\frac{3}{8}$ (251 × 365)
TB CCCLXIV–350, BM 1975(265)
Colour plate 19

Whereas the two late views of Zurich (see no. 93) show the city in full daylight, this equally splendid vision of Lausanne sets off the skyline against a breathtaking sunset. As at Zurich, the thronging activities of the townspeople occupy the foreground of the view; this feature alone makes it very probable that Turner had it in mind to execute a finished watercolour based on this study; but there is no record that he did so. Nevertheless, much of the richness and fullness of content of a finished work is present here; and it is possible that he took the subject no further because he had compressed all that he wished to say into the sketch. The sense of excited expectancy that hangs over a crowd out of doors on a hot summer evening is marvellously suggested. Such summer promenades are among the commonest and oldest-established ways in which people signify their need to identify both with the natural world and with their fellow-men: hence the intensity of excitement that these informal rituals provoke. Here we feel that a form of communal sun-worship is taking place; every part of the drawing is pervaded with the warm brightness of the sunset light.

91 The Moselle Bridge, Coblenz *c.* 1842

Pencil and watercolour, $17\frac{7}{8} \times 23\frac{5}{16}$ (454 × 592)
Yale Center for British Art, Paul Mellon Collection, B1977.14.4651,
Wilton 1520
Colour plate 20

Turner made a number of airy studies of this subject,[1] though none of the others is as large as this one. A more elaborate sketch, worked up into a 'sample' for Thomas Griffiths (see no. 103),[2] gave rise in 1842 to a finished watercolour of the Moselle Bridge at Coblenz which Ruskin owned.[3] It is known today only through copies by William Ward, whom Ruskin gave special permission to reproduce it.[4] It shows the bustle of life on both banks of the river, with the city beyond to the right and the fortress of Ehrenbreitstein in the left distance. Here those elements are indicated only by a few allusive touches, and Turner concentrates on the fall of light on the old bridge. For comment on the series of large colour studies to which this sheet belongs see no. 101.

1. TB CCCLXIV–336 is another (BM 1975, no. 282).
2. TB CCCLXIV–286; BM 1975, no. 283.
3. Wilton 1530.
4. A letter to Ward of 17 May 1882 declares Ruskin 'happy in putting it in your power to produce a facsimile of Turner's mighty drawing of the *Coblentz*'. (*Works* XIII, p. 577–8.)

92 Heidelberg: looking west with a low sun 1844

Pencil and watercolour with some pen and red and yellow colour,
$9 \times 12\frac{7}{8}$ (228 × 327)
TB CCCLII–9, BM 1975(296)
Colour plate 21

Turner made three finished watercolours of Heidelberg in the last decade or so of his life;[1] they show the city from across the river Neckar, clothing the steep hill beyond the water with clusters of buildings and spires. The river bank in the foreground is crowded with figures. When he visited Heidelberg in 1844, during his last tour across Europe, he made a series of exquisitely luminous, sun-saturated studies[2] in which, more than in any other series of city views except those of Venice, the topography is dissolved in light. Forms are suggested by fragmentary outlines, touched in with a pen dipped in the colours of which the washes are pale tints. Turner was particularly alive to the historical associations of Heidelberg, one of the oldest university towns in Europe, and a city which had been severely handled in successive wars, bombarded, fired, and sacked on many occasions during the Thirty Years' War and the campaigns of Louis XIV. The castle, residence of the Electors Palatine of Bavaria, was ruined in a siege by the French in 1693; it was subsequently rebuilt but destroyed by a fire caused by lightning in 1764. When Turner painted a large picture of Heidelberg, probably in about 1845,[3] he showed it in a view roughly corresponding to that in this drawing. Its foreground is densely thronged with figures in historical dress – apparently that of the seventeenth century. After Turner's death this picture was engraved by T. A. Prior and published with the title *Heidelberg Castle in the Olden Time*.[4] It has been suggested that the festivities taking place are those celebrating the marriage of the Elector Frederick with Elizabeth of Bohemia, the 'Winter Queen', herself a figure doomed to a tragic life. The sunny optimism of the oil painting is therefore ironic. But the drawing, as it were, reverses the irony: Heidelberg, as it now is, rises serenely beautiful from its own tribulations, enduring and triumphing, while individuals like the Elector or his subjects cannot.

1. Wilton 1376, 1377, 1554, pls 245, 255.
2. In the *Heidelberg* sketchbook, TB CCCLII.
3. Butlin & Joll 440, where it is dated 1840–5. It seems likely, both on stylistic grounds and because of Turner's 1844 tour, that the picture was executed about the middle of the decade.
4. For the *Turner Gallery*, 1859–61 (R. 732).

T. A. Prior (1809–86), after J. M. W. Turner

93 Zurich 1854

Line engraving, first published state, india proof before all letters,
(R. 672), subject: $11\frac{13}{16} \times 19\frac{1}{8}$ (300 × 486); plate: $16\frac{5}{8} \times 23\frac{1}{4}$
(422 × 590)
Inscr., lower right: in pencil, with engraver's signature; outside plate: *Zurich*. Bears Printsellers' Association stamp.
Yale Center for British Art, Paul Mellon Collection, B1977.14.8077

Like no. 123, this engraving reproduces one of the ten Swiss views of 1845,[1] and presents a subject which Turner had treated earlier in the decade. The 1842 view of Zurich is in the British Museum;[2] the original of this print, now in the Kunsthaus, Zurich, is known as *Zurich: fête, early morning*. Just as the views of Lake Lucerne from Brunnen display an increasing sense of air and space, so the two Zurich subjects mark a progress towards greater aerial freedom, allied to a gradually loosening technique (see *Fluelen: morning*, no. 122). This is indeed Turner's most ecstatic account of urban life, a life that revolves round a vortex of glistening water, radiant sky and distant mountains. Man and his achievements – thronging crowds, toiling horses, the spires and towers of churches, the clustered roofs of city buildings – are all involved in the whirling career of the natural universe. The mood, however, is one of tranquillity; Turner contemplates the wonders of human life with the same reverent ecstasy as when meditating on the still mountains and unruffled lake before dawn. This is his final important statement about the place of man in the cosmos, and it is an affirmative, indeed a joyous one.

1. Wilton 1548.
2. Lloyd Bequest; Wilton 1533.

93

94 Chain of Alps from Grenoble to Chamonix *c.* 1811

Pen and brown ink and wash with scraping-out, $8\frac{1}{8} \times 11\frac{1}{8}$
(203 × 282)
TB CXVII–Y

If a single mountain is sublime, a whole chain of mountains is infinitely more so. Yet to present the vastness of such a concept with concrete vividness is an almost superhuman task. Turner here[1] puts his subject into a context that is natural and proper – he shows the mountains as they appear in the distance to the excited traveller, across an intervening plain of cultivated land, with people engaged in their daily activities. It is not the actual scale of the mountains, but their promise of grandeur, that thrills us in this setting, as all English tourists first saw them. Turner's handling of the splendid recession of the flat landscape in the foreground and middle distance seems to owe something to the technique of John Robert Cozens. He may indeed have had a specific composition of Cozens in mind – his *View from Mirabella in the Euganean Hills* (Victoria and Albert Museum).[2]

1. This is Turner's drawing for a plate of the *Liber Studiorum*, published in 1812.
2. C. F. Bell and T. Girtin, 'The Drawings and Sketches of John Robert Cozens', *Walpole Society* vol. XXIII, 1934–5, no. 216, pl. XVIIIb.

95 Crichton Castle with a rainbow *c.* 1818

Watercolour with traces of pencil, $6\frac{13}{16} \times 9\frac{7}{16}$ (173 × 239)
Yale Center for British Art, Paul Mellon Collection, B1977.14.6299, Wilton 1143

A study for one of Turner's illustrations to Sir Walter Scott's *Provincial Antiquities of Scotland*, a view of Crichton Castle engraved by George Cooke in 1819.[1] There is another colour-beginning for the same subject in the Turner Bequest.[2] The rainbow does not appear in the finished design.

1. Wilton 1059; R. 558.
2. TB CLXX– 4.

96 Grey Mountains (?)*c.* 1835

Grey wash with some yellowish-brown colour, $7\frac{1}{2} \times 11$ (190 × 280)
TB CCLXIII– 262

Both this sheet and no. 97 (*colour 22*) seem to belong to a group of related studies[1] of a mountainous subject unconnected with any finished work. All are very freely handled, and are evocative, not of any specific emotion such as awe or fear, as was the case with the earlier Alpine views, but of a mood of expansion and exaltation in the face of the ineffable and ungraspable reality of nature. It is difficult to date these studies; they may derive from one of Turner's journeys through Europe in the 1830s.

1. E.g. TB CCLXIII– 261, 263, 264, 265, 277, etc.

97 Among the mountains (?)*c.* 1835

Watercolour, $7\frac{1}{2} \times 10\frac{7}{8}$ (190 × 276)
TB CCLXIII– 258
Colour plate 22

A variant of the subject of no. 96.

94

95

96

98

98 A Mountain Valley (?) 1836

Pencil and watercolour, $9\frac{1}{2} \times 11\frac{11}{16}$ (241 × 297)
TB CCCLXIV−276

The handling of watercolour in this study is reminiscent of the technique of some of Turner's views in the Val d'Aosta of 1836,[1] and it may be a sheet that once belonged to a sketchbook in use during that tour. It seems to be a view of the Allée Blanche looking towards the Col de la Seigne, and if this is the case then it almost certainly does stem from that journey. It is in fact a return to the region of *The Battle of Fort Rock (colour 15)*, in which the agitated sublimities of that drawing are subdued into a massively calm vision of peace. Watercolour wash is applied very broadly to convey mass and the play of light, while certain areas have been worked over with the blunt end of a brush, a procedure that Turner seems to have favoured particularly on the 1836 tour.

1. See Wilton 1430−56.

99 The Glacier des Bossons (?) 1836

Watercolour over traces of pencil, with some scratching-out,
$8\frac{15}{16} \times 13$ (228 × 333)
British Museum, Sale Bequest 1915−3−13−49, Wilton 1440
Colour plate 23

Returning to the valley of Chamonix in later life, Turner again found himself impelled to give expression to its insistent diagonal slopes (see no. 24). Here the entire composition is resolved into a single sharply defined slanting line which separates two areas of contrasted tone. The drawing almost exactly mirrors the composition of Ruskin's monochrome study of the same glacier seen from the opposite side, now in the Ashmolean Museum,[1] though Ruskin's careful delineation of geological forms, woodland textures, and the cultivation and settlement of the valley produce a very different kind of work. Turner, for his part, suggests almost all of what Ruskin depicts with a few economical washes. The feathery delicacy of the touches used to render the huge mass of the mountainside vividly conveys the uplifted state of mind in which he contemplated it.

1. Repr. A. Wilton, *British Watercolours, 1750−1850*, pl. 140.

100

101

100 An Alpine Gorge 1836 or later

Pencil and watercolour, $9\frac{5}{8} \times 13\frac{3}{4}$ (243 × 347)
TB CCCLXIV—351

As in many of Turner's studies of the 1830s and 1840s, this sketch is the result of a coalescence of two distinct elements: the pencil drawing, which indicates here a stream and bridge, and some details of the rocks and plants nearby; and the watercolour wash, which describes independently the height and mass of the gorge, conveying simultaneously and in the same strokes such opposite things as a steep cliff and a dark shadow. As usual, Turner's observation is based on the particular, but it is expressed in terms that approach as near as possible to the universal and abstract. The study is 'about' sublime essences – height, steepness, danger – which are propounded with a minimum of specific reference. It is the virtuoso conciseness of Turner's mature technique that makes this possible.

101 Mountainous Landscape with a Lake c. 1842

Pencil and watercolour, $18\frac{1}{16} \times 23\frac{5}{16}$ (458 × 592)
Inscr. lower right: 2nd/Dark(?)
Yale Center for British Art, Paul Mellon Collection,
B1977.14.6300, Wilton 1521

At the end of his life Turner produced a few colour studies that return to the scale of the Welsh studies made in about 1799 (colour 4, 5 and 6). It is not always possible to relate them to finished drawings, but this subject has some features in common with the Pass of Faido of 1843 (no. 104) and perhaps with another sheet from the same series of large studies, that at Leeds known as The foot of the St Gothard.[1] The 'lake' referred to in the title is more likely to be a river. These studies are characterised by their unrestrained generalisation, in which much is conveyed with almost total absence of detailed description; in both scale and approach to subject-matter they come closest of all the watercolours to Turner's very late studies in oil. It is typical, however, that this broad treatment is combined with the rapid note of figures and some detailed effect, added in pencil outline. Another example of the same series of drawings is no. 91.

1. Wilton 1522.

102 The Via Mala 1843

Pencil and watercolour with scraping-out, $9\frac{5}{8} \times 12$ (244 × 305)
TB CCCLXIV—362, BM 1975(290)

Murray's Handbook describes the Via Mala as 'perhaps the most sublime and tremendous defile in Switzerland', and goes on to

102

103

speak of it in terms of the fully-fledged 'terrific'.[1] Turner did not visit it in 1802, and when he saw it on the Splügen route to Italy in 1842 and 1843, made few drawings of it. One rather perfunctory chalk drawing shows the narrow chasm;[2] a rough colour sketch depicts the entrance to it from Thusis;[3] this sheet is the only one that is identified as a view within the gorge, and it is not designed to convey any sense of the threatening narrowness of the chasm. Turner had by this date outgrown the eighteenth-century love of horror, and sought in Switzerland for breadth rather than constriction. The splendour of this study lies in its evocation of sunlight falling onto the steep cliffs of hard rock, and in its sense of imminent release from the confinement of the valley.

1. Murray, *Handbook for Travellers in Switzerland, Savoy and Piedmont*, 7th ed., London 1856, pp. 244–5.
2. TB LXXIV–C; see *Turner in Switzerland*, p. 105.
3. TB CCCXXXVI–19, repr., *Turner in Switzerland*, p. 104.

103 **The Pass of Faido: study 1842 or 1843**

Pencil and watercolour with some pen, $11\frac{3}{16} \times 9$ (285 × 228)
Inscr. verso: *Pass Piolano Tessin No. 14*
TB CCCLXIV–209

A loose sheet in the Turner Bequest, from a dismembered sketchbook used during the tour of either 1842 or 1843, on both of which Turner crossed the Pass of St Gothard, following the river Tessin (Ticino) down towards the Italian lakes. The study was presented to Turner's agent, Thomas Griffith, as a 'sample' to indicate to clients the kind of subject that he might treat for them.[1] The watercolour that he worked up from it is no. 104. As in the case of *Goldau* (*colour 25* and *26*), the differences between study and finished drawing are considerable, but a great part of the intention of the final work is already present in this sketch of Faido.

1. See Ruskin, *Works* XIII, pp. 477–84.

104 The Pass of Faido 1843

Watercolour with scraping-out over pencil, 13¾ × 18½
(305 × 470)
Collection of Mr and Mrs Eugene V. Thaw, New York,
Wilton 1538
Colour plate 24

The study on which Turner based this watercolour is no. 103.
While it was not unusual for him to make such a sketch, the
working up of the idea into a finished watercolour results in a most
unexpected subject. In general, the late Swiss views emphasise the
expansive qualities of the Swiss landscape, taking the eye through
immense vistas of light and space.[1] Here a sense of enclosure is the
dominant note, a claustrophobic obsession with encircling cliffs
that marks a return to the mood of the early Swiss subjects, or of
Gordale Scar (no. 30). In his new relationship with the mountains,
established after a lifetime of technical experiment, and affirming
the liberation of spirit that they conferred upon him, he felt
perhaps that one last full-scale tribute should be paid to the
'terrific' sublime of his youth. In the event he produced two
important essays in this mode, the *Faido* and the *Goldau (colour 24*
and *25*) which strike the most sombre note of all the late watercolours. But such is the metamorphosis of his vision by this date
that the threatening rocks and roaring waters take on a new and
more splendid significance: an exhilarating diversity and excitement, expressed in the swirling lines of the composition, carries us
beyond the Burkean consideration of fear or the Kantian recollection of security to a complete and ecstatic identification with the
elemental forces of nature, which are presented here raw and
unsoftened, yet with a vigorous and compelling life of their own. It
is not by accident that Turner, for once, introduces no figures into
the foreground of the design: if *Regulus* (no. 54) brings the onlooker
face to face with the scorching sun, this watercolour introduces us
without intermediary to the wildness of the mountains: it is we
who breathe the strong air and feel the spray on our face.[2] As
Ruskin observed,[3] the quite unobtrusive suggestion of a carriage
turning the corner on the rocky road is a sufficiently concrete touch
to remind us that it is we who travel that way, and that the
experience is our own. This emphatically personal inference is
supported by Turner's own uncharacteristic comment that 'he
liked the drawing'.[4]

Despite the expressive transformations which Turner wrought
upon his subject-matter here, and which Ruskin analyses at length
in *Modern Painters*, it was still possible for the critic to praise the
work for its truth to nature; he noted that 'The warm colour given
to the rocks is exactly right; they are gneiss, with decomposing
garnets, giving them the brightest hues of red and yellow ochre.'
Ruskin's editors add that he 'brought home an actual specimen of
the rock, which he used to be fond of showing to visitors, in order
that they might compare it with the drawing in his collection.'[5]

1. Ruskin's 'Mountain Glory' as opposed to 'Mountain Gloom'; see *Works*, IV,
pp. 418ff.
2. See the comments of John Tracy Atkyns, p. 26.
3. Ruskin, *Works*, VI, p. 37 ff.
4. Ruskin, *ibid.*
5. Ruskin, *Works*, XIII, p. 207 and note.

105 Goldau with the Lake of Zug in the distance 1841–2

Pencil and watercolour with some pen, 9 × 11⅜ (228 × 288)
Inscr. verso: *Goldau – Rigi – and the Lake of Zug*
TB CCCLXIV–281
Colour plate 25

Like no. 103 this is one of the 'sample' studies presented by Turner
to Thomas Griffiths to enable clients to form some idea of the
subjects they might order from him. Ruskin was the patron who
selected this scene, and even he must have been somewhat sur-
prised by the extraordinary drawing that Turner produced for him
(no. 106). It differs very considerably from the sketch, in which he
saw a direct statement of recognisable weather conditions: 'after
getting very wet at Schwyz, [we] are rewarded by seeing the
clouds break as we reach the ridge of Goldau, and reveal the Lake of
Zug under a golden sky.'[1] Turner's free interpretation of the scene
is already, however, a statement of great grandeur, though it
completely lacks the resonant overtones of the final watercolour.

1. Ruskin, *Works*, XIII, pp. 201–2.

106 Goldau 1843

Watercolour with scraping-out, 12 × 18½ (305 × 470)
Private Collection, U.S.A., Wilton 1537
Colour plate 26

One of the six Swiss drawings of 1843, this subject is derived from a
study in the Turner Bequest (no. 105). The tragic connotations of
this brilliant sunset sky have been compared to those of the sky in
the *Slavers* of 1840 (FIG. XVI). Turner has chosen to commemorate
here an Alpine catastrophe of 1806, when the mountain of the
Rossberg buried the village of Goldau, killing 457 people.[1] A
comparison with the *Avalanche in the Grisons* of 1810 points up the
contrast between Turner's response to such 'terrific' subjects then
and now. Whereas in the early part of his career he sought to
express the Burkean emotion of fear by presenting with inescapable
vividness a scene of natural violence actually taking place, he now
transcends the horror of the subject to pour out a hymn of
exaltation in the ultimate identification of man with the earth to
which he belongs. He frequently depicted man as a kind of organic
element in the landscape (see no. 88), but in no other work does he
present us so forcibly with the very fact of burial, of the return of
the body to the earth: under these huge boulders lie the people
of Goldau, transformed into eternal participants in the cycle of
nature. This is a vision that takes us a stage further than the heaped
corpses on the battlefield of Waterloo (no. 71): their transmutation
has not yet begun; here, after nearly forty years, the tragedy has
become cause for a titanic and primeval rejoicing. There could be
no act of devotion to nature more complete, absorbed and dedicated than that of fishing, Turner's favourite relaxation; hence
the quiet, barely defined figures who passively accept fate as they
wait among the boulders for fish to rise in the lake that reflects the
sunset.

1. Graphic details of the disaster are supplied in Murray, *op. cit.*, pp. 43–7.

107

108

107 **Lake Llanberis with Dolbadern Castle** *c.* 1799

Pencil and watercolour, $21\frac{3}{4} \times 29\frac{15}{16}$ (553×761)
Inscr. lower right: 53
TB LXX–X, BM 1975(20)

Both Dolbadern Castle and Lake Llanberis were to prove recurrent inspirations to Turner in the course of his career. The castle was the subject of his Diploma picture, presented to the Royal Academy on his election as Academician in 1802 (see p. 40), and the lake provided one of the most dramatic of the *England and Wales* views of the early 1830s. Another early study of the castle, from above, is *colour 5*. In this expansive sheet Turner establishes one of the quintessential features of lake scenery: the sense of great space bounded by clearly defined masses of land, the surface of the water taking the eye easily and rapidly over a great distance. As Gilpin realised, the clarity with which the space is enclosed gives us a scale by which to measure its extent, while the uniformity of the still water creates a sense of vastness. Here, tranquillity actually contributes to the sublime mood, and Turner was to repeat the formula innumerable times during his life.

J. M. W. Turner and Charles Turner, after J. M. W. Turner

108 **Lake of Thun, Swiss** (*Liber Studiorum*) 1808

Etching and mezzotint, printed in brown ink, first published state (R. 15), subject: $7\frac{3}{16} \times 10\frac{5}{16}$ (182×262); plate: $8\frac{1}{4} \times 11\frac{3}{8}$ (209×290)
Inscr. above: *Proof.* and *M*; below: *Drawn & Etchd by J.M.W. Turner Esq*. *R.A.P.P.* and *Engraved by C. Turner*; with title, and lower left: *Proof*; bottom: *London Published June 10.1808 by C. Turner Nº 50 Warren Street Fitzroy Square.*
Yale Center for British Art, Paul Mellon Collection, B1977.14.8117

Turner made a finished watercolour of this subject,[1] as well as his usual sepia drawing for the plate.[2] As Ruskin noticed, he retained in all his designs 'the confusion of packages on the shore, by which he had been startled on landing at Neuhaus'.[3] The sudden electric storms that descend on central Swiss lakes were to occupy him rarely in his later visits; though he made one splendid study of a steamer beating through a thundercloud on Lake Lucerne in about 1841 (no 113).

1. Wilton 373, pl. 96.
2. TB CXVI–R.
3. Ruskin, *Works*, XXI, p. 221.

109 **Simmer Lake, near Askrigg** *c.* 1818

Watercolour with scratching-out, $11\frac{5}{16} \times 16\frac{1}{4}$ (287×412)
Inscr. lower right: *I M W Turner RA 4*(?)
British Museum, Salting Bequest, 1910–2–12–280, Wilton 571
Colour plate 27

Turner's sense of the calm splendour of a windless lake here finds full mature expression. He was later to vary and develop the ideas presented here, but he continued to use compositions like this one all his life; compare *Ullswater* (no. 111) and *The Lake of Uri from Brunnen* (no. 121). The elements of foreground, lake and far hills arranged in strips across the sheet provide one of Turner's most stable designs, which is given intensity by the burst of light in the sky above, a radiant benediction on the humble activities that are precisely catalogued along the lake shore, and on its surface. The

numeral '4' which appears after Turner's signature is hard to explain. The drawing belongs to the series of illustrations to Dr Whitaker's *History of Richmondshire* which appeared in 1819–23, with twenty plates engraved after Turner (see nos 34–6). There is no apparent reason to associate the numeral with the project.

James Tibbitts Willmore (1800–63), after J. M. W. Turner

110 **Llanberis Lake, Wales** (*England and Wales*) 1834

Engraving, third state (R. 279), subject: $6\frac{1}{2} \times 9\frac{9}{16}$ (164×243); plate: $9\frac{15}{16} \times 12\frac{7}{16}$ (253×316)
Inscr. below: with names of artist and engraver, and title (as *Llanberis Lake*); lower right: *Printed by Mc Queen*; bottom: *London, Published 1834, by Moon, Boys & Graves, 6, Pall Mall.*
Yale Center for British Art, Paul Mellon Collection, B1977.14.13398

This is a return to the subject of no. 107; like others of the *England and Wales* series, it presents its material more comprehensively than before, forging a mass of information about the landscape into coherence by means of sweeping structural lines: as in the *Llanthony Abbey* (no. 11) the very air itself seems to be broken into vast chunks, apparently by beams of sunlight which create overlapping planes of light and dark against which the topography is disposed in counterpoint. These beams of light fall almost horizontally across the design, giving it a stability that is otherwise absent: while Turner's lake views are usually of emphatic placidity, this is a scene in which the tranquil surface of the water is contrasted with the surging rhythms of the mountains and windblown trees.[1]

1. The original watercolour, in the National Galleries of Scotland, is Wilton 855; Shanes 64.

James Tibbitts Willmore (1800–63), after J. M. W. Turner

111 **Ullswater, Cumberland** (*England and Wales*) 1835

Engraving, printed on india paper, first published state (R. 284), subject: $6\frac{7}{16} \times 9\frac{9}{16}$ (164×243); plate: $8\frac{7}{8} \times 11\frac{5}{8}$ (225×295)
Yale Center for British Art, Paul Mellon Collection, B1977.14.7079

The broad calm of Turner's late lake subjects is here established.[1] Gilpin expatiates at length on the view of Ullswater, 'the largest lake in this country, except Windermere; being eight miles long; and about two broad in the widest part; tho, in general, it rarely exceeds a mile in breadth . . . [descending from Matterdale] the whole scene of the lake opened before us; and such a scene, as almost drew from us the apostrophe of the inraptured bard,
    Visions of glory, spare my aching sight!
    Among all the *visions* of this inchanting country, we had seen nothing so beautifully sublime, so correctly picturesque as this. – . . . "The effect of the *sublime*, Mr Burke informs us, is *astonishment*; and the effect of beauty, is pleasure: but when the two ingredients mix, the effect, he says, is in a good measure destroyed in both . . ." This refined reasoning does not seem intirely grounded on experience. – I do not remember any scene in which beauty and sublimity, according to my ideas, are more blended than in this: and tho Mr Burke's ideas of beauty are perhaps more exceptionable, than his ideas of the sublime; yet it happens, that most of the qualities, which he predicates of both, unite also in this scene . . .'[2]

1. The original watercolour, in an English private collection, is Wilton 860; Shanes 68.
2. Gilpin, 1786, vol. II, pp. 50–4. The 'bard' is Gray's (III l, i).

110△ ▽III

112

112 Constance 1841

Watercolour, $9\frac{5}{8} \times 12\frac{3}{16}$ (244 × 305)
TB CCCLXIV–288, BM 1975(281)

This subject exemplifies the openness of Turner's late continental drawings; its simple horizontal stress and its spaciousness perhaps reflect a deliberate search on Turner's part for the conditions that he had found in Venice in 1840. There, he had made a very large number of such studies in which the open expanse of the Bacino di S. Marco or the Lagoon plays an important part.[1] This view of Constance was submitted to Turner's agent, Thomas Griffith, at the end of 1841 and used as the basis of a finished watercolour,[2] one of the set of ten of 1842.

1. TB CCCXV, CCCXVI, CCCXVII, CCCXVIII. See RA 1947, pp. 154, 155 and BM 1975 nos 216–60.
2. Wilton 1531.

113 Steamboat in a storm (?)1841

Watercolour, $9\frac{1}{4} \times 11\frac{3}{8}$ (232 × 289)
Yale Center for British Art, Paul Mellon Collection,
B1977.14.4717, Wilton 1484

Although this drawing has not been identified as a lake scene, it corresponds closely in its colour and treatment to sheets from a sketchbook of 1841 in which Turner made studies on the Lake of Lucerne. These are now scattered in various collections: one shows *The first steamer on the Lake*,[1] another very atmospheric sheet the *Seelisberg by moonlight*;[2] the subject-matter of this drawing is therefore by no means out of place. Although the shores of the lake are not very apparent, there seems to be an indication of the twin-spired cathedral of Lucerne at the extreme left of the drawing; this would account for the absence of high hills, since the lake shore is comparatively flat at its northern (Lucerne) end. The flash of lightning indicated by a single scratch, partially covered by touches of watercolour, is one of Turner's boldest technical strokes. For an earlier representation of a Swiss lake storm see no. 108. See comments on the idea of sudden storm disturbing a calm sea, p. 100.

1. Wilton 1482.
2. Wilton 1479.

114 The Bay of Uri from Brunnen (?)1841

Watercolour over pencil, $9\frac{5}{8} \times 11\frac{11}{16}$ (244 × 298)
TB CCCLXIV–342

Possibly a sheet from the same dismembered sketchbook as no. 115. For further comment on these studies of Lake Lucerne, see no. 116.

113

114

115 The Bay of Uri from Brunnen 1841

Watercolour, $9\frac{7}{16} \times 11\frac{9}{16}$ (240 × 294)
TB CCCLXIV–354
Colour plate 28

This is the study from which no. 116 (*colour 29*) was elaborated. For further comment on the subject-matter of the drawing, see the note to that work.

116 Lake Lucerne: the Bay of Uri from above Brunnen 1842

Watercolour over pencil, $11\frac{1}{2} \times 18$ (292 × 457)
Private Collection, U.S.A, Wilton 1526
Colour plate 29

The view over Lake Lucerne from above Brunnen was treated more often by Turner than any other Lucerne subject. He made numerous pencil and colour studies of it (see nos 114 and *colour 28*), and at least four finished watercolours between 1841 and 1845.[1] No. 123 is a print from one of the last of these to be completed, and no. 122 a view of the bay of Uri from the southern end. The view from Brunnen includes Grütli, the spot on the opposite shore of the lake where, in 1307, three men from Schwyz, Unterwalden and Uri met to swear fidelity to the idea of liberation from the oppression of the Hapsburg empire. But it is unlikely that Turner's fondness for the place had much to do with this historical association – the scenery itself corresponds precisely to the preoccupations that distinguish nearly all his late work. 'Opposite Brunnen, the lake of the Four Cantons changes at once its direction and its character. Along the bay of Uri . . . it stretches nearly N. and S. Its borders are perpendicular, and almost uninterrupted precipices; the basements and buttresses of colossal mountains, higher than any of those which overlook the other branches of the lake; and their snowy summits peer down from above the clouds, or through the gullies in their sides, upon the dark gulf below. . . On turning the corner of the promontory of Treib, a singular rock, called *Wytenstein*, rising like an obelisk out of the water, is passed, and the bay of Uri, in all its stupendous grandeur, bursts into view.'[2] Murray's handbook quotes Sir James Mackintosh as saying: 'The vast mountains rising on every side and closing at the end, with their rich clothing of wood, the sweet spots of verdant pasture scattered at their feet, and sometimes on their breast, and the expanse of water, unbroken by islands and almost undisturbed by any signs of living men, make an impression which it would be foolish to attempt to convey by words.'[3] The ineffability of the landscape is a quality that is, by contrast, fully conveyed by Turner's repeated essays in rendering it. This series of watercolours serves to remind us that the sublime was for Turner by no means an inevitably literary matter. It was always first and foremost a visual mode, capable of expressing itself without external references or allusion.

1. Wilton 1526, 1527, 1543, 1547.
2. Murray, *op. cit.*, p. 57.
3. *Memoirs of the Life of Sir James Mackintosh*, ed. Robert James Mackintosh, 2 vols, London, 1836, Vol. II, p. 307.

117 The Lake of Geneva with the Dent d'Oche, from Lausanne: a funeral 1841

Pencil and watercolour, $9\frac{1}{4} \times 13\frac{1}{8}$ (235 × 334)
TB CCCXXXIV–2
Colour plate 30

118

118   The Lake of Geneva with the Dent d'Oche, from
       above Lausanne 1841

   Black chalk and watercolour, $9\frac{1}{4} \times 13\frac{1}{8}$ (235 × 334)
   TB CCCXXXIV–7

119   The Lake of Geneva with the Dent d'Oche, from
       Lausanne 1841

   Pencil and watercolour, $9\frac{1}{4} \times 13\frac{1}{8}$ (235 × 334)
   TB CCCXXXIV–10
   Colour plate 31

These are sheets from the *Lausanne* sketchbook, which probably dates from Turner's stay there in 1841. His fascination with Lake Geneva was hardly less marked than his love of Lake Lucerne, and just as there exist long sequences of drawings recording his meditations on the Rigi,[1] or at Brunnen (see no. 116), so there are an equally impressive group of studies made looking across to the mountains of France from Lausanne. These and nos 120 and 121 are five drawings of that view. They were not necessarily all done at the same time, but they all belong to the same profound and tranquil train of thought. Unlike Lake Lucerne, Lake Geneva does not seem ever to have been stormy for Turner: he saw it always – as indeed it frequently is – motionless, vast, stretching its length beyond reach of the eye in either direction, bounded, according to the climatic conditions of the moment, sometimes by haze, sometimes by the peaks of the Dent d'Oche and the Cornettes. Even here, the occupations of men and women have a place in his contemplations: a funeral passes, escorted by a division of soldiers (*colour 30*); or people tend the vines that grow along the terraces overhanging the lake (*colour 32*). Often, a complete panorama of the city is included in the prospect (no. 118). The mind wanders, entirely free of material trammellings, in a landscape immense and immutable, powerful yet benign, eternally energetic yet utterly at rest.

1. For reproductions of several Rigi subjects see *Turner in Switzerland*, pp. 86–91, 94–5.

120   The Lake of Geneva with the Dent d'Oche:
       tending the vines 1841

   Watercolour, $9 \times 11\frac{7}{16}$ (228 × 291)
   TB CCCXXXII–34, BM 1975(276)
   Colour plate 32

Finberg identified this drawing, a leaf from the *Fribourg, Lausanne and Geneva* sketchbook, as a view of Mont Pilatus, opposite Lucerne,[1] but there seems little reason to doubt that it is in fact another of the series of studies looking out across the Lake of Geneva towards the Savoy Alps. For comment on this group, see nos 117–19.

1. This identification was followed in the British Museum 1975 catalogue.

121   The Lake of Geneva with the Dent d'Oche from
       above Lausanne (?)1841

   Watercolour over pencil, $9 \times 12\frac{3}{4}$ (230 × 325)
   TB CCCLXIV–274

No longer associated with any identified sketchbook, this loose sheet probably belongs to the same year as the other drawings of this view. But it is executed in a coarser technique than the rest, using stippling or hatching to suggest the thickening of light and air along the farther shore of the lake. Although such devices are common among the colour studies of the 1840s, the handling here is reminiscent of some of Turner's last finished watercolours,[1] and it is possible that this drawing belongs to the second half of the decade. For further comment see nos 117–119.

1. Wilton 1553–60.

122   Fluelen: morning (looking towards the lake) 1845

   Watercolour with scraping-out, $11\frac{3}{4} \times 18\frac{15}{16}$ (299 × 481)
   Engr: by John Ruskin (outline etching), published in *Works*, XIII, pl. XXIV
   Yale Center for British Art, Paul Mellon Collection, B1977.14.1715, Wilton 1541

Like the original of no. 123, this is a drawing from the set of ten Swiss views made in 1845. It is based on a study in the Turner Bequest.[1] As in other watercolours of this late date, Turner's distortions of scale are violent. The proportion of the little town of Fluelen to its overhanging cliff is much diminished: as in no. 123 the elements of the subject are flung apart by the expansive space between them so that the whole scene seems, as Ruskin put it, 'fading away into a mere dream of departing light'. Ruskin, who saw these late drawings as the valedictions of a pessimist, prophesied that with the 'cliff tunnelled now for the railway' the 'story of the "Sacred Lake, withdrawn among the hills"' would end.[2] Turner's drawing, for him, signals the end of Lake Lucerne, of beauty, of nature, of life; but that is surely not the spirit in which Turner revisited these favourite places so often in his late years. His drawings are certainly those of an old man, experienced, and perhaps saddened by much of life; but they affirm the continuance, not the demise of nature. Ruskin's attitude to the railway was wholly negative – so much so that he never wrote of Turner's masterpiece, *Rain, Steam and Speed*,[3] in all his copious effusions on his art; and when asked why Turner painted it, he replied that it was 'to show what he could do with so ugly a subject'.[4] Much of the pessimism with which Turner is credited is Ruskin's own, attributed by him to the artist because it was impossible for Ruskin to conceive of an alternative view of the world.

1. TB CCCLXIV–282; See Wilton 1540–9.
2. Ruskin's comments are in his 'Notes on his own drawings by Turner', *Works*, XIII, pp. 459–60.
3. Butlin & Joll 409.
4. *Works*, XXXV, p. 601, note.

       Robert Wallis (1794–1878), after J. M. W. Turner

123   Lake of Lucerne 1854

   Line engraving, india proof, second state (R. 671), subject: $11\frac{1}{2} \times 18\frac{5}{8}$ (292 × 473); plate: $16\frac{1}{2} \times 22\frac{13}{16}$ (420 × 580)
   Inscr. below: with names of artist and engraver; centre: *London, Published May 27th 1854: by Henry Graves & Compy. Printsellers in Ordinary to her Majesty and H.R.H. Prince Albert 6 Pall Mall.*; in pencil, outside plate-mark, probably in the engraver's hand: *Lucerne*; bears Printsellers' Association stamp.
   Yale Center for British Art, Paul Mellon Collection, B1977.14.8076

CCCLXIV 274

121△   ▽122

123

When published, this plate bore a dedication to B. G. Windus, the
first owner of the watercolour from which it is taken.[1] The original
drawing is unfortunately severely faded, and this print probably
conveys more accurately now the artist's intentions. Both this, the
Zurich (no. 93) and the watercolour no. 121 are subjects from the
1845 set of ten Swiss views. In all three, Turner revisits familiar
scenes to dilate more expansively than ever on a favourite theme.
The vast spaces of the Lake of Lucerne had attracted him as early as
1802, and a large watercolour made shortly after that first Swiss
tour[2] celebrates the grandeur of the high cliffs that rise from the
lake; their confining and constricting force is strongly presented
there, while in the late views it is the space between the mountains
that becomes the dominant element. In this subject, the viewpoint
is higher than before, and the landscape opened up so that the eye
travels deep into its recesses, swooping and darting across the
serene panorama like the moving sunbeams themselves. Turner
seems to be confirming the observation of another traveller, that
the Lucerne ferry, half-way across the lake, afforded 'a singular and
most beautiful view, composed of the mere elements of landscape –
of water combined with mountains melting into air'.[3]

1. Wilton 1547.
2. Wilton 378.
3. Sir James Mackintosh, *op. cit.*, p. 306.

SELECT BIBLIOGRAPHY

Addison, Joseph, 'On the Pleasures of the Imagination', *Spectator*, London, 21 June 1711 – 3 July 1712.

Alison, Archibald, *Essays on the Nature and Principles of Taste*, 2 vols, Edinburgh 1811.

Allen, Thomas, *A New and Complete History of the County of York*, 3rd ed., London 1831.

Barbier, C. P., *William Gilpin: his drawing, teaching and theory of the Picturesque*, Oxford 1963.

Blunt, Anthony, *Nicolas Poussin*, 2 vols, New York 1969.

Burke, Edmund, *An Enquiry into the Origin of our Ideas of the Sublime and Beautiful*, London 1757, 2nd ed., 1759. New ed. with introduction and notes by James T. Boulton, Notre Dame, Ind. 1958.

Butlin, Martin, and Joll, Evelyn, *The Paintings of J. M. W. Turner*, 2 vols, London 1977.

Diderot, Denis, *Oeuvres Esthétiques*, ed. Paul Vernière, Paris 1959.

Dobai, Johannes, *Die Kunstliteratur des Klassizismus und der Romantik in England*, 2 vols, Berne 1974, 1975.

Du Bos, Abbé Jean Baptiste, *Reflexions Critiques sur la Poésie et sur la Peinture*, 1719.

Finberg, A. J., *A Complete Inventory of the Drawings of the Turner Bequest*, 2 vols, London 1909.

Finberg, A. J., *Life of J.M.W. Turner*, 2nd ed., London 1961.

Finberg, A. J., *Turner's Sketches and Drawings*, 1910, new ed., New York 1968.

Finley, Gerald, 'The Genesis of Turner's "Landscape Sublime",' *Zeitschrift für Kunstgeschichte*, 42, 1979, pp. 141–65.

Friden, G., *James Fenimore Cooper and Ossian*, Cambridge 1949.

Gage, John, *Colour in Turner, Poetry and Truth*, London 1969.

Gage, John, 'Turner and the Picturesque', *Burlington Magazine*, CVII, January 1965, pp. 16–26.

Gilpin, William, *Observations relative Chiefly to Picturesque Beauty, Made in the Year 1772, on several parts of England; particularly the Mountains, and Lakes of Cumberland and Westmorland*, 2 vols, London 1786.

Hagstrum, Jean H., *The Sister Arts*, Chicago 1958.

Hamburg, Kunsthalle, *Ossian und die Kunst um 1800*, exhibition catalogue 1974.

Hawes, Louis, *Constable's Stonehenge*, Victoria & Albert Museum, London 1975.

Hipple, Walter, *The Beautiful, the Sublime, and the Picturesque in Eighteenth-Century British Aesthetic Theory*, Carbondale, Ill. 1957.

Hume, David, *Treatise of Human Nature*, 1739, ed. L. A. Selby-Bigge, Oxford 1888.

Kant, Immanuel, *Critique of Judgement (Kritik der Urteilskraft*, Berlin 1790), trans. J. H. Bernard, London 1931.

Klingender, Francis D., *Art and the Industrial Revolution*, 1947, new ed. [London] 1968.

Knight, Richard Payne, *An Analytical Inquiry into the Principles of Taste*, London 1805.

Lindsay, Jack, *J.M.W. Turner, His Life and Work, A Critical Biography*, London 1966.

London, Royal Academy, *J.M.W. Turner Bicentenary Exhibition*, catalogue by Martin Butlin, Andrew Wilton and John Gage, 1974–5.

McCarthy, J. I., ' "The Bard" of Thomas Grey: Its Composition and its use by painters', National Library of Wales, *Journal* XIV, 1, 1965, pp. 105–13.

Mackintosh, Robert James, ed., *Memoirs of the Life of Sir James Mackintosh*, 2 vols, London 1836.

Manwaring, Elizabeth Wheeler, *Italian Landscape in 18th Century England; a Study chiefly of the influence of Claude Lorrain and Salvator Rosa on English Taste, 1700–1800*, London 1925, new ed. 1965.

Monk, Samuel, *The Sublime*, London 1935.

Nicolson, Benedict, *Joseph Wright of Derby*, 2 vols, London 1968.

Rawlinson, W. G., *Turner's Liber Studiorum*, 2nd ed., London 1906.

Rawlinson, W. G., *The Engraved Work of J.M.W. Turner, R.A.*, 2 vols, London 1903, 1913.

Reynolds, Joshua, *Discourses on Art*, ed. R. R. Wark, Yale 1975.

The Works of Jonathan Richardson, London 1792.

Roget, J. L. and Pye, J., *Notes and Memoranda respecting the Liber Studiorum of J.M.W. Turner*, London 1879.

Ruskin, John, *Works* (Library Edition), ed. Sir E. T. Cook and A. Wedderburn, 39 vols, London 1903–12.

Russell, John and Wilton, Andrew, *Turner in Switzerland*, Zurich 1976.

Russell, Ronald, *Guide to British Topographical Prints*, London 1979.

Shanes, Eric, *Turner's Picturesque Views in England and Wales*, London 1979.

Smith, William, *Dionysius Longinus on the Sublime, Translated from the Greek with Notes and Observations*, London 1751.

Sotheby, William, *A Tour through Wales, Sonnets, Odes, and other Poems*, London 1794.

Stewart, Dugald, *Philosophical Essays*, 3rd ed., Edinburgh 1818.

Thornbury, Walter, *The Life and Correspondence of J.M.W. Turner, RA*, rev. ed., London 1877.

Usher, James, *Clio; or, a Discourse on Taste. Addressed to a Young Lady*, London, 1769.

Warner, Richard, *A Walk through Wales in August 1797*, London 1798.

Whitaker, T. D., *An History of Richmondshire in the North Riding of the County of York*, 2 vols, London, 1823.

White, Christopher, *English Landscape 1630–1850*, New Haven 1977.

Wilton, Andrew, *Turner in the British Museum*, London 1975.

Wilton, Andrew, *British Watercolours, 1750–1850*, Oxford 1977.

Wilton, Andrew, *J.M.W. Turner: His Art and Life*, New York 1979.

Wilton, Andrew, *William Pars, Journey through the Alps*, Zurich 1979.

Wlecke, Albert O., *Wordsworth and the Sublime*, Berkeley 1973.

Woodbridge, Kenneth, *Landscape and Antiquity: Aspects of English Culture at Stourhead, 1718–1838*, 1970.

Wright, Thomas, *Life of Richard Wilson, R.A.*, London 1824.

Ziff, Jerrold, 'Turner and Poussin', *Burlington Magazine*, CV, 1963, pp. 215–21.

Ziff, Jerrold, ' "Backgrounds, Introduction of Architecture and Landscape": A Lecture by J.M.W. Turner', *Journal of the Warburg and Courtauld Institutes*, XXVI, 1963, pp. 124–47.

CONCORDANCE

Numbers in the right-hand columns are those of catalogue entries.

INDEX

Figures in roman refer to page numbers, figures in brackets to note numbers and figures in italics to catalogue numbers.

THE COMPLETE GUIDE TO
KEEPING YOUR
HOUSEPLANTS
ALIVE AND THRIVING

Everything
You Need to Know
Explained Simply

Sandy Baker

THE COMPLETE GUIDE TO KEEPING YOUR HOUSEPLANTS ALIVE AND THRIVING: EVERYTHING YOU NEED TO KNOW EXPLAINED SIMPLY

Library of Congress Cataloging-in-Publication Data

Baker, Sandy Ann, 1976-
  The complete guide to keeping your houseplants alive and thriving : everything you need to know explained simply / by Sandy Baker.
       p. cm.
  Includes bibliographical references and index.
  ISBN-13: 978-1-60138-349-5 (alk. paper)
  ISBN-10: 1-60138-349-5 (alk. paper)
  1. House plants. 2. Indoor gardening. I. Title.
  SB419.B127 2011
  635.9'65--dc22
                            2011014127

Printed in the United States

PROJECT MANAGER: Amy Moczynski
INTERIOR LAYOUT: Antoinette D'Amore • addesign@videotron.ca
PROOFREADER: C&P Marse • bluemoon6749@bellsouth.net
COVER DESIGN: Meg Buchner • meg@megbuchner.com
BACK COVER DESIGN: Jackie Miller • millerjackiej@gmail.com

Printed on Recycled Paper

A few years back we lost our beloved pet dog Bear, who was not only our best and dearest friend but also the "Vice President of Sunshine" here at Atlantic Publishing. He did not receive a salary but worked tirelessly 24 hours a day to please his parents.

Bear was a rescue dog who turned around and showered myself, my wife, Sherri, his grandparents Jean, Bob, and Nancy, and every person and animal he met (well, maybe not rabbits) with friendship and love. He made a lot of people smile every day.

We wanted you to know a portion of the profits of this book will be donated in Bear's memory to local animal shelters, parks, conservation organizations, and other individuals and nonprofit organizations in need of assistance.

– *Douglas & Sherri Brown*

PS: We have since adopted two more rescue dogs: first Scout, and the following year, Ginger. They were both mixed golden retrievers who needed a home.

Want to help animals and the world? Here are a dozen easy suggestions you and your family can implement today:

- *Adopt and rescue a pet from a local shelter.*
- *Support local and no-kill animal shelters.*
- *Plant a tree to honor someone you love.*
- *Be a developer — put up some birdhouses.*
- *Buy live, potted Christmas trees and replant them.*
- *Make sure you spend time with your animals each day.*
- *Save natural resources by recycling and buying recycled products.*
- *Drink tap water, or filter your own water at home.*
- *Whenever possible, limit your use of or do not use pesticides.*
- *If you eat seafood, make sustainable choices.*
- *Support your local farmers market.*
- *Get outside. Visit a park, volunteer, walk your dog, or ride your bike.*

Five years ago, Atlantic Publishing signed the Green Press Initiative. These guidelines promote environmentally friendly practices, such as using recycled stock and vegetable-based inks, avoiding waste, choosing energy-efficient resources, and promoting a no-pulping policy. We now use 100-percent recycled stock on all our books. The results: in one year, switching to post-consumer recycled stock saved 24 mature trees, 5,000 gallons of water, the equivalent of the total energy used for one home in a year, and the equivalent of the greenhouse gases from one car driven for a year.

Dedication

I dedicate this book to all of those struggling to bring plant life into their homes, and to my husband and family for their continued support.

Acknowledgement

Thank you to my editor, Amy Moczynski, for her continued patience and to Douglas Brown and the others at Atlantic Publishing for this opportunity.

Table of Contents

Chapter 7: Growing Plants Chemical Free   203

Introduction

Houseplants evolved more than 200 years ago in England when plant cultivators and traders needed to keep their blossomed beauties indoors. Many of the plants they cultivated were uprooted from warmer, tropical climates, and these new plant specimens needed places to stay warm during northern Europe's winters, or they would not survive. By the 1800s, houses with glass windows became increasingly and permanently popular, which resulted in houseplants being placed in the windowsills of modern European homes. As the practice grew, houseplants became a symbol of middle-class refinement, particularly in 19th century Victorian England. During the Victorian age, industrialization replaced country living. Factories, railroads, and apartment buildings quickly began to define the urban landscape. Indoor houseplants provided the Victorians with a retreat from city life, as well as from the nation's booming populations of people and machines. The United States did not develop a strong affinity for houseplants until the 1960s and 1970s, which is considered America's first green and environmentally active generation.

Today, residents in most middle and upper-middle class communities and subdivisions decorate their lawns and homes with

outdoor and indoor plants. Manicured lawns and gardens are so important to real estate sales and negotiations that home and gardening networks produce several television shows devoted specifically to what real estate agents call "curb appeal." The idea behind curb appeal is to landscape a property with an artful arrangement of colorful, blooming flowers and evergreens. The resulting arrangement should complement and visually enhance a home's exterior and entryway.

Houseplants and indoor gardening has become especially popular among apartment dwellers. Urban and organic gardens filled with fruit, herbs, and vegetables are more than just a trend or a 21st century fad. Annette Pelliccio is a third generation garden business owner. Her company, The Happy Gardener, educates homeowners and apartment dwellers on the health benefits of incorporating plants into their interior living spaces. Pelliccio recommends indoor gardening not just for aesthetics, but economics, too. Pelliccio said, "As consumers become more aware of the health benefits of 'growing your own,' whether it be houseplants to absorb toxins in our homes or growing organic herbs on a windowsill to use in cooking, people are feeling the need to get back to nature."

Indoors, houseplants enhance interior design using a process known as **interiorscaping**, which is the art of using plants to design aesthetically pleasing interior spaces. This book explains how to keep indoor plants flourishing and thriving not just for the plant's benefit but also for the grower's well-being. You will learn how to design interior living spaces skillfully using plants that grow well in particular areas of the house. You will also learn plant care basics, what kind of plants to buy, and where to put those plants so they can grow to their fullest potential. The kinds of plants that best grow in offices, kitchens, and even bathrooms are described here.

Both beginners and experts derive immense personal satisfaction from indoor gardening. Professional gardeners and hobbyists find indoor horticulture much more than an additional element of home design. Houseplants are useful, working creatures that improve the quality of air humans breathe. It would take a roomful of houseplants to completely reduce or eliminate all of the toxins in the air of a room, but it is indisputable that indoor houseplants absorb carbon dioxide and other toxic compounds released by humans and materials such as fabric, wood, and paint. Some plants are so effective at removing toxic materials from the air that the National Air and Space Administration (NASA) tested and approved these plants for use on space stations because they work hard to filter the air of chemical impurities. Because plants improve the physical health of humans, they deserve the best care imaginable.

Before purchasing plants or snipping stems from an outdoor specimen, it is important to reflect a minute on what a plant really needs. A plant that is well cared for will grow green, healthy, and strong. This is great for the plant owner because a plant that is fully bloomed and rich in color is a handsome reward for a job well done. Learning to handle and care for plants properly is easy, but sometimes the work gets a little difficult. Indoor gardening requires tools, time, a good memory, dirty hands, and patience. Plants not only require a grower's personal time and energy, but they also require physical light and space. So, before bringing a plant into your home, be sure you have time to care for it, as well as a sufficient amount of space and light necessary to keep your new addition alive.

Eventually, plants purchased from vendors or nurseries grow and need larger containers. The indoor gardener is responsible for switching out those containers when a growing plant needs it; otherwise, the plant's roots will tangle and choke. When it comes

to plant containers, indoor gardeners looking to beautify their rooms will be drawn to beautiful and decorative plants that add a luxurious intrigue to a living space.

The art of interiorscaping is quite popular in business environments today. Offices decorated with rich, green, and leafy plants give customers the impression of financial success and long-term security. Healthy, thriving indoor plants symbolize life and longevity and help people feel comfortable, relaxed, and satisfied, especially in places like airports, churches, and doctor's offices. Interiorscaping in homes and offices does pose challenges, however. When deciding where to place your plants, you will have to account for **ergonomics**, which is the science of designing and arranging objects, such as desks and chairs, so that the people who use them are as comfortable as possible. The goal of ergonomic design is to increase productivity and reduce fatigue and stress.

Ergonomics gets somewhat tricky when designing and positioning plants and containers in a manner that benefits the people, plants, and in some cases, animals involved. For example, it is ergonomically unfriendly to place a pretty, but delicate or poisonous houseplant in a window where a cat likes to sit. Or, it may be ergonomically dissatisfactory to place a wide-leafed palm tree that has the potential to grow 10 feet in a space too small for it to grow to its fullest. In order to avoid such mismatches, guidelines throughout this book will help you select the right plant for particular spaces inside your home.

Indoor gardening and horticulture is an activity that builds a sense of loyalty and duty. Gardening is a distraction from the time-consuming chores that accompany work, bills, hectic social lives, and other demanding obligations. When inspired by nature, indoor gardening can be a very relaxing and calming hobby.

Chapter 1

HOUSEPLANT CARE 101

Water and light are primary elements that any plant needs to survive, and plants cannot photosynthesize without these elements. **Photosynthesis** is the process a plant uses to feed itself using the sun and water that it is given. The amount of water and light plants need varies with each species. The amount of light a plant gets varies with each home; not every home will have bright windows be-

cause the of the house's positioning in relation to the sun, as well as where windows are located within the home. In a high-rise apartment building, for example, the units with windows

that face south will get bright sun from morning to afternoon while the units that face west will get afternoon sun as long as trees or other buildings that block the sun do not surround the area.

Plants that love natural, outdoor light should be placed in a room where they can receive early morning sun, as well as light that comes during the evening. Other plants can thrive equally as well in artificially illuminated spaces, but caution must be taken when leaving plants under artificial lighting for more than 12 hours a day. Some plants, particularly those that bloom only during certain seasons, need to take a break from the photosynthesis process in order to produce the brightest flowers during their blooming periods.

Finding the direction sunlight enters a room may sound a little complicated at first, but it is really simple and explained in this chapter. In rooms or buildings where there is little or no natural light, artificial lighting is a viable and worthwhile option because some plants will grow under natural or artificial light. Lighting fixtures can be beautiful, modern components to any living space and environment, both at work and home. This chapter contains information that will help you learn more about the direction of light in the home and lists plants that thrive in artificial lights.

Water

Water is a vital element in plant life because it transports chemicals in the plants' cells and moves nutrients upward from the root. Without proper moisture, plants lose their vitality, and they may die from lack of necessary nutrients. When this happens, the cells shrink, and the plant's food supply diminishes. Smart gardeners shop for healthy plants and take a good look at stalks and leaves to make sure they are firm. Firm stems, leaves, and stalks are indicators of a healthy plant that has a strong potential

to survive once it is removed from the plant store and situated into a new environment.

Weak stems, faded leaves, and soft stalks indicate poor plant health, which is the result of too much or too little water. The combination of too much or too little water with the wrong amount of sunlight results in a severe loss of needed nutrients. Solid, firm stalks, stems, and leaves are visual proof of proper nutrients and a good water supply. Undoubtedly, it takes practice and commitment to understand the water and temperature demands of individual houseplants. But it is fair to assume that when a human finds the air dry and cool, the plant and the plant's soil also finds the air cool and dry.

Plants purchased from nurseries or other home gardening centers usually have directions and instructions for watering and the amount of light they need. The information usually is inserted on a tag in the soil, attached to the container, or on the plant's stalk. There are two different classifications for watering requirements of plants: lightly moist and moderately moist.

- "Lightly moist" means the plant's soil does not need to be wet or fully dry. Instead, the plant should absorb water so that its roots and soil are more damp than wet. Plants that are described as lightly moist must be watered frequently but delicately. The water must be distributed evenly throughout the plant container. Plants that come from tropical and temperate climates generally need to be kept lightly moist.

- Plants that are labeled "moderately moist" need moisture often. This group of plants, which typically come from tropical environments, includes most indoor flower-

producing plants, most of which grow quickly and require a good deal of light.

There is no need to water the leaves of the majority of household plants. The roots gather water that travels upward to deliver moisture to the leaves. Watering the leaves of a plant may be a well-intentioned gesture, but it often results in unappealing, sickly looking brown spots on an otherwise healthy specimen. It is best to water the soil and allow the roots to transport the water to the plant's leaves.

Once a gardener determines how to care for his or her plants properly, watering becomes a small task in the endeavor to preserve the plant's good health and promote its growth. Interior gardeners discover early on that many plant species need more water from spring through summer. Plants that need more water in the spring and summer do not need much water during winter months. Many plants go through a period of dormancy or rest during winter. During this time, cooler temperatures place less demand on potting soil, so plants need less water and fewer disturbances.

Many resting plants are gathering strength as they prepare for springtime blooming. Plants speak loud and clear about their physical health. A wilting, withered plant with flimsy, brown edged leaves and soft stalks and stems is initiating conversation about its physical health. Plant owners must learn to read the signs their plants give. Drooping leaves, for example, indicate the plant's physical needs are not being met.

When you water your plants, the goal is to keep the soil moist without drenching or drowning the roots or the soil. The surface soil of a plant should not become hard and dry due to lack of water. A drowned plant and a drought-stricken plant will both die

with no hope of revival. Plants placed in windowsills, particularly windowsills where the sun peers through bright and hot, should be watered early in the day or in the evening when the sun sets. Plants that sit in windowsills with direct sunlight risk drying out and scorching if watered during hours that the sun is hottest.

Be thorough when watering because frequent, small doses of water do not benefit a plant; in fact it does the plant more harm than good. Small doses only moisten the surface, rather than deliver the water deep down below the soil's surface where the rootlets grow. When watering a plant, the water should fall in different locations of the plant's container so the water is distributed evenly to the roots. Unless directions state otherwise, the leaves of a plant do not need water. Usually only plants that thrive in humid conditions appreciate having their leaves misted.

After the roots receive water, it then travels up the stem and flows to the leaves. You can easily check to make sure your plant is receiving enough water. Gently remove the plant from the container after it has been watered and look at its roots. A plant that needs more water will have dried roots and the soil at the bottom of the container will be dry. A plant that has been overwatered has soggy, graying, and sometimes moldy roots. Looking at the roots gives you a good idea of how much water is needed to moisten the plant soil and the plant's roots successfully. After inspecting the roots, place the plant back into the container or plant it in a new one.

Check plants once a week and rewater them when the top of the soil is dry. In the spring, plants need more water because they experience a new growth. Depending on the type of soil the plant is growing in, a thorough watering may not last long. All plants experience a period known as the **growth period** when the plant undergoes a growth spurt. The growth period also refers to the

time of season when the plant is in bloom. During growth periods, plants use more water than usual, but two weeks after the growth period, the plant reverts to its regular water intake.

Older plants may not grow as fast as younger specimens, and when owners have their plants for years, they are aware of whether the plant needs a higher water intake during the spring months. As nature would have it, most plants bloom from spring through summer so most houseplants need much more water during this time than during the fall months. Plants that are flowering or blooming, as well as plants that need repotting, also need more water during those periods of change.

Water temperature

The water given to a plant should be room temperature so you do not shock or disturb the soil. Leaving water on a counter at room temperature for a day is a safe way to achieve equal water and soil temperatures. The watering can should not be left near a windowsill where the air tends to get cooler or hotter than the room's actual temperature.

Watering while away

Summer vacations can be hazardous to a plants' health. Ideally, a neighbor with a bit of a green thumb would be ideal, but if no one is available to help water your plants while you are away, an automatic watering apparatus may be ideal for the health and lifespan of the plants. You can do an online search for automatic watering systems and see which type will work best for you. Try Indoor Gardening Supplies (**www.indoorgardensupplies.com**) or The Happy Gardener (**www.thehappygardener.info**) to get an idea of available supplies and prices. Annette Pelliccio of The Happy Gardener recommends adding a Store n' Feed Mat after

repotting. The mat absorbs up to 4 cups of water at a time, and plants can take up water as they need it. This makes vacationing easy. Plus the mats provide organic plant food, which also eliminates worry especially over flowering plants that need an extra shot of fertilizer to rebloom.

Indoor Gardening Supplies also sells inexpensive and uncomplicated self-watering devices like self-watering pots and watering globes. Watering globes are available in gardening supply centers of stores such as Home Depot. Although tempting, it is never advisable to drench a plant with water before going away because drenching a plant might drown it.

CASE STUDY: WHY WATER MATTERS

Carin Froehlich
Author, Laundry Wisdom: Instructions
for a Greener and Cleaner Life
Perkasie, Pennsylvania

Carin Froehlich's indoor gardening experience began in her childhood when she spent several summers working with her aunt and uncle. She also worked part time at a nearby nursery. She prides herself on her violets and orchids, and she said her favorite plant is the geranium.

"Watching a tiny little seed grow into a full plant still amazes me to this day," Froehlich said. "The success that you continually receive for your efforts keeps you happy."

Froehlich said watering plants is the most important chore in caring for these plants. Although most people who care for houseplants know too much or too little water can be lethal for plants, that is not the only problem water can cause. Perhaps one of the most important factors to keep in mind regarding water is the source of the water. Is the water from a well or is it public water? Luckily, those homeowners using well water to care for their plants will not have the same difficulty as those who use

public water unless the homeowners use a water softener. (Salt, which is used in most water softeners, is poisonous to plants or trees.)

For those who use public water on their houseplants, the chlorine used in the water supply that is deemed safe for human consumption is actually lethal for plants. Even bottled water can be problematic for houseplants, although the reason for this is still unclear. Froehlich said the best way to prevent both of these water options from harming your houseplants is to fill watering containers and allow them to sit out overnight before watering plants. This allows the water to reach the ideal temperature and allows some of the residual chemicals to dissipate.

Light

Areas near windows are often the most convenient living spaces for houseplants. Light is crucial to plants because the amount of light a plant gets not only determines the amount of food it receives but also whether the plant will produce flowers in its blooming period. Plants need light in order to process their food and complete the photosynthesis process. **Chloroplasts**, which are the cells found inside leaves, absorb and change light into energy during a successful photosynthesis process. Leaves, stems, and flowers absorb light from the sun and store it away for the plant to survive. When plants do not receive enough light, no amount of fertilization and water will keep the plant alive. The location of windows in a home is the first and best way to understand what room a plant should be placed in so that it will grow to its maximum height and potential.

South-facing light

The sunlight that enters a home with south-facing windows will deliver the strongest and brightest spectrum of rays to a living space and the plants inside of it throughout the day. Southern exposure is the strongest light because southern-facing windows

receive the sun's rays from the time the sun rises until the sun sets. South-facing windows tend to be rather hot, so there is danger of scorching and drying out plants that are left in windowsills during the summer. Flower-producing plants are especially fond of sun and grow well in bright rooms with south-facing windows; these plants like direct light and appreciate the shift from full sun to evening shade.

East-facing light

Typically, windows facing east get the strongest dose of sunlight in the morning followed by long shadows and no sun later on in the day. East-facing windows are good matches for those plants that adjust well to low and moderate levels of light. If a plant that needs moderate sunlight is situated in a room with east-facing light, use artificial supplemental lighting. The photosynthesis process works best when plants receive eight full hours of light, but rooms with east-facing windows cannot provide that much light without additional artificial lighting.

North-facing light

Indirect sun from a north window provides a cool, shaded light that plants like ferns will survive in. North-facing windows provide enough sunlight to grow houseplants that thrive in low light, but in the winter, plants need supplemental artificial light, or need to be relocated to a space where the light is stronger. Plants that have an original habitat shaded by trees and cooled by rains appreciate northern-facing lights, but these plants still must be watched carefully in the winter months. In the winter, a room with north-facing sunlight may be cooled to as little as 55 degrees, which is beneficial to the hardiness of spring-blooming houseplants like cacti and other plants that need a break in the winter. Ideally, most homeowners would rather rest such plants

outdoors rather than suffer harsh cold air in a northern exposure for the sake of spring blooms.

West-facing light

Windows that face west get the brightest sun in the early afternoon, and the light lasts until evening. The afternoon sun of a western window is strong and increases room temperatures, which make these environments good places for plants that thrive in sunny spaces and grow strong in warmer environments.

Dealing with over/underexposure of light

Plants that are overexposed to natural sunlight will lose their vibrant green colors and fade to pale, sickly yellows, similar to when a plant drowns or dries out. This loss of color indicates the plant has not been able to properly nourish itself, and overexposure to the sun prevented the plant's roots from carrying water and nutrients to its leaves, stems, and flowers. Just as gardeners must learn the levels of moisture required to keep a plant healthy and happy, they must also study the amount of light individual plants require to thrive in living spaces where light is not always bright or direct.

Regardless of how much or how little natural light a room gets through windows, the light in a living space can be increased with reflective materials and decreased with shading objects, such as blinds or screens. Reflective materials can be as simple as the natural elements inside of a room, such as white paint and other light-colored walls that reflect light so well that rays bounce around the room. Rooms with reflective lighting materials will help larger plants grow not just in size but quality. You can use mirrors to illuminate and reflect both natural and artificial light in a room. A plant placed in front of a mirror located a good dis-

tance from the window will enjoy the strong reflection of natural sun rays that emanate from the window.

Using artificial light

Artificial lighting is a great alternative when natural sunlight is not available or strong enough to keep plants thriving. This lighting is effective when the light bulb's intensity and the spectrum of wavelengths available are enough for plants to carry out its photosynthesis processes. You can use artificial lighting as a supplement to natural sunlight, and it may enhance the décor and appeal of a living or working space because many lamps and other lighting objects are stylish and sleek. When an interior space is shaded by outside factors, such as tall buildings or thick, leafy trees, the rays provided from artificial lighting will keep the plants fed and healthy. Plants will tell you if their artificial lighting is insufficient by the way they grow, or do not grow. Weak stems and leaves that are stiff with brown edges that fall off a plant are indicators that the plant does not have the nutrients it needs to survive and grow properly. The following are some examples of the different kinds of lighting available for houseplants.

Incandescent lights

Incandescent lights have warm, red rays that release heat and cannot be placed too close to the plant because the soil may dry out and kill the plant. Incandescent lights are more useful in the winter because they give plants the warmth and light similar to long summer days. One incandescent light suggestion is a 200-watt floodlight because it will supply the plant light it needs without drying out its soil.

Fluorescent lights

Although houseplants are not very fond of incandescent lights, they do well under fluorescent lights, which provide blue and green rays — the rays necessary for plants to manufacture food. They cost less and last twice as long as incandescent lights, which make them much more energy efficient.

Fluorescent lights are sold in various watts and wavelengths so they can be used alone or in addition to the natural sun in any given living space. Fluorescent lamps can sit closer to plants without burning or drying the plants or the soil, and there are several types of fluorescent bulbs on the market. There are long, tube fluorescents that are often found in offices, as well as special growing lamps that are usually sold as wide-spectrum and/or full-spectrum lamps. Full- and wide-spectrum lamps are the best substitutes for natural sunlight because the bulbs emit light in every range of color on the light spectrum, yet they only release a tiny amount of ultraviolet light. If you have a room that does not pull in enough natural sunlight, experiment with the distance between the lamp and the plants. Some plants can be as close as 1 ½ inches to a fluorescent light. Other plants that prefer medium to low light need at least 4 to 12 inches of distance from the leaves. Plants that have not been given much light should respond positively to the supplemental energy that artificial light sources provide.

Artificial lights kept on for 12 to 14 hours in a day will sufficiently substitute for natural sunlight for foliage plants. However, flowering plants need a lot more light, a total of 18 hours in a 24-hour time frame. The leaves of the plants provide excellent clues as to how much light a plant needs to survive. Light-colored leaves usually need much more sunlight than some of the plants with deep, waxy green foliage like the snake plant. Waxy, deep green leaves found on the snake plant and the weeping fig have more chlorophyll and do not need eight or more hours of sunlight to photosynthesize. Leaves that change colors during certain periods need intense light during certain seasons.

Now that you know more about the direction of natural light and the effect it has on a room's temperature and lighting, you can make more informed choices about the type of containers you will need to grow healthy indoor plants. Container size, material, shape, and color all vary greatly because they serve different purposes. Plastic pots often have holes in the bottom and drain over-watered plants fairly well. They are cheap and easier to move unlike clay pots that are porous and absorb water on the sides. Clay pots are much heavier when wet and serve the houseplant and the plant owner best when kept still. Ceramic pots are often a designer's or decorator's choice because of the crafted designs and variety of colors.

Choosing Your Plant's Container

Plants will grow in almost any waterproof container that has drainage holes for excess water. Urns, baskets, pots, kettles, cans, boxes, and wine casks, which are huge wooden barrels that store wine, are a few of the items available to house a plant. Containers are a plant's primary home, but for some homeowners, plant containers can be a key element in interior design. If

a unified space is the goal, then choose matching or identical plant containers.

In addition to considering these factors, consider the types of plants you plan to purchase. The plant's size and growth needs are important to consider. Many plants will require repotting from time to time, but in nearly all situations, starting out with an appropriate pot size is critical for the plant's growth and development. The first step is to consider the plant you want to display, and then consider the appropriate pot. A good estimate is to look at the root ball of the plant and to provide at least 3 to 5 inches of space around that root ball in all directions so there is space for the roots to grow upward, downward, and to each side.

Plastic

Plastic containers are common because they are inexpensive, and they lock and seal in moisture better than other containers. Plastic also endures the shipping process as the plants make their way from the grower to the market and then later to the gardener's home. One handy feature of many plastic

pots is a snap-on tray used for drainage. The snap-on tray is located underneath the actual plant container, holds excess water, and prevents water damage to floors and tables.

Plant containers come in all sizes and shapes. Some are oddly shaped, such as oblong planter boxes, which typically are used to situate plants comfortably in windowsills. Plastic pots come in a number of colors, and some are imitations of more expensive

clay and ceramic containers. Another advantage of plastic is that it is easy to clean and care for, especially when the plant is larger.

Plastic pots with drainage holes are critical. Because plastic is not porous, a drainage method is critical because waterlogged plants can cause root rot. In addition, monitor the plant's growth in a plastic pot. Because it is flexible, plastic can bend and crack if the weight within it is too much. Heavy plants, even with smaller root balls, should not be placed in plastic pots unless the plastic is thick enough to support it. Many of these pots will provide information on their bottoms about the appropriate size of plant to use within the pot, or the weight the plastic pot can withstand.

Clay

Many decorators feel that clay and ceramic planters possess a unique, sophisticated, and elegant beauty. Clay pots are common plant containers, and even the simplest clay pot is visually intriguing. The earthy tone of clay pots creates a strong and natural look when paired  against a plant's deep green and vivacious foliage. These pots are available in diameters as large as 24 inches or as small as just a few inches. Most are inexpensive compared to ceramic pots or other options.

Because clay containers are quite porous, they absorb water quickly so the soil in a clay pot dries quicker than it would if it were in a plastic container. The type of clay and whether it is glazed plays a role in this process. Some clay pots are more porous than others. Those that feel lighter, for example, often are

more porous. If the pot is glazed, it is less porous and, therefore, will not allow evaporation to occur as easily as non-glazed pots.

Clay helps plants and their roots absorb air easily, which helps the plants grow a healthy stalk. Once a clay pot is filled with soil and water, it becomes heavy and vulnerable to cracking. Clay pots also need to be cleaned and sterilized because their porous nature makes them susceptible to harmful pests and disease.

Terra cotta

Terra cotta is a type of unglazed ceramic clay. Terra-cotta containers are made of baked earth; they are inexpensive, brick colored, waterproof, and very popular as plant containers. They are usually for sale anywhere plant pots are sold. When placing a plant into terra cotta, monitor the soil's moisture level carefully. Because the pot's walls are porous, this can cause the soil to dry out quickly. The benefit of using a terra-cotta pot is it is more difficult for plants to become waterlogged. If you select this type of pot for your plant, soak the pot overnight prior to placing the plant within it. This helps to slow down the amount of moisture the pot extracts from the soil, which allows you to have more control over the soil's moisture level.

A number of variations are available in these pots. You can purchase cylindrical containers or those pots meant for specific tasks, such as strawberry jars that have small openings along the sides to allow the strawberries to grow and spread properly. Italian

terra-cotta pots are similar, but often have unique rims in various shapes. Some have beveled edges whereas others are wavy or have a rounded edge. Venetian terra-cotta pots are also widely available. These have a barrel shape to them and often have a band design along the sides. Yet another version is the Spanish terra-cotta pots that have an outward sloping side and often feature flared lips along the top. This particular type often has a thicker wall that offers more stability. These pots are available from 8 to 12 inches in diameter.

Another version of the terra-cotta pot is a three-legged pot. These pots have an elevated bottom, which helps to display the pot better. These range in size from 8 inches to 20 inches or more in some cases. Use these to display plants that are slightly larger or have longer span of leaves. Some are called bulb pans or seed bowls, which is a term that describes the size and shape of the types of plants to put in them. Seed bowls are smaller and excellent for starting out new plants from seed. These are often smaller, often no larger than 6 inches in diameter.

Ceramic or glazed pots

Ceramic planters, also known as glazed pots, are sold in a variety of finishes, textures, and glossy colors. Smaller plants tend to thrive inside of ceramic pots because most ceramic pots do not have draining holes. Like plants, ceramic containers are diverse and should be handled with care. Ceramic containers chip easily, so they should be placed in a permanent location and moved only when absolutely necessary. Ceramic pots do not tolerate cold and should not be left outdoors during the winter months. When compared to terra-cotta clay pots and plastic, ceramic containers are costly, but with proper care, ceramic can outlast the life of the plant. If you have a ceramic pot that is larger, and you want to

use it for a plant, place the plant into a plastic or terra-cotta pot first and then place this into the ceramic pot. This creates the necessary drainage the plant requires to thrive.

Cachepots

When people include plants in interior or exterior design, the pot can make a big impact on the space's look and feel. Although terra cotta and other types of pots are excellent options for plants because of their strength and ability to drain water away, many pots are very basic and less decorative. A solution to this is to  use **cachepots**, which are decorative, rather than functional, pots that you can place plainer pots with drain holes into.

You can purchase cachepots virtually anywhere pots are sold, including many home garden centers. To use these pots, place a layer of pebbles or gravel at the bottom of the plain pot so there is a bit of space between the bottom of the cachepot and the plain pot to allow water to drain properly. Then, place the plain pot within the cachepot, and display where you would like to.

Cachepots come in numerous designs and color schemes. Some are brass and copper to add a luxurious look to a space, though most are not too expensive. Consider purchasing a porcelain cachepot for a higher value, more color, and often, more design features. Another option is a more natural teak or mahogany cachepot. These are high end and expensive, but may work well in rooms with these types of woods already in the space. Some cachepots have feet, similar to those found on the bottom of a

bathtub, which add to the decorative elements of the plant. When buying a pot, you should consider the size and the weight of the plant. A well-made cachepot should last for years and, often, will outlive the plant itself.

Metal pots

Metal containers are unique planting choices that fit well in both traditional and contemporary living areas and office spaces. Holes can be drilled into metal pots for draining and potting, but metal gets hotter faster than other materials, especially in a room with direct sunlight, and this could overheat the pot. In the winter, they cannot gather sufficient heat, and plants that normally tolerate cooler temperatures actually may experience a frost if not moved to a warm, lighted area. Still, the containers are fine if they are used in a room where the temperatures remain steady year round.

Bamboo and wood containers

Bamboo containers are rare and work best in spaces that are African or Asian themed. Bamboo pots need waterproofing with plastic sheets because bamboo is a delicate wood that needs protection from excess water. A bamboo pot can be waterproofed by lining the container with thin plastic, such as a plastic bag from the grocery store. Wooden con-

tainers are diverse decorating pieces. Like bamboo and even metal, wood containers can be painted or left in their natural state. Bamboo containers can be found at trendy stores like IKEA and Pier 1 Imports.

Using urns, tubs, and boxes

Urns can be a beautiful and formal option for displaying plants, or inexpensive and informal, depending on the material and style of the urn itself. Most will have a pedestal base or a footed bottom to elevate the plant off the ground by a few inches. Some are stone while others are fiberglass but have a faux wood look to them. Stone can be expensive, but fiberglass options can be inexpensive. Other options include bronze and concrete. Many interior designers use urns when the plant will be at eye level because this gives these planters more visual appeal. Select urns for flowering plants because the colors of the flowering plants can often look beautiful in this style of pot. When using pedestal urns, you should do so in larger rooms or even on patios. Because these are often very large, they can take up a larger amount of space and may dominate the look of the space, too.

Tubs are an option for many homeowners and businesses. These are round or hexagonal in shape. Some of these are wood, while others are stone or concrete. If you are purchasing wooden tubs, be sure to select varieties that are durable and have rotting protection. Those made from cypress or redwoods are naturally rot resistant and make good choices. Consider using Japanese soy tubs for an informal space, such as a living room. These are inexpensive but decorative. Another option is a Japanese porcelain tub. These tubs are often more ornate and glazed, whereas soy tubs are often more rustic. These are very luxurious and formal. Use them for more sophisticated plants, such as a jade plant, for

a formal-looking display. Some tubs have drainage holes while others do not. If the tub does not have drainage holes, place a plain pot within to allow for drainage, similar to cachepots.

Boxes are yet another option for displaying plants. If you wish to grow indoor trees or shrubbery, these boxes can be a great choice for displaying them. These boxes, which are available in numerous styles, often complement the look of these larger plants because the wooden box will match well with the wooden trunks and stems of the plant. The box shape also creates a visual base for the larger plant within it. To ensure the box does not become too overpowering, top the soil with a layer of sphagnum or unmilled peat moss, commonly available at garden centers. Keep in mind that filled boxes can create a heavy pot. To move these, use a dolly or a wheeled trolley to allow you to move them properly.

Plant stands

Furniture stores carry attractive plant stands, pedestals, and other decorative pieces. Plant trolleys and dollies enable growers to move plants from room to room, either for light or decorating purposes. You also can use these dollies to move plants to ensure they receive the proper amount of heat and light in the winter and summer months. Dollies keep planted pots off the floor and prevent water damage and stains to floors and carpets.

Most plant stands are wood, wrought iron, or plastic; they elevate plants to eye level and add interesting décor to the living space. Pedestals are a simple, yet elegant design idea. If pedestals are out of your price range, wooden barstools or stools with flat

metal surfaces are good substitutes. Stepladders are also acceptable options.

Any grate-like stand or a platform display will provide plants with health benefits, too. These help air to get to the plants roots. In some cases, the stands allow for the branches of the plant to cascade downward, keeping them off the ground but still giving them room to grow. These stands can vary in the height of the actual stand, from as small as 1 foot to as large as 5 feet. Some stands display just one plant while others have shelves to accommodate as many as six to eight smaller plants.

Hanging Baskets and Pots

A popular option for displaying plants is using hanging baskets or hanging pots. Hanging a plant from the ceiling or from the side of a doorway frame extending to the side of the door itself is a good idea, especially for plants that have longer branches or those that spread out. The pot will house the roots of the plant and soil, and the branches and leaves will come up out of the pot and hang over the edge, creating a beautiful display. This also provides the plants an easy way to grow without many restrictions. Those who have limited window space or tabletops near windows may be able to hang these plants from the ceiling in front of windows, or from the window framing.

These are available in various types of materials, including ceramics, baskets, and plastic. Using a woven basket with a plastic liner to catch water may be a good option, or you can use a plastic or wire basket and line it with peat moss before placing the plant within it. Whatever material you select for the hanging pots, be sure it offers a way to catch water. The soil will still need a way to drain off excess water to ensure that the water does not become stagnant.

Another aspect to consider with these baskets is the actual method of hanging them. This suspension needs to be strong and stable, especially if the plants or the pots are heavier. You can purchase chains that create a strong hold while also offering an appealing design feature. Otherwise, you can choose other types of roping for this process. Macramé hangers or woven ropes can also work well.

The hanger choice depends, in part, on the amount of weight it can support. The roping must not only be strong enough to support the plant, but it is also necessary to have a dependable at-

tachment for the ceiling. One option for hanging the pot from the ceiling is to use a screw hook. When you purchase the hook, look at the size of the hook to ensure the roping you select will fit properly into the hook. A larger hook is recommended for larger plants, as it will hold more weight. Some hooks may provide weight information on the packaging. Otherwise, select a larger hook for plants weighing more than a few pounds. When placing the hook into the ceiling, consider the amount of support present in the ceiling. Look for a ceiling joist to screw the hook into for security. Otherwise, ensure there is plywood or another strong surface to install the hook into to ensure the screw threads can anchor properly. Do not depend on gypsum or any other type of ceiling panels, such as drywall, even for lightweight plants.

Another option to consider if you do not want to use a ceiling hook is to attach a hook to the wall. Wall brackets allow you to hang lightweight to moderate weight plants from the wall. Swinging arm brackets have an arm that swings outward or inward, giving you more flexibility on where the plant will actually hang. Attach these to the side of a window frame then rotate the arm. This will allow you to display the plant in front of the window. Fixed arm brackets, on the other hand, remain stationary; so only use these when you do not need movement. The stability and overall design are also things for you to consider. For heavier pots or baskets, select a thicker or larger bracket with larger screws. Consider the coloring and material for its attractive appeal in the space. To install these types of support, be sure to look for a wall joist or another strong material to anchor the brackets into for support.

A variety of plants work very well as hanging container plants, but for the best look, consider any type of cascading plant, or plants that trail. Ivies, for example, will cascade over the edge, creating a beautiful and natural display. Avoid hanging plants that need frequent attention because you will need to climb up to manage the plant. Other good varieties of hanging plants include rosemary, purple queen, and most types of ferns.

How to choose the right plant container and display

Whatever plant pot you purchase, remember that plants speak when they are uncomfortable, thirsty, and when they need to be repotted. Plants also change in appearance when they are not receiving enough light. When choosing a plant container, consider the soil and fertilization process. In addition to water and light, soil and fertilization are vital aspects of plant care and plant life

because soil and fertilizers provide the daily nutrients that all plants need.

When choosing a plant's container, select one that complements all of the needs of the plant, including its growth habits, its appearance, and its other needs, such as being elevated. If you are planting a bushy plant or a rounded plant, choose a dish-like pot with a rounded design. You may want to consider using more cylindrical containers if you are planting taller plants or those with more vertical growth.

The depth of the pot is important to consider in the selection process. Learn how the plant's root system will grow. Some plants with shallow roots will do well in shorter pots. Those with longer roots need wider pots, even if the portion of the plant you see is small. Choose a container that can comfortably accommodate the plant's root system. Avoid pots that are too large because they can dwarf the appearance of the plant, creating a visually unappealing look. Also, if there is too much unused soil in the container where roots are not developing, this can lead to soggy, unhealthy conditions for the plant.

The color of the container should make a difference, too. If you are using a pot that has neutral colors, this will allow the colors of the plant to come through well and be displayed prominently. This is a good option for vibrantly colored plants or plants that flower. For plants that are less spectacular in color, choose a more ornate planter that adds more visual interest to the space. Consider other elements in the room, too, to ensure the plant fits in. If you have a specific wood tone in the space, for example, select a wooden planter that complements or matches that wood tone.

Also, consider the surface you plan to place the pot on. If you are using pots with external drainage holes (as opposed to a pot like

a cachepot), you may damage the surface of a tabletop or windowsill unless you place a tray or catch underneath the planter. You can often purchase plastic or terra-cotta trays to place under the plant that will match the pot. If you choose terra-cotta saucers to catch drainage, realize that these will absorb moisture and can damage wooden surfaces as a result. To remedy this, choose terra-cotta saucers with a glazed bottom.

As for displaying these plants, choose what works for your space as well as for the plant. Displaying on a tabletop or windowsill is an easy option if you have the space. If the plants need to be near a source of outdoor light, consider using a plant stand near a window. Another option is to use a hanging basket to display the plant. Many larger plants can sit on the floor in a cachepot or box for display. You can often choose a container from a range of colors and sizes to fit your tastes. Consider the interior surroundings and the plant's particular shape to find the right blend of options. If you have trouble finding options in local garden stores, consider purchasing these plant containers from websites such as Amazon. com (**www.amazon.com**) and PlantContainers.com.

SOIL AND FERTILIZATION

Just as plants need water and sun to survive, they also need soil and fertilization. Unlike outdoor plants, houseplants cannot send their roots deep into the soil to get their water and food. So, plant owners must supply the right diet of nutrients and moisture by providing the plants with good quality potting soil. Plants need nitrogen, phosphorous, and potassium, and they get these nutrients through fertilizers sold in plant and gardening centers everywhere.

Soil

The houseplant soils sold in stores and garden centers are not the same as the soil found outdoors. There is actually very little, if any, soil in these potting mixes. Potting mixes are actually growing substances commonly referred to as "growing media." The particles potting soil comprises are manufactured just for houseplants to help them grow strong and healthy. Indoor growing

media does not host earthworms, insects, or microorganisms associated with outdoor soil. Using outdoor soil as a growing medium is not recommended because houseplants will die when exposed to the troublesome microorganisms that are routine with outdoor plants and soil.

There are very few remedies to help potting soils that are overrun with dangerous outdoor inhabitants, so avoid adding outdoor elements to potting soil mixes. Potting soils are composed of materials that will not allow soil-borne disease to take over, and particular ingredients are included in potting soil that keeps the plant free from the harm of contaminating microbes. Potting soil also feels light and fluffy, while outdoor soil is heavy, clunky, and filled with particles that may or may not be good for your plants.

Potting soils are filled with varying ingredients, but most are blended from peat moss, bark compost, sand, vermiculite, or perlite. **Peat moss** usually has its pH fine-tuned with ground limestone so that the soil's pH balances out at 7, which is a neutral reading. Many potting soils are sold with small amounts of fertilizer, which is highly beneficial for the initial growth of the plant. When choosing a soil, make sure it is dark with a spongy texture, and be sure that it does not have an odor.

Good potting soil will satisfy a plant's needs. The best potting soils are sold in large plastic bags that prevent the soil from drying out and lock out unwanted organisms and creatures that may destroy the soil's balance. Try to purchase the amount of soil that you need without having excess left around because storing unused potting soil could lead to the growth of harmful bacteria or other organisms. Potting soil is available in 2-, 5-, 10-, and 20-quart bags. Three or four plants in 6-inch pots will be fine with a 2-quart bag of soil. The 5- and 10-quart bags will be enough for 12 plants in 6-inch pots. If the plant container is 10 inches diam-

eter or wider, then purchase a 20-quart bag. Remember to choose soft, black soil.

Potting soil only lasts a couple of years inside of a plant container because water, minerals, and other nutrients inside of that soil change over the years. For the plant, being left in the same soil for several years is akin to eating leftovers for an unreasonable period. It is only natural that organic matter will decompose in the pot and then be absorbed by the plant. After a while, the potting soil is unable to perform the duties it did when it was initially purchased, so you will need to repot plants periodically. The old potting soil cannot be recycled among your other houseplants, but it can be thrown outdoors, and it will integrate itself into outdoor garden soil.

A plant's roots will develop properly as long as the plant fits well inside its container. Pots that are too large or too small, potting soil that is much too heavy, has a musty smell, or an awkward soil mix will negatively affect a plant's growth. Indoor gardeners occasionally will use a fork to loosen the soil and remove algae, moss, or mold deposits. Not everyone agrees on the type of soil combinations necessary to grow certain plants. Many feel a peat-based soil and fertilizer is fine while gardeners that more particular recommend soil compost mixes to grow specific specimens.

There are a few additives that, when combined with potting soil, create ideal root-growing conditions for a number of household plants. If a plant demonstrates that it is still thirsty after watering or shows signs that it is overwatered after a simple dousing, then its soil content needs adjusting. Gardeners who are familiar with these next six substances are able to tailor their potting soil mixtures to those plants that beg for more attention than potting soil, water, fertilizer, and sunlight provide.

Peat moss

Peat moss is developed from moss in exceptionally water-absorbent bogs found mostly in Michigan and Canada. Peat moss's greatest asset is its ability to eliminate a number of root destroying fungi. Pure peat moss is highly acidic; therefore, it becomes a good match for azaleas and gardenias that thrive in acidic soil. Lime added to peat moss offsets its acidity, so it becomes a suitable soil environment for African violets that fully appreciate the way peat moss offers enough moisture. The fine texture of peat moss, which is meticulously broken down into a coarse, brown powder before it is packaged for the market, makes it an ideal soil to seed plants that have new roots and are waiting to dwell in a permanent container. Although peat moss holds water rather nicely, once it dries out, there is not much chance of reviving it. Peat moss needs to be moistened with an equal measure of lukewarm water before adding it with another soil medium. You may often run across plants that need **sphagnum**, a peat moss that is compacted with stringy and fibrous contents from other plant debris. Sphagnum helps the plant retain water, which is good for the plant soil and good for plants that are allowed to dry out between watering.

Composted plant materials

In general, composted plant materials are recycled waste from your kitchen and garden, such as egg shells, tea bags, coffee grounds, banana peels, chicken bones, and leaves from trees. When you repot plants grown at nurseries or other indoor gardening sites, the potting soil usually contains bits of bark, sticks, and other decomposed plant materials. The decomposition is advantageous to the plants that are seeking nutrients and firm soil. The coarse products mixed in with the potting soil help the water drain nicely and prevent the roots from compacting because it

provides the roots plenty of air. Indoor gardeners can compost themselves by gathering stones, leaves, and wood chips from their backyard to add to the potting soil. The website Eartheasy (**http://eartheasy.com**) offers good instructions for composting in its lawn and garden section. The Happy Gardener's website (**www.thehappygardener.info**) offers excellent composting tips for indoor gardeners and novices who like information delivered fast and easy. *Chapter 7 goes into full detail with ideas and tools needed to compost in the kitchen.*

Indoor gardeners and those who grow plant nurseries like bark-based compost because it provides excellent drainage and it is inexpensive. This form of compost also decomposes slowly and mimics soil conditions in places between tree branches where many bromeliads and orchids originally take root. Dark-colored potting soil indicates a good presence of composted plant material.

Sand

Grains of sand are actually rather large when compared to other soil particle types; therefore, water tends to flow quickly through soil mixes that contain a fair amount of sand. Sand's primary purpose in potting soil is to facilitate drainage. However, a very sandy soil mix needs to be watched carefully because this mixture will dry out too quickly. Cacti, succulents, palms, as well as plants that have natural habitats near the ocean, such as the screw pine (*Pandanus utilis*), do really well with a sand and soil combination. If it appears that your plant's roots are drying out unnecessarily or if the plant is suffering because it does not drain very well, amending the soil mix to include sand is an ideal solution to restoring a houseplant with poor drainage. Sand helps with draining because it is a dense mix that tends to exclude air.

Whenever you purchase sand for a soil mixture, you will need to wash the sand so you can remove salt and other impurities. Sand packaged in aquariums, for example, is salty. Sand used in children's sandboxes is also good, but it needs a good rinsing with fresh water before combining it into your planting mix. Sand does not contain any nutrients for a plant to feed from so any plants stationed in a sandy potting mix will need to be fed extra nutrients in the form of fertilizers.

Perlite

Perlite is another option to improve a plant's drainage. Perlite resembles small, broken pieces of popcorn, and its particles are composed of volcanic rock that explodes at 1,600 degrees during the manufacturing process. Perlite has a neutral pH, and because it is chemically inert, meaning the chemicals inside of it do not combust when mixed with other elements, it influences water and oxygen regulation. With proper nutrition, plants can grow in full perlite. Mixes created specifically for cacti and succulents often have a good deal of perlite, which is available at most garden centers. Indoor gardeners use perlite to root their cuttings and to lighten up heavy soil.

Vermiculite

Vermiculite is also a good material to improve a soil's water drainage. Like perlite, vermiculite is composed of mineral deposits that are mined, crushed, and heated to a breaking point. Vermiculite mixes very easily with peat moss, and this mixture is the basis for most seed-starting mixes. Pure vermiculite, or its mixtures, must be dampened when handling it because some vermiculite has small amounts of cancer-causing asbestos, which is likely to become airborne and inhaled if the soil is not wet.

Vermiculite is not a health risk when mixed with potting soil, or when used to root cut stems or start seeds.

Mineral nutrients

Soil contains 13 mineral nutrients, all of which dissolve in water and are absorbed by the plant's roots. Because there are not always enough minerals present in soil for a plant to grow healthy, gardeners use fertilizers to add nutrients to soil. Plants use primary nutrients nitrogen (N), phosphorous (P), and potassium (K) so quickly that they must be replenished with fertilizers. Typically, gardeners use commercial potting soil mixes that are enriched with these three minerals.

Calcium, magnesium, and sulfur are secondary nutrients, and generally, these minerals are prevalent enough in soils that you will not need fertilizers to introduce or replace them in a potting soil. As a finishing touch, most potting soils include a dusting of various minerals, such as lime, gypsum, or rock phosphate. Lime, which is ground limestone, raises the pH of mixes that are too acidic and provides plants with slow-release calcium. Calcium and magnesium levels increase in plant soils when limestone is added to the mix.

Gypsum and rock phosphate also serve as very slow-release fertilizers. As a casual houseplant grower, the only mineral amendment you need is a little lime if you mix your own peat-based potting mixes. A pinch of extra lime in a pot helps some plants cope with the uptake problems associated with chemically tainted water. Never add lime to soil used for plants that like acidic soil conditions, such as azaleas, gardenias, certain rhododendron, and most ferns. In rare instances, a batch of potting soil may be so acidic that plants have trouble taking up nutrients. If plants fail to grow well after they are repotted and do not respond to an in-

crease in fertilizer, then you can try giving them a drench of lime water, which you can make by mixing a teaspoon of powdered lime with a quart of water. Try using this solution once before discarding or giving up on the soil and the plant.

Special Potting Mixtures

Once indoor gardeners find a favorite plant and stick with the plant over the years, they know what their plant needs and what it likes, from water to soil to sunlight. Plants such as orchids and palms thrive very well when their soil mix or plant media is specifically mixed for their species. Special mixes are available in garden centers, home improvement stores, and online nurseries.

Orchid mixes

Orchids need porous plant soil that does not contain many nutrients because they are **epiphytes** — meaning they are plants that live on other plants. Orchid mixes are byproducts of coarse peat fiber, bark media of European pine and cork, or the bark of American evergreens. Another mix, known as "Meranti," is composed of shavings from a South Asian tree. These basic ingredients are combined with perlite, tile shards, pumice, mica granulate, clay aggregate, and other inorganic materials that help the soil remain firm. Charcoal added to an orchid mix will help prevent rot and

disease. A fertilizer for orchid mixes called Orchid Quick is available in home repair stores or gardening centers.

Fern mixes

The fern's natural habitat is loose soil filled with organic materials. There is a mix for ferns that mimics their natural environment. The mix is not commercially available, but it is easy to make. It requires:

- Three parts coarse peat moss

- Three parts leaf mold or sterilized compost, which is compost that is baked in the oven or under the sun to rid it of all outdoor bugs and germs

- Two parts coarse sand or perlite

This mixture is also ideal to grow epiphytic ferns. Epiphytes, like ferns, grow above ground and are supported by another plant, but an epiphyte does not feed off the plant it lives on. Instead, epiphytes get their nutrients from rain, dust, and air. You can use lightly fertilized regular potting mix if you are unable to make this particular mixture. However, ferns do not like lime bases, so be sure to use a lime-free potting mix.

Bromeliad mixes

The first bromeliad brought to Europe from South America was the pineapple. Bromeliads are newcomers to houseplants, as they were grown only in conservatories of wealthy Europeans in the 1800s. Members of the bromeliad family grow in tree limbs, forest floors, and some anchor themselves to rocks. All bromeliads bloom a colorful flower when they are three to five years old. After it blooms, the plant dies. During those three to five years while you are waiting for colorful flowers to bloom, the plant

will have produced several seedlings. Neither orchids nor bromeliads can be grown in packaged potting soils or homemade mixtures. Both plants thrive if grown in fir bark, which is available from gardening centers in three grades: fine, medium, and large. The medium-grade bark bits that are not large or small are easiest to work with, and orchids like them immensely. To imitate the trees in which bromeliads grow, they will need soil that consists of equal parts of peat moss and sand. You also can add pine needles from your yard or a park. Pine needles add acidity, which the bromeliads like, and will promote good drainage. You also will need wood chips from a lawn and gardening center to add to your mix.

Repotting

Plants need to be repotted, even if they have been in their pots for years, because the soil wears out after a while and is no longer able to absorb nutrients properly. Roots, after a while, will grow too large and spiny for their containers, and when this happens, they accumulate salt from the fertilizers, which is toxic for most plants. Older plants that are housed in pots or containers 10 inches in diameter or smaller need repotting annually. Plants that are housed in containers larger than 10 inches in diameter should be repotted every two years. Young plants need to be transplanted more frequently than older, more situated and established plants because the gardener must be sure the plant's roots are able to grow freely. Plants that grow quickly need transplanting frequently, but no matter how fast or slow a plant grows, it must be placed in a pot that is a good deal larger than its previous pot.

Repotting is a less messy process when using soil that is slightly dry, rather than trying to repot wet soil. By tapping the side of a container that has dry soil inside, the mixture will loosen quite

easily. Loose soil enables the plant to disassemble from the container much easier without harming its roots. The old soil must be replaced with new soil, and if there are dead roots on the plant, they need to be trimmed from the plant and discarded.

Clean pots make healthy plants, and terra-cotta containers especially need to be thoroughly cleaned during the repotting session because these pots are most susceptible to germs, bacteria, grime, and calcium buildup. The terra-cotta pot should be soaked for a few hours in water before it is repotted, otherwise the clay will absorb water from the soil. Reused containers can be disinfected with a solution composed of nine parts water and one part chlorine beach. Give the pot a thorough rinse with clear water, add soil to the pot, center the plant in the soil, and then fill the rest of the potting mixture around the plant.

In a container, the roots still grow and reach deeper beneath the topsoil surface, but the container restricts the roots' ability to expand as far as they are meant to stretch, and unless more space is provided, the roots become cramped and jammed causing a condition termed as **pot bound**. A pot-bound plant does not produce healthy flowers and grows much slower than a plant that has roots that experience the freedom of space to move deeper into its container, particularly during a growing or blooming season. Repotting plants into a slightly larger pot with fresh soil mix usually happens once a year in the spring when the new growth for the season starts.

When replanting, be sure that new containers have drainage holes. These drainage holes prevent water from clogging the soil that weighs heavily on a plant's roots. Ideally, the new plant container should be 2 inches larger than the previous container so as not to increase drastically the amount of soil and room the plant is accustomed to. Plants that are placed in larger pots than needed encourage root, rather than plant, growth. Sometimes the roots of plants that are housed in container larger than necessary will rot because the roots are overwhelmed by excess soil and water. When planting or repotting, place newspaper across the base of the pot so the potting mix does not seep through the drainage holes. Stand the plant inside to get an idea of container space and add more soil mix underneath the plant if necessary. Fill the sides of the container and pat the soil gently with your hands and fingertips. The pot should be filled at least 1 inch below the rim. When the potting is done, add water to the plant to tighten and secure the soil mix, and if any holes appear, add more water and even out the soil.

Overgrown roots are quite easy to detect; they usually are growing through the base of the pot or growing upward, sticking their

way out of the topsoil. Plants that dry out quickly may have too many roots compacted in the bottom of the pot, too little soil mix, and possibly, too little room for the plant. If you see either one of these scenarios, it is time to repot. If the plant stops growing and if the top growth becomes unpleasantly lopsided, then the plant should be removed and replaced in the center of a larger pot. Poorly anchored plants are letting you know they need new plant facilities.

Fertilizers

Light is a plant's primary energy source, but plants need nitrogen (N), phosphorous (P), and potassium (K) to help them grow strong. Fertilizer bags often contain three hyphenated numbers. The amount of each of these chemical elements in relation to the others in a compost or fertilizer is shown on the bag as the N-P-K ratio. For a balanced, general fertilizer, the number is the same for each element, for example 5-5-5. However, some plants need different quantities of each element. Foliage plants have a lower potassium requirement, but flowering plants need a healthy dose of potassium when the buds begin to develop.

The first number on the bag represents nitrogen. Nitrogen supplements plant growth and assists with strong leaf color. Young plants particularly are helped by nitrogen, as are plants that are experiencing a rapid growth spurt. Fertilizers with high nitrogen content benefit leafy plants.

The second number found on the fertilizer label represents phosphorous. Phosphorous helps plants grow strong roots and produce healthy seeds and fruits after the flowering period. When you find that the phosphorous is higher than the number for nitrogen, you found a fertilizer designed specifically to promote blooming. When looking for a high phosphorous food for bloom-

ing houseplants, look for a fertilizer that has a phosphorous count that is twice as high as the other two ratios. For example, 1-3-2 or 8-14-9 would be ideal for a blooming plant.

The third number represents potassium, which builds the plant's immune system by helping the plant absorb other nutrients and resist disease. Potassium strengthens root function and aids the plant's ability to spread moisture and nutrients to its leaves and tissues. Kelp and green sand are ideal fertilizers rich in potassium. They are especially beneficial when making compost for rose plants.

Organic fertilizers

Natural or organic fertilizers consist of an animal or plant base, and plants tend to absorb organic fertilizers slowly. Natural fertilizers can be sprayed upon the leaves, dissolved in water, or mixed into the potting soil. Organic fertilizers are good sources of nitrogen, and they tend to last longer than their inorganic or synthetic counterparts because the living organisms in the plant's soil must break the materials down before the plant is able to use any of it. Organic fertilizers usually have a clean, earthy smell and, in general, organic fertilizers have less potassium, which can be compensated for by adding small amounts of potassium magnesium sulfates into the fertilizer. Some examples of organic fertilizers include cottonseed meal, fish emulsion (fish protein that acts as a fertilizer), and blood meal, which is made from the blood of dead animals and is high in nitrogen.

Inorganic fertilizers

Synthetic or inorganic fertilizers contain mineral-based ingredients, such as salt and organic materials. Synthetic plant fertilizers are sold as tablets, sticks, granules, or in liquid form. The purpose of synthetic fertilizer is to act quickly with as minimal damage as

possible. Because the synthetic fertilizer acts quickly, there is a tendency to overuse it, which is damaging to the plant. There is a danger that salt inside of synthetic fertilizers will settle in the soil and kill all of the soil's living organisms.

New soil mixtures have enough nutrients that fertilizer does not need to be added. It is better to wait at least six weeks after repotting plants in fertilized soil before feeding them fertilizer again because the soil is already heavy in nutrients. When it is time to fertilize, add fertilizer to moist soil because plants that are alive but stressed out in dry soil conditions are going to use more of the fertilizer's nutrients than they need. Before fertilizing, be sure the plant is between 2 and 4 inches tall. As a rule, plants should be fertilized when they are actively producing. Most plants undergo growing and blooming periods from the spring through the fall. Other experts recommend fertilizing three to five weeks after the plant finishes germinating. Healthy plants benefit from fertilizer, but sick plants will not have the strength to absorb the nutrients.

The amount of fertilizer a plant needs depends on several factors including light, age, the time of year, temperature, the size of the root mass, and the overall rate at which the particular plant grows. During resting periods, plants need little fertilization and water. As with water and sunlight, plants will tell their gardeners if they are receiving too much or too little fertilizer. Plants that do not have enough fertilizer grow, but they grow weakly. Weak plants have pale, small leaves and yellowing veins. After two or three feedings, weak plants will perk up and take better color within three to five days. When plants are given too much fertilizer, their leaves are very dark and, the edges of the leaves brown and curl. A blooming houseplant that is overdosed with nitrogen may not produce any buds. Before you conclude that a plant has been overfertilized, take time to assess light and watering meth-

ods as well to ensure it is fertilizer that is harming your plant. It is clear that fertilizer is doing its job when the newly formed leaves are equal in size, shape, and color as the older leaves.

Plants do not use every nutrient that fertilizer supplies. Moisture tends to evaporate in the topsoil, which is where salt tends to build up. Sometimes the salt deposits are visible on the rims of the plant containers and, in some cases, salt is visible on the topsoil, also. Salt destroys root tissues and hinders the plant's ability to absorb and distribute nutrients and water.

The drenching process is one way to remove excess salts that compromise the integrity of the houseplant. Pots need to be flushed out every four weeks in a practice called double watering or **drenching**. The drenching procedure requires gardeners to water plants thoroughly two or three times with douses of clean, lukewarm water. The excess water then drips through the drainage holes for 30 minutes, and then the pots are drenched in water a second time. If the plant is especially sensitive to salts, drench for a third time. It is important to remove the accumulated excess water from the pot trays when the drenching process is complete. Allow the plant to dry out after drenching. When the plant is dry, it is fine to resume its regular watering and feedings. Without the excess salt in the soil, the plant will absorb food and water heartily.

CASE STUDY:
INFO FROM AN
INDUSTRY EXPERT

Mark Whittier
Pike Nurseries
Color, Foliage, and Sod Buyer
2675 Breckinridge Blvd, Suite 300,
Duluth GA 30096
www.pikenursery.com
770-921-1022

Mark Whittier, who works with Pike Nurseries and is the color, foliage, and sod buyer for the company, provided some interesting viewpoints and information about houseplants from his wealth of knowledge. When asked about his experience, Whittier said that he has 12 years of experience as a grower of specialty interior plants, which include plants such as topiary ivy, topiary herbs, topiary tropicals, indoor citrus, poinsettias, and forced bulbs. He also has experience growing annuals, perennials, and roses. He has 24 years of experience as a buyer of interior grade tropical foliage with the last four of those years being with the largest independent garden center in the United States, Pike Nurseries.

Perhaps one of the most interesting bits of information that Whittier offered was about what attracted him to the horticulture and interiorscaping industries. "Although my education is in business, specifically management sciences, my love of nature and the outdoors quickly won out. I did not even last a year with my first job out of college, sequestered in a windowless office behind a massive CRT monitor. My brother had worked with an interiorscape maintenance firm in Atlanta, but it was not for him. He suggested I might enjoy that type of work. I found the opportunity to work with incredibly beautiful, exotic, and even fragrant plants, and was able to work with them often outdoors. Along with it came far more interaction with interesting people, some travel, and a chance to employ and develop my skills."

Many people who have a passion for this industry and work in the career bring business home with them. Whittier is the same. When asked about his houseplant collection, he said, "I have always kept houseplants

throughout my 24-year career. At first, my home was like the Hanging Gardens of Babylon. I sought out every manner of discount plant to nurse back to thriving — everything from fuchsia to Australian tree ferns to Juniper bonsai to one of my all-time favorites, a lemonquat. It has been some years since I gave that lemonquat tree away, and I have not been able to find one since. As the name implies, it is a hybrid between a lemon and kumquat, with tart fruit larger even than a Eureka Lemon and the most wicked thorns ever, similar to Poncirus trifoliate thorns."

Plants are a part of his life, and he likes to keep them close by. How does he accomplish this in his home and space? "Both my wife, whom I met through the industry, and I like to keep the majority of our houseplants in the great room and kitchen where we spend the most time. There are a wide variety of light conditions, so we position the most light-demanding species near the room's southern exposure windows, and other plants rotate back and forth into other locations. We like an organized, architectural space where we relax; we tend to use plants like Dracaena deremensis, Crassula argentea, and Sansevieria cylindrical."

The impact houseplants have on a home is important on the humans that live there. According to Whittier, "Humans have a primal need to stay connected with life and nature in general. Not only do indoor plants fulfill that basic need, but they also enhance the beauty of our home and work environments in a way no art or décor ever could. Furthermore, the research continues to mount to support the notion that, in addition to converting CO_2 to oxygen, plants are natural air filters, crucial to cleaning our increasing toxic atmosphere. As we add more and more toxins and carbon to the air, the need for plants becomes greater and greater."

Although we stress the importance of choosing the right container for the plant, Whittier offers a different view on the way that he selects plants. "Often plant choice begins with the container. We usually find a container we love and then decide which room's décor it is best suited to and where it will sit. Next, we look for plants that have the right habit for that placement (upright, bushy, or trailing) and will not outgrow the container too quickly. Of course, the relative natural light level is also considered (low, medium, or high). I am a believer that artificial light contributes little to the general health of houseplants, so natural light is the

key. Still, there are plenty of beautiful and interesting options for low light. For us, the number of plants in a room is determined by a combination of the volume of space (not only length and width, but also height), the exposure and amount of glass, and the amount of time we spend in a room."

Like a pet, houseplants can hold some people back when it comes to taking trips. However, Whittier recommends using a self-watering container. These can be just as good, he says, as using a trustworthy friend to water plants. "Depending on the variety, most houseplants will be fine untended for two up to four weeks in a well-designed, self-watering container. For interior plants, I find these less risky than automatic drip systems, slow-release bottles, or well-meaning inexperienced friends."

Like most growers, Whittier is all about the organic soil options available. Soil is so important, and this is why he prefers using "organic potting media since it is partly composed of living organisms such as mycorrhizae and beneficial bacteria that symbiotically benefit the plant." He also provides insight into what he uses at home. "I use organic fertilizers as well to feed the soil, which in turn helps the plants absorb the full gamut of nutrients, just as nature intended. While it is certainly possible to grow and maintain perfectly lovely plants using synthetic media and fertilizers, it can be a constant battle to adjust pH, maintain nutrition, and avoid salt buildups."

Many people are investing in herbal gardens and bringing fruit trees indoors. This can be an ideal investment in some cases, but as Whittier recommends, you have to know what you are doing to make it work. He offers some key advice for growers who plan to do this type of horticulture indoors. "Herbs and citrus make fantastic houseplants. With both, the most critical factor is an absolute minimum of four hours direct sunlight. For herbs, high light is important to maintaining compact, vigorous growth (and regrowth as you harvest). Floppy, stretchy plants will not produce much edible foliage, and will not recover well from cutting, if at all. With citrus, high light is necessary for bud initiation. Without flowers, there can be no fruit. This typically, takes place during the transitions from winter to spring and summer to fall when the day length is right, and when days are warm and nights are cool.

With his experience, Whittier provides this final piece of advice for the beginner in houseplants. "The first, most important lesson I learned is that it is far better to underwater than to overwater. 'Overwatering' refers to the frequency of watering. I tell people that you cannot give a plant too much water at once, but you can water too often. So, water deeply and thoroughly, but allow the soil to dry somewhat before the next watering. The soil and roots need to breathe just like we do. Aquatic and bog plants are the exceptions because they have specially adapted roots that allow them to extract gasses from water without suffocating."

THE RIGHT PLANT FOR YOUR HOME

Houseplants are available by the thousands, and every plant has a unique purpose. Fragrant plants and flowers release scents into the air, and blooming plants have vibrant, joyful colors that immediately brighten an environment. Flowering houseplants are equally fun in work environments or places in the home. The right houseplant lends exotic energy to bedrooms, halls, entryways, and stairwells.

There are endless varieties of houseplants, and they are for sale almost everywhere. Evergreens, such as pothos, a common vine-like houseplant, and ivy stay green all year long. They are tremendously popular houseplants because they are easy to care for and manage to grow without full or direct sunlight. Chain stores such as Target and Walmart, grocery stores, and drug stores sell various plants throughout the year, and many home improvement stores, such as Lowe's and Home Depot, have their own garden centers. Countless online nurseries such as the North Car-

olina retailer Plant Delights Nursery Inc. (**www.plantdelights. com**) and Accents for Home and Garden (**www.accentsforhome- andgarden.com**) will deliver plants to your home. Beware that shipping costs may become a little pricey.

Many experts recommend getting new houseplants from a full nursery. Experts work at nurseries, and their livelihoods depend on the growth and sale of their cultivated plants, so you are sure to receive reliable information from the staff at these gardening centers. For homeowners who wish to fill their homes with hard to find, exotic, or tropical plants, online mail order nurseries are their best bets because many species of plants are difficult or im- possible to find in local nurseries.

How to Choose Your Plant

The health of a plant when it is purchased is an important compo- nent in plant care. The average consumer assumes store owners are selective shoppers, like themselves. However, this is often not the case, and unsuspecting consumers often end up buying plants that are less than ideal because they are unhealthy. When buying plants from retail outlets, you must check the vitality of the plant, and you also must be sure the plant does not have bugs, spiders, or any other pests or small creatures nesting and building in it.

Choosing a healthy plant sounds simple enough, but in order to actually do so, a novice gardener must be fully aware of what a healthy and strong plant looks like. A strong and healthy plant stands up straight, has a firm stem, and its foliage is so eye-catch- ing that it pops with healthy and vibrant color. Plants that are weak and pale with a sad and droopy look are not likely to perk up simply because they are in a new home with a new owner. Removing the weak plant from its current habitat, whether that is a grocery store or a sidewalk sale, will likely increase that plant's

current stress. There is little hope such a plant will grow to become a healthy specimen.

Similarly, it is not a good idea to purchase plants with flowers already in bloom because the flowers may fall off during the ride home. Buying an annual that has flowers that fall off is a waste of money because the plant will die within a year and never bloom again. If a perennial's flowers fall off, the grower has to wait another year to see the blooms again. In each scenario, it is better to have the plants bloom indoors where homeowners can experience nature's beauty.

Unhealthy and diseased plants are easy to spot because they are gray and have hairy mold or pale, blotchy spots on their leaves. These are clear indications of disease and root rot. Plants that have yellow leaves, rather than bright or deep green leaf color, have not been given enough light; avoid purchasing a plant that looks like this. Plants that have worn and nibbled edges are infested with pests. If infested plants enter a home, the pests will procreate and destroy healthy plants already living in the home. Round, brown lumps on a plant's stems indicate disease and poor health.

Do not be timid about checking the roots of a plant because a plant with weak roots will not grow properly. Purchasing pot-bound plants is also a problem. In extreme cases, the roots of pot-bound plants travel upward and situate themselves at the top of the soil. Pot-bound plants are likely to have rotten, discolored, flimsy roots. Such a plant is a growing challenge best resolved by experienced gardeners, and even experienced gardeners may not be able to remedy the problem. It is easy to check for healthy roots of small plants. If the plant is in a 6-inch container, put your fingers in the plant's soil, lift the plant from its container, and look at its roots.

It makes good sense for beginner gardeners to purchase plants that are 6 to 12 inches tall. Usually, these small plants are common houseplants and are relatively inexpensive. Smaller and younger plants adapt quickly to new environments and to new caregivers who may overwater or who may be a little absent-minded when it comes to light and nutritional needs. Smaller houseplants are wise investments because they grow with their owners over time.

It is tempting for new growers to purchase large, expensive houseplants because they dramatically and immediately change the appearance of a particular living space. However, large houseplants and indoor trees are not good investments for new growers because if they are improperly cared for, they die quickly. When purchasing larger plants, know exactly where that plant will sit inside of your home, and make a commitment not to move it. Larger and older plants take longer to adjust to new environments because their roots, stems, and leaves have fully adapted to a certain quality of life. A new environment means different air, different lighting, and differing watering periods, so the best way to help the mature plant adjust is to keep it in one position for a while.

When purchasing plants for design and decoration, prioritize and organize your decorating and growing strategies. Does your home have sufficient light and space for a new plant? Living rooms and dining rooms are typically ideal spaces to grow houseplants because, generally, these are larger rooms that offer open, natural light and steady temperatures. Tall, upright plants with slender branches, such as the dragon tree (*Dracaena concinna*), are good fits in long and narrow living and dining room areas because they do not take up much room.

Before purchasing a plant, find out how large its leaves and stems will grow. Be sure the room in the home, apartment, or office is tall enough and for the plant to mature to its maximum height.

Some of the larger, indoor houseplants are similar to trees and can grow taller than 8 feet. If allowed, vines, ivy, and ivy-like houseplants, such as pothos and philodendrons, will crawl to lengths well over 35 feet. Take advantage of decorating a small, empty vertical space by hanging plants from the ceiling.

Cascading vines look lovely when placed atop mantels, china cabinets, or file cabinets. Other plants, like hydrangeas, are better suited for tabletops because they are much more beautiful when viewed from above. If your room's wallpaper or background has strong horizontal lines, then a vertical plant, like a snake plant (*Sansevieria trifasciata*), will contrast nicely. To create vertical accents in a large and airy living room space, place a row of the same tall plant behind a sofa. Be creative and spontaneous with decoration and design, but always keep size and scale in mind. Medium-size plants that are at least 1 to 3 feet tall work well in smaller spaces and, often, cost less than mature and taller trees or plants.

Easy-to-Care-for Houseplants

Easy-to-grow plants thrive without a lot of help from humans, little water, and without full sunlight, which is great because full sunlight is difficult to find in some interior living spaces. The following is a compilation of common houseplants that are easy to work with and easy to grow, primarily because their major requirements are indirect sunlight, normal household temperatures, and regular humidity levels. These plants are ideal for the novice gardener who occasionally forgets to perform plant care basics like watering. Note, propagate is a term used throughout plant descriptions within this book. This describes the process of encouraging plants to reproduce.

- **Snake plant** (*Sansevieria trifasciata*): This tall, upright green plant enjoys both direct and indirect sunlight. It is considered one of the most carefree houseplants because it adapts quickly in homes, workplaces, and shopping malls. It tolerates neglect, but responds to good maintenance by growing sturdy, sword-shaped leaves. The plant needs to be cleaned for dust periodically, and sometimes, a very old snake plant will produce white flowers in the winter. Interiorscapers use the snake plant to decorate rooms that have strong horizontal lines. Water the snake plant only when the top ½ inch of soil dries out. In the winter, water it less frequently because standing water will kill this plant quickly. Provide the snake plant with cactus food one time per month. If the leaves of the plant soften, this is an indication of overfeeding. Repot the plant each spring into a pot one size larger than the previous pot. To propagate, use a leaf cutting, using only healthy, green portions of the leaves.

- **Paper plant** (*Fatsia japonica*): This evergreen has wide and large leaves. It can be grown both indoors and outdoors. This plant grows quickly and requires a fair amount of vertical and horizontal space because it can grow as high as 5 feet. To care for this plant, provide even watering throughout the summer months to keep the soil moist. During the winter months, allow the soil to dry somewhat, but keep the root ball moist by ensuring the soil closest to the root bulb is damp. Feed this plant weekly from spring through fall. Propagate using a cutting from the woody stem, softwood, or from semi-hardwood cuttings. This plant requires sun to partial shade. Repot if it grows to fill the pot in the spring.

- **Swiss cheese plant** or **taro vine** (*Monstera deliciosa*): The Swiss cheese plant is a large plant with elephant ear leaves. It is called "Swiss cheese" because of the holes near the veins of the plant. It can grow to be 10 feet tall. The Swiss cheese plants like sunlight and partial sun, but it needs very little watering and can tolerate dryness between watering. For overall care, keep the soil moist,

not overly wet. Feed this plant one time every two weeks or less. From time to time, use a damp, clean cloth to wipe off the plant's leaves. This encourages proper respiration for the plant. In addition, thin roots may form and grow out of the soil. Turn these roots downward, pushing them slightly into the soil. Avoid cutting these roots, but try to keep them underground if possible. Repot as the plant grows, using a quality potting soil, and ensure the pot allows proper drainage. Propagate through seed, suckers, or stem cuttings.

- **Oleander** (*Nerium oleander*): Oleander is a large evergreen shrub with dark, leathery, and attractive green leaves.

Oleander produces fragrant and colorful flowers, but every part of the plant is poisonous. Oleander is one of the easiest plants to care for because it needs little attention. It will thrive when the soil remains damp throughout the summer months. You can allow water to sit in a saucer for this plant without a problem. Feed it weekly or every other week. Prior to overwatering the plant, avoid removing any fresh flower shoots or the dead blooms from the plant, as this will stress the plant too much. If the plant becomes overrun with roots, prune several of the roots down to the soil

level to keep it from spreading too much. To propagate this plant, use cuttings in water. This plant does best in full sun, but will tolerate partial sun. Separate the offsets as they grow for propagation of the plant. Repot only when plant grows to within a few inches of the pot's edge.

- **Kaffir** or **bush lily** (*Clivia minata*): The Kaffir lily has beautiful, dark green leaves that can grow as long as 24 inches. It also blooms reds flowers. This is an easy-to-care-for plant because as long as it is left alone, it will grow beautiful red flowers. The Kaffir lily does not need a lot of water because, like most plants with big green waxy leaves, the water absorbs well through the roots, which allows the plant's soil to dry in between watering. Feed this plant once every other week or less. This plant prefers shaded or filtered light. Propagate by seed or by removing suckers. Repot the plant if it becomes pot bound.

- **Cast iron plant** (*Aspidistra elatior*): The cast iron plant is a relative of the lily family and is a favorite among interior gardeners because this plant is capable of surviving in very dry conditions. It prefers to grow in an area where the light levels are low. The cast iron plant actually earned its name because it is capable of growing and surviving in the worst of conditions, which include deeply shaded outdoors. Fully domesticated for years now, its leaves grow up to 3 feet tall and 4 inches wide. The cast iron plant should be potted in a large pot with standard, all-purpose houseplant soil that must be kept evenly moist, except during the winter when the plant is resting and can withstand dry conditions. Repot this plant every two to three years as necessary due to the growth of the plant. Repot during the spring months for best result. Use a

standard potting mix to replant. Avoid waterlogging this plant even in short term. Propagate by division; each portion of the plant needs to have at least two leaves when divided. Feed this plant lightly in spring, and then as needed through the late summer months.

- **Christmas cactus** (*Zygocactus* or *Schlumbergera*): Most easy-to-care-for plants are typically deep green waxy leaf plants, but the Christmas cacti come with a lot more characteristics. There are so many types of cacti plants available because crossbreeding them has long been a popular and common practice among growers and plant traders. The Christmas cactus is popular as a holiday plant because it blooms near the holidays. Flowers of this cactus are deep pink or red and appear in the early winter season. Growers who do not leave the plant in cool temperatures before the holiday season will not experience these flowers bloom. Its flowers blossom when kept in cool temperatures under 65 degrees during the month of November. This one temperature requirement may be a difficult accommodation for people who live in Southern states.

However, because the cacti do not need much in terms of food or water, a plant of the cacti family is always one of the easiest plants to care for. This plant likes bright light and direct sunlight during the winter, and even though the instructions for maintaining this plant sound tedious, the Christmas cactus is a common and popular choice among growers because it does well when left alone. Like other cacti, the Christmas cacti prefer to spend their summers outdoors until the night temperatures drop to 40 degrees. This plant experiences best results when it is moved to its indoor holiday display area once the buds begin to sprout sometime in early December. The Christmas cactus in bloom does not like to be disturbed, and if the plant loses flowers, that means it has been stressed or handled more than necessary. It is wise not to purchase this plant while it is in full bloom because the flowers may not survive the transition from the store to its new location. Feed this plant one time every two weeks. You also want to spray the leaves of the plant, without wetting the flowers, once every month while keeping the soil moist as well. Allow a period of rest after blooming. You can force a bloom by decreasing the watering and lowering the temperature. Do this for three months before you want the plant to bloom. Once the blooms show, water weekly. To propagate, use stem cuttings. Repot this plant in the spring to a larger pot as it outgrows smaller pots.

- **Lucky bamboo** (*Dracaena sanderiana*): Lucky bamboo is not really a bamboo plant but is actually a member of the lily family. Feng shui enthusiasts are particularly enamored with this plant because it is believed that the lucky bamboo brings good energy. This is an interesting plant to grow because it will last in water as well as soil. It also grows

well in rocks and water rather than a soil. If you gather rocks or pebbles from outdoors to grow bamboo, be sure to sterilize the rocks first. Its leaves and stalk will reach as high as 3 feet without much fuss while sitting in indirect sunlight. The plant needs lots of light, even if the light does not shine directly on the plant. If the plant is grown in water with pebbles, the water pot should be changed every other week. In potted containers, the lucky bamboo thrives with irregular watering from spring through autumn. Irregular watering may mean once every two or three weeks. After the summer season, however, it needs enough water to keep the mix from drying out. Use stem cutting for propagation. Repot in the spring whenever the plant's root ball grows too large for the pot. Feed lightly during watering.

- **Pothos** (*Epipremnum aureum*): This common and inexpensive plant is what some consider the easiest to grow, and its vine stems, if allowed, will trail well over 10 feet. Popular in homes and offices, this plant's glossy, heart-shaped leaves can climb up a moist moss pole or cascade down from a high planter or hanging basket. Pothos plants grow faster under bright light, but this plant will die if overwatered because its roots will succumb quickly to drenched and clogged soil. Keep soil just moist. Even during the repotting period, the pothos demands dry conditions while it adjusts in the new container. These are quite vigorous plants, and they flourish in offices where there is fluorescent light. They work hard at clearing air in new houses that have air pollutants such as formaldehyde and other contaminants from plywood or carpets. Feed this plant only once every month or so. Propagate using stem cuttings.

- **Spider plant** (*Chlorophytum comosum*): This South African plant grows best in pots, and it needs to stay in the pot until it clearly outgrows its container. If positioned in a room with insufficient light year round, the plant must be  fed fertilizer to assist with its growth. The popular spider plant is not a finicky plant and is fully capable of growing unaided in indirect light, with light feedings. Ideally, feed the plant every few weeks and keep it in indirect sunlight. Spider plants are safe in dorms, apartments, and offices because they can be left alone for days and not suffer. When the roots of the spider plant fill the container, which will occur once every couple of years, the plant is ready for repotting. The spider plant is usually reproducing dangling baby plants, or plantlets, at the roots. The plantlets can be removed by cutting and can be planted to dwell in their own containers. Visually, this is a dramatic plant, particularly when placed in a hanging basket or on a pedestal where the leaves are free to sprout and fall. The soil of this particular plant should remain moist in the spring through autumn months, but during the winter, the plant needs less moisture, and the plant will maintain its healthy condition as it withstands drier soil. Once this plant gets dried out, however, its leaves become a permanent brown. Saving a browned plant at this level is

unlikely. If maintained properly, the green leaves on the spider plant grow to heights of 2 feet.

- **Philodendron** (*Philodendron bipinnatifidum*): The philodendron has been used as a houseplant since the Victorian age. It is a popular and hard-to-kill houseplant. It has waxy green leaves, and it is a vining plant. If a stick is placed in its soil, the vines can be trained to grow up and around the stick. This tropical plant requires some sun, but if sunlight is not available, the plant is equally satisfied to grow in an artificial light. It can go for days without being watered, but it does prefer warm, moist air. Avoid allowing this plant to dry out. Use a damp cloth to wipe down the leaves once every two weeks to help encourage respiration. During the spring to fall season, feed the plant one time every two weeks. In the winter, feed one time every month or less frequently. Faster growing plants will need more watering and a higher humidity level. Never cut aerial roots, but otherwise, you can prune this plant back. To propagate, do so by tip or stem cuttings. Repot rarely, only when the plant's roots become compact.

- **Jade plant/money tree** (*Crassula ovata*): This gorgeous, waxy-leaf plant needs bright sunlight to grow and does not tolerate humidity. It can grow to be 30 inches or more and does not require much care. The plant will sunburn if it is moved from subdued lighting to full sun, so growers must be sure not to dramatically change its light and heat exposure when searching for better light. The jade plant likes moderate temperatures, between 75 and 80 degrees during the day, and it likes cool nights when temperatures do not fall below 40 degrees. Every two years, the healthy jade needs repotting. The plant's soil

should be kept slightly moist during the spring and summer months, and its soil should be completely dried out before its next watering. Jade is dormant in the winter, and its soil should be kept dry. This plant needs fertilizer to grow, but experts recommend they not be fertilized

from November through the end of March because the plants rest during that time. Around September or early October, money trees should be moved into a room where there is natural light; exposing jade to lights at night will prevent its Christmas bloom. Having the plant engage in photosynthesis outside of its natural waking hours will limit the colorful blooms that make this plant special. Propagate using stem cuttings.

- **Chinese evergreen** (*Aglaonema commutatum*): The Chinese evergreen's thick and leathery leaves grow to 12 inches and are olive colored with gray-green edges. This plant likes cool light and needs to be kept thoroughly moist from spring to autumn and slightly drier in winter. This is a slow-growing plant that does not need repotting very often. The Chinese evergreen will not survive a drowning, so it is important that this plant does not experience overwatering and that it is placed in a container that permits sufficient drainage. It is a common houseplant choice because it will thrive without a lot of attention. It tolerates the cold very well, but will die in temperatures

below 55 degrees. With its low tolerance for salt, use a 3-1-2 ratio (3 percent nitrogen to 1 percent phosphorus to 2 percent potassium) of slow release feed for this plant and do so only once every other month. Repot in the spring.

- **Ivy** (*x Fatshedera lizei*): The x in front of the Latin name for this ivy indicates that the plant is a crossbreed. The *x Fatshedera* is an evergreen ivy, and its waxy green leaves have five points that resemble a claw or a small hand. Ivy is easy to grow and care for, as it only needs light and water to thrive, which is why it is considered a hard-to-kill houseplant. Keep the soil of this plant evenly moist. If the plant is kept in a moderate temperature room, mist the plant with cool water once a week. During growth periods, the plant needs feeding one time per week. A young plant will need repotting every year. As the plant grows and ages, repot one time every two to three years instead. This plant will likely avoid branching out on its own. If you want it to begin to branch out, prune it back to encourage the new growth to continue. Ivy tolerates partial to direct sunlight. To propagate, wait until spring, and then use tip cuttings, or propagate through seed.

- **English ivy** (*Hedera helix*): This plant climbs to lengths of 100 feet, but it makes a great indoor plant because it can be positioned to grow as a decorative frame around fireplaces, kitchen cabinets, bathroom mirrors, and similar interior ornaments. In the summer, ivy thrives with light and cool temps, but it does not benefit from direct sunlight. With weekly watering and monthly feedings, the ivy will climb and grow well. Every two or three years, the healthy ivy needs repotting. Ivy is a very easy plant to take care of in your home, but because it grows so long, it is important to

have enough room for it, or to have friends and family who would love to have your pruned stems. This is another great houseplant plant because it is known to clean and improve air quality inside homes. To propagate this plant, do so by tip or stem cuttings for the best results.

- **African violet** (*Saintpaulia*): African violets add a wonderful burst of color to interior spaces, particularly interior spaces composed largely of neutrals. This small, flowering plant has fleshy, rosette-forming, hairy leaves, and its flowers are white, pink, or purple. The plant comes in shades of pink, blue, and red with multicolored hybrids. African violets grow in warm light and partial shade, and  they are easy and popular houseplants because they grow flowers that do not need strong sun. The violets need to be watered once a week, and it is best that the plant is able to dry out before being watered again because it does not like to be held down by soggy, water-bogged roots. In the winter, keeping the plant dry and cool for a while will give it a rest. The wilted flowers of African violets should be removed immediately. Propagate through leaf cuttings. Feed every time you water using a high-phosphate soluble feed to encourage blooming. Repot in the spring as needed.

- **Cacti** (*Cactaceae*): There are many varieties of cacti, but there is one characteristic that earns the cactus plant a place in the *Cactaceae* family, and that is the presence of

areoles — the specialized buds where spines and new bodies, or stems, grow. Nine popular species of cacti are recommended for easy growing:

1. **Rat tail cactus** *(Disocactus flagelliformis)*: The rat tail may be considered by some to be a trailing or creeping plant because its stems are so long that they can grow to be 4 feet long. This plant blooms in the spring when it is exposed to bright light, and it blooms in half shade in the summer, fall, and winter months. During the spring and summer, the rat tail needs thorough watering, and it will not need more moisture until the soil is completely dried. In the fall and winter, less water is needed, but the soil must not dry out completely. The leaves of the rat tail hang, and the plant is a great ornamental piece that decorates and complements a room when potted in a hanging basket or placed on a pedestal or ledge. The needles on this plant are sharp, so beware when positioning in high traffic areas. Feed one time per year, in the spring, using a water-soluble fertilizer. Propagate using seeds or cuttings in the spring or summer. Only repot if the plant outgrows its container.

2. **Peruvian apple cactus** *(Cereus peruvianus)*: The most common Peruvian apple cacti are tall and linear. These plants like being outdoors in the summer. A full-grown plant is heavy, and its spiny needles hurt. From the late spring to early fall, the plant needs bright light, and it probably thrives better outdoors so it can absorb the natural sunlight and higher temperatures. Cacti in general are easy to care for because they rarely need water. In the winter, it needs a bright light from a south or west window. This cactus prefers indoor

temperatures. Feed this plant one time per month. To propagate, do so by seed or through cuttings. The cuttings will root easily after you allow them to dry for a day. Repot this plant each year to prevent the plant's root from becoming pot bound.

3. **Powder puff, snowball,** or **golden star** *(Parodia nivosa)*: This plant has several different common names. Powder puff cacti are easy to grow, bloom at will, and adapt to homes and office environments quite well. Yellow, orange, pink, or red flowers appear atop these plants. In their natural habitat, warm rain falls and waters the plants, and in the winter, the powder puff endures long, dry, and temperate zone conditions. It would be wise and fun to duplicate the plant's natural growing conditions and watch it mature into a healthy houseplant. Like most other cacti, this plant loves to spend its summer outdoors in a half-shaded area. Feed this plant cactus food one time every three weeks. To propagate, use only seed, but the process is difficult because it is slow. Only repot if the plant overgrows container.

4. **Aloe** *(Aloe vera)*: Most people do not realize that aloe is a member of the cactus family. It is a succulent plant like other cacti because its leaves retain moisture longer than the average houseplant. The sap of the aloe plant has medicinal properties and relieves pain from minor burns and scratches. The aloe plant needs direct sunlight and should not be moved from bright to dim lit areas because the leaves of the aloe suffer when forced to adjust to rapidly changing environments. This plant needs only moderate watering when the soil dries out.

 It does not require watering during the winter months, or water once every month if the conditions are very dry. Do not wet the rosette during watering, and avoid standing water or waterlogging this plant. If you feed this plant, feed it very lightly. With a standard potting mix, this plant will do well on its own without feedings. You can repot, if necessary. If you decide to repot, do so in the spring. To propagate, do so without damaging the rootstock.

5. **Prickly pear** *(Opuntia)*: This cactus must have well-drained soil and be placed in a sunny location. It has sharp thorns and barbed bristles that prick and stay in the skin. It produces a yellow-orange colored flower and an inedible, deep red fruit. It cannot withstand standing water. However, this plant requires regular watering in the summer months to keep the soil moist. In the winter months, it needs water when the soil dries out. Feed this plant once a week with cactus food. You will need to repot in spring months anytime the plant grows significantly from one year to another. To propagate, use separated segments after drying them.

6. **Rose cactus** *(Pereskia grandifolia)*: This ancient cactus is perhaps the only cactus that has leaves like plants

outside of the cacti family. However, it also has spines like other cacti. Oddly enough, this cactus is different from other succulents because it does not have tissues to store water, so it has to be cared for like other houseplants. These plants may be drought resistant, but it is best to keep their soil moist and spared from completely drying out. To propagate, do so by herbaceous tip cuttings. The plant does best in sunny conditions. Water this plant regularly through the summer and less in the winter. With a good potting soil, you should not have to feed this plant. However, repot each year in the spring.

7. **Starfish/carrion flowers** *(Stapelia hirsuta)*: Known as African starfish flowers, the *Stapelia* is best known for its foul-smelling flowers. It blooms a large star and it is almost 1 foot wide. The stems are usually erect and green to reddish, depending on the amount of time it was exposed to full sun. The plant is propagated through stem cuttings taken in the spring. Position the plant in full sun. It needs moderate (without standing) watering throughout the growing season. Keep moist throughout the year otherwise. Use a fertilizer one time during the growing season, and repot only when the plant outgrows the pot.

8. **Easter cactus** *(Hatiora gaertneri)*: The Easter cactus

is a close relative of the Christmas cactus and has flat, segmented stems. The Easter cactus blooms in early spring. The flowers have multiple pointed petals and are usually red or pink. Less winter watering helps the plant bloom strong in spring. This plant needs light to partial shade. It needs to remain slightly moist throughout the year. Propagate this plant using its shoot segments and feed every two weeks.

9. **Torch cactus** (*Trichocereus peruvianus* also known as *Echninocereus candicans*): This particular cactus is easy to grow and tolerates drought. It is the miniature version of typical desert cactus found in American southwestern deserts, although it is a plant native to Argentina. The torch cactus is a slow grower, needs direct sunlight, and can be grown in a sand and soil mix but will not tolerate only sand. The soil needs to be barely moist year round. It is a large columnar plant that should grow to be 40 inches tall. Propagate using woody stem cuttings. Allow the surface to callous over before planting cuttings. Feed once during the growing season. Repot to keep the plant from becoming pot-bound by repotting one time yearly.

Shade-thriving plants

Plants usually come with instruction tags inserted in their soil or an instruction sheet is looped onto their stems. Read those instructions carefully, and if the instructions are not there, as may be the case with plants purchased at a nursery, ask the florist, nursery owner, or salesperson what type of living conditions the plant needs. Often, the first-time indoor gardener and the impulsive shopper will choose a plant because it will look good in a

certain space at home or in the office. Many novice gardeners do not notice that the plant they choose for a shaded corner of the living room is a plant that needs 12 full hours of sunlight in order to survive.

Some interior spaces are shaded, and therefore, cooler. Shaded does not mean dark or void of light; rather, a shaded space, like a covered patio, is not exposed to full sun. In shaded spaces, the light surrounds, rather than hovers, over an area. Temperatures are lower in these spaces because of the window's location, or because objects such as leafy trees or buildings prevent sunlight from beaming directly through a window. In situations where a room receives shaded light, plants with leathery or waxy green leaves are good growing matches. Shade-thriving plants tend to retain moisture very well. Hallways and entryways are often cooler locations that do not receive direct sunlight and are ideal locations for plants that do not need full sun exposure in order to grow well.

Although plants are able to grow in shade, they must have forms of light in order to photosynthesize. Any plant left in dark shade will die because lack of sunlight reduces its ability to produce food. If left in the dark, a plant's strong stems and firm leaves will become weak. Plants will get the light they need if they are allowed to sit outside in the sunlight or if ceiling lights that are aimed directly at the plants are used to create light.

When decorating a shaded room with plants, several houseplant specimens will happily grow in a home without coming into contact with full and direct sun:

- **Cast iron plant** (*Aspidistra elatior*): This plant is called "cast iron" because it is almost impossible to kill this plant. It is tolerant of bad light, gas fumes, and extreme temperatures. This plant was very popular in Victorian

England, and today, it is considered a common houseplant that grows in clumps. Its leaves can grow up to 2 feet long. Keep this plant evenly moist throughout the summer but do not overwater. Feed it just one time per month with a weak feeding solution. You will need to repot every two to three years in the spring. Propagate through division, with each division having at least two leaves. The plant needs partial light to do best.

- **Bird's nest fern** (*Asplenium nidus*): This plant is a true fern with tall, leathery leaves and a fibrous root-like growth in its middle. The plant cannot be left in direct sunlight and needs to be watered often. Keep this plant evenly moist throughout the year. You also want to feed it every two weeks during the summer months for the best results. This plant also needs a higher level of humidity. To propagate, divide the root ball. Repot if the plant grows to fill the pot.

- **Ivy tree** (*x Fatshedera lizei*): *Fatshedera* is an evergreen and like most ivy, it is easy to grow. Its waxy green leaves have five points that resemble a claw or a small hand. From spring to autumn, you need to keep this ivy moist and offer it cool light. Cool light is similar to partial shade, which means the plant enjoys sunlight, but not direct or full sun. To propagate, do so with tip cuttings with the use of bottom heating. Repot young plants each year or mature plants every two to three years. Feed one time per week during the growing season.

- **Creeping fig** (*Ficus pumila*): The creeping fig grows low, meaning it is a short plant. Its stems and leaves climb and trail similar to vine plants. This plant has small, abundant green leaves that grow in partial shade. The ficus is easy to care for because it does not require a lot of water and

enjoys staying barely moist. To propagate, use seeds, suckers, or cuttings. Feed once every other week during the growing season. Repot in the spring every other year or as the plant grows too large for its container.

- **Paper plant** (*Fatsia japonica*): This is a tough evergreen with shiny, leathery leaves. It can cope with little or no direct sunlight and is an excellent choice for growing in shaded corners. The Fatsia needs to stay moderately moist. Propagate from woody stem or softwood cuttings. Repot in the spring. Feed during the growing season one time every other week.

- **Kentia palm** (*Howea forsteriana*): This plant tolerates a wide range of indoor conditions except deep shade. (Deep shade is associated with forest growing conditions where the sun is blocked by larger foliage. In deep shade, temperatures may be lower than normal because the area does not receive direct sunlight.) This grassy palm grows as tall as 8 feet and needs sufficient living space to grow really well. If growing plants from seeds, be sure to research the growing height of the plant before purchasing. The Kentia palm would not be an ideal plant for areas where the ceilings are less than 10 feet tall. This plant needs repotting in the spring if the plant becomes pot bound. Keep this plant evenly moist. Use a fertilizer for houseplants regularly, one time per week. Do not fertilizer during the winter months. To propagate, use stem cuttings.

- **Prayer plant** (*Maranta leuconeura*): This plant thrives in partial shade, which means it needs about two to four hours of sun during the day. It requires moderate room temperatures. This plant is called prayer plant because its waxy, veined leaves, which are light green in the center

with deep green edges, fold together at night and resemble praying hands. This plant grows to 12 inches; its leaves are shaped like large ovals and can be 5 inches long. The prayer plant needs moist soil except in the winter when the soil likes to dry out between watering. Give this plant half diluted plant food about every other week. To propagate, do so by division when you are repotting. Repot when it becomes pot bound.

- **Swiss cheese plant** or **taro vine** *(Monstera delicio)*: You can place this plant away from direct sunlight, and it will thrive with minimal water all year round. As it grows, you can train the stem against a moss pole, if you wish. **Training** means wiring or wrapping the stem and its leaves up a pole until it learns to grow there without help. Leaves on the *Monstera delicio* are large, and the plant reaches heights of close to 10 feet. Feed this plant every week with a houseplant fertilizer. To propagate, use stem cuttings or tip cuttings, using bottom heating to encourage growth.

You also can grow these plants from seed. Repot if the plant becomes pot bound.

- **Boston fern** *(Nephrolepsis exaltata)*: This common fern needs warm, partial shade and must be kept away from direct sunlight. It looks great in hanging baskets or tall pedestals. Boston ferns like humidity and should be misted with a spray bottle once every three or four days. The plant's soil should be kept moist. Feed this plant from early spring through the summer months, but only lightly, such as every other week. You can repot into a larger container when the plant becomes pot bound. To propagate, do so using offshoots or through division.

- **Tree philodendron** *(Philodendron bipinnatifidum)*: This is a tree-like shrub with a single stem and long, many-fingered leaves that become floppy as the plant ages. This plant can grow as tall as 15 feet and enjoys indirect sunlight or partial shade. This plant enjoys thorough moisture during the spring through autumn. Repot as

this plant grows out of its pot. To feed, consider the rate of growth. Plants growing faster need feedings weekly. Slow growing plants need feed just in the spring and summer months. To propagate, use tip or stem cuttings after pruning the plant.

- **Mother of thousands** (*Soleirolia soleirolii*): This small evergreen plant produces many more small plants. The little plantlets that sprout on its leaves can be cut and placed into water or soil and grown into new plants. Mother of thousands produces clusters of white flowers in the late summer and early fall. The plant likes normal room temperatures, partial shade, and indirect sunlight. The plant will do well with moistened and well-drained soil. To propagate, divide rhizomes or do so from leaf or stem cuttings. Feed the plant every other week using a houseplant fertilizer. Repot if it becomes pot bound.

- **Little club moss, spike moss** (*Selaginella martensii*): In addition to shade, this moss-like miniature evergreen must be kept in a warm, humid environment to survive. To increase humidity for a plant, place the plant container atop a tray of pebbles or water. The pebble tray is only effective in plant containers that have drainage holes at the bottom. In most homes, a warm humid bathroom may be an ideal location for this indoor plant. Repot if it becomes pot bound and use a high-quality fertilizer. Feed this plant every other week through the growing season. Propagate this plant through seed.

- **Natal ivy** or **wax vine** (*Senecio macroglossus*): This plant copes well in partial shade. Keep this plant's soil moist, but during the winter, keep it watered only enough to prevent it from drying. The natal ivy resembles the same

type of ivy that grows alongside buildings and homes, but its leaves are fleshier; some are pale yellow, while others are deep green with strong veins. Propagate through stem cuttings. Only repot when this plant becomes pot bound. Feed lightly throughout growing season.

Choosing Plants According to Location

If a plant is to last as long as it naturally can, then it must be placed in a room where the conditions best meet its needs. Temperature, light, and humidity are key factors that professionals use to determine where they wish to grow particular plant types. When considering plants for a home or office, be sure the growing conditions meet a plant's needs. A colorful, sun-loving black-eyed Susan would die in a shadowy basement den, but it would love to show off its color sitting inside a sunny windowsill in a living room, bedroom, or sunny office. The following section lists numerous plants that grow well in specific areas of the home or workplace.

Plants for foyers and hallways

Some plants need especially stable living conditions and will only grow well in rooms that are not loud, busy, or incredibly varying in light and temperatures. In most spaces, hallways and foyers are indoor locations with steady temperatures and slow traffic. In lobbies and sitting areas of schools and office buildings, stationary plants dwell peacefully and grow strongly. Situating plants in a hallway is only a viable option when there is enough space so the plant will not interfere with human traffic. Hallways are also second homes for plants that grow too large for windowsills. Unless the plant is a tall, tree-like specimen,

plants in hallways usually are placed atop pedestals, or placed in a group on the ground near an entryway. The following is a list of more plants that thrive well in quiet hallways. Smaller homes that were built around the turn of the 20th century often do not have hallways that receive natural light. Modern and more contemporary homes are usually well lit with natural and artificial lighting and generally, have wide walkways. Often, business and homeowners keep their walkways well lit with artificial lighting throughout the day, and this can be an ideal location for housing certain plants. Some of the plants in this section may sound familiar because they are repeats of plants already mentioned in the previous section.

- **Marguerite** (*Argyranthemum frutescens*): This flowering plant resembles the daisy, and it blooms in summer. Marguerites like cool environments, and they grow well in a hallway or foyer with good light. The average room temperature for houseplants is between 70 and 75 degrees, but with good light and cooler temperatures, the Marguerite's flowers will grow rich with strong color. The Marguerite is an annual and must be replaced yearly. Propagate by tip cuttings in the spring. Keep the root ball moist, and feed this plant weekly.

- **Cast iron plant** (*Aspidistra eliator*): Cast iron plants tolerate dust, drought, dimly lit areas, as well as the heat and cold. Its shiny green leaves grow to be 2 feet long. *More details on the cast iron plant can be found in the section on shade-thriving plants.*

- **Persian violet** or **florist's cyclamen** (*Cyclamen persicum*): It is best to purchase this plant from a nursery because other vendors may accidently or unknowingly expose the violet to freezing temperatures. When it undergoes temperatures

below 40 degrees, the plant will not bloom the way it should. The plant has several shapes, and its leaves are fleshy and dark green. It produces fragrant flowers, and it comes in a variety of colors, including white, purple, red, and pink. This plant thrives in humid conditions and needs plenty of water, bright, but not direct light, and two hours of direct sun or light in the winter months. The Persian violet is ideal in a sunny foyer, or in the foyer or entryway of a business or

school hall where the front doors are usually glass and let in the appropriate amount of light. Propagate through seed with bottom heat. Repot this plant every other year, using a new soil mix. Feed every 14 days.

- **Prairie gentian** (*Eustoma grandiflorum*): This is a popular flowering plant because when cut for a floral arrangement, its leaves and flowers remain solid and healthy for a while. Its summer blooms may be purple, blue, pink, or white, and it thrives in cool temperatures and indirect sunlight. The prairie gentian has average to moderate water needs. It can survive for extended periods without water, but thrives best when it is watered well. Plant in rich soil. No other feeding is necessary. Repot every year in the spring. To propagate, do so from seed during summer months, but the process is difficult.

- **Ivy tree** *(x Fatshedera lizei)*: This is an evergreen plant, and like most ivy, it is easy to grow. Its waxy green leaves have five points that resemble a claw or a small hand. This plant must be kept moist from spring to autumn. The more light this plant receives, the greener its leaves will be. This plant also likes cool light. Repot these young plants every year and mature plants every other year. Propagate by tip cuttings with bottom heating. Feed once a week while growing.

- **English ivy** *(Hedera helix)*: This popular plant needs to be moist from spring to autumn and only needs enough water in the winter to keep from drying out. This plant is a household favorite because it tolerates indirect sunlight and has the ability to withstand varying temperatures. In dry, indoor climates, the plant needs to be placed atop a plate of wet pebbles to steady soil humidity levels. Feed one time a month. Repot every two to three years. To propagate, do so with tip or stem cuttings, and use bottom heat where you place a source of heat under the plant.

- **Florist's cineraria** *(Pericallis x hybrida)*: This is an annual plant, meaning it dies after a year. It produces blue, white, pink, maroon, violet, purple, and red flowers. Most gardeners discard the plant after one season. It will grow in either sun or indirect sunlight and prefers a cool room temperature, which helps it produce vibrant flowers during its blooming period. The florist's cineraria adds color to an arrangement that is mostly or all green. Feed this plant every other week lightly. It will self-sow, so propagating happens naturally. Keep the soil moist when caring for this plant.

- **Polyanthus** *(primula x polyantha)*: The polyanthus prefers lightly shaded locations and cool temperatures as low as 50 degrees. The  soil must be watered consistently so that it remains moist at all times. Its flowers are white, yellow, pink, orange, red, and blue. Divide the root ball to propagate this plant. Feed the pot infrequently, and repot if the plant becomes pot bound.

- **Fairy rose** *(Rosa)*: Roses are not always outdoor plants. After it produces summer flowers, the indoor rose can be planted outdoors or kept inside. The soil mix must remain moist from spring to summer. Its humidity levels should be stabilized with a tray of water pebbles underneath. This plant will grow in full sun or partial shade. Feed during the growing season and repot each year in the spring. Propagate this plant using softwood cuttings or by budding.

- **Mother of thousands/strawberry geranium** *(Soleirolia soleirolii)*: This small, evergreen plant likes higher humidity, which is achieved by placing it atop a moistened pebble tray, and for at least half of the day, the plant needs direct sunlight. This plant also requires consistently wet soil Mother of thousands is another plant for foyers and entryways that are well lit or receive plenty of sunlight. Propagate by dividing the rhizomes or do so from leaf or stem cuttings. Feed the plant every other week using a houseplant fertilizer. Repot if it becomes pot bound.

- **Black-eyed Susan** *(Rudbeckia hirta)*: This cute plant needs some direct sunlight every day for a good display of its  orange, yellow, or white flowers. You must keep the soil moist all year round. The black-eyed Susan needs a bright foyer hallway in a home or office building to thrive. To propagate, do so from seed, starting the seeds in the winter. Feed this plant every two weeks, and repot the plant if it becomes pot bound.

- **African hemp** *(Sparmannia Africana)*: If this plant is placed in a cool room with indirect sunlight, it can grow to be 7 feet tall. This plant also does well on porches. It must be kept moist from spring to autumn. In winter months, it needs enough water to prevent the soil from completely drying out. Feed every other week during growing season. Repot when the plant becomes pot bound. Propagate through stem cuttings for best results.

- **Pickaback plant** or **youth on age** *(Tolmeia menziesil)*: Like the geranium plant named mother of thousands, the pickaback plant is named because of its overlapping leaf development. New forming leaves piggyback onto the older leaves, which gives the plant the appearance of a vine. It needs to be moist from spring to autumn and watered enough to keep the soil from drying out during the winter. This plant tolerates most light, except intense

mid-day sun and deep shade. You can propagate this plant by dividing the root ball or from leaf cuttings. Feed every other week. You will only need to repot the plant if it becomes pot bound.

- **Spider lily/wandering Jew** *(Hymenocallis)*: The stems of this plant will trail and hang abundantly from a hanging basket. Its leaves curl upward, and it produces flowers with three petals in the spring and summer. This plant is tolerant of most light situations. The spider lily needs moderate moisture, and overwatering this plant should be avoided. Feed this plant every two weeks during the spring and summer months. You can propagate the plant using tip cuttings in the soil or in water. Repot if it becomes pot bound.

Plants for a bathroom

Several plant species will grow in the bathroom primarily because these species will absorb as much water as they can take and soon after want more. Bathroom environments mimic natural habitats because their climates range from tropical to temperate. In most bathrooms, the air is hot and steamy while someone is bathing, or the bathroom is cool and dry when it is unoccupied for an extended period. Temperatures often fluctuate in bathrooms, so plants like ferns and ivy that fare well in climates where the air fluctuates between humid and cool are good fits for a bathroom. The common thread among the plants listed here is that they all thrive in humidity and desire moisture much more than other plants. Most, but certainly not all, plants love water, but bathroom plants thrive with extra humidity and are refreshed with the cool air. These plants can also withstand being misted with warm moisture at any point in the day.

- **Cupid's bower/nut orchid/magic flower** *(Achimenes longiflora)*: This trailing plant has green leaves and produces red or purple flowers from June through October. A **trailing plant** has vines like ivy and eventually trails long enough to wrap around poles that are placed in the soil. It tolerates indirect sunlight and temperatures between 60 and 80 degrees. Its soil must be kept moist, but if the plant owner chooses, the plant will not need watering at all during the winter because it can survive during this dormant period without water. It can grow as tall as 2 feet. Divide rhizomes for propagation. Feed this plant every other week lightly during the growing season. Repot only if it becomes pot bound.

- **Maidenhair fern** *(Adiantum)*: This fern needs moist soil all the time. This plant has long, thin branches with narrow leaves coming off of it. This plant can be light to dark green in color. It thrives in humid conditions but does not like its roots to get too wet. Keep moist, but do not allow standing water to occur. This fern likes indirect sunlight and should be stored in minimal temperatures of 50 degrees. Divide the root ball to propagate. Feed throughout the growing season. Repot this plant if it becomes pot bound.

- **Basket plant** *(Callisia fragrans)*: This plant has large, fleshy green leaves and trailing stems. It produces pretty orange-yellow or dark red flowers that grow to 4 inches. It needs lots of water during its blooming period, and it must be grown in humid conditions. Even when grown in humid conditions, this plant does not rest and must be watered all year. To propagate this plant, use stem cuttings. This plant needs sun to partial sun. You should feed it during

the growing period of spring through summer, and repot only if the plant becomes pot bound.

- **Flamingo flower/tailflower** *(Anthuriam scherzerianum)*: These pretty flowering plants with long, bright orange and red flowers are similar in appearance to miniature orchids. From spring until autumn, its soil must be thoroughly moist. It survives in indirect sunlight, and the lowest temperature it can survive in is 65 degrees. Repot this plant when it grows too large for its pot. Feed it a slow-release fertilizer during the spring and late summer. Propagate from stem cuttings.

- **Emerald fern** *(Asparagus densiflorus)*: This plant looks like a fern, but its stems are woody, and they arch straight up. It likes indirect sunlight and needs thoroughly moist soil in the spring and summer months. It will tolerate little water during winter as long as the soil does not dry out. You can divide this plant to propagate. Keep the plant in a healthy soil, and repot each year in spring. Feed lightly through summer.

- **Begonia** *(Begonia bowerae)*: There are many begonia species available, but the *bowerae* loves high humidity. The *bowerae* is a bushy, stemless, flower-producing plant, but because it loves high humidity, it is susceptible to gray mold that accompanies high humidity. To grow begonias, use a wet pebble tray and clean its leaves regularly. This plant grows best in indirect sunlight. Keep moist throughout the year, and feed every two weeks. You can repot if the plant becomes pot bound, using a flower soil mixture. Propagate this plant from tip cuttings.

- **Yesterday, today, and tomorrow** *(Brunsfelsia pauciflora)*: The macrantha is a shrub with deep purple flowers that change from a deep purple to lavender to white in a three-day time span. It likes direct sunlight, does not tolerate mid-day summer sun, and craves high humidity. Keep the soil evenly moist. Feed this plant biweekly during the growing season. You can propagate it using tip cuttings, but the process can be slow and difficult. Repot the plant if it becomes pot bound.

- **Gardenia** *(Gardenia ellis)*: This beautiful, flowering shrub needs moist soil, high humidity, and indirect sunlight. It is an interior gardening favorite because of its beautiful, white flowers and deep green, waxy leaves and fragrance. Feed this plant every other week using a non-alkaline fertilizer. You can repot the plant when it becomes pot bound. To propagate, do so from tip cuttings during the fall or spring.

- **Boston fern** *(Nephrolepsis exalta)*: The Boston fern's native habit is the tropics, which is one reason this is also a good bathroom plant. It likes sun and warm, humid air all year. Unlike other ferns, Bostons do not react negatively when

their exposure to sunlight is increased. The Boston fern has light green, cascading leaves that grow in arches. This lush plant looks good hanging in a basket or placed atop a pedestal. It grows in indirect sunlight and partial shade and it needs moist soil year round. Feed this plant from spring through early fall lightly. Propagate by offshoots or through division. Repot if it becomes pot bound.

- **Baby rubber plant/American rubber plant/pepper-face** *(Peperomia obtusifolia)*: This plant likes high humidity and thoroughly moist soil, but it cannot tolerate standing in water. It needs indirect sunlight and cool temperatures. The rubber plant grows wide, so it will work in well-ventilated bath and sauna rooms. Feed this plant every two weeks from spring through the middle of summer. Propagation  is done by leaf, tip, or stem cuttings. You can repot the plant if it becomes pot bound.

- **Table fern/Cretan brake** *(Pteris cretica)*: This is a small fern with delicate roots. The table fern is a less leafy fern than the Boston fern, and it needs moist soil all year. Table ferns like humidity and indirect sunlight or warm, partial shade. Feed this plant during the growing season one time every other week. Repot if the plant becomes pot bound. Propagation is possible through stem cuttings.

More plants that prefer humid environments

A number of plants prefer humid and damp environments. Saunas, balconies, patios, and screened porches in front of a pool are ideal locations to grow plants that thrive in humidity. If you are growing plants that consistently need humidity, and you live in a rather dry area, it is best to mist these plants or place them on pebble trays that add humidity to their growing environment.

- **Fan maidenhair** *(Adiantum tenerum)*: This delicate and lacy upright fern usually does not grow over 2 feet tall or wide. Place this plant on a pebble tray, and mist it daily. Feed this fern monthly while it is actively growing in the spring and summer months with a balanced liquid plant food or fertilizer. During the winter, feed the plant bimonthly. To propagate, do so by dividing the root ball. Repot if the plant becomes pot bound. This plant needs light shade to grow well.

- **Lipstick plant** *(Aeschynanthus speciosus)*: The lipstick plant grows best in indirect sunlight. The plant has colorful, bright orange flowers and needs to be misted frequently, at least one time per week, with warm water. A pebble dish is good for increasing humidity levels. Feed this plant every other week lightly. Repot it only if it becomes pot bound. You can propagate this plant using softwood cuttings.

- **Yellow plume plant/zebra plant** *(Aphelandra squarrosa)*: The zebra plant has noticeable green leaves with white veins running through it. The plant needs humidity at all times and will benefit from a wet pebble tray. Plant the zebra plant in a large 12- to 18-inch round pot because once situated, the zebra plant does not like to be removed. Its leaves are the most spectacular aspect of the plant and they

may need to be kept clean and shiny with a damp cloth. This plant needs light shade. Keep the plant evenly moist, and water less after it blooms. Propagate by tip cuttings with bottom heating. It does not need fertilizing.

- **Bird's nest fern** *(Asplenium nidus)*: This plant is a true fern with tall, leathery leaves and a fibrous root-like growth in its middle. The plant cannot be left in direct sunlight and needs to be watered often. The best temperature for the bird's nest fern growth is 70 to 90 degrees. Temperatures slightly outside of this range will not reduce plant quality, but will reduce growth rates. You should maintain a high level of humidity for this plant. Feed this plant lightly every two weeks in the summer only. You can propagate using spores, but the process is difficult. Generally, this plant does not need repotting unless it becomes pot bound.

- **Rex begonia** *(Begonia Rex)*: This colorful, flowering plant has different leaf shapes and a variety of color options. It likes cool, moist conditions and high humidity. All begonia species thrive in humidity. The begonias do not like direct sunlight nor will the plants need to stay wet all of the time. It prefers to dry out between watering, and one sure way to kill a begonia is to give it too much water. You can propagate the plant from cuttings. Repot if it becomes pot bound, and feed during the spring and summer growing months.

- **Earth star** *(Cryptanthus bivattatus)*: This plant is a South American native with modest flowers and colorful leaf rosettes. It likes light and warmth all year but does not tolerate midday sun. You can set this plant outside in the early morning and bring it inside before noon, or you can place it in a bright room that provides bright light but not direct sunlight. They must be sprayed with water regularly to survive indoors because of their need for humidity. Set in a tray of pebbles to surround these plants with humidity. Repot this plant as the soil mix depletes, usually about one time per year. Use offsets to propagate the plant. Feed lightly every two weeks.

- **Sago palm** *(Cycas revoluta)*: This is a slow-growing and attractive palm that takes one to two years to form one ring on the outside of its trunk. It needs light year-round, and its soil must remain moderately moist. If grown in a dry room, the plant must be sprayed frequently. Organic fertilizer is recommended once a week during the spring. Sago is a very decorative and ornamental plant respected for its leafy, feathery foliage, it grows to about 6.5 feet. Propagate this plant from fresh seeds with bottom heating. Repot this plant every three to five years using a humus rich soil mixture.

- **Florist's cyclamen** *(Cyclamen persicum)*: This herb is native to the Eastern Mediterranean area and needs full sun to partial shade with a rich, well-drained soil mix. The florist's cyclamen grows 8 inches tall and needs high humidity, even in the winter months. This is an excellent plant to grow in a glass terrarium. *Instructions for growing in glass containers are in Chapter 12.* During the summer months, cyclamen plants rest and benefit from shade. In the winter, and while

in full bloom, cyclamen need bright, indirect light and a nitrogen fertilizer during the winter and early spring months. Cyclamen flowers are red, white, or pink with streaks of gray outlining its green leaves. Propagate from seed with bottom heat; the plant's roots and soil remain warm as it grows due to the source of heat. Feed it every 14 days, and be sure to keep the root ball moist. Repot only when it has become pot bound.

- **Holly fern** (*Arachniodes* or *polystichum*): This plant requires consistently moist soil and cannot dry out between watering. Its leaves are shaped like holly leaves. It has a coarse texture, but it is a handsome fern that grows 2 to 3 feet tall. The holly fern is usually found in moist, rocky areas or woodland in central and eastern Asia. If it is not easily found in gardening centers, the holly fern is available from retail outlets online. The holly fern does well in partial shade when outdoors, but indoors, it thrives underneath a sunny window or in a sunny room. For this plant's needs, be sure to feed half-diluted plant food one time per month. You can repot the plant if it becomes pot bound. As for propagation, division or spore methods work best.

- **Dendrobium species** *(Dendrobium)*: This is an orchid family member plant that enjoys full morning sun, but requires shading between 11 a.m. and 3 p.m. Use this

evergreen plant to add color to your home. It has blooms of various colors. It needs less shade in the late afternoon. An overhead light source is the most effective artificial lighting source. Allow the soil of these orchid relatives to dry out before watering again. This plant needs repotting every two years in the spring. Feed every two weeks lightly. Propagation is possible from seed.

- **Flame violet** *(Episcia cupreata)*: This plant has oval, wrinkled, green leaves flecked with copper tones. It has scarlet flowers and makes a good hanging basket plant. The flame violet blooms from June to September. It requires plenty of light but cannot tolerate the strong rays of the sun. It takes moderate amounts of water during the summer months, but slows down and needs water only sparingly in winter. Let the soil dry in between watering. Flame violets need high humidity but cannot tolerate water on their leaves. They need to be fertilized every two weeks during the summer months. This plant can be propagated by tip cuttings or from offshoots. As for repotting, only do so if the plant becomes pot bound.

- **Cape jasmine** *(Gardenia augusta, G. jasminoides)*: This evergreen blooms fragrant white, near white, and tan flowers in the late spring and early to midsummer. The plant needs water regularly, but cannot withstand overwatering. It likes heat, humidity, and a lot of light. If natural sunlight is not available, keep the cape jasmine under artificial lighting for most of the day. Cape jasmines will grow as tall as 6 feet. Feed this plant in the summer months lightly. Propagate using softwood cuttings, and repot only if the plant becomes pot bound.

- **Dancing lady orchid** *(Oncidium* species): This plant's original habits are Brazil, Costa Rica, Guatamala, and Trinidad. This plant features large, single leaves with various color choices. It likes high humidity and indirect sunlight coming from the south, east, or west. This plant will tolerate drenched potting mix, as long as the soil is allowed to dry between watering. This orchid also needs orchid fertilizer, which is a plant food found in gardening sections designed specifically for orchids. This plant will not tolerate the strength of the midday sun. Because this is not a very large plant, it only needs a small pot and is ideal for a hanging basket. Repotting is not necessary. To propagate this plant, use division.

- **Goldfish plant** *(Nmatanthus* species): Noted for its bright orange flowers that look like goldfish and its glossy green foliage, this plant requires high humidity and bright light but will not tolerate direct sunlight. It must be grown in temperatures above 60 degrees. If this plant begins to sulk or lose healthy leaves, allow its soil to dry in between watering. Propagate this plant by seed or from cuttings. Repot once the plant outgrows its container. Feed this plant weekly, giving it an easy, water-dissolving solution.

- **Boston fern** or **sword fern** *(Nephrolepsis exaltata)*: This plant is popular because it is so versatile. With its narrow,

light green fronds, the plant's fullness is striking. The lush plant looks good hanging in a basket or placed atop a pedestal. It needs increased humidity and grows in indirect sunlight and partial shade. Its soil has to be kept moist year round. This plant needs light feeding from spring through summer. Use offshoots or division to propagate. You will need to repot the plant only after it outgrows its pot.

- **Philodendron** *(Philodendron bipannatifidum)*: The philodendron loosely translates to mean "tree loving" in Latin. It has been used as a houseplant since the Victorian age. The philodendron is a tropical plant that requires some sun, but if sunlight is not available, the plant is equally satisfied to grow in an artificial light. It can go for days without being watered, but it does prefer warm, moist air. The philodendron is a popular and hard-to-kill houseplant. The leaves are shiny and dark green. Most are heart-shaped and not necessarily large. Feed this plant weekly in the spring and summer months. Repot if the plant becomes pot bound. Propagation is by tip or stem cuttings.

- **Shield aralia** *(Polyscias scutellaria)*: An ornamental houseplant with exotic, branching patterns and luxurious airy foliage, this plant can be kept small by trimming it back, or it can be allowed to grow several feet. This plant needs high humidity and can withstand light as long as humidity levels are maintained. It does best in indirect sunlight from a north, east, or west exposure. Feed this plant biweekly from the early spring through summer. Propagate using tip cuttings. Repotting is only necessary if the plant becomes pot bound.

- **Moses-in-a-boat** or **boat lily** *(Rhoeo spathacea)*: This easy-to-grow, small- to medium-size plant does not require

bright lighting. This plant is a Mexican native with small, white flowers that are tucked inside of the base of the plant. It needs bright to moderate light without direct sun and needs sufficient water. It grows to 20 inches and has deep purple leaves among deep, waxy green foliage. Feed this plant weekly. Repot if it overgrows its pot. Propagate from seed, or use cuttings from tips or the stem.

- **Leather fern** or **iron fern** *(Rumohra adiantiformis)*: The leather fern grows 8 to 10 feet in partial shade. This plant is nonflowering and has narrow fronds. It requires consistently moist soil that cannot dry out between watering. This plant is usually found in bogs and water gardens where the humidity levels are highest. This plant needs shade. The plant needs to be fed lightly once a week. For propagation, use division. Repot only if it becomes pot bound.

- **African violet** *(Saintpaulia* hybrids)*: This easy-to-grow houseplant does not need direct sunlight. This plant has a small flowering center and pale green underneath leaves. The flower is white, pink, or violet. The African violet needs good light, but hot, direct sunlight can scorch it and cause unsightly blemishes. This plant also needs to be fertilized regularly. It is native to tropical Africa and typically found on floors of rain forests where the air is always warm and humid. Place this plant atop a deep pebble water tray to improve humidity. This plant needs to be kept moist. Repot if it becomes pot bound. The plant can be pot bound if it grows quickly. Repot in this instance. Propagate from leaf cuttings.

- **Gloxinia** *(Sinningia speciosa* hybrids)*: This plant has a large, bell-shaped flower with a velvet feel and has round, dark green leaves. The gloxinia needs a lot of light, loves

sun, but does not tolerate direct sunlight. It needs regular and thorough watering, and the soil should dry slightly between watering. This relative of the African violet loves humidity, needs soil that drains well, and general houseplant fertilizer. The plant can be propagated using leaf or shoot cuttings. Repot in the spring each year.

- **Peace lily** *(Spathiphyllum* species): The peace lily has a frank way of signaling when it needs water because its leaves begin to wilt. If this plant, which stores water in its leaves, wilts severely, then it likely will perish. The peace lily is an easy-to-grow houseplant because it only needs a little light. The plant has no stems, and its leaves are a very attractive dark green that grow 14 inches long and 4 inches wide. It has a striking white flower that forms on its stalks. The flowers are 12 inches long. The peace lily needs consistently moist soil and fertilizing every two weeks from spring through autumn, and it needs a solid humidity level that can be achieved by placing its container on a pot full of moist pebbles. Repot as the plant becomes pot bound. Propagation is possible using division.

- **Cape primrose** *(Streptocarpus* hybrids): This plant blooms purple flowers from mid-spring through the early fall and has evergreen, velvet, and fuzzy-textured foliage. It

needs light shade or partial to full shade and consistently moist soil, as well as day and night temperatures between 60 and 75 degrees. Feed this plant weekly in the spring and through the summer. Propagate the plant by division. Repot in the spring is necessary if the plant becomes pot bound.

- **Air plant species** *(Tillandsia)*: *Tillandsias* come from semi-arid environments that are lit with full sun. The *Tillandsia* is a strange-growing plant, and most growers are attracted to the plant for this reason. *Tillandsias* have thick, succulent leaves that develop a gray hue when it craves light. They are not dependent on fertilizer to survive, but when fertilizer is added to its growing medium, the plant tends to grow and flower faster. In addition to bright light or full sun, the *Tillandsia* likes humidity. Keep these plants lightly moist. Repot these plants when the plant becomes too large for the pot, using an acid-rich soil. Propagate using offsets.

- **Nepenthes** *(Nepanthes)*: This plant sits quite well in a hanging basket, and it is only recommended to grow in very humid spaces. If there is a small bathroom or other area in the home that stays humid, the nepenthe with its large, floppy, waxy green leaves will grow well in the space. Like the Venus flytrap, this plant is an **insectivore**, which means it eats insects. It likes light, but does not care to be situated in sunny spaces. Aside from humidity and constant moisture, this plant needs special soft water. Soft water contains less magnesium and calcium compared to hard water. Feed this plant biweekly during the growth season. Propagate by cuttings. Repot this plant each year using a rough peat product.

Plants that thrive in sunny locations

Some plants, especially flowering plants, fare best in rooms that are bright and sunny. This list compiles plants that thrive in bright rooms. Thriving in a bright room does not necessarily mean sitting in the direct sunlight of a windowsill because only a few plants can thrive and withstand a glass window's exaggerated heat.

- **Silk Oak** *(Grevilea robusta)*: This plant has dark green, fern-like leaves. The bottom sides of its leaves are covered with silky hairs. This plant enjoys direct, but not too intense, sunlight. It can grow to be 7 feet tall, and its soil should be kept moist, but not overwatered. This plant needs repotting in sandy soil if the plant becomes pot bound. Feed this plant during the growing season. Propagate using seeds, because cuttings will take too long.

- **Jasmine** *(Jasminum* species)*: This climbing plant has white and pink flowers that appear in the winter and spring. It is best positioned in a sunny and cool room, but the plant never needs direct sunlight. The jasmine plant only  needs water when the topsoil is very dry. As long as the soil is never soggy, its flowers will bloom properly. Feed this plant every 14 days. Repot each spring in larger containers. Propagate using semi-hardwood cuttings in the spring months.

- **Rose pincushion** *(Mammillaria zeilmanniana)*: This cactus plant is different from most other cacti because it grows in small, needled clusters. The stems of the plant are small, and it produces violet-pink or purple flowers in the spring. It enjoys warm rooms and direct sunlight. This plant needs a sunny location during the summer months. Feed this plant once a month. Propagation is by seed or offsets. You will not likely need to repot unless the plant outgrows its container. Water every other week, but keep soil moist for best results.

- **Oleander** *(Nerium oleander)*: This is a large evergreen shrub with dark, pointy green leaves. The oleander produces fragrant flowers and grows up to 6 feet tall. The oleander is a pretty plant and often is grown in front living room windows because it needs direct sunlight and is a beautiful ornamental piece in a room. The oleander is an easy-to-care-for plant and will tolerate irregular watering and dry periods in between watering. Propagate this plant by cuttings in water. This plant needs little feeding, generally once every month. Repot if it becomes pot bound.

- **Blue crown passion flower** *(Passiflora caerulea)*: This is a strong climbing plant that blooms beautiful amethyst flowers and small, edible, egg-like orange fruits late in the summer. It needs direct sunlight and moderately moist soil. Feed this plant weekly. Repot young plants, those under two years of age, in new pots each spring. Older plants do not require repotting unless the plant becomes pot bound. Propagating this plant occurs through tip cuttings or by offshoots.

- **Touch-me-not** *(Impatiens)*: This plant is not too large and has dark green leaves. This low-maintenance flowering plant needs moist soil year-round, direct sunlight, and

normal room temperatures. Flower colors include pink, orange, and yellow. This plant's propagation is through softwood cuttings. The plant needs to be fed once every other week lightly. Repot if the plant becomes pot bound.

- **Star flower** *(Pentas lanceolata)*: This is a soft-wooded shrub, meaning its stems are wood sticks. It has thick, star-like pink flowers that are surrounded by deep green pointed leaves. Keep this plant moist and in direct sunlight. Feed this plant every week, and propagate using tip cuttings or seed. Repot this plant if the roots overcome the edges of the pot.

- **Leadwort** *(Plumbago auriculata)*: Another evergreen shrub, it has white to sky blue-colored flowers and dark green leaves. It needs direct sunlight and a normal room temperature of 70 degrees. The leadwort should be watered regularly, but it will not do well if overwatered. Feed this plant weekly from spring to the end of summer, and repot only if the plant outgrows its pot. Propagation is by herbaceous cuttings during the summer.

- **China rose** *(Rosa chinensis)*: This is an indoor, miniature rose plant. It offers bright, fragrant red roses in direct sunlight at normal room temperature. Make sure the plant's pot is placed in pebbles because the plant thrives in high humidity and moist soil. Propagate this plant from softwood cuttings or from semi-hardwood cuttings. Repotting is only necessary if the plant outgrows its container. Lightly feed this plant each week.

- **Snake plant** *(Sanseveria trifasciata)*: The plant has sword-like leaves of green to yellow coloring. It has small flowers. This tall, upright, green plant enjoys both direct

and indirect sunlight. Snake plants that are more than two or three years old can go weeks without water. Newer and younger snake plants should be watched and watered before the soil gets too dry. Snake plants that are grown in sunny locations are greener and grow much faster than snake plants grown in dimmer or softer natural or artificial lighting. Repot this plant each spring. Feed the plant cactus food one time per month, and propagate the plant through division.

- **Madagascar jasmine** *(Stephanotis floribunda)*: This climbing shrub with thick, waxy white flowers enjoys indirect sunlight. Madagascar jasmines need moderately moist soil. Feed this plant every two weeks, and propagate through tip cuttings. Repot the plant only if it outgrows its container.

- **Black-eyed Susan** *(Rudbeckia hirta)*: These need some direct sunlight every day so that their orange, yellow, or white flowers bloom to their fullest potential. Its soil must stay moist year round. This plant needs feeding every two weeks and can be propagated by seed. Repot only if the current pot is too small for the soil to surround the root bulb in soil.

- **Kaffir lily** *(Schizostylis* species): The kaffir lily has beautiful, dark green leaves that can grow as long as 2 feet. It blooms reds flowers. This plant must be kept still, and it prefers indirect sunlight. This plant takes a winter break,

meaning that it rests and shows no visible signs of growth, for about six to eight weeks. Kaffir lilies like water and will react well with a drenching once each month. This plant needs to be fed every other week in the summer months. Repot this plant every two to three years, and propagate through offsets.

There is no shortage when it comes to the variety of plants you can cultivate indoors. It does not matter whether the room is bright and sunny or if the room is shaded; the key to any successful and thriving houseplant is to research the environment the plant likes best. The world of houseplants becomes larger and more diverse when the creative grower focuses on recreating an outdoor growing environment inside his or her home or office.

Plants to Purify Your Home or Office

Certain plants, such as spider plants and pothos, are tremendously popular in many homes, foyers in school buildings, workplaces, and classrooms. Studies in England and the United States prove a direct correlation between houseplants in learning and working environments and increased productivity and efficiency. Studies also show that student performance improves when houseplants are added in the area. In classrooms, the carbon dioxide level is much higher than what it should be because a large number of students in one space are breathing in oxygen and exhaling carbon dioxide. Plants in offices and other spaces with fair to heavy volumes of human traffic absorb carbon dioxide and release oxygen, thus creating a healthier environmental balance.

Air-filtering plants

Here are a several species that work particularly hard at improving air quality. Not only do plants release oxygen into the environment, but also their transpiration processes naturally remove gaseous chemicals from indoor environments. Electrical equipment and furniture release trace chemicals into the air that cause headaches and lethargy. Paint, furniture, carpeting, and fabric release chemicals that potentially build up to toxic levels in areas that are heavily insulated. Houseplants are suggested for new homes because they are able to filter and remove air pollutants found in new building, cleaning, and construction projects. Houseplants help reduce toxic air qualities, but it would take a large number of houseplants to clean air where the toxic residue is particularly strong. Aggressive environmentalists believe that new homes and buildings where the chemical pollutants are always strong should be filled with as many green plants as the space allows to filter the air.

The plants reduce three primary chemicals: benzene, trichloroethylene, and formaldehyde — chemicals that promote unhealthy environments. These chemicals are used in construction, cleaning products, and in fuel-burning gas stoves and ovens.

The following plants help reduce levels of benzene, formaldehyde, and trichloroethylene in your home or office space:

- **African hemp** (*Sparmannia Africana*): This plant increases humidity, which is great for modern offices that are generally chilled with air conditioners that may release any of the previously mentioned three chemicals. The quick-growing, tree-like shrub has large evergreen leaves that are vibrant green and grow to be 9 inches long. The plant itself will grow to 7 feet. African hemp produces

flowers in long clusters, and if growing conditions are right, the flowers will appear year round. Good growing conditions for this plant include indirect sunlight and normal room temperatures in summer and winter. The plant must be moistened thoroughly from the spring throughout the summer months. In the winter, the plant needs only enough water to keep its soil mix from drying out. It needs liquid fertilizer every two weeks from spring through autumn. This plant also needs sufficient space to grow. Repot when the plant becomes pot bound and propagate through stem cuttings.

• **Paint drop tongue/Chinese evergreen** (*Aglaonema*): This plant reduces benzene. Its thick and leathery leaves grow as long as 1 foot. The leaves are an olive green with green edges. Other variations of the *Aglaonema* have dark, gray-green-edged leaves with deep silvery and white cream middles. This plant functions to purify air quality. Most Chinese evergreen owners position this plant in a group of many other plants to mask its oddities and imperfections. This plant needs feeding every two weeks in the spring through the fall. Propagate through stem cuttings, and repot only when the plant overwhelms its current pot. It also needs indirect sun and moist soil.

• **Aloe** (*Aloe vera*): This plant reduces formaldehyde. The sap of the aloe plant relieves the pain of minor burns and scratches. Aloe has plump, vertical leaves filled with medicinal sap and needs direct sunlight. The aloe produces little yellow tubular flowers, but these flowers are not known to bloom when the plant is cultivated indoors. Aloe plants grow to be about 3 feet tall. They need plenty of water from spring until autumn and can be

watered sparingly in the winter while they rest. Propagate this plant through careful division of the rootstock. Feed this plant lightly and rarely, no more than one time per month. Repotting is only necessary if the plant overgrows the pot. It needs full sun in the summer months especially.

- **Zebra plant** *(Aphelandra)*: This attractive indoor plant increases humidity. Its deep green leaves are 8 to 10 inches long with thick, yellow-white stripes throughout. A golden yellow flower blooms in the middle of the leaves. The flowers are relatively short lived. In addition to being a pretty plant, it does not take up a great deal of space. It grows to be 12 to 18 inches tall and 12 inches wide. It needs indirect sunlight and thoroughly moistened soil from spring to autumn. The zebra rests in the winter and does fine if the top half of the soil is allowed to dry out before it is watered again during the resting period. This plant needs feed weekly during the growth season. Repot it in the spring months annually, and propagate through cuttings.

- **Banana** *(Musa balbisiana)*: Dwarf banana plants grow fast, reaching heights as tall as 8 feet. The plant increases humidity and reduces formaldehyde. The dwarf version will grow 5 to 6 feet tall, and it has big, shapely, leathery-looking leaves. Many banana plants are grown outdoors as well, because the plant is exceptionally pretty. The soil mix of a banana plants must be kept thoroughly moist in spring to autumn and moist in the winter. In order for fruit to grow, the plant must be kept in temperatures above 65 degrees at all times of the day. It is a safe bet that the banana plant will tolerate the same temperatures all year round as an indoor houseplant that humans do. Propagate

this plant from seed. This plant needs repotting often in a rich soil and large containers, at least annually. It needs full sun. Due to the frequent repotting, this plant does not need feeding.

- **Croton, St. Joseph's coat** *(Codiaeum variegatum)*: Crotons are one of the most commonly sold foliage plants. The leaves are yellow, orange, and yellow-green combinations. These plants transpire heavily, which for plants is similar to sweating, so they are water-seeking plants that require frequent watering. The Croton needs bright light and warm temperatures; the lowest temperature this plant

will tolerate is 60 degrees. The croton helps clear the air by creating humid conditions that help break down toxic chemicals in the air. Feed this plant lightly one time per week, and propagate through tip cuttings. This plant does not require repotting unless the plant becomes pot bound.

- **Devil's ivy** *(Epipremnum aureum)*: This plant reduces formaldehyde and grows under fluorescent light or moderate to bright sunlight. It has a long-standing

reputation as one of the easiest houseplants to grow. The stems, which are long and vining, trail for more than 8 feet, and the plant has glossy, heart-shaped leaves. It will not tolerate overwatering or drenched soil. This plant needs feeding only monthly during the growing season. Repot as it grows out of its container, and propagate through softwood cuttings.

- **Golden pothos** (*Epipremnum pinnatum*): This popular and dependable houseplant reduces formaldehyde, benzene, and trichloroethylene. These excellent hanging plants quickly cascade their bright yellow and green leaves. This plant is not fussy, easy to grow, and can be trained to climb wooden mounts or moss-covered sticks. This plant needs light but not strong sun. It needs watering regularly to keep the soil moist. Lightly feed this plant biweekly. Propagate through tip and stem cuttings, and repot if it outgrows its pot.

- **Ivy tree** (*x Fatshedera lizei*): This plant has three to five lobed, shiny leaves, and the plant is bushy. This plant reduces toxins in cool light with moist soil from spring to autumn. In dry locations, increase humidity for the plant by placing it atop a tray of wet pebbles. The ivy tree crawls and hangs and can be trained to grow up a moss pole. The plant needs feeding every week for growth. Repot the plant every year while it is growing, and propagate through tip cuttings.

- **Pygmy palm** (*Chamaedorea*): The pygmy palm is very attractive, small, and grows slowly. It is a popular accent plant in tropic areas. They adapt well, growing in containers, and they reduce formaldehyde and trichloroethylene. The pygmy palm should be watered regularly, and careful

attention must be paid to make sure the plant's soil never dries out. It grows best in sunlight and partial shade. This plant propagates through offsets or from seeds. The plant needs half-diluted plant food every other week. Repot it when the roots overgrow the edge of the container.

- **Philodendron** *(Philodendron bipinnatifidum)*: This tree-like shrub has a single stem and multi-fingered leaves that tend to fall over and lie horizontally as the plant gets older. The popular philodendron reduces formaldehyde and can grow as long as 15 feet. It enjoys indirect sunlight or partial shade and needs thorough moisture from spring through autumn. Feed this plant weekly in the spring and summer months. Repot if the plant becomes pot bound, and propagate by tip or stem cuttings.

NASA-approved plants

Some plants are so proficient at filtering air they are taken into space to improve air quality in small areas. The National Air and Space Administration (NASA) studied plants that would improve the air quality in space stations, and the following are plants NASA approved to use on space station:

- **Green spider plant** *(Chlorphytum elatum)*: The green spider plant has darker leaves than the spider plant. The green spider plant needs plenty of light. It is a plant NASA studied and approves for its space stations to clear the air of formaldehyde and benzene. The green spider plant does

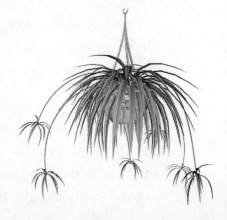

not need much water and can tolerate being dry in between watering. This plant needs to be fed every week during the summer and every other week in other seasons. Propagate by planting the offsets of the plant. Repot this plant only when the plant's root crown protrudes over the soil.

- **Mass cane/corn plant** *(Draceaena massangeana)*: This plant topped NASA's list when the organization studied plants that remove toxic chemicals from the air in space stations. It does well in low light conditions; its wide leaves are long and arc gracefully from the stalk. The massangeana is popular due to the dramatic yellow color that runs down the center of its leaves. This plant needs feeding weekly from spring to the fall and then, once a month after. The plant needs to be kept evenly moist. Repot it if needed to ensure it remains in loose soil. To propagate this plant, use stem cuttings.

- **Warneckii/Janet Craig** *(Dracaena deremensis)*: This NASA-approved plant helps filter the air and has stiff, tapered leaves with gray, green, and white stripes. It may develop weak color and narrow, strappy leaves when overwatered and become incapable of fertilization. This plant prefers low to medium light and just enough water to keep the soil moist. Feed this plant weekly during the summer growing season and then monthly, after summer ends. Repot if the plant becomes pot bound; propagate through stem cuttings.

- **English ivy** *(Hedera helix)*: The plant has small, dark green leaves with a pointed shape and grows on a vine. English ivy reduces benzene and trichloroethylene, and NASA uses English ivy to clean air in space stations. This popular plant needs to be moist from spring to autumn and only needs enough water in the winter to keep from drying out. This

plant grows in indirect sunlight and is able to withstand varying temperatures, which makes it a household favorite. In dry indoor climates, the plant needs to be placed atop a wet pebble tray to steady soil humidity levels. This plant needs to be fed weekly. Repot it every two to three years, and propagate through tip or stem cuttings.

- **Gerber daisy** (*Gerbera jamesonil*): The Gerber daisy reduces formaldehyde, benzene, and trichloroethylene. This is a NASA-approved air-filtering plant that is sold in a wide variety of seed selections. A popular flowering plant that grows to heights between 1 and 2 feet, it produces red, orange, pink, and white flowers that appear from May to August. Daisies like indirect sunlight and will tolerate some direct sunlight in fall, winter, and spring. The Gerber daisy needs moist soil and must be fertilized every two weeks. Propagation of this plant is through seed or by division. You may need to repot this plant each spring as long as it continues to grow.

- **Dragon tree** (*Dracaena marginata*): NASA approves this plant for use on space stations to help filter the air of harsh chemicals. This is long-leafed plant has green, cream-striped centers edged with red. The marginata resembles a palm with its airy, arching leaves and woody stems. Its soil must be kept moist

from spring through autumn. It only needs just enough water in winter to keep its potting soil from drying out. This plant likes indirect sunlight and will grow as tall as 5 feet. Feed this plant weekly during the growing season and one time per month after that. Repot as needed to ensure the plant has loose soil. Propagate through stem cuttings.

- **Bamboo palm** *(Chamaedorea seifrizii)*: NASA approves this plant to clear the air of formaldehyde, benzene, and trichloroethylene. This is a beautiful, tall, green indoor plant that can reach a height of 3 to 6 feet. This plant does well in brightly lit rooms. This plant should have moist soil at all times, so do not let it dry out. Fertilize this plant during the growing season. This plant does not like excess water and always needs to be moist, never wet. Propagation is by division. Repot this plant if it becomes pot bound.

- **Snake plant:** *(Sanseveria trifasciata)*: NASA studied and approved this tall, upright, green plant for its space stations. The snake plant enjoys both direct and indirect sunlight to clear the air of benzene and trichloroethylene toxins. It is considered one of the most carefree houseplants because it adapts quickly in homes, workplaces, and shopping malls. The snake plant tolerates neglect, but responds to good maintenance by growing sturdy, sword-shaped leaves. This plant needs to be cleaned for dust periodically, and sometimes, a very old snake plant will produce white flowers in the winter. Interiorscapers use the snake plant to decorate rooms that have strong horizontal lines. Water when the soil is dry to the touch. Give this plant cactus food each month, and repot each spring. Propagate through division.

- **Peace lily** *(Spathlphyllum)*: The peace lily reduces benzene and trichloroethylene, and it is an easy-to-grow houseplant because it only needs a little light. The plant has no stems, and its leaves are an attractive dark green that grow 14 inches long and 4 inches wide. A striking, 12-inch-long white flower forms on its stalks. The peace lily needs consistently moist soil, fertilizing every two weeks from spring through autumn, and a solid humidity level that can be achieved by placing its container on a pot full of moist pebbles. Propagate this plant through division, and repot when it becomes pot bound.

Once your home is filled with plants that mirror your sense of style and complement your living space, there may be an urge to experiment more. It is great to have houseplants that heighten the beauty of our home, but imagine having a kitchen or space full of indoor plants that produce the same foods purchased at grocery stores and chain food markets.

Indoor gardening is a term applied to growing fruits, herbs, and vegetables within the comfort of your home. The same basic rules that apply to popular houseplants also apply to growing and keeping those viable food sources alive. If you stay on top of water, food, and light requirements, then your edible plants will fare wonderfully.

Growing edible plants indoors fosters a great sense of accomplishment, independence, and pride. For indoor gardeners who find that their houseplants are a source of joy, growing herbs, vegetables, and fruits indoors is a productive hobby that brings about similar delight.

CASE STUDY:
CREATING AN
INDOOR KITCHEN GARDEN

Owner, IndoorGardener.Org
www.indoorgardener.org
and www.indoorherbgarden.org
Phone: (646) 341-2743

Having advice and guidance from professionals is critical when it comes to starting a houseplant garden in your home. Steve Liu offers some insightful and helpful tips and tools to help individuals create that environment within their homes. His experience is quite varied. As the owner of two websites, IndoorGardener.org and IndoorHerbGarden.org, and with years of experience under his belt, he offers information and advice worth reading.

Liu said, "I was an avid flower and vegetable gardener for many years, but in the last few years, I moved into an apartment and had to give up my victory garden. I turned my green thumb to raising houseplants. Because I love to cook, I decided to specialize in indoor herb plants and indoor vegetables." And, when asked what attracted him to the horticulture and interiorscaping industry, he said a few things did, including the following.

"A living plant can be a decorative item in the house that is just as beautiful as or more so than any sculpture, painting, or artwork. It changes every day, and literally breathes new life into any space. You can choose plants of any nationality, size, and shape to fit into any décor."

Health also played a role in his attraction to this industry. "The health benefits of plants are well documented. They clear the air, reducing ground-level ozone while providing fresh oxygen. Studies show that rooms with plants contain less airborne mold and bacteria than rooms without them. Other studies have shown that workers in offices with windows and plants are happier and more content than workers in offices without them."

There are also economic factors that played a role in Liu's use of houseplants. "I got tired of paying several dollars for a handful of herbs, only to use a tablespoon and throw it away. With indoor herbs, I snip off what I need while the rest continue to grow for the next recipe."

In addition, education is an important reason to consider houseplant care. He says, "Especially if you have kids in the house, it is a wonderful way to teach them about creation and the miracle of life."

He also states that it is a great hobby to have. "There is something just very satisfying about taking a living thing from a tiny seed or seedling and growing it into a healthy adult plant. It gives you a nice sense of accomplishment."

It is helpful for readers to know what is growing in Liu's home. He provides a description of his personal indoor garden. "I have been growing indoor houseplants for the better part of 30 years. My favorite plants range the gamut, from cacti and succulents, to green plants, to trees, to indoor herbs. Every time I travel, I buy a local houseplant to being home. It is great to live in a time when you can get plants from all over the world in your home. Not long ago, this was a luxury reserved for royalty. "

Because much of Liu's focus is on herbal gardening, it makes sense that his favorite place to keep his plants is in the kitchen. "While others have spice racks of old and dried herbs, I have a "living" spice rack with fresh basil, mint, thyme, oregano, sage, and much more. Aside from being convenient to use in cooking, they add color and a conversation piece to the kitchen."

Aside from just herbs, though, how does Liu choose the plants he will put into his home? He has a specific process he uses. "I approach choosing plants as I would any other artwork to decorate the home. In a family room with more of a southwestern feel, I will put more cacti and succulents."

If he is traveling, caring for his plants remains important to him. Instead of having a friend come into the home to water his plants and risk that person's inexperience, he said a better option is to use a different system. "For things like indoor herb gardens, I, generally, will use an aeroponic or hydroponic type system such as the AeroGarden. These can go up to two weeks without adding water, sometimes even double that. As a bonus, when its lights go on and off, it doubles as a burglar deterrent. For houseplants, I have had success with the glass water globes that release water slowly to your plants as it is needed. If you do not want to pay for the glass globes, you can do the same by drilling small holes into the tops of soda or water bottles."

Caring for plants is an important part of raising them and reaching that level of accomplishment Liu speaks of, but doing this is often a harder process than what one expects. He offers a few different tips to make houseplant growers more successful. When it comes to watering in

sunlight, Liu said, "I think the notion that this causes damage or leaf burn is a myth. I have never had an issue with watering at any time of the day." Deciding which type of fertilizer to use is also important. He states, "I prefer organic soil and fertilizers. I have always found that plants grown in organic soil come out fuller and richer. I think organic soil is much richer in nutrients, and I like the idea of keeping harmful chemicals outside of my house, my soil, and my plants."

Many people who grow herbs and other plants in their homes face challenges along the way. This happens even to professionals in the industry, including Liu. He offers a variety of tips to help people to overcome the challenges. The first challenge he addresses is bugs. "Especially if you grow herb in an aeroponic unit, chances are eventually you will have to deal with bugs, from whiteflies to aphids to spider mites. If you are not careful, they will hijack their way into your house through houseplants. Or, if you have a grow light, they will be attracted to that. Generally, I keep my indoor herbs separated from my other houseplants and only open the windows in the daytime."

Dust is another problem with some indoor kitchens. "House dust can make indoor herbs very unpalatable to say the least. This is why I keep my garden in a dust-free environment (the kitchen is usually good for this), and I spritz them with water from time to time."

Another area that some struggle with is pruning. "This is perhaps the most important thing to know about indoor herb gardens: You need to prune them constantly. This helps them continue to grow rapidly and full. It feels counterintuitive to chop off half a basil plant, but you'll soon find your herbs grow much faster when you do," Liu said.

One of the challenges he says is knowing which herbs are right for you. "Certain herbs are hardier than others in different climates. Where I am, rosemary refuses to grow at all, but basil grows like a weed If any given plant does not succeed, try, try again; you will find the ones that grow well in your area."

Finally, when asked to provide a bit of advice for the novice on indoor garden care, Liu said, "Try different things and do not give up. You will go through periods when you are dealing with bug infestations or plants that just refuse to grow. But online you will find dozens, even hundreds, of people who have gone through the same things and have great advice for you."

GROWING HERBS, FRUITS, AND VEGETABLES INDOORS

After you have successfully grown houseplants for the fun of it, the beauty of it, or for the health benefits, almost instinctively you will want to grow plants for food. Experts caution that sun exposure is the most difficult component of growing fruit, vegetables and herbs inside. "You have to work with your plants to be sure they are getting enough sun or not too much," says Pelleccio.

The leaves and flowers of certain plants have fragrant oils or herbs that are released when they are touched. Many of these plants are used in cuisine and grown in kitchen windowsills and indoor gardens. Other fragrant flowers — lavender, lemon geranium, and gardenias, for example — produce natural scents that often are reproduced or partially derived and then packaged into bottles and sprays for commercial use. Lantana, a plant that

releases scents, is often placed in doorways, as its aromatic fragrances are more noticeable when people brush past it.

These are a few fragrant foliage plants suitable to grow in your kitchen:

- **Calamondin orange** *(Citrofortunella)*: This plant has deep green glossy foliage; it produces plants when it is young and bears fragrant flowers.

- **Citrus** *(Citrus* species): If grown in warm environments, small citrus trees will bear fruit and flowers all year.

- **Shrubby verbena** *(Lantana camara)*: This plant has semi-green leaves and multicolored summertime blooms but a coarse and dull skin.

- **Bay laurel** *(Laurus nobilis)*: a small tree or shrub that has dark, glossy green fragrant producing leaves.

- **Spearmint/garden mint** *(Mentha spicata)*: fragrant and popular herb often used in cuisine.

- **Lemon geranium** *(Pelargonium crispum)*: Geraniums are not always easy to grow; this plant is grown specifically for its lemon scent.

- **Lemon thyme** *(Thymus x citriodorus)*: an herb and shrub plant that releases a sharp lemon scent when it is crushed.

Fruits and herbs can be grown in kitchens as long as the right growing conditions, primarily temperature and sunlight, are available. Twenty-first century kitchens, generally, are large and located near a living room, den, or a morning room where there is plenty of incoming light. Herbs do well indoors and in kitchens provided they get enough light. The humidity in kitchens from cooking is a plus for plants. Planter pots can sit in windowsills or

underneath lights. Other potted plants can sit atop shelves and cabinets in kitchens where they will grow well. Indoor gardeners who place their plants high atop cabinets and shelves are usually people who spend a lot of time in the kitchen, often cleaning and wiping down counters, particularly after cooking. For indoor gardeners, daily housework chores would include using a stepladder to reach, water and feed plants placed high. Plants placed in hard to reach areas are difficult to water, so it would be best to place those plants that do not require much water in high areas.

Typically, kitchen temperatures and humidity levels rise and decrease in homes where the kitchen is used a lot, and herbs that grow indoors generally are milder than those grown outdoors. One recommendation for herbs grown indoors is to turn the plants every couple of days so they can grow taller and stronger as they reach for the light. Basil, bay, chamomile, mint, oregano, parsley, rosemary, sage, and thyme are the typical herbs planted in outdoor herb gardens, and they are popular with indoor growers. Herbs will grow heartily in 6-inch pots and all-purpose potting soil equally mixed with soil, sand, and peat moss. They are similar to vegetables and thrive well in soil that is one part peat, one part vermiculite, and one part perlite. Another suggestion is to place separate herbs in one large pot that has separate growing holes for each plant to compensate for space lost planting in several different containers. When growing herbs, it is good to consider that what is good for the plant yields better food for the gardener. Herbs do not like soggy soil from overwatering, and chefs will not like the taste of herbs that have been overfertilized. Herbs like to get a little dry before their next watering, and they experience optimal growth in temperatures between 65 and 68 degrees. After cooking, the kitchen tends to get greasy, and plant leaves develop a waxy build-up. Greasy plant leaves have to be cleaned and wiped down for the health of the plant.

The most common herbs and spices grown by indoor gardeners include the following:

- **Basil** *(Ocimum basilicum)*: Basil is the most popular herb, and it is grown in almost every indoor and outdoor garden. It is reputed to be an easy grower that thrives in sunny windowsills, but basil also is capable of surviving with partial shade. Basil is grown from seed and can grow up to 18 inches tall. The plant needs to be watered only enough to prevent its soil from becoming dry. Feed this plant lightly each week. Propagate the plant through division, and repot the plant each spring.

- **Rosemary** *(Rosmarinus officinalis)*: Rosemary is an evergreen shrub that will grow 3 to 6 feet tall. Rosemary is a member of the mint family and has attractive, dark green leaves and pale blue flowers. Growers find rosemary easy to grow because it tolerates drought, dry soil conditions, and grows in full sun to partial shade. Rosemary seeds are hard to start for planting and should be soaked and  softened in water a few hours before sowing. Feed this plant from spring through summer. Propagate through cuttings in the summer, and repot only if the plant becomes pot bound.

- **Oregano** *(Origanum vulgare)*: Oregano is common in Italian and Greek dishes. It has a distinctive aroma that some people do not like. Oregano is not a difficult plant to grow as long as it is placed in a sunny window. Oregano grows in dry areas, so it is fine to let the soil of an oregano plant dry out. To grow an oregano plant, purchase a baby plant from a nursery and grow more plants from saplings or branches of the original plant. Feed this plant weekly during the growing season, and propagate through stem cuttings. Repot only if the plant outgrows its pot.

- **Spearmint** *(Mentha spicata)*: Spearmint is popular with indoor gardeners, but it grows rampant and needs its own container. It has a savorier flavor than peppermint and tastes excellent when freshly speared. It is easier to cultivate spearmint from cuttings rather than seeds. The **seedlings** (plants grown from a seed) usually are available at a nursery. It thrives in moist soil and will not tolerate overwatering. It needs bright, direct light and will grow 12 to 18 inches tall. It also grows fine under strong fluorescent lights. Spearmint seeds are poisonous and people should not eat them. Keep this plant fed weekly while it is growing. Repot the plant only if it outgrows its container. Propagate through stem cuttings.

- **Bay Leaf** *(Laurel nobilis)*: The bay leaf is easier to grow when rooted from 12-inch cuttings rather than grown from seeds. Potted bay leaf plants can grow as tall as 6 feet in containers and need a large container. The older the leaves, the stronger its flavor. Bay likes good sunlight or hours underneath a fluorescent lamp and humidity. Bay leaf soil should stay moist. The herb grows best in a well-draining soil mix. Propagate through tip cuttings in

the spring or fall and feed weekly. Repot as it grows if it outgrows its container.

- **Chives** (*Allium schoenoprasum*): Chives are members of the onion family. They make excellent window plants and are cultivated for both their ornamental and culinary properties. Chives grow quickly and easily from seed. The growing seeds will need to be planted in the suggested vegetable or herb soil potting mix, watered, and then set in a sunny window or underneath bright plant lights. If someone has given you a large chunk of chive for growing, then you need a 5-gallon container, and the little bulbs must be separated before planting. The plant looks like long blades of grass. When it gets too tall and thick, it can be trimmed; cut leaves are fit for consumption. Chives need to be watered once a week. Keep this  plant fed every other week, and repot only if it outgrows its container. Propagate through seeds.

- **Marjoram** *(Origanum majorana)*: This perennial herb is usually grown as an annual for its fragrant foliage, which is used to flavor dressings and meat dishes. Marjoram grows 2 to 3 feet tall and usually sprouts one to two weeks after planting. Marjoram needs full sunlight but will grow indoors under standard fluorescent lamps. The stronger the light intensity, the better marjoram grows. Marjoram will thrive in dry soil. Divide the root ball to propagate, and keep this plant fed weekly. Repot as it grows to ensure soil remains loose.

- **Parsley** *(Petroselinum crispum)*: Parsley is one of the most popular culinary herbs. It is a flavorful ingredient in savory dishes and is an attractive addition to any indoor gardening scene, but it can be very difficult to grow. The seeds have a hard exterior that must be softened before they will grow. Soak parsley seeds in hot water for a few hours or overnight before starting them in vegetable gardening soil. Be sure to use either of the recommended potting soil mixes of sand, perlite, vermiculite, or peat moss. When the plants begin to grow, select seedlings for planting that have vigorous growth and sturdy glossy leaves. The soil must be thoroughly moist, and the seedlings must be planted 8 inches deep. Parsley should be planted in a deep container; its moisture must be consistent, and it must have full sun. Feed the plant every other week, and propagate by seeds. Repot only if it grows out of its pot and roots show.

- **Tea** *(Camellia sinensis)*: The tea leaf is a bushy plant that blooms in the winter and spring. It has dark green, shiny leaves, and it produces small white flowers each winter. It is a wonderful potted plant that grows in full or partial sun but requires cool night temperatures lower

than 55 degrees in order to bloom. The plant is relatively inexpensive, perhaps because of its popularity, and sells for less than $10 at most online retailers. The leaves of the plant are meant for harvesting, even when the shoots are very young. The soil of the tea plant should remain moist daily. Propagate through seed, and feed it every other week. Repot only if the plant outgrows the container.

- **Coffee** *(Coffee species)*: The coffee plant produces coffee beans for growers to make their own coffee. It also has deep waxy green leaves that make it a very attractive houseplant. The coffee plant looks like a small tree; it has leaves that grow red, fleshy berries, and its white, blooming flowers produce a handsome fragrance. The coffee plant needs a bright window with full or partial sun. It should be grown in a 3- to 5-inch pot, and its temperature must remain above 55 degrees all year round. Coffee plants' soil must be kept moderately moist; overwatering and dryness will kill the plant. Feed this plant every three weeks, and propagate it from seed. Repot as it grows out of its pot.

- **Curry Leaf** *(Murraya koenigii)*: The leaves of the curry plant are somewhat delicate and rather easy to harvest. It needs

full sun or a southern exposure, as these plants are native to Sri Lanka and India. A clay pot will best maintain the curry plant's finicky water needs, because in between watering, the plant likes dry topsoil while the roots remain moist. Feed this plant monthly, and repot only when it becomes pot bound. Propagation is from seed.

- **Patchouli** *(Pogostemon heyneanus)*: This is a fragrant herb used to make scented oils. When the leaves are rubbed together, an exotic scent is released. The patchouli plant quickly reaches heights of 12 inches and recovers quickly after it is pruned. It grows best in full sun and tolerates periods of dryness, which means it can be watered well one day and then left alone for six or seven days. Propagate by dividing the root ball. Feed this plant monthly while it is growing, and repot if it becomes pot bound.

- **Cinnamon** *(Cinnamomum* species): The cinnamon tree grows rather slowly, so it is a good container plant with reddish-bronze leaves that develop a spicy smell as it matures. White flowers appear in the spring and summer, and these flowers make way for a small purple fruit. Once the plant is developed enough, the outer bark is scraped off, and then rolls of the inner bark are cut to make cinnamon sticks. Cinnamon is known to reduce blood sugar. The cinnamon plant grows to heights between 3 and 6 feet, so it should be planted in pots that are 8 inches or wider. The cinnamon plant grows best in full or partial sunlight and needs an acidic potting mix that is half peat moss and half perlite. Cinnamon needs light to moderate water. This plant requires light feeding in the growing season. Repot if it outgrows its current container, and propagate through seed.

Herbs and fragrant flowers always have been popular gardening plants, but fruits are becoming very popular contained plants. If they are not used for medicinal or culinary purposes, fruit trees are often handsome additions that lend authenticity and beauty to a kitchen or any other well-lit area.

The Banana Family

At his website, **www.beginner-gardening.com**, award-winning gardening author Doug Green warns gardeners who are considering growing banana plants to be mindful of the banana plants' need to feed. The plant needs to be fed regularly for it to grow well. Green recommends putting a thin layer of compost on the top of the potted plant and feeding the potted banana plant once every week or every two weeks with a liquid plant food. Miracle-Gro, Schultz, and a variety of others manufacture liquid plant food, which is easy to find in gardening sections of local stores. Amazon.com also sells liquid plant food. The banana plants need full sun or strong indoor lights. In addition to heavy feeding, the banana plant likes water, but the plant is fragile and will rot quickly in heavily watered soil or standing water. Some gardeners use a 30-percent partial sand mix to grow their banana plants.

If tended to properly, banana plants should grow new leaves every week. The banana plant is a popular plant because it is an overpoweringly beautiful plant with a strong resemblance to a miniature palm tree with wide leaves. The banana plant can be grown indoors without losing its ability to produce fruit. The biggest problem with the banana plant is pests, particularly spider mites. *Chapter 6 goes into full detail on recommended pesticides, both chemical and organic, to treat indoor houseplants that have been attacked by pests.*

- **Banana plant/dwarf cavendish** *(Musa acuminata)*: This plant is often erroneously referred to as a tree, but it is a large herb with a succulent, juicy stem. With its thick, but short, stalk, the banana plant is a popular choice for homes. The plant grows to between 4 and 7 feet tall. The leaves make this plant a standout for the home because the leaves are large. Also, the banana plant grows new fruit constantly, making for an interesting display. Some experts recommend placing the banana plant outdoors in the summer for improved sunlight. Even though the banana plant only needs a little water during the winter season, it must be kept warm and never subjected to cold all year round. This plant needs full sun and should be fed monthly. Propagate through seed. Repot in rich soil and larger containers as it grows.

- **Flowering banana** *(Musella lasiocarpa)*: This lush plant is overlooked as a houseplant. When grown indoors, this plant will not produce fruit, but it does add a colorful note thanks to its rich green leaves and attractive yellow flowers. It needs plenty of room to grow, because over the years, it can grow as tall as 6 feet. It should be planted in a tub container. It rests in the winter months, at which time the soil needs to be moistened enough to keep the plant from completely drying out. This is a tropical plant, but it withstands cold temperatures very well. It fares fine in outdoor weather that drops as low as 45 degrees. Feed this plant each week, and repot into larger containers as it grows, usually every few months. Propagation is through division of rhizomes or bulbs.

- **Parrot plant** *(Heliconia psittacorum)*: This plant is a large vertical plant with beautiful orange and red vertical

flowers and handsome leaves. The *heliconia* is a large genus from Brazil and a member of the same family as the banana plant. There are many different plants under this particular genus name, but the parrot plant's regal, tall flowers resemble the bird of paradise, and this plant is much more compatible to indoor growing. The plant grows to be more than 4 feet tall and can be moved outdoors in the summer where it  will receive plenty of sunlight. It needs to be grown in a bright location, and its soil must be evenly moist all year. These plants thrive in warm environments, and this plant will chill in temperatures lower than 55 degrees. Feed this plant once a week, and repot it annually. Propagate through rhizome division.

- **Japanese fiber banana** (*Musa basjoo*): This is a fast-growing tree, and the plant flowers when it has 35 or more leaves. It bears inedible fruit. This banana plant will tolerate cold temperatures as low as 20 degrees in the winter. This plant needs full sun and should be kept moist. This plant propagates through division of the root ball. Repot as it outgrows its container. Feed it monthly.

- **Darjeeling banana** *(Musa sikkimensis)*: The Darjeeling is a rare banana plant that grows as tall as 14 feet. This plant can survive cold weather and can be moved outdoors in the winter seasons of almost any climate. It is originally from the Himalayas of northeast India and has been grown successfully in Germany, Britain, and Switzerland. This plant needs full sun and regular watering to keep soil moist. Propagate through division. Feed this plant every other week. Repot as it outgrows its container and the soil is no longer loose.

Citrus, Berries, and Other Fruits

The best part of growing fruits indoors is that fruits like strawberries are available and growing in your home during the winter months. Citrus trees can make attractive indoor houseplants for those homeowners who have the space and the access to natural light indoors to support their growth. Limes, kumquats, and calamondins are smaller members of the citrus family and great choices for houseplants. All citrus plants will adapt to containers until they reach a certain size. Plants too large to remain indoors can be planted in outdoor gardens, or their cuttings can be made to grow fresh plants. All citrus plants are evergreens, and overall, they will not tolerate winter weather or cold. Most citrus trees grow to be taller than 10 feet, so they must be pruned and scaled back if left inside.

- **Orange tree** *(Citrus sinensis)*: The orange tree arrived in North America from Europe, but it is originally from China. Indoor citrus trees must be pruned because the plant can grow anywhere from 22 to 33 feet tall. Its dark green, pointed leaves are 3 to 5 inches wide and live as long as three years. It produces white flowers and can be

cultivated to bear seedless fruit. Like all citrus trees, the orange tree will not tolerate cold. The orange tree needs a lot of light and supplemental lighting if possible. Its soil should be kept moderately moist and well drained. Propagate through tip cuttings. This plant should be fed every two weeks. Repotting this plant is necessary as it outgrows its container and becomes too leggy.

- **Grapefruit tree** *(Citrus paradisi)*: A mature grapefruit plant can reach heights of 30 feet. Its leaves are 3 to 5 inches long with pointed tips at the base and last for two years. Grapefruit at maturity are bright yellow with a thick peel with white, pale yellow, pink, or red flesh. Grow in sunlight or full artificial light, and keep soil moist. Propagation is through tip cuttings with this plant. Repot this plant as it outgrows its container, and feed it every other week.

- **Mandarin, satsuma, tangerine tree** *(Citrus reticulata)*: Very old mandarin trees are at least 22 feet tall. When ripe, the mandarin is bright orange or an orange-red. The fruit is smaller than an orange and easier to peel. Tangerines and satsumas are a part of the mandarin tree clan. Grow mandarin under bright artificial lights if it cannot sit directly in front of a windowsill. Keep soil moderately moist. Propagation is through stem cuttings. Feed this plant every other week, and be sure to keep it in loose soil, repotting as necessary.

- **Lemon tree** *(Citrus limon)*: Mature lemon trees generally reach heights between 20 and 30 feet. Lemon twigs are often thorny with dark green, elliptical-shaped leaves that have fine teeth. The underside of its leaf is a lighter green. Its flowers are white with purplish undersides. The fruit of the lemon tree has a yellow peel and ranges in length

from than 2 to 5 inches. The lemon tree needs plenty of light, whether the light is artificial or natural, and be sure to keep soil moist. Feed this plant monthly. Keep it growing in loose soil, so repot as necessary. Stem cuttings are the best option for propagation.

- **Lime tree** *(Citrortunella)*: The lime tree is a more popular indoor citrus plant because the tallest it will grow is between 6 and 12 feet. Its branches are slender with sharp spines. Flowers on a lime tree are white and the fruit only one to two inches wide. The lime tree has dark green leaves with a prickly undersurface. Keep soil moist, and grow in bright light. Propagate through stem cuttings for this plant. Repot as it outgrows its container. Focus on feeding it once a month.

- **Kumquat tree** *(Fortunella* species): The kumquat is not really a member of the citrus family, but it shares many of the physical characteristics of typical citrus trees. Kumquat trees reach heights between 8 and 15 feet. Its dark green leaves range from a little over 1 to 3 inches long. It produces white flowers and small fruit with an orange or reddish peel. Unlike the other citrus trees, the kumquat is cold tolerant and is known to survive in 20-degree temperatures. Kumquats need plenty of water

and plenty of light. Propagation is through grafting or budding. **Grafting** is often a propagation method left to the professionals because it is the most difficult of propagation methods. It involves removing part of one plant and attaching it to another. Feed this plant monthly. Repot it as it outgrows its container and the soil becomes too dense.

- **Sunquat** *(x citrofortunella)*: The sunquat is a cross between the kumquat and a lemon. The sunquat tree is a small evergreen tree, and it produces small, seedy, pear-shaped fruits that can be eaten whole after peeling. The sunquat is a very fragrant tree that blooms several times in one year. The plant is small and is an excellent container plant. It needs full sun, consistently moist soil, and should be fertilized once a month with water soluble, acidic fertilizer with high nitrogen content. Sunquats are easier to find online. Sometimes Logee's, an online retailer that specializes in tropical plants (**www.logees.com**), sells them in 2 ½-inch pots. Repot it as it outgrows its pot, and propagate through grafting or budding.

- **Black pepper** *(Piper nigrum)*: The black pepper plant is a beautiful houseplant with vines and deep green leaves. It produces chains of small red fruit that can be harvested and dried for its spicy black, white, green, and red peppercorns. Black peppercorns are harvested when the seeds are nearly ripe and then dried at room temperature. The black pepper plant needs warm temperatures and a lot of light while fruiting, but its beautiful leaves also appreciate the shade. The plant is known to bloom freely in the summer months, and its fruits appear the next year. The black pepper plant is a slow-growing specimen; it

may take as long as four years before it blooms. But when it does, the plant can be expected to yield hundreds of peppercorns. Online nurseries sell the plant between $15 and $20. Black pepper plants like water, but the soil must be a well draining, and it needs to grow in a container with holes for drainage. Feed this plant every month and propagate through stem cuttings. This plant will need light shade. Repot it when the plant becomes pot bound.

- **European elderberry** *(Sambucus nigra)*: Although the elderberry plant is not the most attractive plant because its leaves resemble weeds, its flowers are small and fragrant. The dark purple to black-colored fruit is sweet and ripens late in the summer. The berries contain antioxidants, and the elderberry fruit is good for building up immune systems. Elderberry syrups on the market treat colds, coughs, and upper-respiratory infections. The plant needs full sun or direct light. Elderberries need even moisture and a well-draining soil. They are usually sold in small pots, but will need a medium-sized pot that is 4 to 8 inches tall and wide as it blooms. Feed this plant monthly. Repotting is only necessary if the plant becomes pot bound. Propagation is through woody stem cuttings.

- **Vanilla plant** *(Vanilla planifolia)*: The vanilla plant is an attractive, slow-growing vine and is best grown indoors. The flower of the vanilla plant grows into a bean. Vanilla is a member of the orchid family and is the only orchid that produces edible fruits. Vanilla is one of the most expensive spices because the process of converting the vanilla bean into a spice is long and complicated. Vanilla should grow near a window where the sun does not shine directly. The plant's soil must remain moist at all times. The plants

can be grown from the cuttings of another vanilla plant, or they can be ordered from a tropical plant nursery on the Internet. Propagate this plant through seeds or from stem cuttings. Feed this plant one time a month at most while it is growing. Repotting is only necessary if the plant becomes pot bound.

• **Black olive** *(Olea europaea)*: Olives are easy to grow because they can withstand dry soil, humidity, and varying temperatures. For the olive plant to flower, it needs full sun and cool evenings consistently during the winter season. The olive is a great potting plant, and it flowers when it is about 12 inches high. At this height and stage of its development, it produces dark olives in the spring seasons. Internet stores usually sell black olive plants for $20. An olive plant thirsts for water and should be watered daily, but it is also an easy-to-grow plant because as long as it has sunlight, it tolerates periods of watering neglect. Propagate this plant through woody stem cuttings, and feed it monthly. Repot it into a larger container if the plant becomes too large for the container and the roots top the plant's container edge.

• **Pineapple** *(Ananas comosus)*: Although it takes two full years for the pineapple plant to produce fruit, the pineapple is a great container plant. Pineapples grow fastest if they are grown in full or partial sunlight and its coolest temperatures do not drop below 60 degrees. The plant

only needs a 1- to 2-inch container and grows upright with long, exaggerated spidery leaves. Pineapple is a fragrant and easy-growing plant because it tolerates saturated watering and does not mind drying out its topsoil in between watering. Propagation is through division. Feed this plant monthly, and maintain the soil quality by repotting it every year.

- **Seedless kishu** (*Citrus reticula*): The seedless kishu is a mandarin, and it grows in full sun and produces small, sweet, seedless fruit during the December holidays. Mandarins grow after one or two years, and fragrant flowers appear from late winter to spring. The tree will grow between 1 and 3 feet, and it has thorns that can be removed without interfering with the plant's growth. The kishu needs fair amounts of water or should be kept moderately moist, but the fruit should be planted in a container that drains well. Feed this plant every two weeks, and use stem cuttings for propagation. Repot as the plant grows and the roots fill the soil.

- **Strawberry** (*Fragaria species*): Strawberries grow easily and are a favorite among indoor gardeners. They last for years and produce at least 1 quart of strawberries in optimal growing conditions. The fruit produces according the grower's schedule, not the weather, so home growers enjoy having fresh strawberries in the middle of winter. Strawberries need full sunlight and a potting mix that drains water well. To grow the strawberry plant, visit a garden supply store, pick up a large container and strawberry seeds, and fill a container with vegetable soil mix. Add plant fertilizer according to directions. Stick holes in the potting soil with your fingers and drop a few

strawberry seeds in each hole. Place the container in a sunny south-facing window or a porch that receives direct sunlight. Water the pots plentifully, and fertilize the plant every ten days with a mixture diluted to half strength. Plants bloom with white flowers and then fruit grows in a few months. The plant will produce flowers and small, but sweet fruit for three years. Propagation is done through seeds. Repot whenever the plant's roots become visible.

- **Raspberry** *(Rubus idaeus)*: To start a raspberry plant, purchase raspberry plugs from a nursery. You can choose between summer- and fall-growing varieties. Summer-bearing plants produce fruits in the early summer, and the fruit-bearing season lasts about five weeks. Ever-bearing varieties will produce two crops each year, one in the late summer and the other in the early summer of the next year. You can choose red, gold, purple, or black raspberries for your container garden. Fill a 5-gallon container with a mixture of equal parts sand, vermiculite, perlite, and peat. Make sure that the container has drainage holes in the bottom because raspberries do not like wet roots. Set the pots on a gravel bed and allow the raspberries to thrive in summer sun. If the indoor area gets cool in the winter, surround the plant with straw to keep it warm. Raspberries begin to grow after six weeks. Propagation is through seeds, and repotting is necessary only when the plant grows out of the pot. When kept indoors, keep in full sun, and ensure the soil remains moist. Feed this plant every month.

- **Honeyberry** *(Lonicera caerulea)*: The honeyberry is a member of the honeysuckle family. The plant is easy to grow and very similar to blueberries. Although they grow fine

in containers, they need to be placed in cold temperatures below freezing for several weeks as this helps them bloom and produce fruit the next year. Honeyberry needs well-drained soil, which means the soil should be moderately moist. It also likes partial shade in the afternoon and warm late morning sun. Feed this plant once a month, and repot it only when the plant overgrows the container. Propagate this plant from seed.

The economic and nutritional benefits and convenience of growing fruits, herbs, and vegetables indoors are unbeatable. Edible gardens provide fresh, healthy additions to breakfast, lunch, and dinner servings. Growing fruits and vegetables indoors is not only fun, but also productive and economically advantageous for large and small families.

Vegetables

Vegetables can be grown indoors, preferably in kitchens that get as much as six to eight hours of natural sunlight. A determined gardener will make good use of artificial light whenever possible. In most cases, artificial light is fine as long as the plant responds well under the lamps. There are delightful advantages to growing vegetables indoors, including the following:

- Food is available when you want it, and it is in season when you want it.

- Growing your own produce reduces dependency on grocers and vendors who have transported produce for several miles.

- Indoor vegetable gardens and plants are a lot less prone to bugs and other pests, such as cucumber beetles, tomato hornworms, and cutworms.

- Indoor gardens will not be hassled by squirrels and other animals that nibble and destroy produce. Indoor vegetables are not completely immune to pests, however. They do pick up spider mites, whiteflies, and sometimes, mealy bugs, so it is recommended to keep an insecticide handy.

Every vegetable grown indoors requires more attention and water than other houseplants because the water, light, and soil conditions are demanding. Indoor vegetable plants need a lightweight soil mix rather than the usual gardening potting soils found in stores. Chapter 2 discusses fertilization and soil further, but it is important to know that indoor garden vegetables need one part potting soil, one part vermiculite, one part peat, and one part perlite. This mixture can be made easily by purchasing the separate ingredients at a home gardening center. Vermiculite and perlite are compounds available at gardening stores that blend with potting soil to create a sustainable environment for particular and choosy indoor plants.

- **Spinach** *(Spinacia oleracea)*: Spinach has a deep taproot so its seeds need to be planted in 10- to 12-inch deep containers. Spinach plants need to be potted in one part vermiculite, one part peat, and one part perlite. Spinach should grow in rooms where temperatures do not fall below 65 degrees. After one or two weeks, the spinach plant will grow, and it will need to sit in a window. Keep the soil evenly moist as the spinach grows. If the direct sunlight from a window only lasts a few hours, the plant will need to sit underneath artificial lighting to maximize its growth. Propagate through seed, and repot this plant when it overgrows the pot or each year. Feed this plant once a month during the growing season.

- **Eggplant** *(Solanum melongena)*: The eggplant should be planted in full sun or underneath warm lamps because it likes hot weather between 75 and 80 degrees. It takes two to three months before the eggplant matures. The most common eggplants are dark purple, sometimes near black in color, and they be either globe- or round-shaped. Eggplants are considered especially suited for container gardening because they taste better grown indoors, and they harvest quickly. It is recommended that they are planted in 5-gallon containers with drainage holes. Eggplant needs moderate moisture and a good draining pot. Eggplant propagation is through seeds. Repotting is not usually necessary during the growing season, but start plants from fresh soil in the spring. Feed this plant every other week.

- **Avocados** *(Persea americana)*: Although it is unlikely that an avocado will sprout from an indoor tree, people love to plant avocado seeds and watch their roots sprout. Poke three toothpicks into the avocado pit, evenly spaced around the middle circumference of the pit, and then place the seed in

water with a few pieces of charcoal in the bottom. Only the bottom half of the seed should be immersed in the water, and the container should be placed somewhere warm but not in direct sunlight. In two or three weeks, the roots and stem should grow. That seeded plant should be should be potted in the recommended vegetable garden plant soil mix. The plant needs direct light and features attractive purple flowers. Be forewarned, however, it is difficult to sprout a plant from an avocado seed. Once a plant does grow, the soil should remain moderately moist. Propagate through seed, and repot as it grows out of its container. Feed this plant once every other week during the growing season.

- **Broccoli** *(Brassica Oleracea, Botrytis cymosa)*: Broccoli can be grown indoors from seeds. The seedlings should be grown in starter planters, and once they sprout, they should be transplanted in a large 5-gallon container. Dig a hole that is 4 inches deep, and plant the seedlings in a warm area and if possible, near an electrical outlet where the broccoli can sit under a lamp. Water the containers well because broccoli grows better in wet, but not soggy, soil. Broccoli is best propagated through seed. This plant needs full to partial sun and needs repotting whenever the plant becomes pot bound. Feed it every other week during the fruit-bearing season.

- **Carrot** *(Daucus pusillus)*: Carrots grow in containers nine months out of the year. When planting carrots, use a container that is 12 inches deep and large and round enough to allow a full-size carrot to grow. Be sure the container has holes at the bottom so the plant will drain

easily. The carrot seeds are tiny, so the seeds should be spaced an inch apart. Water the soil evenly, and then place the pot in a sunny area or under good artificial lighting. After a week or two, the carrot plant should begin to grow. Carrots propagate best from seed. Repotting is not necessary more than annually in the spring. Feed every two to three weeks.

- **Cucumber** (*Cucumis sativus*): Cucumber seeds must be purchased online or in a plant nursery. Cucumbers require warm weather so be sure the kitchen temperatures do not drop below 60 degrees. When you consider that cucumbers are grown in bulk by farmers outdoors in the extreme heat, it is safe to say that the warm temperatures in an oven-heated kitchen will delight the cucumber plant. Sow single cucumber seeds in pots that are at least 3 inches deep, and cover with compost. The compost should be completely damp because cucumber seeds have hard shells and without a good amount of water, the seed may not germinate. The containers, compost, and seed should

be covered with a plastic cling film and stored in a warm room where the temperatures are 70 degrees or higher. After the seeds sprout, remove the cling wrap, and keep the plants in a warm, sunny area with steady temperatures. Cucumbers need to be watered regularly, and they need moderately moist soil. Cucumbers and vegetables do not like soggy soils. A combination soil mix that drains well is always best for growing vegetables indoors. Feed this plant once every two weeks to improve fruit growth. Repot this plant whenever the plant grows over the edges of the container. Propagation is through seed.

- **Tomatoes** *(Lycopersicon esculentum)*: Tomatoes can be grown in one 6-inch pot in direct sunlight. If you want to grow tomatoes throughout the winter, start one or two new plants from seeds every two weeks. The seeds should be planted in starter mix about ¼ inch deep and watered. The mix should stay moist but not soggy, and the seedlings should appear in one to two weeks. When the seedlings reach 3 inches tall, remove the plants from the starter soil, and place them in vegetable soil compost. Tomatoes grow best from seed or stem cuttings and need full sun. Feed the plants one time every week during fruit-bearing season and once a month after. Repotting is necessary if the roots extend to the bottom of the container.

- **Potatoes** *(Solanum tuberosum)*: Growing potatoes indoors requires a lot of light and moisture in order to produce strong tubers, which are the bulbs that form to produce the actual potato. If direct natural sunlight is not available, be sure to grow vegetables under a light that will stay on for the duration of the day. Use a deep container with holes in its bottom for planting potatoes indoors. Potatoes

can be placed atop a pebble tray, and you can use the peat moss soil compost for growing. When the potato plant reaches 6 inches, add more soil and continue to add soil until the tuber reaches the top of the container. The soil must be mounded around each plant in the container if you have planted more than one tuber. Any flowers the potato plant produces are not edible. These flowers help the tubers grow and indicate that the potatoes in the soil are ready for harvest. The potato takes up to three months before it harvests. Keep the soil evenly moist and feed this plant during the growing season once every other week. Repotting in the spring is recommended. Propagation through rhizomes is best.

- **Green beans** *(Phaseoolus vulgaris)*: Green beans grow as vines and bushes. It is best to plant a bush bean variety indoors because they are smaller and adapt well in containers. Green beans need six full hours of sunlight. Purchase green bean seeds online or at a nursery and plant them in long, narrow, 8-inch containers. Use the vegetable gardening compost, and if a fertilizer is desired, use a high phosphorous fertilizer like a 10-20-10, and work the fertilizer into the soil two weeks before planting. Greens often grow as vines so they need long and narrow containers with plenty of holes in the bottom. A newspaper and draining tray would be handy to prevent the soil from slipping out of the holes. When natural sunlight is being used as the primary lighting method, plant the beans in the spring when sunlight is more available. Green beans will grow in temperatures between 50 and 85 degrees, and they harvest 50 to 60 days after being planted. The green bean grows every year, so the entire plant can be plucked during harvest, picking the

beans individually. Green beans are best repotted each year in spring. Propagation is best through seeds. Keep the soil moist throughout the growing season, and feed this plant one time every other week.

- **Onions** *(Allium cepa)*: Onions are an attractive plant for windowsills and other interior spaces. They sprout tall, long green leaves and will grow year round. Choose a plant container, and get three green onions and three red onions that have their long green stems still in place. Cut the bottoms off and make sure the roots are still attached. You will use the top portion for  cooking, but you will plant the bottom portion that has the roots. You will do this for both red and green onions. Place dirt in your container, preferably the soil mix used for growing herbs and vegetables, and make 3-inch holes with a large spoon. Plant the three onions, but leave sufficient space in between them. The larger red onions should be planted in a medium- to large-sized container because those bulbs need more room to spread out. Onions sprout

quite easily and quickly, and results should be seen in less than week. Like all plants and vegetables that grow indoors, onions need plenty of direct sun, and the hotter the indoor area gets, the more water the onion plant will need. Onions propagate best through cuttings. Feed every other week. Repotting is necessary annually prior to fruit-bearing season.

- **Radishes** *(Raphanus sativus)*: Radishes harvest in two weeks and are very easy to grow and reseed. They do well in damp and cooler climates, but they do not need much care. Seeds should be planted with enough space for its long carrot-like bulbs to develop in the container. Radishes propagate best through seed or cuttings. They require partial sun and need to remain moist as they grow. Feed this plant once every other week. Repotting is necessary if the plant becomes pot bound.

- **Cress** *(Lepidium sativum)*: This is an easy vegetable to grow indoors in a flat container or shallow pot. It should be watered regularly. The seeds should be sown evenly and heavily in the potting mixture, and then pressed flat. Cress needs to sit in a sunny spot, preferably a windowsill when temperatures are sure not to drop below 65 degrees. Within two weeks, the seedlings should be ready for harvesting. Cress is notably one of the easiest crops to grow indoors. Cress is best repotted annually and should be propagated through seeds. Feed this plant every other week.

Growing foods indoors is fun, easy, and convenient because out-of-season fruits will be available in the winter. No matter if you are growing fruits, herbs, or vegetables, all of the indoor crops need plenty of light whether the light is natural or artificial. Pay

attention to the soil mix requirements for growing foods. Herbs will grow heartily in 6-inch pots and all-purpose potting soil equally mixed with soil, sand, and peat moss. They are similar to vegetables and thrive well in soil that is one part peat, one part vermiculite, and one part perlite. Most experts recommend growing citrus in commercially available citrus potting mixes that are available in stores. Like other soils in which foods grow, citrus potting soils should drain well and store nutrients well.

CASE STUDY: BASEMENT BANANAS

Sandy Burrell
Owner, Northern Tropics Greenhouse
www.northerntropics.com

Sandy Burrell has enjoyed growing plants for several years. She has an indoor garden in her basement where she supplies her plants with adequate artificial lighting. She grows aloe, Victorian water lilies, and banana plants, and she said she first purchased her banana plant while on vacation and wanted to keep it alive all winter. She said this decision is what began her interest in growing tropical plants, especially banana plants.

Burrell finds tending for her plants an enjoyable and relaxing hobby. When considering growing plants as a profession, however, she said it requires more hard work and dedication, especially during the winter months when long hours are required.

"When growing plants indoors, you have to match the plants to their growing conditions," Burrell said. "The most attractive plant in the world will not stay attractive if you place it in the wrong location. You have to give each plant some space to grow, or it will not grow into a beautiful plant."

She uses a potting mix made of perlite, composted bark, beat, and vermiculite, and she said she does not notice a difference between organic and conventional gardening supplies. She said the most important thing to consider when buying fertilizer and soil for plants is to ensure the plant's needs are being met.

One of the most important facets of gardening is ensuring the plants receive the proper amount of water. If plant owners must leave plants unattended for an extended period of time, such as on vacation, Burrell suggests grouping the plants together in a shady place and watering them well. She also said plant owners can use inexpensive drip irrigation kits that run on timers. It is best to set these up a week or two prior to using them to ensure they function properly before leaving the plants unattended.

Burrell offers the following pieces of advice for those who may not be experienced with houseplants: do not overwater them, use a water-soluble fertilizer, and make sure the plants are placed in good light.

ALL THE PRETTY FLOWERS

There are two plants types that most houseplant owners are concerned with: plants that remain green year-round (foliage plants) and plants with bloom that add powerful color. Colorful plants that bloom add excitement and vibrancy to a household that green foliage cannot. Now that you know about the foliage plants you can choose to include in your home, it is a good time to learn which flowers you may be interested in adding to brighten up any room in your house.

Choose the plants you like, and find the seeds at a local or online nursery to begin your blooms. Before you purchase seeds, be sure to check the plant's needs, just as you did when you first brought a houseplant into your home. Be sure the seeds will grow in the light and temperatures that your space provides. The more seeds you plant, the larger and more colorful your blooms and indoor décor will be. This list, while it is intended to be exhaus-

tive and varied, is far from comprehensive. There are thousands of blooming plants to choose, so consider this a sampler from a much larger menu.

Indoor Plants that Bloom

- **Flowering maple** *(Abutilon hybridum)*: The *Abutilon* is not a maple but is named because its leaves resemble that of a maple tree. With good light and the correct maintenance, the flowering maple will produce yearlong blossoms that are red, yellow, pink, orange, or peach. Water thoroughly and grow in bright indirect sunlight with temperatures between 65 and 70 degrees year round. The plant grows to be at least 36 inches tall. Feed this plant every two weeks, and repot the plant if it becomes pot bound. Propagation is through tip cuttings in the spring.

- **Flamingo flower** *(Anthurium andraeanum)*: Tropical plant with colorful waxy, heart-shaped **spathes**, which are tube-like growths that develop inside a flower. Calla lilies, like the flamingo flower, are particularly noted for the spathe that grows inside of its flower. The flamingo flower needs bright to moderate sunlight, but not direct sun, and cool to warm temperatures between 60 and 80 degrees. It needs fertilizer high in phosphorous content every month and plenty of water during the spring and summer months. The flamingo flower grows to heights of 18 inches. Propagation of this plant is best through dividing older plants. Repotting this plant every two to three years in the spring is best.

Begonias

Begonias need a lot of fertilizer and moist soil throughout the year. They like humidity and warmer temperatures between 65 and 75 degrees. Begonias are widely considered outdoor plants, but there are three types of begonias that are excellent for indoors: angel-wing begonias, fancy-leafed begonias, and winter-blooming begonias. Their flowers are yellow and pink.

- **Angel-wing begonias** *(Begonia x corallina)* grow 1 foot tall and bloom in the late winter and spring. They need bright light in the summer, but not direct light, and every two weeks it needs to be fertilized with a product that is high in phosphorous. It is possible to allow the soil to dry out, but do not allow it to remain dry for longer than a day or two. Propagating this plant through tip cuttings is best. This plant needs to be repotted when pot bound.

- **Fancy-leaf begonia** *(Rex begonia)*: Fancy-leaf begonias like high humidity and bright sunlight or direct bright light. The plant rests during the winter, will survive with one watering per week, and will not need fertilizer. Fertilize the fancy-leaf during its blooming period. Most plants that like high humidity crave consistently moist soil, so it is important to keep the soil moist, particularly when the plant is in full bloom. Propagate this plant through tip, or leaf cuttings are possible. Repot this plant if it becomes pot bound.

- **Winter blooming begonias** (*Begonia x hiemalis*) are incredibly attractive houseplant flowers because they resemble pale-colored roses. These need a cool bright window and have the same water and fertilizing needs as angel-wing begonias. Propagate this plant through tip cuttings. If the plant becomes pot bound, repot in the spring.

Bromeliads

Bromeliads are popular blooming plants that belong to the pineapple family. Some bromeliads sink their roots into the floors of the forest, and others cling and grow onto rocks. Many of the bromeliads grow in between limbs of trees. When grown indoors, bromeliads need a moderately moist environment and direct sunlight for at least half of the day. Bromeliads also need high humidity, which can be achieved by placing a pebble tray underneath the plant's draining container. Keep the soil moderately moist, and remember that on average, bromeliads like temperatures between 60 and 80 degrees. A well-balanced soil is recommended.

Bromeliads grow heartily when given generous amounts of fertilizer in the summer seasons. Adding magnesium to a bromeliad's water or fertilizer will encourage the plant's blooms. Placing a plastic bag over a bromeliad plant with a ripe apple or several apple cores for seven to 14 days will produce ethylene gas that encourages the flowers of a bromeliad to bloom. Do not allow a bromeliad with a plastic bag tied around it to sit in the direct sun.

Here are a few bromeliads you may wish to consider for growing colorful species inside your home.

- **Urn plant, silver vase plant** (*Aechmea fasciata*): The urn plant is found on the floor of South American rain forests, or the Amazon. The plant with long, green leaves produces a large pink bloom that lasts four to six weeks in the spring. Urn plants need bright light and temperatures between 70 and 85 degrees. Keep the plant soil lightly moist, and keep the arched, inside leaves of the plant (the urn) filled with water. Feed this plant once every month. Repot the plant if it becomes pot bound. Propagation is through division.

- **Queen's tears, friendship plant** (*Billbergia nutans*): This easy-to-grow and popular bromeliad will tolerate a brief winter chill and temperatures of 40 degrees. Queen's tears grow in partial shade, make an excellent hanging plant, and need bright light in the fall and early winter. The flowers produce nectar drops that resemble tears. The plant is called the friendship plant because it is so easy to propagate. The offsets are easy to pinch from the plant and give away to friends. The plant is popular because it tolerates dry soil in fall and winter, and it does not cringe if it is left to grow without high percentages of humidity. If the friendship plant is raised in a dry area, mist the leaves to increase humidity. Feed this plant weekly in the

summer and one time every two to three weeks the rest of the year. Repotting is necessary if the plants outgrow the containers.

• **Scarlet star** *(Gusmania lingulata)*: The Scarlet star is easily the most beautiful bromeliad available. One thick, colorful scarlet flower that resembles a pineapple grows in the center. Scarlet stars like high humidity, and unlike their peers, scarlet stars will grow underneath artificial lighting in homes and offices. The roots of the scarlet star should be kept lightly moist all season long, and the plant should be fed fertilizer once each month. Repotting this plant is necessary if it becomes pot bound. Propagating through dividing rhizomes is the best option.

• **Air plant, sky plant** *(Tillandsia* species): *Tillandsias* are miniature versions of the scarlet star, but these plants are unique because they do not have roots. *Tillandsias* absorb water and nutrients through their leaves and are ideal plants to store in a greenhouse or a cold frame during the winter when they take a rest and benefit from cool temperatures, which help provide more brilliant color during the bloom period. The *Tillandsia* needs to be grown in a glass container, a bowl with wood or sphagnum moss, or even inside of a seashell. These are small and thin plants that grow about 6 inches tall. It will tolerate direct light every season except summer. A high phosphorous fertilizer will help the plant achieve its full potential in the spring and summer, but the air plant will not need fertilizing during the fall and winter season. Tillandsias should be sprayed until they are wet, and because it absorbs water through its leaves, the base of this rootless plant does not need to be wet or soaked. Misting this plant two to three times per

week is enough to keep this houseplant alive and thriving. Even less water is needed in the winter, and misting can be reduced to once every week. Repot this plant in orchid soil when it is necessary. Propagation by offsets is best.

- **Flaming sword, painted feather** *(Vriesea splendens)*: Flaming swords are interesting because they have wide, long leaves and a tall, erect, red flower ejects from their centers. The plants grow to be just under 2 feet tall, and the spike that grows in the center of the plant will last for several weeks. Once the spike at the center of the plant withers back, the plant produces one or more offsets, which can be propagated right away. The parent plant should be exhausted before propagating, however. Flaming swords need bright indirect sunlight from January through December and warm temperatures, between 70 and 80 degrees. They are a perfect indoor plant to decorate bare walls, long tables, and fireplace hearths. Fertilizing once a month and keeping the soil lightly moist will keep the dramatic colors alive and the plant hearty. Repot if the plant becomes pot bound.

Bulbs, corms, and tubers

Bromeliads and begonias are cute, but plants grown from bulbs are beautiful. There is no denying the natural and exquisite beauty that plants such as tulips, clivias, and lilies add to a home, a doorstep, or an area of the office. The colors are vibrant, memorable, will liven up a room, and boost a mood for weeks on end. And, if you have the time to propagate plants year-round, the mood and flowers can stay throughout the year.

Bulbs, corms, and tubers do not have the same tolerance for cold, so they have been categorized into two distinct groups: spring-flowering bulbs and warm-natured bulbs. Spring-flowering bulbs are bulbs that are planted in the fall and flower in the spring. The bulbs need time to stow away underground in cold weather, which helps bring about magnificent spring color. Warm-natured bulbs, corms, and tubers do have to be chilled, either in the refrigerator or a cold greenhouse in order to bloom. **Corms** are similar to bulbs in appearance, and corms, like bulbs and tubers, store food for the plant in order to help it grow. The corms die and are replaced during the plant's growth process. Gladiolus, tuberous begonias, and crocus are plants that bloom at the expense of their corms. Some of the warm-natured bulbs will bloom in the winter and spring, but, in general, these are considered summer bulbs that need a dry period, usually in the fall where it takes less water and no fertilizer. The dry periods occur after growth period.

Spring-flowering bulbs are available in garden centers in the late summer and early fall. Once you purchase the bulbs, store them in the refrigerator or a cold frame. In the refrigerator, the bulbs should not be kept near apples and other fruits because the ethylene gas that those fruits release are harmful to the bulbs.

Bulbs from the warm-natured group are from tropical places or arid climates. Most bulbs from this group need a period of bright light or cool temperatures that will help them grow well indoors and produce colorful blooms. Before the blooming periods begin, and while these plants are in bloom, they need to be fertilized with a high-phosphorous plant food and watered regularly.

There are countless warm-natured bulbs to choose from and with the proper planning, interior environments can be decorated with colorful plants like calla lilies, amaryllis, and caladiums throughout the year.

- **Cupid's bow** (*Achimenes* species and hybrids): The delicate leaves of the cupid's bow appear in the summer and throughout the fall, and this plant fares best in a hanging basket. Plant the bulbs in the spring, and they will bloom in eight to 12 weeks. *Achimenes* need bright, unfiltered light and steady temperatures between 70 and 75 degrees. A high phosphorous fertilizer during its growing season and a constant supply of lukewarm water to keep the soil evenly moist are ideal feeding habits to grow heartily. In October, or the mid-fall, let the plants dry. When the leaves turn brown, gather the rhizomes, and store them in a bag of peat moss or vermiculite. Store the bulbs at 60 degrees and replant them in the spring. Repot this plant if it becomes pot bound.

- **Caladium, angel wings** (*Caladium* hybrids): Caladiums are pretty because they are pink and green, but they are not typical blooming and flowering plants. They are foliage plants with colorful leaves. Caladiums are grown in the warmth of the summer seasons. They do not like temperatures below 60 degrees in the day or evening and need bright to moderate light in order to thrive. Feed a

high-nitrogen, foliage plant food to caladiums, and keep soil constantly moist in an area with high humidity levels. The plant's colors last as long as six months. Propagate caladiums in the spring. Repotting is necessary if the soil becomes compact.

- **Kaffir lily** *(Schizostylis* hybrids): When the Kaffir lily is three years old or older, it will produce clusters of red, yellow, orange, or white winter flowers. The Kaffir lily needs to be stored in cold during the fall and allowed to rest with a dry soil until midwinter in temperatures that are cool or below 65 degrees. The blossoms arrive in February or March. Moderate light in the winter and shade in the late spring to fall make this plant a popular favorite. Keep the soil lightly moist during the spring season, and in the fall, the water needs are reduced significantly. Only enough water to keep the soil from going completely dry is needed. In the winter, the plant does not need fertilizer, but during the spring to the fall, fertilize the plant every two weeks with a highly phosphorous plant food. Most Kaffir

lilies are grown from seed, but if you wish to propagate, cut from the stalk when the blossoms begin to shrivel up. Repot this plant as the roots overgrow the container.

- **Freesia** *(Freesia corymbosa)*: Freesia is a fragrance-bearing plant. But freesia bulbs need adjusting before blooming. The freesia corms should be kept in a warm spot over the summer for at least eight weeks and temperatures should remain at 80 degrees. Some store the plants on top of the hot water heater or the refrigerator. Use well-drained, clean pots to plant the corms, and water. After one month of sitting in a room with average room temperatures, freesias need to be removed into a brightly lit area where temperatures remain a steady 60 degrees. The buds should form during this period, and when the buds arrive, the plant will need direct or bright sunlight near a window, but the window and the outdoor temperatures cannot be hot. The stems of freesia plants often grow 18 inches tall. The flowers are delicate soft lavender; the stalks are a bit lazy and may need to be held up with ties, tape, or stake for display. High phosphorous fertilizers every ten days and slightly moist soil during the growth period are sure bets to keep this plant healthy during its dormant and growing season. Propagation is through division. Repot this plant if it overgrows the container.

- **Amaryllis** *(Amaryllis* species and hybrids): Exotic and popular, this plant is a wintertime favorite. The bulbs usually are sold in kits and marketed for the December holidays because their blooms are festive, royal, and red. The amaryllis is not difficult to grow and will bloom six to eight weeks after it has been planted. When the bulb is planted, it needs to be stored in a cool, dry place (60

degrees) for a period of four to eight weeks or until a shoot appears. Then move the plant to a place where there is bright light and make sure the amaryllis has an all-purpose plant food every ten days and a slightly moist soil. When the amaryllis fades out, take the bulbs, store them away for ten to 15 weeks, and then replant them. Propagation is through bulb offsets. Repotting is necessary if the plant overgrows the container.

- **Hyacinth** *(Hyacinthus* hybrids): Hyacinths are popular outdoor plants and need to be manipulated into blooming indoors by allowing the bulbs to sit in cool soil (temperatures of 65 degrees or less) until the roots form. They are a favorite because of their colors and their scents. Hyacinths need 12 weeks of cold time before blooming. Hyacinths will grow in soil or pebbles (even decorative pebbles) and plain water. The flowers only last two weeks when kept in a cool room, but indoor-growing hyacinths cannot be repotted; they must be thrown away after their season ends. Fortunately, they are not expensive. They like bright cool light, and fertilizer is not necessary. The plant only needs enough water to keep soil slightly wet, but if grown in water, the roots should be suspended in the water.

- **Easter lily** *(Lilium longiflorum)*: Easter lilies bloom in the summer, but the species is quite popular around Easter to commemorate the Christian holiday. Greenhouse growers force Easter lilies into springtime blooms with extreme light and water routines. If you are purchasing the Easter lily because you want to watch it grow in your home, buy the plant when it only has one or two buds that appear ready to bloom. Otherwise, buy the plant when it has

completed its growing cycle and there is nothing left to enjoy except the final stages of bloom period. Keep the plant in temperatures that are between 60 and 65 degrees. The plants need bright light and use fertilizer every two weeks; water lightly and often to keep soil lightly moist. Propagate through dividing rhizomes. Repot this plant if the soil becomes compact.

- **Daffodil (narcissus** species and hybrids): Like hyacinths, daffodils are grown most often outdoors and are considered popular outdoor plants. The larger daffodils that are typically found outdoors can be force bloomed in container pots after 12 weeks of being stored in cold temperatures. If daffodils are purchased in pots, be sure to choose plants that are not yet in bloom because it gives the indoor gardener the opportunity to watch the plant grow and enjoy it in its liveliest state for as long as possible. Paperwhite narcissuses do not need chilling before they go to into bloom. The bulbs can be planted, and three weeks later, fragrant blossoms will appear. The flowers last two to three weeks, and if they are purchased to decorate or fragrance a home, propagate accordingly so that

newer blooms are ready as the last batch begins to wither. Daffodils need bright light, moderately moist soil, cool temperatures (45 to 65 degrees), and weekly all-purpose plant fertilizer while the plant grows. Repot this plant annually in the spring.

- **Tulip** *(Tulipa* species and hybrids): Tulips are lovely for indoor growing because they come in so many colors. All tulips can be grown indoors, but Triumph tulips are probably the best bulbs to plant indoors because they will grow to maximum heights without leaning over. Triumph tulips are hybrids that have been cultivated to withstand harsh temperatures and bloom in an almost endless assortment of colors: red, orange, pink, purple, and yellow. Tulips need to be chilled for 14 weeks, and because tulips grow long roots, the bulbs should be planted in deep containers. Keep tulips in a cool room because the warmer the environment, the faster the flowers will fade. Tulips need bright light, and a little liquid fertilizer is optional but not necessary. The soil should be kept lightly moist while the plants are growing. Propagation is done through bulbs. Repot these plants each spring for the best blooms.

- **Calla lily** *(Zantedeschia* hybrids): Calla lilies are beautiful, but they are not the easiest blooming plant to grow and keep alive because without bright light, the right food — a highly phosphorous plant food — temperatures, and humidity, the Calla lily will die. When properly cared for, calla lilies should last four to six weeks. Container plants will grow at least 12 inches high. Calla lilies will bloom again the next season if they are given a proper resting period late in the summer. The plant can be stored away or the bulbs can be removed and stored in a cool, dry place.

The plants should dry until the leaves wither. Remove old foliage, and place the containers in a cool, shaded place. Keep the soil lightly moist until winter comes. In the winter, give calla lilies a new pot of soil, warmth, bright light, and if you have removed the bulbs, replant them, and add moisture. Calla lilies need a cool growing environment, and temperatures between 60 and 65 should keep the plant firm in the spring and winter season. During the summer, the plant will not respond well to temperatures over 85 degrees. Providing highly phosphorous plant food every three weeks when the plants are growing, and slightly moist soil will help keep the calla lily alive and thriving.

- **Goldfish plant** *(Columnea gloriosa* hybrids): The *columnea* has green, waxy leaves and red flowers that resemble goldfish splattered throughout its busy leaves. The *columnea* does most of its blooming in spring and summer, and mature plants produce dozens of red flowers. When the soil is kept mostly dry during the winter months, the early spring season blossoms are prompted to grow. The *columnea* does well in hanging baskets and should be kept indoors in the summer seasons because it will wither and die in hot weather and harsh light. Moderate light or fluorescent light, temperatures between 65 and 75 degrees, and fertilizer from spring through summer every two weeks with plenty of water during that period should produce healthy and lifelong goldfish plants. The goldfish plant can grow wildly so it is easy to propagate this plant while trimming because it needs to be manicured and trimmed for a neat appearance, as the plant gets older. Repot this plant if it becomes pot bound.

- **Florist's cyclamen** (*Cyclamen persicum* hybrids): Cyclamens bloom in midwinter. Instead of throwing cyclamen away after their blooming period, allow the foliage to dry until the late spring and the leaves have dried out. Clear the dead leaves; place the plant in a cool, dark place for three months; and give it water just enough to keep the roots from drying out. Late in the summer, retrieve the container, and place it in a bright location. The plant should be repotted into new soil. When the new growth appears, begin to fertilize the plant every two weeks with a high phosphorous plant food. Keep the cyclamen in bright light and direct winter light for at least two hours each day. The soil should be kept lightly moist. Propagation is best through seeds.

- **Chrysanthemums** (*Leucanthemum maximum*): Mums are sold as perennials and annuals. Annuals are the most typical, and they flood florist's corners and nurseries in the fall. Mums, whether perennials or annuals, need bright light, cool temperatures around  65 degrees, and slightly moist soil. Chrysanthemums are great plants for window boxes, and if grown from seed, plant many of them to create a full and rich look. If you purchase a chrysanthemum plant, try and buy those plants that are just coming into bloom or have not yet

bloomed to enjoy the shelf life and the blooming period more. Perennials will return after their blooming period, and annuals are usually thrown away or discarded, primarily because people plant their mums outdoors and once it experiences a frost, the plant dies. Propagate this plant from tip cuttings in the spring. Repot in the spring, and feed it once every other week.

- **Poinsettia** *(Euphorbia pulcherrima)*: More than 75 million poinsettias are sold every year, mostly during the winter holiday season. In October, poinsettia bulbs and containers have to be stored in darkness for 14 hours every night for eight to ten weeks because that is the only way poinsettias will produce buds. Poinsettias need bright light, but not outdoor or direct sunlight. They will survive in room temperatures between 60 and 70 degrees, and if the plant is situated in a cool room, the bloom time will last much longer, for at least the second half of winter. Fertilizing the poinsettia is not necessary, and the soil should be kept slightly moist. The poinsettias live one season, but with diligence and a greenhouse, can be propagated for future growing seasons. Repot this plant if it becomes pot bound.

- **Regal or Martha Washington geraniums** *(Pelargonium x domesticum)*: This plant has larger flowers that are pink, red, white, or speckled. It has large, serrated leaves. Geraniums are very popular outdoor plants. Indoor regal geraniums are often sold as winter flowering houseplants. The most popular plants are the plants that are not hard to keep alive, which explains why the regal geraniums are a very popular brand indoors and out. This plant needs full sun and needs to be kept moist throughout the year. Feed it once a month during the growing season. Repotting is

not necessary, but these plants often will need replacement every three to four years.

Orchids

Orchids are beautiful flowers. They are expensive and rather difficult to grow without a good deal of experience. There are tens of thousands of orchid species out there, and the species is evolved from tropical rain forests as well as dry alpine rocky areas. Only certain varieties of orchid will grow successfully indoors because orchids have extreme light and temperature needs. Most orchids grow best in bright, indirect light. Suitable temperatures for orchids are 75 degrees in the day and 65 degrees at night. Because the day and night time temperatures vary by 10 degrees, it is important to choose an appropriate growing location in order to produce healthy flowering orchids.

Orchids will do fine outdoors in the summer season. Plants that show signs of bloom should stay indoors because the buds attract insects and pests. If the summer nights are sweltering, bring the orchids indoors where the temperatures are cooler. Orchids do not grow in potting soil but rather bark or wood chips and special orchid mixes mentioned in Chapter 2 on soil and fertilization. When purchasing an orchid plant, it is wise to purchase orchid fertilizer as well. The Internet is a good go to place for orchid fertilizers, and be wary because there are many. There is one recommendation, however, for organic orchid fertilizer products. Everything

Orchids website has good product for a value price; the website can be found at **www.everyting-orchids.com**; their fertilizer prices begin at $10.

- **Corsage orchid** *(Cattleya)*: Beginners do not grow this plant typically because the corsage orchid is a high-maintenance plant. Gardeners who live in warm temperatures with high humidity will do well with this plant because it originates from tropical jungles. The corsage orchid needs bright light every season and high humidity all year round. The leaves should be medium green, which indicates the plant likely will bloom. Use an orchid potting mix, and fertilize the plant every two weeks from late spring to early fall. In the winter, the plant should be fed every month and watered to keep the soil slightly moist in summer. It will thrive in temperatures between 60 and 85 degrees all year round. When corsage orchids do bloom, it is best to display them in a warm windowsill. Propagation of this plant is best through dividing the rhizome. Repot this plant every two to three years using orchid soil.

- **Dendrobium, spray orchid** *(Dendrobium* species and hybrid): The flowers of spray orchids have the potential to last for many weeks. The spray orchids come in a several colors — yellow, violet, red, and pink — and often, the blossoms have a fruitful scent. They may grow to heights of 18 inches and may need a stalk to keep the plant upright. These orchid species likes bright warm summers, plenty of fertilizer, and consistent watering. During the winter season, they like cool temperatures, and the soil should almost go dry before they are watered again. Rest the orchid for one month by letting the soil become dry, and leaving the plant in a cool area without direct sunlight will

encourage strong flowering. Repot every two years in the spring. Propagation is best by dividing the rhizome.

- **Dancing ladies orchid** *(Onicidium* species and hybrids): This orchid species and their closest relatives tend to bloom when they are ready and often, bloom more than once in the year. They are fast growing and produce more than 100 small blossoms at a time. They like year-round bright light and outdoor summer weather as long as there is shield from the direct sun. The orchids need fertilizer in between every three waterings and should be watered as often as needed during the summer, but left to dry in between watering during the winter. Propagate using division, and repot if it overgrows the container.

- **Moth Orchids** *(Phalaenopsis)*: Moth orchids are easy-to-grow orchids that will thrive under natural and artificial light in homes and offices. The graceful arc of the moth orchid makes it an interesting design concept. It craves comfortable temperatures between 65 degrees at night and 80 in the day. Moth orchids stay indoors all year round. It needs fertilizer once every seven or eight days in the spring and summer months, but only needs fertilizer and enough water to keep the plant from drying out in the winter. These roots need room, so repot the plant any time the soil becomes too densely packed with roots. Propagate offshoots in new pots.

- **Paph, Lady's slippers** *(Paphiopedilum* species and hybrids): Most of the paph orchids are ground dwellers and do not need a lot of light. The plant will thrive in the shade outdoors in the summer in cool to moderate temperatures between 60 and 80 degrees. The blooms of the paph last at least eight weeks, and the single white flower rises from

a wreath of spotted green leaves. Fertilize every three weeks in the winter and every third watering during the summer. The potting medium should remain lightly moist at all times, even during the winter season. Propagate by dividing rhizomes or tubers. Repotting is necessary if the plant becomes pot bound.

- **Primrose** (*Primula* species and hybrids): Primroses are cute blooming plants that have more than 425 species of wildflowers and garden flowers cultivated as houseplants. Primroses are colorful and charming plants grown from seed and planted and chilled in the summertime to make winter blooms. Primroses need a lot of water; the plants must be watered constantly, or they wilt fast. They take bright indoor light without direct sun and like cool temperatures between 50 and 70 degrees. Feed this plant every two weeks, lightly. Propagation is best done through seeds, though it is difficult. Repot this plant if it becomes pot bound.

- **Cineraria** *(Cineraria)*: Cineraria is popular with greenhouse growers because the seeds are started in greenhouses during the summer, and the colorful blooms burst four months later. Nurseries sell cinerarias from January through April. The blooms are stronger when the plant is kept in temperatures that are cool and do not get higher than 65 degrees at night. Cinerarias like bright sunlight, constant moisture, and high humidity. They do not need fertilizing, and their blooms last four to six weeks. Propagate from seed late in the summer months. Tip cuttings also may work. Repot this plant every year during the spring.

PESTS, INSECTICIDES, AND DISEASE

When insects attack a plant, the best way to keep the plant alive is to identify the causes, find a solution, and deal it with it quickly. Not every pest situation requires chemical pesticides as a solution. Sometimes a plant dipped in soapy water may be all that is needed to destroy insects that have inhabited the plant.

Insects occasionally will attack houseplants, particularly those that are not growing in the best conditions possible. The best way to prevent pest problems is to give plants fresh air, increase the humidity in a room, and keep the temperatures between 65 and 75 degrees.

Bringing Plants Into Your Home

As a precaution with new plants entering a home, check the underside of the leaves because bugs nestled there are difficult to see. You can bring insects to the surface by soaking plants in a tub full of water that reaches up to the pot's rim. After a few minutes, the insects

in the soil will rise to the surface. Indoor gardeners who leave their plants out for the summer have to make sure to inspect these plants thoroughly for bugs before bringing them back indoors.

When houseplants are moved outdoors for the summer, a number of insects, including caterpillars, earwigs, and other pests that usually remain outdoors may feed on leaves or buds. Taking one or two preventive measures when bringing plants back indoors will significantly decrease the possibility of insect infestation. The following are some tips you should follow before bringing your plants indoors:

- Aphids, earwigs, fungus gnats, mealy bugs, scale, spider mites, thrips, and whiteflies colonize on plants quickly. Before using a pesticide on a houseplant, check the label and warnings to be sure the chemicals are the appropriate treatment for both plant and pest. Insecticides should only be used on the plants and pests listed on the label because there are no general, all-purpose insecticides. If your plant is not listed on the label, that particular insecticide is not intended for your plant.

- Most insecticides should be sprayed outside, in the garage, or any other well-ventilated area outside the home. Spraying insecticides in the home allows the insecticide to linger in the air. Avoid inhaling insecticide fumes, even if the product is organic. If using powders, wear a face mask and goggles when adding them to your plants.

- Apply insecticides in the shade, if possible. After spraying a houseplant with insecticide, place the plant in a shady place because many insecticides lose their effectiveness in sunlight, and the combination of light and pesticide injures plant leaves. Be sure the plant soil is moist before applying so that

it can absorb the insecticide. Carefully follow directions for use, storage, and disposal. You may need to apply insecticides more than once to kill all of the insects. Keep the products stored away from pets and children.

Pests

The following are some of the pests your houseplants will likely encounter, as well as ways you can prevent or treat a pest infestation.

Ants

Ants cause a plant to wilt and can be a nuisances if they invade your home. Peppermint oil will deter crawling insects. Ant traps are also useful because the ants will eat the poison and take the chemical to the nest, which will kill their young. Ants transmit disease, and they pick up aphids while eating the honeydew that aphids excrete.

Aphids

When aphids attack the leaves and new sprouts of a plant, the plant will get distorted. Aphids are the most bothersome of plant pests because they cluster in leaf axils, along the stems, and on the underside of leaves. Axils are tiny folds in a leaf that hold water and aquatic life, and other animals grow in those folds. The aphid is a green, black, or red insect that pierces stems, leaves, and buds. When aphids are done with a plant, they leave a sticky honeydew coating that may have black sooty mold that covers the leaves. Plants attacked by aphids should be removed and burned; just be sure the aphids are destroyed immediately and not left to linger and move to another plant. Smaller plants can be

soaked in cool soapy water. Larger plants should be sprayed with an aphid-control pesticide.

Caterpillars

When caterpillars attack a plant, they leave holes in the leaves, flowers, or seed pods. Caterpillars are hairy, tubular creatures, and whether the caterpillars are moth or butterfly larvae, they are visible to the naked eye. To avoid bringing caterpillars into the house, inspect the plant before bringing it indoors. Larger worms can be removed by hand. A larger plant with massive infestation will need a pesticide that poisons the attacking creature and its offspring when the poison is ingested. Some people are opposed to toxins and poisons and prefer natural pesticides, but that will not work against caterpillars. Some people make a solution of water and dish soap to kill horned-worm caterpillars that have infected food plants. Others use spearmint because it kills lar-

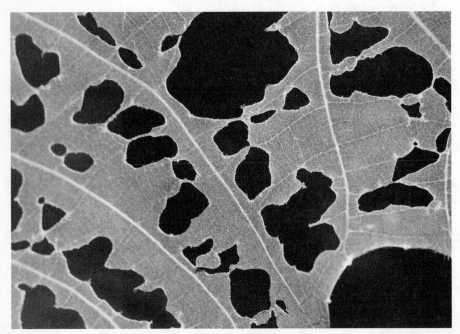

Photo courtesy of the USDA

vae. BT, which is an acronym for *bacillus thuringiensis*, is a form of bacteria that farmers and gardeners have used since the 1930s to control caterpillar populations.

Cyclamen mite

A cyclamen mite is a minute insect that looks like dust on a houseplant. When these pests attack the stems of the cyclamen plant, the plant gets brittle and distorted. The insects cause leaves and flowers of African violets, begonias, and cyclamen to wither and lose their shape, size, and color. Before bringing plants indoors, check for these mites. Infested plants should be isolated immediately and destroyed because there is no way to salvage a plant after it has been infested with cyclamen mites. The best way to kill these mites is by submerging the infested plant foliage in 110-degree water for 15 minutes. This method is likely to kill the plant as well, so in most cases the plant should be destroyed.

Earwigs

Earwigs are attracted to the cool dampness beneath plant pots. When notches or holes appear in the leaves and flowers, an earwig has attacked the plant. To prevent earwigs from coming indoors after a houseplant has been outdoors, check the stems and leaves. Most indoor conditions are usually too dry for earwigs so the insects do not reproduce indoors. Small earwigs can be removed by hand, but larger infestations should be taken care of with systemic insecticides.

Scales

Scales are tiny, oval-shaped insects that have soft bodies. Scales do not move, but instead they stay in one spot and grow larger, developing a waxy coating that becomes a hard shell. The scale will reproduce hundreds of its young in one place. They suck

the plant sap and leave a sticky substance on the leaves, causing the leaves to discolor. Most scale species are exclusively female; when males occur, they live for a shorter period than females. Several species of scale attack houseplants, including those scales that normally live on outdoor trees and shrubs in mild climates. Other scales are tropical and inhabit greenhouses. Scales can attack hundreds of houseplants, but they give ficus and ferns the greatest difficulty. Most indoor gardeners recommended getting rid of a plant infested with scale because the pests also get onto furniture and floors. Those who have tried to save their plants have used alcohol, water, and oil swabs but this has not proven effective in large infestations. Some have recommended an organic pesticide called Simple Green. But, most recommend getting rid of a plant with a significant scale infestation.

Fungus gnats

Fungus gnats are slender, dark gray flies that hover above the plant soil. If young plants and seedlings wither and die, fungus gnats have invaded the plant. The best way to avoid these pests is with a fresh soil mix. Drench the soil mix with a systemic pesticide to kill heavy infestations. These bugs enter the house through open doors or windows, and they breed in the damp soil of plant containers. Adult fungus gnats lay about 300 eggs at one time, and these eggs hatch only one week later. The larvae feed on the minerals and nutrients of rotting soil, and they attack plant roots. They become adults two weeks after feeding. Soil affected by fungus gnats should be dried out between watering so as not to encourage gnat growth. Like all living creatures, the gnats will die of dehydration if there is no water for them.

Leaf miner

If leaves develop white wiggly lines or become a pale green, the plant has experienced a leaf miner. Check the plants for insects before bringing the plant indoors after the summer. Affected leaves should be gently plucked from the stem of the plant; larger infestations can be treated with a systemic pesticide.

Mealy bug

The mealy bug is a common, small white, cotton-like pest that leaves patches of black sooty mold and a sticky substance on a plant's leaves. It forms colonies and destroys plant tissue. An infestation of mealy bugs will wilt and yellow a plant and, eventually, kill its leaves. Mealy bugs attack tender new shoots and leaf axils. Checking the plant before bringing it indoors is the best way to prevent the bugs from attacking your plants, but in the event of infestation, use a systematic insecticide.

Thrips

Silvery spotting on leaf surfaces and white spots on the flowers indicate thrips. Thrips make their way indoors from outside. A systematic insecticide will rid plants of the bugs. Thrips are tiny sucking insects, and although they are not very common, they are real nuisances when they do appear because they reproduce in large quantities. When a thrip infestation is severe, the leaf

may pucker or curl around the insects, and sprinklings of black feces, which look like finely ground black pepper, appear. Thrips travel on humans, pets, and plants to get indoors. Once they are inside, their food choice is limited to plants. Underneath a strong powered magnifying glass, the thrips' feathery wings are visible.

Vine weevil

When the edges of plants are nibbled and the plant collapses, it is likely a vine weevil has attacked the plant. The vine weevil not only eats the plants, but it also feasts on roots. Large infestations must be sprayed with a systemic insecticide, but small clusters of adult vine weevils can be removed by hand.

Whiteflies

When leaves turn an unhealthy yellow and fall off or clouds of tiny white flies appear like snowflakes around the plant when it is shaken or disturbed, whiteflies have infested the plant. Adult whiteflies are tiny, moth-like insects with greenish larvae that suck on leaves. They cling in groups to the underside of leaves. The best way to prevent an infestation is to closely inspect the plants, especially underneath its leaves, often. A systemic insecticide will remove the bugs from plant effectively. Whiteflies infest and feed on more than 60 plant species. Whiteflies need to be eliminated quickly because they reproduce quickly.

Spider mites

Spider mites are dreaded arachnids. They are closely related to spiders and ticks, and they spin webs on the underside of plant leaves where they often remain unnoticed for a while. These tiny insects pierce plant leaves with their needle-sharp mouth parts and then suck the sap from leaves or flowers. Spider mites leave plants with sickly yellow leaves that fall off. They are prone to at-

tack in areas that are hot and dry. Spider mites are capable of killing one plant and then moving on to nearby plants, but because they are so tiny, they are not harmful to humans or pets. Spider mites are invisible to the naked eye, and under magnification, they appear to be green, red, yellow, black, or colorless. However, their webs are visible, especially on the underside of plants. A complete life cycle for this pest can pass in two weeks. Spider mites typically enter the home via new houseplants so it is a good idea to find them and treat them with any of the following recommended chemical or organic pesticide treatments before situating new plants with plants already in the home.

Chemical Treatments

This list details chemicals and home remedies available to treat certain plants and particular pests. Insecticides and pesticides are available at any garden centers. Pesticides that are placed in the soil and then absorbed by plants are called **systemic pesticides** because they introduce a new toxin to the plant's system. The insects that feed on the toxins are poisoned by the plant's juices. Systematic pesticides are used for invasive pests like scales and other sucking insects. Systematic pesticides not only introduce plants and insects to new toxic chemicals, but they also enter and permeate closed indoor environments. It is important to read and follow directions on pesticide products. As a safety precaution, it is highly recommended to treat plants with pesticides outdoors in the shade. Plants sprayed with chemical treatments should be allowed to dry outdoors, and remember never to use systematic pesticides on edible plants.

Imidacloprid

Imidicloprid is a pesticide that kills pests on contact. Most newer products use imidacloprid as their bases. It also mixes with plant sap and poisons insects that feed on the plant. Plants with delicate leaves should not be sprayed with this product because it may harm the leaves. Instead, the roots of this plant should be soaked with pesticide or repotted into a soil that has been amended with imidacloprid. Bayer Company makes this product, and it is widely available under the Bayer brand. Imidicloprid, particularly in concentrated form, should not be sprayed indoors. It must not be used on herb plants or any other food-bearing plant.

Neem/Azatrol

Neem and Azatrol are natural pesticides. Neem is made from a tree that destroys a pest's desire to eat and disrupts the insect's maturation process. Neem can be applied safely indoors, and the products are usually sold with neem in their name. Neem's active ingredient is azadirachtin, but several popular houseplants — African violets, begonias, crown of thorns, ferns, geraniums, ivy, jade plants, palms, the schefflera, and other succulents — are sensitive to neem. Azatrol also contains the pesticide azadiracthin, which kills a variety of pests. Pests feed off of the azadirachtin and then die. Azadiracthin's selling point is it is better on the environment because the product does not contain toxins. Azatrol is used as a preventive pesticide treatment because it does not kill bugs as fast as poisons kill. Azatrol takes 21 days to effectively destroy infestations.

Carbyl

Carbyl is also known as sevin, an insecticide that kills a wide range of pests, including thrips. Carbyl should be applied out-

doors. It has been known to damage the leaves of the aluminum, arrowhead, English ivy, ferns, peromia, and schefflera plants. Follow the directions for Carbyl; the product should be safe for plants except where otherwise stated.

Orthene

Orthene is a synthetic pesticide that poisons and kills most insects. Orthene can be applied indoors, but precautions must be taken with this pesticide because it causes leaf damage to the African violet, chrysanthemums, ferns, ficus, geraniums, nerve plants, palms, piggyback plant, poinsettias, prayer plants, and the shefflera; it is considered safe for other species.

Homemade Remedies

Homemade remedies are often the best solution for ridding a houseplant of pesky insects because pests often develop a level of resistance to synthetic chemicals. Test the leaves of a plant with the solution before applying it to the entire plant. The following are some homemade treatments you can use on your houseplants.

Insecticidal soap

When a large cluster of insects are present, use insecticidal soap with sodium and potassium salt. Insecticidal soaps come in packages, so follow the directions and use with caution. One homemade recipe combines 1 ½ tablespoons of liquid dishwashing detergent with 1 gallon of water. If desired, add 1 cup of regular rubbing alcohol to the recipe. Insecticidal soaps and homemade soap sprays kill insects by cutting through their protective coatings. When that coat is cut, the bug dries up. The insecticidal spray is effective when it covers the body of the pests. Insecticidal soaps can cause leaf injury to begonias, crown of thorns, ferns,

the jade plant, and palms. The soap cannot be used on newly rooted cuttings because the leaves of new cuttings are usually so young and frail that they cannot handle harsh chemicals yet. Insecticidal soaps are not harmful to people and pets if they are used at the recommended dosage.

Hand picking

To hand pick pests off your houseplants, use a toothpick or tweezers to remove visible insects from plant leaves and stems. After the insects are plucked off the plants, drop them in a container of soapy water to kill them. Remove any dead, rotted, or discolored leaves. Use rubbing alcohol to clean tweezers and scissors or pass the instruments over a flame to kill the insects and prevent them from moving from one part of the plant to another. Mealybugs can be removed by hand quite simply. Use a cotton swab dipped in rubbing alcohol, or pick mealybugs from plant leaves and stems with tweezers.

Damp wiping

Use a damp cloth to wipe the top and the bottom of plant leaves. Wiping plants carefully eliminates and prevents pests that like dry conditions. A soft cloth dipped in warm, soapy water will remove scale from leaves and stems.

Water spray

Squirting plants with water from the kitchen sprayer or bathroom showerhead will remove small groups of pests from plants. Using a water hose will thoroughly target and hit the pests with

a greater force than a water bottle. The spraying should be gentle but forceful enough to remove bugs. Spraying the leaves of plants that will tolerate it will deter insects that like dry conditions. Keep in mind that some houseplants will not tolerate being sprayed with water. For example, the leaves of a philodendron may not be too keen on showers, but a palm plant, fern, or a bamboo plant will not mind being sprayed. Be careful when watering leaves of plants that are growing flowers because the flowers are not likely to tolerate the rushing water from a sprayer or a showerhead. A snake plant is an example of a plant with strong leaves that can tolerate showers from a water spray. The leaves of a bamboo plant will tolerate sprays from the sink as long as the leaves are sprayed very gently. Thrips are the easiest pest to control with water sprays. Water spray treatments should be repeated every five or six days until the bugs are gone. Remember that water spraying prevents insect infestations if the insects like dry plants. Water is a necessity for all life forms, including bugs, so it is better to water the plant's soil or growing medium, rather than watering the leaves of a plant for other predators to feed from.

Rubbing alcohol

Aphids, mealy bugs, and scale will die when alcohol touches them. Dab the insects with a cotton swab soaked in rubbing alcohol and repeat the application every two to three days. This is an effective method that works over time, but covering an entire plant with alcohol will damage the plant tissues. If it appears that the plant needs to be doused in a bucket of alcohol to save it, it may be time to let the plant go. The alcohol treatment is best for plants that are beleaguered by pests but not infested with them.

Tobacco tea

Steep tobacco in water for several days, and then dip a cotton swab into the tea. This tobacco tea mixture will kill scales. This highly toxic tea should be sealed in a jar and stored away from children and pets. Tobacco tea mixes can be made from cigarettes or chewing tobacco. Use 1 cup of tobacco per 1 gallon of water.

Sticky traps

You can make a sticky trap by coating a piece of blue or yellow cardboard or plastic with petroleum jelly or motor oil. Prop the sticky trap on the plant, or tape the trap to a toothpick, and insert it into the soil. Thrips are especially drawn to bright blue traps. It is a good idea to monitor the presence of whiteflies with sticky traps for several months by keeping the sticky traps on the plant or nearby for precautionary measures. Whiteflies are attracted to yellow. You also can purchase sticky traps from nurseries or an indoor gardening center. Fungus gnats are attracted to yellow sticky traps that are placed near lights. Sticky traps also will attract earwigs.

Soap-oil treatment for spider mites

You can treat light to moderate spider mite infestations with soap oil. Mix 1 tablespoon of dishwashing liquid; add 1 tablespoon vegetable, canola, or corn oil; and then add 2 quarts of lukewarm water. Before using the soap-oil solution, give the plants a shower to remove the largest spider mite clusters. Gently bathe plants in the soap oil solution, or dip a cotton ball in the soap oil treatment and wash the plant's leaves. A philodendron, for example, would be much easier if bathed in the soap oil rather than washing each of its leaves. Rinse the plant well, and be sure that the solution does not mix with soil.

Plant Diseases

Bacteria and fungi cause diseases in houseplants, but the good news is that well-cared-for houseplants rarely develop diseases. Fungi and bacteria enter a plant through a wound or natural opening and force their way into a plant's stems, leaves, and flowers. Fungi cause most houseplant diseases such as leaf spots and rotting stems.

Leaf spots that fungi cause may have a sunken middle or dark space in the middle of the spot. This spot is the fruiting site and that will produce the next generation of spores. Leaves with suspicious spots on them should be removed to disrupt the fungi's life cycle. Leaves that are spotted because of fungus should be kept dry because fungi thrive in warmth and wetness.

Bacterial diseases tend to be problems in greenhouses where humidity levels are high, and other conditions that invite disease to inhabit are present. In most homes, bacteria benefit the soil and help plants absorb the soil's nutrients.

Fungal diseases

Fungal spores are transmitted by wind, water, air, and gardening tools. In damp, low-light conditions, fungi tend to multiply rapidly because moisture and low light are essential growing conditions for fungi. Today's plants are bred to be disease resistant, and fungi tend to occur in a garden room full of plants where there is high humidity. Spots, rusts, mildew, and streaks on leaves are signs that disease has invaded the plant.

If a plant has a gray, moldy growth on its leaves, stems, or flowers, botrytis blight may be the cause. This disease develops and stays on plants that have been overwatered, overfed, and overcrowded. Clip off the affected leaves and stems, and decrease the

plant's doses of water and fertilization. Crowded plants need to be divided, or their shoots should be trimmed, so the plants have more room. If it is not bitterly cold outside, open a window, or install a fan near the plant to improve ventilation in the room.

A wilted plant that has become brown and mushy near its base is close to death. Plants that have been badly overwatered and suffer from rotted roots and damaged stems will not revive. If a plant is shriveled or collapsed, and rot root is suspected, inspect the roots. Rotted roots are black, and they have been disintegrated by a soil-borne disease that destroys the fine root hairs leaving fragile, stripped, and ineffective fibers. Other fungal diseases leave roots intact until they have attacked the stem near the soil, leaving dark brown spots and wilted stems at the plant's base. Roots that are darker than others likely have been damaged by fungi. Clip spoiled roots while repotting or root inspecting.

White fuzzy growth that later turns brown indicates powdery mildew. When mildew is present, cut off all parts of the plant that have been infected, and use a fan or open windows to improve ventilation. Powdery mildew is treatable with a solution of baking soda and water. Mix 1 tablespoon of baking soda and 1 tablespoon of horticultural oil (available at garden centers) in 1 gallon of water. The oil helps the baking soda stick to the leaves. Completely saturate your plant with the spray. Once you have finished handling an infected plant, wash your hands, and sterilize any tools or containers that were used on the affected plant to prevent spreading the disease. Baking soda also is used by outdoor gardeners to treat similarly affected roses.

Before reusing a fungus-infected container to grow a new plant, give it a thorough scrubbing with hot, soapy water; then dip the container in a solution of ½ cup chlorine bleach per gallon of water, and let the container dry in the sun.

Aside from fungi and bacteria, mold, mildew, rot, rust, virus, and a condition known as black leg are all diseases with grave symptoms to a houseplant. Plants afflicted with black leg turn black at their bases and then, die. The best preventive measures are using clean, sterilized tools and keeping plant cutting areas clean.

The best way to prevent plant diseases is offering your plant a clean environment, good and healthy growing conditions, and fresh air. Ask your gardening department or local nursery for horticultural charcoal, which deters fungal disease, mildew, and many bacterial diseases. You also can use fireplace ashes. Sprinkle the charcoal or ash onto the leaves of affected plants.

Whenever a plant begins to look sick or unhealthy, ask yourself a few questions about its recent environment and living conditions. When was the last time the plant had water or fertilizer? Have the humidity levels in its living area dropped or increased over the past several days? Has the room been too hot or too cold for the plant? Are pests visible on the plant? Is there evidence of pest presence on its leaves and stems? Correctly identifying problems with a plant is the first step in effectively and properly resolving the plant's issue.

CASE STUDY: IMPORTANT HOUSEPLANT CONSIDERATIONS

Nikki Phipps,
senior gardening writer/researcher
Gardening Know How
www.gardeningknowhow.com

Nikki Phipps is a garden writer and researcher, and a gardening hobbyist. She recently provided some interesting information on the subject of houseplants. Her passion stems from her grandfather's natural green

thumb and love of plants. She said the plant world is fascinating in that there are many unique types of plants available to the grower. In addition, she says it is a great way to relax.

When asked about her favorite types of plants she grows indoors, Phipps said she "loves growing philodendrons, so easy and carefree they practically grow by themselves nearly anywhere." When asked about how plants have changed her life, she says, "Others might think it strange, but I find them to be quite calming and refreshing to have around."

Phipps also provided information on how to interiorscape living rooms, specifically how to choose the number of plants and the types of plants to include in the space. According to her, a variety of factors play a role in this process, including the lighting, the mood you want to accomplish in the space, and the amount of space itself.

Some growers place stipulations on when to water plants, based on the amount of sunlight the plant is getting. When asked about her preference in terms of when to water plants, Phipps states, "I typically do not water anything in full sun. Always wait for sun to go down."

Another factor that changes so frequently from one grower to the next is the preferred types of soil products used in the houseplants. Because soil is the main component for obtaining nutrients, it is critical to have the best mixture. When asked about her preferred soil mixture, Phipps states that several types can be used. "I like soilless potting mix and organic type fertilizers used sparingly." Organic is a better option because it is much healthier for the plants, Phipps provided.

For houseplants, the right container is also an important factor. When asked about her favorite types of containers to use for medium- to larger-sized plants, Phipps states, "Nearly anything can be used with adequate drainage and enough room to accommodate the roots. I especially like using unique items whenever possible."

Finally, Phipps provides a bit of advice for anyone who is just starting out in houseplant care. "Choose plants wisely beforehand to ensure that they are given the most ideal growing conditions. Also, do not jump into exotic species right off — get some experience first, as many of these tend to have more maintenance involved."

GROWING PLANTS CHEMICAL FREE

O rganic growing means indoor gardeners must make the necessary changes to their container soils so that their plants have nutrient-rich soil. When you first purchased your plant, the soil was probably rich with compost and nutrients. As time goes on, those nutrients have to be replaced. Amending the soil is the best way to do it. Many fruit and vegetable container plants are grown organically or completely without chemicals. Natural gardening advocates contend that plants, fruits, and vegetables grown in organic soil produce stronger, healthier plants and produce. Organic soils are preferred because they are highly resistant to insects and diseases. Highly organic soil is also much better for gardeners who occasionally forget to water their plants because organic soil is especially capable of keeping plants thriving even in drought-like conditions.

The Best Soil Media for Organic Growers

Fertile, moisture retentive soil that is highly composed of organic matter is the best soil media for growing indoor plants. However, man must create this soil because it does not occur naturally. Adjusting soil is not so complicated as long as there is a basic understanding of the soil properties and the way it helps plants grow.

Indoor gardens and houseplants are grown in containers, and few people grow indoor plants with outdoor soil. The typical indoor plant soil is an organic medium made of peat moss, perlite, or vermiculite. Home gardening centers also sell organic growing media. The outside of the bag will say organic growing soil and usually will indicate the product is intended for produce-growing plants.

Soil as an organic growing media

Sand, silt, and clay comprise soil's mineral particles. Each particle has a different size, and in addition to sand, silt, and clay, soil has organic matter, air, and water. Plants grown in the sand need more water because sand dries fast, and fertilizers do not last long in sand. But the sand's coarse texture is great for roots because the air helps promote good root growth. Sand is a good organic growing medium because it is unlikely to develop soil-borne disease.

Clay soil, which is heavier than sand, is better than sand at holding water and nutrients, but clay soil does not drain very well because it is so tightly compacted. Unlike soil, clay does not allow air to strengthen plant roots; clay does not aerate as well as sand because clay particles are so tiny.

Silt particles are smaller than sand but larger than clay, and silt particles hold water and nutrients very well. Water drainage also is good with silt soil. Plants grow very well in silt when mixed with sand and clay.

Amending Soil

The bottom line about growing organically is that plant soils must be created to produce the optimum growing conditions for plants. The best soil mixture is known as loam. **Loam** is a mixture of sand, silt, and clay. Once sand, silt, and clay are combined to make the loam, the mixture is primed to add an organic soil amendment. Organic soil amendments strengthen the soil and provide nutrients needed for plant growth.

Humus: the best organic soil amendment

Humus — decomposed plant and animal matter — is considered the best organic matter to include in soils. Humus helps clay soil become airier and helps improve the soil's drainage qualities. When added to sand, humus improves its ability to retain moisture and nutrients.

Bags of humus waiting to be transported

When organic matter is added to a plant's soil, the organic matter goes to work supplying growing media with necessary nutrients and encouraging microorganisms to grow inside of it. The microorganisms have a positive effect because the organisms break down nitrogen, which benefits the soil. The roots are able to absorb nutrients much better with the broken down nitrogen particles. The result is stronger plants and hardier fruits and vegetables.

Alternative organic soil amendments

Organic amendments are natural and organic products from soil amendments to pesticides to fertilizers that are in their natural state without the presence of chemicals or preservatives. In order to ensure that all the products used are organic, they need to be certified and gathered from places that only use all organic products and procedures. Organic byproducts, wood ashes for example, are still organic because they do not contain a chemical into the final product. Cow's manure is organic only if the manure is from cows that have only consumed and eaten organic materials, meaning that as long as the cows only graze in certified organic fields the manure that they produce can be considered organic. Cow manure is used in container gardening because cows are animals that graze without eating meat, and the waste is not a combination of digested products similar to that a dog would devour.

Quite a few organic soil amendment choices are available in the quest for organic indoor gardens and houseplants. Sphagnum peat moss, leaf mold, and ground bark are among the most popular options. Garden centers sell bark and other organic soil components. Typically, outdoor gardeners use backyard compost

to grow plants and vegetables, but indoor plants also will grow heartily when fed organically created composts.

Wood ashes: Adding wood ashes or charcoal to your plant or soil will help improve the way the plant holds water and nutrients. Wood ashes are a natural fertilizer for plants. Although it sounds odd that something burnt and useless would complement a plant's livelihood, it long has been used as an addition to plant soil to lower the soil's pH balance and promote good and healthy plant life.

Tree bark: Indoor gardeners need to sterilize their outdoor components before bringing them indoors. Some gardeners bake tree bark they get from outdoors, and others boil it and let it get almost dry before using it. Sterilizing outdoor bark guarantees dangerous pests or diseases that may have contaminated or infected the bark or wood are destroyed. Like wood ashes, tree bark improves water and nutrient retention, and it is a decent fertilizer that works in a 4-2-4 nutrient ratio. Bark compost can be purchased in gardening centers. Use bark that has already fallen from trees or bark that has been shredded instead of taking bark off of a tree. Taking bark from a tree without having a good idea of the tree's health condition can pose a risk to houseplants because houseplants are a manicured and isolated species with no defense against outdoor environmental hazards such as pests and disease.

Cow manure: Cow manure is not heavy in nitrogen content and has good moisture and nutrient retention. It is not necessary to compost cow manure, and it is best used dried. Manure can be

purchased from gardening centers or online and has been found as a suitable match for vegetable and rose plants. Cow manure has become increasingly popular among container plant growers because it is natural and does not adversely affect plant soil once amended to soil. People mistakenly believe cow manure as a soil amendment creates a stench, but the decomposed matter takes on a new form that has a weakened smell. If the manure is not decomposed, it would burn the plant and the soil.

Sphagnum peat moss: Inexpensive and popular, sphagnum peat moss is popular because it improves water retention and nutrient retention. This soil amendment should be moistened before it is added to soil in order to refresh its nutrient properties, which the moss then releases into the soil. Most bagged potting soil mixes have peat moss as their primary ingredient but specimens planted in peat moss need plant fertilizer because the peat moss is not a nutritional growing media. As time goes on, peat moss becomes highly acidic. A soil test must be done to balance the pH or, with container plants, it may be easier to replace the soil with a newer medium.

Leaf mold: Leaf mold is excellent at improving nutrient and moisture retention properties of the soil. Leaf mold is probably the most valued of organic compost materials because it is easy to make, and you do not have to purchase it. Leaf mold is dark with a rather earthy smell and can be created by taking a pile of leaves and allowing it to decompose. Leaf mold is far superior to any store-bought soil amendment because it provides a good habitat for soil life. Oak leaves are the most recommended soil amendments to use for leaf mold because of their nutrient value. The leaves should be chopped and left to sit for six to 12 months to become leaf mold. You can compost by putting the leaves in a plastic bag, or you can make a leaf pile in a sectioned area of your yard.

Making Your Own Compost

Composting is one way to offer plants nutrients and fertilizer without having to visit a garden supply source and spend money. **Compost** is decayed material used to condition the soil. When waste materials thoroughly decompose, compost is created. Gardeners who compost have learned to feed their plants and large gardens by preparing decomposed organic or natural materials such as coffee grounds, leaves, and food scraps to feed their plants. Composting is particularly important for fruit and vegetable growers because fertilized plants produce abundant and large crops.

Outdoor gardeners use large heap piles to compost or to allow leaves to decompose until they become mold. Outdoor gardeners use huge bins filled with leaves and other materials that sit and rot over several months. That pile is carefully tended to in the same way a master chef tends to a stew. Gardeners take a shovel and turn the compost pile, which allows it to cook in the interior and take in oxygen at the top.

Indoor gardeners can compost in their homes using special containers made to conceal and hide compost ingredients. To create your own compost pile, you will only need a storage container, time, and the willingness to turn over the pile in the compost container until the decomposed matter is ready for use as a plant food.

Outdoor gardeners create compost piles and devote a section in their garden to composting. However, for gardeners who only cultivate houseplants, an outdoor compost heap may not be a feasible option. Indoor gardeners who want their houseplants to reap the nutritional benefits compost can offer can purchase compost pots that are found easily at online retailers. Compost pots are available in ceramic, stone, and stainless steel, and they are usually attractive containers that seal your compost and allow you to create a compost heap indoors. Nextag is an online retailer that sells a variety of kitchen compost slow cookers for $30 or more; the website is **www.nextag.com**. Plow and Earth and eBay also sell compost slow cookers for as low as $10.

After you have been gardening, and it is time to repot your plants and change the soil to improve, composting is a natural and inexpensive way to add nourishment to your soil. Bacterial microorganisms help compost decompose, and these microbes eat dead and decaying matter. Once the microbes have digested the organic matter, gardeners can add compost to plant soil, and the compost's microbes will reduce the reproduction of soil diseases.

Outdoor gardeners do a lot of composting for economic and organic reasons. Compost piles are not only a good way to improve a garden plot, but they are also an environmentally friendly way to dispose of kitchen scraps and other household items that might otherwise be sent to a landfill. Compost also offers a significant cost savings as the materials needed to form compost can be found in any household. Indoor gardeners may not graduate or

acclimate to the idea of composting until they have had several months' experience growing fruits, vegetables, and plants indoors. When indoor gardeners actually see and reap the benefits of adding compost to their plants, it becomes a mainstream part of growing and feeding houseplants, fruits, vegetables, and herbs.

Indoor gardeners can create their compost in bins or storage containers. There should be draining holes in the container because without drainage, the compost pile suffers aeration deficiencies. Some compost slow cookers have aerating holes, but most have tight lids. If the compost is not given the proper aeration, the pile will soon start to smell foul, which will be rather unpleasant for indoor gardeners.

All of the compost items — leaves, food scraps, straw, sawdust, newspaper — should be chopped and free of large clunks that will not blend easily into the soil. You can alternate layers of high-protein sources (green) with high-carbohydrates (brown) materials. The material should get hot when it starts to decay, but to speed up the decomposition process, some indoor gardeners actually bake their compost. The natural heat of a compost pile destroys disease organisms, insects, and weed seeds. But indoor gardeners cannot risk outdoor pests in their indoor soils, so when adding compost from an outdoor pile to your houseplants, bake the soil between 140 to 150 degrees. When the oven temperatures are steady at that temperature, usually after ten or 15 minutes of baking, it is time to turn the pile. If you are not baking the compost, use a meat thermometer to check the compost pile's temperature. Turn the pile over at least four times in a week or ten-day period. Compost that gets hot without using an oven has enough nitrogen (or green) products inside to nourish the soil without possibly contaminating the soil with various diseases.

Your compost pile needs water if it is dry. Your compost is too dry if it crumbles and if water does not release when pressed between the fingers. When a compost mix is too wet, water drips from the mix, and the compost starts to smell. You will know your compost has enough water when you can squeeze the compost and only a few drops drip out, similar to a damp sponge. The compost is ready when the ingredients inside of it are no longer recognizable. The compost will be dark and crumbly, its contents will not be warm, and it will have an earthy smell.

Compost alone is not enough to keep plants healthy. *Chapter 2 discussed organic fertilizers to a small extent.* The next section explores alternative natural fertilizers you can make at home or purchase from gardening centers.

Natural Fertilizers and Amendments

In Chapter 2, nitrogen (N), phosphorous (P), and potassium (K) proportions in fertilizer were discussed. Each mineral is represented by a number, for example 8-3-5. Eight represents nitrogen percentage weight, 3 represents phosphorous percentage weight, and 5 represents potassium percentage weight. Consider nutrient value when you choose particular natural fertilizing methods. Some plants are more sensitive to alkaline mixtures, and some plants cannot tolerate acid. Before adding natural ingredient fertilizers, be sure the plant you are fertilizing does not have an aversion to the fertilizer's pH content. To test your soil's pH content, purchase a pH test kit from a garden center, and carefully follow the directions. A soil's pH balance is measured between zero and 14, and the lower your soil's pH, the more acidic it is. Higher numbers on the pH scale represent more basic, or alkaline, pH levels. Most soils should have a pH from 6 to 7, and you

can add any of the following natural amendments to ensure your pH levels are ideal for the houseplant you are trying to grow.

The following are natural fertilizers you can add to your houseplants.

- **Wood ashes** are a natural fertilizer with a high alkaline pH, which makes them good at neutralizing overly acidic soil. Wood ashes are low in nitrogen but high in potassium. Five to 7 percent of wood ashes contain potassium and 1 to 1 ½ percent of wood ashes contain phosphorous. Wood ashes also have 25 to 50 percent calcium compounds.

- **Banana peels** have high calcium and phosphorous content that satisfies a plant's nutritional needs. Banana peels are an excellent substitute for potassium fertilizers, which can be rather costly. To compost with banana peels, slice the peels, and add them to the compost slow cooker or compost bin. Banana peels help speed up plants' growth and ability to produce fruit. Banana peels are an alkaline-based fertilizer, so add them to your plants if their soil is too acidic.

- **Coffee grounds** help sandy soils retain water. Coffee has acidic pH properties and is one of the more accessible natural fertilizers around.

- **Sawdust** can be used as a soil amendment, but because the microorganisms inside will use much of the nitrogen content, sawdust amendments will require a nitrogen-rich fertilizer. If you use sawdust on your houseplants, you should add a nitrogen supplement. Sawdust is not valued for its fertilizer properties, but rather for its ability to retain moisture and loosen tightly compacted sandy soils. It may help acidify soils that are high in alkaline content.

- **Bone meal** is a long-lasting organic fertilizer, but it has no potassium content. Adding bone meal to vegetable plants encourages root growth, and it has an average fertilizer ratio of 4-12-0 with 20 percent total phosphate and 24 percent calcium. Bone meal works slowly as a fertilizer, and the bone can be fed to plants either steamed or raw. Bone is alkaline, so it will raise the pH of your soil.

- **Rock phosphate** is an alkaline-based fertilizer that contains many trace elements of phosphorous. Rock phosphate is slow acting with 22 percent phosphorous levels. Rock phosphate works inside of soil for many years because it does not dilute in water.

- **Seaweed** encourages beneficial soil bacteria and is good for root crops like carrots and turnips. Seaweed is acidic, and it begins to work on container crops very quickly.

Organic soil amendments are not all-in-one fertilizer solutions because some are high in potassium like banana peels, for example, and others are high in phosphorous, like rock phosphate. Combining fertilizer combinations, like chicken bone, banana peel, and rock phosphate, to balance the NPK content is a viable and cost-effective option for organic and inorganic home gardens.

Growing plants indoors is perfect for organic gardening. Soil from outdoors should not be used to grow plants in containers because outdoor soil is heavy, drains poorly, and exposes houseplants to insects and diseases.

Growing Fruits and Vegetables Organically

Organic home growers are not eating fruits and vegetables grown using synthetic chemicals and pesticides. Instead, they are eating foods fresh picked from the plants or trees in their homes. If you have considered growing any of the fruits, vegetables, and herbs mentioned in Chapter 4, use the organic nutrient components mentioned in this chapter, and revisit the natural pesticides reviewed in Chapter 6. The plants will grow healthier and stronger and produce the best fruit and vegetables for you if you can manage not to add chemicals in the effort to maintain a plant or indoor garden's livelihood.

Growing plants organically is a cultural movement that falls in line with the effort to preserve and protect the environment. Not using pesticides or chemical fertilizers is only a minor inconvenience considering that the many compost and fertilizing nutrients — leaf mold, bone meal, and banana peels, for example —

are readily available in the kitchen and in parks and backyards during the fall season.

Furthermore, when organic growers are growing food indoors, they are primed to compost from indoor materials. Kitchen waste, such as vegetable peelings and coffee grounds, can be recycled rather than thrown away. Fallen leaves from other plants in your kitchen garden also can be used to compost. Gather the materials that you want to compost, and let them dry. Remember, wet compost releases an odor, so keep it dry until it has been thoroughly composted. Also, do not forget to turn the compost pile over regularly.

As your houseplants get older, you will need to provide them with nutrients to keep them healthy and strong. The work needed to keep houseplants alive for the first years is basic. As the plant grows into your home, its nutritional needs become more sophisticated. If organic gardening and growing does not initially appeal to your indoor growing regimen, then the idea may catch on a year or so later when it is time to change potting soils and assess what has and has not worked for your indoor garden during the past year.

One of the benefits of growing organically and using organic fertilizers is that the indoor gardener controls how fast and how green their plants grow by using more or less of the natural ingredients as nutrients to feed their plants. Fertilizing sounds like a hassle and an added expense, but fertilizers that indoor plants need to stay healthy and strong are ingredients that can almost always be found somewhere around the home, such as leaves, bark, wood ash, and apple cores. Using natural ingredients or recycled home materials saves money and time spent back and forth at garden centers searching for particular elements, potassium-rich fertilizer for example, that are at home and available to compost.

Growing organically can begin right from the start. Ask nursery owners for their organic seeds or browse the Internet for organic seed retailers. Seeds of Change (**www.seedsofchange.com**) and Park Seed (**www.parkseed.com, www.organicseed.com**) sell organic seeds of many varieties.

Organic growers are particularly concerned with improving soil quality and making the soil as healthy as possible to produce better fruits and vegetables. Organic growers incorporate soil amendments and compost into their growing regimens. There have been many studies done that compare fruits grown in soil and fruits grown organically. *Consumer Reports* magazine confirmed the superiority of organically grown foods, as have other institutions such as the Rodale Institute, the Soil Association, and The Pesticide Action Network. Johns Hopkins University and the Washington State University are only two of the many universities that have studied and proved that organic grown foods surpass those grown with pesticides. The organic fruits scored higher with people because the colors are brighter, and with apples, for example, the fruit is sweeter.

You may notice organic sections in the grocery store and may wonder why organic produce is more expensive. Organic farmers have to find alternative ways to deal with pests and weeds in the natural environment without resorting to common chemical sprays or pesticides in order to save crops that may become at risk. Organic growing has been the traditional method in which food and plants were grown. Chemicals or pesticides similar to roach and ant sprays were not introduced to the growing process until the mid-1800s. Organic fertilizers and organic pesticides were touted by J.I. Rodale in *Organic Farming and Gardening*, in the early 1940s as a newer and safer way to grow and keep the environment safe. *Organic Farming and Gardening* magazine is still in publication.

One extra tool needed in organic growing is a container to store the recycled food and animal waste. Planet Natural, a website dedicated to organic lifestyles, has a kitchen compost crock, which is essentially a stylish storage can. The metal container stores recycled matter from the kitchen that you wish to use as compost. You can order an attractive compost container from Planet Natural (**www.planetnatural.com**) if you are unable to find a suitable storage container for your kitchen. Ideally, a composting container should keep the recycled animal and plant products dry, and the container should seal tightly to avoid emitting unnatural smells. The compost crock at Planet Natural sells for $25.

Most people grow houseplants because there is a sense of reward and accomplishment that coincides with watching small plants grow into taller, stronger, and greener ones. Mastering the fine art of growing foods — fruits, vegetables, and herbs — indoors lends an unparalleled sense of security to families and growers.

The rewards for cultivating abundant and healthy indoor crops are enormous. Growing plants organically heightens the sense of reward and accomplishment. Organic growing is a movement that has caught on in the United States and taken on its very own cultural identity among gardeners and gardening communities.

Organic Pesticides for Houseplants

Creating a healthy, organic soil for your plants is the first step in protecting the plants from disease and damage from insects. When a plant has an organic base to start from, it is able to extract more of the nutrients it needs from the soil, thus creating a stronger, healthier plant that is more capable of resisting disease and pests. Follow the instructions provided thus far to help you to create an organic soil composition.

Even when you take the best steps to create an organic base, it is still possible for plants to become victims of pests. Pests may invade from nearby plants or from the environment surrounding the plant. Pests can thrive in organic conditions, and may damage a plant or root system of these plants, too. Because pests can invade, it is important to take steps to treat the pests as soon as you notice a presence. This ensures the plants are able to overcome any damage and reduces the number of actual insects doing damage.

Why never to use chemical-based pesticides

Chemical pesticides are readily available on the market, but using these just one time can severely damage the plant. If you have developed a nonchemical soil base for the plant, adding a chemical-based pesticide will change the structure of the soil and kill off the microorganisms growing within the soil. Microorganisms create a unique environment within the soil that contributes to the health of the plant. One application of pesticides could destroy that foundation, leading to a plant being unable to use the nutrients found within the soil.

Chemicals can also harm the plant. Depending on the type of chemical used, the pesticide can damage root systems. The plant itself may face stunted growth, too.

Be careful buying organic pesticides

Purchasing organic pesticides is possible in some home improvement stores and garden centers. You can find these available through most of the websites listed in this section for organic products, too.

USDA Organic Seal. Photo courtesy of USDA National Organic Program

When buying, learn what you are purchasing and whether the product is truly an organic pesticide. In the United States, specific labeling requirements limit the terminology a manufacturer can use to sell a product as an organic pesticide. The USDA National Organic Program standards state that manufacturers can only use natural substances and some nontoxic synthetic pesticides, such as soap products, within products labeled as organic. Reading the label of a product may offer better insight into what is actually included. If the manufacturer labels the product all-natural, this does not indicate the product is organic. The product may include non-organic plant material, such as plant material treated with chemical pesticides, within it. A manufacturer may label the product organically based but this, too, does not mean the product is chemical-free.

Because it can be difficult to find truly organic pesticides specific for houseplant care, it may be best to use your own methods to improve the pest problems you have. Before you do this, first learn how organic pesticides work.

The Basics of Organic Pesticides

In nature, plants have a natural ability to repel most insects. Plants living indoors, on the other hand, face a unique environment and new pests that may not have been present in the plant's natural setting. Because of this, there is a need to help household plants fight off insect invasions.

Organic pesticides work by providing houseplants with the natural protections available to fend off insects. One product on the market is called Orange Guard, and it features a citrus and fruit peel blend. Using this product can be helpful for the plant because this combination of lemon and orange peels naturally helps to kill insects. This product is helpful at killing most flying insects

and many crawling insects commonly found within a home. The citrus contained in the organic product destroys the wax coating that lines the respiratory system of insects, thus killing the insect.

Another effective way to use organic products to protect plants is to use them as a repellent. Rather than killing pests, the ingredients in the organic product work to repel insects that would otherwise invade the soil or damage the plant's leaves. A common repelling product, for example, is garlic or hot peppers, as their smell repels the insects. Essential oils, which are the natural oils found in plant products, can also be useful as repellents. Cloves, for example, are helpful at repelling most household insects from plants.

While this book provides excellent examples of effective pesticides useful to most household plants, the National Sustainable Agriculture Information Service offers more information and a list of potential organic pest management products on its website at **www.attra.org/pest.html**. Use this as a tool if other treatments are ineffective.

Prior to using organic pesticides

Although the organic pesticides listed here are safe to use on most plants, it is still a good idea to try other methods to prevent pests from invading plants. One method to do this is to use a process called companion planting. Companion planting creates a scenario in which you have two or more plants that offer benefits to each other to create a mutually beneficial environment. More information on companion planting is provided in the next section. Use this method as a prevention tool.

Do You Have a Problem with Pests?

Prevention tools are helpful, but not if you currently have a problem with pests. In those situations, it is best to use an organic pesticide to kill or to keep away insects and other pests. The following pesticides are highly effective for most indoor houseplant insects.

Diatomaceous earth

One of the most effective natural methods for getting rid of insects in any planting medium is using diatomaceous earth. Manufacturers create this product from the fossils of tiny sea creatures called diatoms. This all-organic product is an abrasive powder when purchased. It comes from soft sedimentary rock (this rock forms through the decomposition of sea creatures over the years) that crumbles easily into a fine, white powder. Its composition is similar to pumice powder. It has an iron oxide level ranging from 0.5 to 2 percent, alumina percentage of 2 to 4 percent, and the rest is silica.

Although this product is useful in various applications, it is a highly effective pesticide because it works to kill pests. The powder absorbs lipids from the outer layer of the pests' exoskeleton, causing the pests to dehydrate. It works well against gastropods, such as slugs. It can work well against any arthropods, which die due to the water pressure deficiency present. In some cases, it has been useful as a bedbug treatment, though it can take several weeks to work in this application. Yet another application for it is as a treatment of fleas within the home. Farmers commonly use it in grain storage to control insects there. It works and is safe to both plants and humans.

In the household plant arena, diatomaceous earth works well on silverfish, slugs, millipedes, centipedes, ants, cockroaches, and

earwigs. If your pest problem extends outside of the plant, including into carpeting or even outdoors, use this product. Unlike other products, including chemical products, this organic pesticide works mechanically so pests cannot become resistant to the product. You can use this continuously or use it whenever the presence of insects is evident.

Diatomaceous earth is available in various home garden centers. You can also purchase it online at websites such as Amazon.com and EarthWorksHealth.com. Follow directions provided by the manufacturer if the product is specifically for treating pests indoors. Otherwise, sprinkle a fine layer onto the soil of the houseplant. Place the powder any other place you have seen pests crawling or living. Leave the substance on the surface and replace as needed. Most pests will die within 48 hours of the application.

Garlic pesticides and fungicides

Another product that is highly effective at treating pests is garlic. It is the same product you may use in food preparation as a flavor enhancer. It is essential that you purchase food grade garlic extract because products sold as additives or with additives are not effective enough. Garlic is a natural insect repellent because its strong smell keeps pests away, but it also does not harm the plant. Farmers use garlic as a way to prevent pests, including insects, from invading crops. It also keeps larger animals away. If your pets, for example, tend to

nibble on the houseplant's leaves, using a garlic pesticide will keep the pets away from the plants and will not harm your pets.

It may be possible to purchase a garlic pesticide like this, but you can make your own. To do so, you will need an empty spray bottle. Be sure it is rinsed well before using. Create a mixture containing one garlic bulb, a medium onion, and 1 tablespoon of cayenne pepper. Crush the garlic and mince finely. Mince the onion in the same way. Add both to about ½ gallon of water, then add the cayenne pepper. Allow the mixture to sit for at least an hour before using. You can store it for up to a month in the refrigerator. To use, spray the mixture onto the houseplant's leaves and the top layer of soil. Do so two or three times per day. This product will work to repel many insects, especially slugs, and also will work as a natural fungicide.

Neem insecticidal spray

Another organic product effective as a pesticide is neem. Neem is a plant native to India. The plant naturally repels most common household pests, so you can use this on your houseplants. A variety of organic pesticides sold on the market contain neem extracts. These are safe to use whenever the manufacturer labels the product as organic.

Many distributors sell neem in an oil form. Neem contains a variety of active ingredients that interact with insects, including a product similar to a hormone that interacts with the insect's brain. This ingredient blocks the real hormones from working properly, causing the insects to stop laying eggs and to stop feeding. Neem works to disrupt the cycle of insects laying eggs within the soil, and the insects eventually die off.

Interestingly, neem only affects chewing and sucking insects, which are the most common problems for plants. Other insects, including the microorganisms within the soil composition, remain healthy.

To use this product, follow the organic pesticide's labeling when available. Use a very small amount of neem oil to treat pests, usually no more than one part per million. Unlike chemical poisons, organic products like this take time to disrupt the life cycle for the pests, which means it can take a few days to weeks to see a noticeable difference in the plant's pest level. You can purchase organic neem products on websites like Amazon.com or find them in some garden centers that offer organic products.

Orange Guard

Another product to use as an organic insecticide and pest control is Orange Guard. This product will kill ants, fleas, silverfish, cockroaches, scale insects, spider mites, and similar insects. You can use it safely on the plants, and within reach of your pets. It is 100 percent biodegradable and water-soluble. This product is readily available in many hardware stores that sell organic insecticides. You can purchase it online as well through websites such as Amazon.com. Follow the directions provided on the manufacturer's bottle.

Orange Guard has d-Limonene, which is an extract from the orange peel. This destroys the wax coating that covers the insect's respiratory system. You can spray the product directly onto the insects to suffocate them if you see them. It can be sprayed on the leaves of the household plant, on the soil, and on other surfaces. When the insect consumes the product, it destroys the insect's respiratory system, killing the pest. This product works almost immediately when insects come into contact with it. In addition,

the citrus smell of the product works as a repellent. The insects smell the orange citrus scent and avoid the plant as a result.

You can spray Orange Guard on most surfaces, including carpeting. If you have pests invading your houseplants, the pests may be in other areas of the home, including in carpeting or on countertops. This product is safe to use on those surfaces. After spraying, allow it to remain. You can wipe it off countertops using a damp towel.

For a less potent but effective repellent, create your own orange-based product. To do so, add orange extract to water. You can purchase the extract from most grocery stores or health food stores. Choose a food grade product. About 1 tablespoon of orange oil to 1 quart of water is effective. Spray on plants once a week as a repellent.

Organic Lawn and Garden Bug Spray

The product, Organic Lawn and Garden Insect Control Spray, is another option and is useful for treating lawns and gardens outdoors, but it also can be safely used on houseplants. The product repels and kills many insects. It is highly effective at treating fleas, ants, ticks, pill bugs, mosquitoes, and grasshoppers, but can help with most insects and pests. The product is an organic mixture of ingredients such as clove, sesame, and thyme oils. As such, you can make a product similar to it using these oils from your kitchen cupboard. However, it may be more cost effective to purchase this product because some of these oils can be expensive when purchased separately. You can purchase it online at Amazon.com or find it in some garden centers. If you do make your own, you need to combine equal parts of each oil in 1 quart of water. Place in a spray bottle.

Follow the manufacturer's suggestions for use outdoors. If you decide to use this product indoors, add it to a spray bottle and spray on the leaves, stem, and on the soil of the household plants, including plants nearby other plants with a pest infestation. Repeat as needed. The product will kill the pests present, but you may need to treat a second or third time to get rid of larvae from these insects.

Other homemade pesticides and repellents

Your kitchen cupboards may be a good place to find a variety of organic pesticides. You can create your own, and many require using a mild dish detergent. This works as a glue, of sorts, to help the product to stick to the leaves of the soil. Any water-soluble mild detergent without any abrasive chemicals can be helpful. However, if you want a truly organic product to treat your plants, avoid using any detergent-based product.

For those with problems with aphids, caterpillars, or small worms, use a tobacco treatment. Add 1 cup of tobacco to 1 gallon of water. Allow the mixture to sit for at least 24 to 36 hours. If the water is a weak tea color, it is ready to use. Spray a light misting of this product onto the leaves of the plant and onto the soil. The product will kill the pests present. If you have problems with mealy bugs, a helpful solution is an alcohol-based spray. To make it, combine ½ cup alcohol with 2 to 3 tablespoons dry laundry soap and 1 quart warm water. Spray onto the leaves of the plants. This is not a truly organic solution, but it is an effective treatment.

A salt spray can be an effective treatment for spider mites and cabbageworms, among other types of pests. To create, mix 2 tablespoons common salt in 1 gallon of water. Shake well. Add to a spray bottle, and coat the leaves of the plant and the soil lightly.

Organically treating the pests invading your houseplants is the best step to take because it helps to increase the overall health of the plant while still getting rid of the pests. Organic products are becoming more readily available in the marketplace. Choose carefully based on the label of the product to ensure a 100-percent safe product.

Companion Planting

Though commonly used in crops and gardens, companion planting is beneficial within the sector of houseplants, too. The process involves placing two different types of plants near each other and the plants benefit each other in some way. Some plants may produce products the other plant needs to be healthy and to thrive, for example. An example to use in companion planting would be tomatoes with basil because it will improve growth and flavor.

Organic cabbage is being grown in the wooden cages. Marigolds were planted next to the cabbage as a companion plant to help deter pests.

Radishes and peas are a good combination as the peas will deter insects from the radishes, and planting petunias and beans is another good combination as the petunias will protect the beans. The micronutrients these plants create can benefit each other.

Another reason to use companion planting is as a deterrent for insects. Some plants provide protection against insects not only for that plant but also for the plants nearby. When you plant a few of these natural insect-repelling plants near other plants you wish to protect, you create a safe zone for all plants in the vicinity.

One example of this is with food crops. If you are attempting to grow fruits and vegetables in your home, try to plant those crops that provide for each other. Basil, for example, is an excellent choice to plant near marigolds or peppers to help deter flying insects, including mosquitoes, from the plants. The scent of the basil helps work as a deterrent in this instance.

If you want to incorporate companion planting beyond just the fruits and vegetables, you have a few options. You can incorporate any of the listed herbs above into your household plants to get the benefits of insect repellent. You can use other plants as well, including the following combinations:

- Use catnip as a beetle and flea deterrent.

- You can use peppermint to keep white cabbage bugs at bay.

- Use wormwood to help keep your family pets away from your houseplants.

Companion planting may mean combining the plants within the same pot. If this is the method you plan to use, be sure that the plants you plant together have the same or very similar needs for water, sunlight, and soil. In addition to this, the plants need to be able to work together. Some plants grow roots very quickly, making it difficult for the other plant to become well established. Choose a large enough pot to accommodate the needs of each plant.

Keeping this in mind, realize that close proximity planting may help, too. Planting two plants next to each other but in different pots allows you to better protect all plants involved but allows you to group plants that have different requirements next to each other. By placing these plants next to each other, the plants are able to have separate living spaces but will still benefit from the companion planting relationship.

To learn more about companion planting, visit the National Sustainable Agriculture Information Service at its website: **www. attra.org/attra-pub/complant.html.**

PROPAGATING HOUSEPLANTS

P ropagate means to cause an organism to multiply or reproduce. Buying more plants is one way to increase a collection, but those who have successfully taken care of their houseplants for a while propagate from the healthy plants already in the home. Propagating is economical and a lovely way to share indoor gardening successes with friends, family, and other parts of your home.

Houseplants are not usually grown from seed, but many of those mentioned in Chapter 4 — herbs, fruits, blooming plants like tulips, and some vegetables, for example — often are. Once you start growing beans and parsley or basil from seed, the speed at which these plants grow makes propagating from seed child's play. Propagating blooming plants like tulips or amaryllis calls for a bit more effort and a cold, dry place to store the plants until blooming begins. This chapter examines ways to propagate from seeds, leaves, cuttings, and bulbs.

Propagating Methods

Peat pots

Peat pots are the most biodegradable way to start growing plants indoors. Peat pots are pots filled with peat moss. Start growing plants with seeds in containers of various sizes. Kitchen herbs often are started in peat pots with rows of four and five. That way, varying herbs and spices can grow simultaneously in a con-

venient and small space. Peat pots are small and convenient enough to sit neatly under lamps in case the larger, flat containers often used to start plants do not conveniently sit under windowsills.

Peat pots should be soaked in water, filled with a soil mix, and the seeds should be placed in the soil. Once the leaves grow, it is time to transfer the plant into its permanent and larger container. Peat pots are good for propagation because the roots grow safely inside the small pots and experience the least amount of shock once the plant makes the leap from a tiny living space to a larger one.

Seed pellets

The seed pellets are disks made of peat moss that expand when placed in water. The seed pellet is like shell that will house the seed until it has germinated. Use a seed pellet to begin plants. Nixa Hardware & Seed Company (**www.nixahardware.com**) sells seed pellets for less than $10. Add seeds to the pellets and

once the leaves grow, the plant and the pellet should be placed in the larger container with soil. Seed pellets are useful because they become containers once water is added.

Sowing seeds in regular containers

Planting citrus seeds in traditional growing containers such as terra-cotta clay pots or plastic plant pots will produce handsome citrus trees, even if the seeds do not bear fruit. The seeds should be taken fresh from the produce and pressed gently into

the soil mix. Just water, and watch for the leaves of the new plant to grow. Seeds that are small and fine do not need to be buried deep into the soil mix. Fine seeds, cucumber and herb seeds for example, should be sprinkled evenly throughout the soil mix. Seeded containers can be covered with a plastic bag and sealed with an elastic strip to retain moisture.

Large seeds can be planted and left to grow on their own. In fact, planting too many of the larger seeds close together is not a good way to grow plants because they will overlap, and the roots will tangle. Larger seeds can grow in their own containers with compost until they become large and strong. Growing a seed in the pot that you expect it to live in at least until the plant is two or three years old, rather than choosing smaller containers for when

the plant is still a seedling, allows the plants to remain still and firm without interruption and without risking root health.

Stem cuttings/vegetative propagation

Growing plants from seeds is not the only way for plant lovers to start plants. Plants will grow from stem cuttings, also. To grow a plant from stem cuttings, cut a stem of the plant and place the plant stem into a growing medium until its roots sprout. You will know the plant has developed roots inside of its growing media because the plant resists when tugged. Cut stronger and older stems, and do not worry too much about the mother plant, or the plant from which you have taken the stem because that plant will be fine. Do however, avoid cutting off several stems at once from plants that are smaller than 1 foot and not yet a year old. Doing so can stress the plant too much, leading to death.

A plumeria cutting has flowered after being potted for nine weeks.

Vegetative propagation is the practice of making new plants from plant parts. Most feel that growing plants from an original plant's parts is easier and faster than growing plants from seed because growing from an original plant part means not having to wait the additional two or three weeks for the seed to sprout,

grow strong, and wait the additional months it takes to produce fruit or flowers.

But, the plant has to survive the propagation to be successful. Not every plant part that is taken from its original stalk or stem will grow to live successfully. **Offsets** are the new plant parts taken from the original plant and planted into soil for growth. Offsets are easy to cut in some plants, scheffleras for example. After the offset is cut, it should be planted. The most that needs to be done with woody plants is to cut the stem beneath a growing leaf or a node. The **node** is the place where the leaves attach to the stems. But in other plants, the spider plant, for example, proper propagation from offsets may be more difficult because the plant does not have nodes anywhere other than the root of the plant. Scheffleras have stern, woody stems while spider plants have floppy leaves that grow from a single stem. Plants with woody stems tend to bear offsets at its base, which makes propagating easier. With spider plants, however, the plant must be old enough and strong enough to produce a **runner**, which is a stem that grows alongside the long floppy leaves of the spider plant.

Purchase rooting powder from a garden center when propagating stems. **Rooting powder** accelerates root growth by stimulating plant hormones. The powder is usually sold in small plastic jars. When stems are cut, they need to develop roots as fast as possible so the cuttings will not rot. It is never recommended to stick stalks or cuttings in water and allow plant roots to grow because while the roots sit in water they are susceptible to disease and overwatering, which may lead to root rot. Ideally, plant cuttings should be placed into a growing medium that stimulates root growth, like a root tray filled with rooting mix. **Rooting mix** is a soil mixture of two parts potting soil, two parts peat moss,

and one part vermiculite. The combined ingredients are loose, but hold water rather well, which is what the cutting needs.

After the cutting is dipped in rooting hormone powder and inserted into the rooting mix, take a plastic bag and cover the containers. Covering the plant with a clear plastic bag will increase humidity and help the cuttings form roots. Typically, gardeners will take cuttings from blooming plants in order to form a new plant. When plants are resistant to tugging or pulling once inserted into the potting soil, this means the cuttings have grown roots. At this point, the new cutting is ready to be placed into its permanent growing container.

Air layering

Plants with woody stems, such as rubber trees, can be propagated using a method called air layering. Here are the steps, and keep in mind this method works for plants with branches that are thick and woody.

1. At the base of the plant, cut the leaves from the primary woody stem or the main stalk of the plant. Use a sharp and sterile knife and make a diagonal cut halfway through the stem. Be sure your cut is just below the leaf node. Place a toothpick in the slot you have just cut to keep the gap open.

2. You will need a plastic wrapping. Use plastic wrap or something similar to create a tent or a bubble around your cut stem. Fill that bubble with sphagnum peat moss (*discussed in the previous chapter*) and then tie the open end of the bubble with a ribbon or a bag tie. The moss should be compacted around the slice that you have made into the plant's stem. After the moss has been compacted around the stem, seal the lower half of the plastic bubble.

Recall that sphagnum peat moss is good for new plants, and often, new plants are sold in sphagnum peat moss.

3. Once you see roots forming at the lower half inside of the plastic bubble, you are ready to separate the stem from the rest of the plant and the container.

4. Remove the plastic bubble, and then insert the newly rooted stem cutting into a fresh potting mix and container.

Propagating leafy plants

Here are propagating steps for plants leafy plants like spider plants and sansevieria.

1. Use sterile materials. To make a new plant from the leaves of an existing plant, use a sharp stencil knife and slice the leaf down near the base of the plant.

2. Place the leaf on a wooden board, and then cut the leave into 2-inch sections.

3. Fill a pot with the proper growing soil and then place the leaf cuttings (you should have at least three) into the container.

4. Place the cuttings upside down so that the piece that you cut is in the air, leaving the tip inside the soil. Be sure to keep your water and soil moist until roots form.

Propagating bulbs

Plants that grow from bulbs are easier to propagate because much of the work has already been done. Bulbs have the proper nutrients needed to grow and produce beautiful and healthy new plants. After the bulb produces the plant, flowers, and then dies, the bulb can be repotted into fresh soil and grown again the next season. Just remove the dead leaves, store the pot in a cool and

dry place at 60 degrees until spring, and then place the bulb in new soil. To propagate plant bulbs, use the following steps:

1. Make sure the bulbs are healthy and fresh. Dark coloring on bulbs or moldy growth on the bulb indicates rot.

2. Plant the healthy bulb into the proper potting mix.

3. Water the bulb and its new soil, and keep the container in a warm area. Avoid direct sunlight, but be sure the container is in a bright room or in a room that is well lit with artificial lighting.

Forcing Winter Blooms

Indoor growers have a moderate amount of control over their blooms. Throughout this book, you have read instructions for caring for plants that bloom bright flowers in the winter. Those plants must be stored in a cool place before winter arrives in order for the plant to bloom with magnificent and memorable color.

The concept of forcing winter blooms is a fun indoor gardening idea that alters the way Mother Nature originally intended a species. For example, tulips and summer blooming plants can be propagated to grow in the middle of winter. Imagine a room full of bright yellow lilies alongside poinsettias during the winter holiday season. Or, imagine poinsettias in the summer. Those looks are possible to achieve and loads of fun.

To force winter blooms from your houseplants, purchase healthy bulbs from a nursery or garden center. If you purchase amaryllis bulbs that you wish to bloom in February near Valentine's Day, you will store those bulbs away three months before you wish them to bloom. You would plant the bulbs two to three months

from the date you want to see a room full of amaryllis. In this case, propagation would begin in mid to late November.

You can store hardy bulbs that are tough and firm in the refrigerator. Softer bulbs should be stored in a cool, well-ventilated location. Do not place either of those bulbs in the freezer because they will not survive without soil to protect them from the cold. When you are ready to grow, you should plant the seeds using these step-by-step instructions.

1. Use 5- to 6-inch diameter pots with draining holes and a well-draining, porous soil medium to plant bulbs. Use a soil mix of equal parts peat moss, potting soil, and sharp sand. Three bulbs of a hyacinth plant or a daffodil will fit inside 6-inch pots. Six-inch pots will hold five to six tulips bulbs as well.

2. Scrub used container pots to completely remove algae, dirt, and salt buildup. The pots should be soaked in one part chlorine bleach and nine parts water. Thoroughly rinse the pots, and if the pots are clay, let them soak overnight in clear water to prevent the walls from drawing moisture from the potting mix once the bulbs are planted.

3. Plant the bulbs and leave the tips exposed. The bulbs do not need to be buried completely unless directions state otherwise. Plant as many bulbs as the container can hold with 1 ½ inches of space in between each bulb. This planting method produces rich and beautiful pots full of brightly colored plants.

4. Water the plants well, and then cover the plants with a cloth or some other material to avoid light exposure.

5. Place the pot in a cool location where the temperatures range between 35 and 45 degrees, but not below freezing.

6. Every week, check to be sure the soil is moist. The soil should not be wet, and it does not need a fertilizer. After the chilling period, bring the pots into bright lights, but still keep temperatures cool. The evenly moist soil should be maintained throughout the growing period.

Here are ten plant bulbs and specific directions for wintertime propagating. The following instructions teach growers how to successfully propagate these plants from bulbs in time for spring blooms. Before you grow certain flowering plants successfully, the bulbs must be stored in a cool area before they are planted. The cold helps produce strong, hardy, and vibrant colors in the spring. If you wish to grow these plants in the winter, follow the directions in the previous section, and allow your plant two to three months to grow.

- **Tulips** (*Tulipa* species): Store the bulbs in 35- to 45-degree temperatures for 12 weeks. Plant the bulbs ½-inch deep, and keep tips above soil. These plants need bright light, but not direct sun. Keep these evenly moist throughout the year. Feed once a month or less. Propagate this plant's bulbs. Repotting these plants is necessary each spring for the best blooms.

- **Narcissus** and **daffodils** (*Narcissus* species): Store bulbs in 35- to 45-degree temperatures for 12 weeks. Let the

plants grow in temperatures between 60 and 65 degrees. These plants need direct to indirect sunlight. Do keep evenly moist, especially during summer. Feed once every two months, especially in the spring months. Repot this plant if it becomes pot bound. Propagate by offset bulbs or from seeds.

- **Dutch crocus** (*Crocus* species): Store bulbs in 35- to 45-degree temperatures for eight weeks. Keep the soil moist until plants have fully bloomed. Then keep the plants moderately moist. In winter, move plants to a cool, light room. Water these plants sparingly, and do not feed any type of solution during winter. During summer, use a humus rich garden soil to feed. Repot this plant if it becomes pot bound. Propagate by removing the young bulbs and planting them in a new pot.

- **Corn lily** (*Ixia* species): Store the corn lily bulbs in their soil for eight weeks at 50 degrees. The bulbs of the corn lily can be recycled. Store them away over the summer, and reuse them again the next season. You can uproot the lily and take its bulb for safekeeping. Keep the plant's soil moist, and provide plenty of light. Feed this plant lightly once every other week. Repot if the plant becomes pot bound, and propagate using division.

- **Freesia** (*Freesia* species): Store freesia plant bulbs for eight weeks at 50 degrees. Plant the corms deep in the soil mix, and cover them. The plants need 40-degree night temperatures. Propagation is through division. Repot this plant if it overgrows the container. Keep this plant in partial sun, and keep the soil evenly moist. Feed the plant every other week during the growing season.

- **Enchantment lily** *(Lilium Enchantment)*: Keep in the cold at 50 degrees for three to four weeks, and as the plant gets taller, it will need an all-purpose fertilizer. The lily is a springtime plant that enjoys cool temperatures but should avoid a frost or temperatures below freezing. Feed it once a month. Keep this plant evenly moist throughout the spring and summer months. Propagate this plant by dividing the rhizomes. It needs full sunlight during most of the year. Repotting is only necessary if the plant overgrows its container.

- **Persian buttercup** *(Ranunculus asiaticus)*: Store these bulbs at 50 degrees for eight weeks. The tubers must soak until they are soft before planting. The buttercup should be grown in cool indoor temperatures between 65 and 70 degrees. Keep this plant evenly moist, and enjoy; it gets moderate sunlight. You will need to ensure its fertilizer remains well balanced, or feed it once a month. Propagate this plant by dividing the rhizomes. Repot if the plant becomes pot bound.

- **Paperwhite narcissus** *(Narcissus papyraceus)*: This bulb planting will not need a cold period and can be forced in soil or a bowl full of pebbles and water. Grow this plant in average room temperatures. Once it blooms, keep this plant in a warm room only for short periods of time. It prefers cool temperatures. Keep moderately moist, and avoid waterlogging the

plant. You will need to supply feed in the spring and summer months. This plant needs partial sun. Propagate through offset bulbs. Repotting is necessary if the plant becomes pot bound.

- **Hyacinth** *(Hyacinthus orientalis)*: Store at 40 to 50 degrees for eight weeks. This is also an easy plant to force, and it will grow in water or soil. Hyacinths are a springtime plant and will do well in temperatures between 60 and 68 degrees. Water moderately, keeping the soil from drying out. The plant will only allow one force of the bloom. Plant in a garden after the first year in organic soil for the best results. This plant needs full sun. Feed the plant every two weeks while growing or blooming. Repot the plant if it becomes pot bound, and propagate from bulbs.

- **Amaryllis** *(Amaryllis)*: Rest the bulb for eight weeks in a dark and cool location where temperatures are 65 degrees or lower. This plant will sprout in late fall or winter. Keep half the bulb above ground when planting. Keep the soil moderately dry for the best results. Once it sprouts, increase the water until the stalk is just about hand high. Water freely after that. Keep the bulb dry during watering. You will need to provide this bulb with partial to full sun for the best results. Propagation is through bulb offsets. Repotting is necessary if the plant overgrows the container. Feed this plant every other week during the growing season.

CASE STUDY: CARING FOR YOUR HOUSE- PLANTS — WHILE AT HOME OR AWAY

Mike Rimland, director
of business development
Costa Farms
22290 SW 162 Ave
Miami, FL 33170
www.CostaFarms.com
305-247-3248

Mike Rimland works as the director of business development for Costa Farms and has 34 years of experience in the industry. As part of his career, Rimland has tested indoor plants in his own home for research and development for his company and for the company to sell to consumers. This experience in growing and selling plants can provide others with insight into what to expect when they begin to explore this option.

Those who work in this industry often have a few favorite plants. When asked about his favorites, Rimland said, "My favorite indoor plants are anthuriums because the flowers last two months indoors, and there are many colors of flowers." When asked about which room in his home is the best place for plants and why, he stated that his choice was the kitchen because it offered great eastern window exposure so plants located there thrive. He also said, "I like to use plants in east and west exposures that are high light plants, and I use low light plants more in the center of rooms in my home."

One of the things some people do not know about using household plants is that these plants do more than just offer a visual impact, but they also provide improvements to the mental health of those around those plants. To that extent, Rimland said, "The studies from a few leading universities has shown they have great physiological impact."

How does Rimland take care of plants when he travels? Besides having a friend come into the home to take care of the plants, he has some additional recommendations. "I would say today the only thing you could use that is cheap would be a saucer, and fill it full the day before you leave on vacation, but any time over 14 days you would still generally need to rewater."

When it comes to soil selection, Rimland thinks keeping it simple is best. "I believe your common houseplant mixes found in the retail garden center are excellent for the end customer." These products are readily available in specialized formulas for houseplants.

For a first-time houseplant grower, what is the best advice that can be given? "Do not overwater them. Wait until the soil is dry, and then water the soil very, very slowly, like rewatering a dry sponge. Make sure you get it fully wet again." That method can help to protect the soil, the plant, and keep the water from overflowing onto your floor, too.

TABLETOP
GARDENS

Tabletop gardens, like window boxes, are growing spaces for a number of plants, rather than a single plant. Window boxes are a confined space filled with nature's brightest and most beautiful forms of plant life, and indoor tabletop gardens are a similar idea. The idea for tabletop gardens enclosed and displayed in glass containers formed back in 1829. Dr. Nathaniel Ward was experimenting with a chrysalis moth that he left inside of a corked bottle. The bottle had garden soil and a few seeds that began to grow once moisture from the garden soil evaporated and left drops of water on the sides of the glass. The droplets watered the soil, and the germinated sprouts grew. Ward wasted no time bringing outdoor plants that could not survive the cold indoors into the miniature greenhouses. Ward's discovery sparked the houseplant revolution that dominated the Victorian age.

There is no creative limit on growing ideas for glass gardens. Some growing enthusiasts use bell jars, cake dishes, hurricane lamps, or outdoor lanterns as covers. Others grow their miniature green plants inside of fishbowls and round glass jars perhaps meant to house candles. Whatever the notion for the glass container, there are two important points to remember: First, the plant must not be deprived of air, and second, the plants must not get too moist.

Tabletop gardens are a unique way to display unusual or rare plants. Typically, plants grown inside of containers are smaller than the average houseplant because tabletop gardens are decorative living elements in a room and, therefore, small to accommodate living spaces. A philodendron or a spider plant would not make good tabletop garden plants because the plants are too big. The combination of glass containers and hydroponic grow-

ing media, rocks for example, as part of the living display is an intriguing, tranquil, and inspiring design. The combination of green grassy plants with potting soil looks like a small piece of a healthy green lawn displayed indoors.

You can create indoor gardens anywhere in the home where light and temperature are conducive to growing. In modern homes and historic homes where bathrooms have thick window ledges, tabletop miniature gardens are refreshing. Unused space on kitchen countertops and islands are also excellent growing spaces. Tabletop gardens can be as small or as large as a designer desires. Many grow several gardens on bookcases in well-lit areas for display, as well as space convenience.

Before choosing plants for a container garden, be as familiar as possible with the plant and its growing needs. Humid environments can be created with closed glass containers and artificial light, for example. But it is important to know whether the plants chosen to create tabletop gardens are capable of growing under the environmental circumstances that each home provides. Tabletop gardens can be created with glass containers, gravel, trays, dishes, and water as long as the plants chosen for the tabletop garden grow well in this particular medium.

Tabletop Gardens Made with Glass Dishes, Jars, Lanterns, and Bowls

Glass is a beautiful element that lends grace and beauty to a room, and glass also retains humidity and moisture for good plant health. Like greenhouses, plants that grow underneath glass encasements absorb light. It is preferable that indoor plants grown under glass containers have natural light. Plants growing under a glass cover should be small or dwarf varieties. Miniature

flamingo lily *(Anthurium andraeanum)*, rare begonia, African violets *(Saintpaulia)*, or miniature gloxinias *(Sinningia speciosa)* are all prime candidates for growing in glass-covered gardens because of their small size and dependence on humidity.

Each glass container should be raised off of the counter or tabletop to accommodate for airflow. You can use any design element that complements the glass container as a way to elevate the tabletop garden.

Portability, or the ability to move the garden, is the most convenient aspect of glass gardens. They can be moved into different areas of the home, which is very good for the plants. Plants that get too much moisture will not fare well, and all plants need fresh air. In glass gardens, there are no roof vents so it is important to consider the ventilation in the room when creating glass gardens. You will need to remove the top of a glass garden so the plants have fresh air occasionally.

A soft and beautiful mixture of an African violet plant, a maidenhair fern *(Adiantum* species), and Irish moss *(Sagina sabulata)* is a pretty combination as the violets provide the color burst and two shades of green surround the African violet. The pretty combination looks splendid when planted inside of a hurricane lamp, outdoor lantern, or lamppost.

When shopping for glass cases to hold plants, choose those with hinged lids and removable glass panels so the plants will get fresh air without having to remove them from their container. Just as with the greenhouse, keep the glass clean. This is healthy for the plant and keeps the display looking most attractive.

A terrarium garden can be made from a variety of thick glass containers. A **terrarium** is nothing more than a large glass house for a plant, similar to a fish tank. Glass candleholders and fishbowls, for example, blend almost anywhere in a room. Inside of the glass containers should be plants that do not need a lot of maintenance. Plants that lose petals often will be difficult because the glass containers magnify beauty and life, and falling leaves sends the opposite message.

Miniature tea rose *(Meil-landine)* is an ideal terrarium plant because roses need humidity, which the glass provides. There is nothing difficult about these gardens or these plants because they are so small and convenient to maintain. Because tabletop gardens are decorative pieces, one would likely clear fallen leaves or petals while talking on the phone or dusting.

Humidity and sunlight combined keep miniature tea roses alive and healthy inside of terrarium containers. Primroses *(Oenothera biennis)*, because they are a smaller species, grow well and look

great in terrarium glass containers. Plush vines *(Mikania scandens)* are well recommended for terrarium growing. The vine-like, flower-producing plant is exquisite inside glass. Scotch moss *(Sagina sabulata)* is an excellent example of bringing the front lawn inside of the home in very small doses. Scotch moss planted in a terrarium with potting soil looks great and lasts a long time. Moreover, Scotch moss meets the very definition of easy gardening because it needs very little care and works great either as a background plant for colorful blooms or as an individual plant display.

Water Gardens

Plants that grow in water are easy to care for and interesting to look at. Clear and colored glasses are among the better choices for water garden containers because they help display the plant's underwater growth in a creative way. Three choices for water gardens are the corkscrew rush *(Juncus effuses 'Sprialis')*, the Chinese taro *(Alocasia cucullata)*, and willow twigs *(Salix 'Flame')*, which are simple plants with complex, but interesting, root growth.

Water gardens should be filled with plants like the three above-mentioned plants because they do not need long periods of sunlight. Instead, these plants will thrive in bright but indirect light and rainwater or distilled water in average room temperatures. If plants are transferred from a soil garden to a water garden, take care to rinse the roots thoroughly in tepid water. The roots may not survive the shock of the change, so once a plant is removed from its soil, place the plant in its water container, and keep it in a shaded area for a couple of days. After a few days, the old roots should wear off, and new ones will form.

Plants and their roots need oxygen, even in water gardens. In container plants or plants growing in water vases, changing the water provides the oxygen the plant needs to thrive. Crushed

charcoal effectively keeps water inside of the containers clean longer. A ½-inch layer of crushed charcoal should be at the bottom of the container to help keep water clean. Marbles, stones, or rocks can be added to the container for decorative purposes.

Water gardens need nutrients. After the plant has adjusted to its new environment or has been situated in the home for a couple of weeks, add fertilizer to the water. Be sure that the fertilizer is compatible with the type of plant growing in the water garden.

Gravel/Japanese Gardenscape

Plants that grow well in water also are sustainable in gravel gardens. Gravel is a primary growing medium found in Japanese gardens that are centuries old. Japanese gardenscapes are especially complementary inside of modern living spaces and environments. Outdoor living scenes are easy to mimic with Japanese gardenscapes. Water, green, and gravel combine to create Japanese gardenscapes or gravel gardens. *Eleocharis*, also known as spikerush and hairgrass, grows fine in gravel and looks great. Spikerush and hairgrass are grassy plants that resemble tall, very thin blades of grass.

Trays no more than 1 or 2 inches tall make nice gardens for plants grown in gravel. Gravel trays and gardens look good in offices and have a calming effect on those who see them. Caution is warranted, however. Gravel, pebbles, rocks, and stones are all attractive and appealing to toddlers. Gravel gar-

dens, no matter how beautiful, should be kept out of the sight and reach of children.

Lucky bamboo is the most common and most popular houseplant grown in gravel and water. A single stalk can grow in a glass with gravel and water. A more complicated form of the *Draceana* plant, the ribbon plant, is usually placed inside of a low-edged vase with gravel and water. The ribbon version of the Lucky bamboo has several intertwined stalks. The Lucky bamboo with deep green leaves and stalks, needs bright light to grow. Fertilizer will strengthen its stalk and help the plant grow strong.

Tray and Dish Gardens

Plants with shallow roots are perfect for tray and dish gardens. Tray and dish gardens are usually shallow containers, much shallower than any of the other containers mentioned here. Serving trays, for example are not as deep as bowls, glasses, or fish tanks. The appeal of each dish or tray is often its shape and color. Tray and dish gardens are easy to build and easy to maintain. Moreover, they are literally mini-gardens inside of a living room or living area of the home. They can be decorative pieces much like statuettes and crystal.

With stones or gravel, gardeners can create designs inside of the tray to resemble checkerboards, or horizontal, vertical, and diagonal stripes. Stones can form one line while the plant occupies the inside space. Geometric shapes are an important element in designing neat and interesting tray gardens.

Sand polished stones, clear beach glass, terra-cotta balls, and aquarium gravel are all good materials to place inside of a gravel garden as a growing medium and decorative element. The color of the rocks or other chosen growing medium should blend well with plants and the home's décor. Garden shops, landscape suppliers, and your local arts and crafts stores carries many of the materials needed to create tray gardens.

Before purchasing any item for the tray garden, draw out a design scheme and color palette that interests you and complements your room. Then set about finding the right materials to help bring your ideas to life.

Here is a sample of plants that grow nicely inside of tray gardens with decorative stones, beach shells, and other growing media that work well with interior elements inside of a home. These outdoor elements are good growing media that help keep plants healthy and thriving.

- **Baby's tears** *(Soleirolia soleirolii)*: This is a fast-growing and moisture-loving plant that reaches heights of 6 inches. It grows in sun to partial shade. The roots of the baby's tears should always be moist. Because this plant grows quickly, it is probably best grown in a container alone. When grown with other plants, the baby's tears tend to overtake other plants. Baby's tears make an excellent indoor houseplant because the moisture and humidity derived from water and gravel or pebbles in the tray keep the plant healthy. Feed this plant monthly during the summer and every other month the rest of the year. Repot the plant annually in the spring, and propagate by division.

- **Wooly thyme** *(Thymus pseudolanuginosus)*: Wooly thyme is an herb, but is grown for ornamental purposes, not culinary reasons. It is a low-growing, shrub-like plant that needs full sun. Wooly thyme grows fast and naturally in rocks and produces small and pretty lavender-purple flowers in the summer months. Thyme needs to be kept moist, but keep in mind that plants grown in rocks and gravel are akin to plants being grown in a pond. Repot this

plant if it becomes pot bound, and feed the plant every other week at most. Propagate by division of the root ball.

- **Mondo grass** *(Ophiopogon japonicas)*: Mondo grass is an ornamental grass with a deep, rich green color. Mondo grass is an evergreen member of the lily family. Essentially, it is a tall blade of grass that produces small blue berries in the summer. Mondo grass grows well in full shade and direct sunlight because it is very adaptable. This is an easy-to-care-for plant because it does not need a lot of water and tolerates heat and drought. Dwarf Mondo grass species only grow 2 to 4 inches and are an ideal mate for gravel tray and dish tabletop gardens. Propagate this plant by division or from seed. Feed the plant every month, and repot this plant if it overgrows its pot.

- **Netted iris** (Iris reticulata): With its green stalks and purple flowers, the Netted iris is a wonderful specimen for garden trays. They are delightful because they are colorful and fragrant. They grow in rock trays or gravel gardens. The iris needs full sun or partial shade. Propagate this plant using offsets. Repot the plant during the spring if needed. Feed the plant every other week at most, and keep the soil moist.

- **Cacti:** Cacti and succulents are great for tabletop gardens because they are the most recognizable,

interesting, and unique plants around. Everyone will recognize these tabletop indoor houseplants as some form of the cacti species. Cacti are the easiest houseplants to grow because they grow in bright sunlight with very little water. They do not need soil, will survive in sand and rocks, and go for extended periods without any water.

o **Window plant** *(Haworthia cymbiformis)*: In direct sunlight, this cactus plant will grow into short, balloon-like succulent leaves. The window plant appreciates shade and a little more water than its cacti counterparts. The leaves seem to glow from the inside while sitting under the sun. This plant is propagated using side rosettes or offsets. Feed the plant monthly. Repotting is necessary every spring using cactus soil.

o **Black Prince** *(Echeveria)*: The black prince grows in full sun and reaches a height of 6 inches. The flower looks like a two-dimensional rose and is dark red or scarlet in color. It is an ideal container plant and survives well on tabletops or windows because it takes up little space. It needs normal room temperatures and should not be subjected to cold or frost. Feed this plant with weak fertilizer monthly. Propagate using leaf cuttings. Repotting is necessary if the plant becomes pot bound. Keep the soil moist.

o **Blue Cereus** *(Stenocereus pruinosus)*: This is an expensive and exotic cactus that needs full sun. It is a tall blue plant that has the potential to grow between 10 and 20 feet tall, but inside of a container the plant will grow especially slow. Like traditional desert cacti, the blue cereus has prickly spines. Propagate through

woody stem cuttings, and keep this plant evenly moist. Feed a weak mixture every month, and repot only if it becomes pot bound. This plant needs partial sun.

o **Bunny ears** *(Opuntia microdasys)*: Bunny ears are named for their round pads that call to mind the floppy ears of a bunny. They grow in full sun, and although they can reach heights of 3 feet, they spread wide 6 feet across. In containers, however, the growth potential of succulents is thwarted because the roots are not encouraged to grow fast or wide inside of a shallow dish. Among the many cacti recommended for container growing, bunny ears are the most recommended and among the most popular container plants because they are cute and add a fun, creative element to a living space. Propagate from woody stem cuttings. Repot this plant if it becomes pot bound. Keep the soil moist, and feed this plant every month.

Appendix A

This section represents plants that are not your typical "garden variety" houseplants. These plants are rare, and some only will grow in special facilities. One growing suggestion for those growing rare varieties to is to keep their original habitats in mind and mimic those environments as best possible.

The following rare plants are listed in alphabetical order. From A-Z, these rare plants are difficult to find in typical gardening centers, but often are available during certain seasons from on-line retailers:

A

- **Actiniopteris** (*Actiniopteris australis*): This is a fern genus found in tropical Asia and Africa that needs sun and shade all year long while situated in room temperature and humidity. Every month, this plant needs fertilizer, soft water, and a good drainage system. Repot this plant if it becomes pot bound. Propagate using spores or division.

- **Aerangis** *(Aerangis fastuosa)*: A member of the orchid family, this is an attractive plant with light green leaves and white, three-pronged flowers that bloom in spring. The plant likes bright, but not full, sun and should be kept in a greenhouse in possible; it thrives with humidity and its winter threshold is 59 degrees. Feed this plant weekly during the summer. Propagation is difficult in most cases, so it is not recommended. Repot the plant if its roots become compact in limited soil. Water to keep the soil moist.

- **Apache beggarticks** *(Bidens ferulifolia)*: A member of the aster family and accustomed to Southern temperatures, this native Mexican flower needs plenty of sun, warmth, and water. It flowers in the summer through the end of fall with bright yellow flowers on long, thin stems. Feed this plant weekly, and propagate from tip cuttings. Repot only if it overgrows its pot.

- **Aztec lily** *(Sprekelia formosissima)*: This delicate red flowering plant blooms in spring, prefers light to partial shade all year round and happily spends its summers outdoors. It needs generous moisture during the summer, but once summer ends and throughout the winter, it will need less water. Its minimum winter temperatures are in the 55- to 60-degree range. This plant requires weekly fertilizing, and you can propagate it through side bulbs. Repotting is necessary as it grows out of its current container.

B

- **Barrel bottle tree** *(Brachychiton rupistris)*: Australia is the natural habitat for this member of the cacao family. It

needs light sun and warmth but tolerates cool winter air with a cold air threshold of 54 degrees. This plant needs consistent watering but will not react well to overwatering. Propagate this plant through tip cuttings or by seed, and repot the plant only if it becomes pot bound. Feed the plant every two weeks during the summer months only.

- **Barren strawberry** or **Indian strawberry** *(Duchesnea indica)*: This rose plant blooms in the early summer to fall, but its fruit lacks taste. It must stay hydrated during the summer and kept dry during the winter. It likes a light room, but not bright sunlight. This plant rests in winter and is best kept above 50 degrees during its winter rest period. Its native habitat is East Asia and India. Feed this plant one time per week, and repot it if it becomes pot bound. Propagate through rooted runners or use seeds.

- **Bertolonia** *(Bertolonia houtteana)*: This plant's native habitat is Brazil; it seldom blooms anywhere other than in its natural habitat. It likes light and warmth or partial shade and warmth all year round. Its cold threshold is 73 degrees. It needs plenty of warm and humid conditions to grow its pink and green, veiny leaves. Fertilize this plant monthly, and repot it only if it becomes pot bound. Propagate by tip cuttings.

C

- **Carob tree** *(Ceratonia Siliqua)*: The carob tree's natural habitat is the Mediterranean. It flowers in the early summer through the fall. Its fruits are used to make artificial, or carob, coffee. This plant needs sunlight and partial shade

during the summer months. It likes the outdoors and needs to be kept warm. It will tolerate days during the winter months, but prefers warmer temperatures. Feed this plant once a month or less, and repot the plant in the spring if it becomes too large for its container. Propagate by seed. Keep the soil evenly moist.

- **Common caper** *(Capparis spinosa)*: The caper grows in well-drained soil and hot, sunny windows. The ethereal mustard oil in this bush is the same active ingredient in mustard, horseradish, and cress. Withered buds can be preserved in vinegar or oil as long as they are not crushed. This will maximize the plant's fragrant aromas. The caper's original habitat is Southern Europe and the Middle East where it grows in the cracks of walls and on the side of buildings. When cultivated, it grows best in full sun and can be grown in stones and water. It needs to be watered sparingly and fertilized once every two or three months. Propagate through tip cuttings, and repot minimally.

- **Crown-of-thorns** *(Euphoribia milii)*: This plant is a relative of the poinsettia. Its winter blooms of red, pink, or yellow are attention getters. This dense, shrubby plant needs to grow in a windowsill for full sun, and should be planted in a 6- to 8-inch pot. The soil should be evenly moist all year, and careful attention must be paid to its water needs during the fall while it prepares for winter bloom and is thirstier. This plant has thick, green leaves that should not be watered, and the plant should not be left in temperatures below 60 degrees. Feed this plant regularly, about once a week. Repot this plant every two years using cactus soil, and propagate by tip cuttings.

G

- **Gardenia** *(Gardenia augusta)*: Gardenias are not rare plants; however they are not the easiest plants to grow indoors. This is an acid-loving shrub with waxy, white, flagrant flowers. It survives in indirect sunlight and grows to be 18 inches tall, but this plant cannot be subjected to drafts because it will lose its buds. The soil mix must remain moist from the spring through autumn using soft water or rainwater. In order for the flowers to grow, the plant needs high humidity and must be kept on a tray of moistened pebbles that gets misted frequently. Feed this plant every other week using a nonalkaline fertilizer. You can repot the plant when it becomes pot bound. To propagate, do so from tip cuttings during the fall or spring.

H

- **Hairy zygopetalum** *(Zygopetalum crinitum)*: This is an orchid that needs to be fertilized every two weeks from spring to fall. This plant likes light to partial shade and humid locations that do not fall below 60 degrees. Keep the plant's soil moist, and repot if it becomes pot bound. Propagate by separating off the leaves.

J

- **Japanese shield fern** *(Dryopteris erythrosora)*: This plant's native lands are China and Japan. It is grown in well-lit spaces but does not like direct sunlight. This plant is rarely seen inside of homes, although it is a good houseplant. It needs soil made of humus that drains well. This plant must

be catered to because this plant thrives when consistently moist. Propagate this plant through division of the root ball. Feed the plant every other week, and repot only if the plant becomes pot bound.

L

- **Lace flower** *(Alsobia dianthiflora)*: This plant vines and makes an excellent hanging plant. It does not require a full sun and does well in partial shade and room temperatures that are warm all year round. During its summer growth period, this Mexican and Costa Rican native does best when fertilized every two weeks. It also likes high humidity. This plant needs moderate moisture. Repot it if it becomes pot bound. Propagate through cuttings.

M

- **Moses-in-a-boat** *(Rhoea spathacea)*: This is a new variety of the other Moses-in-a-boat plant described in Chapter 3. This plant has striped multicolor red, green, and yellow leaves. This dwarf plant is from Mexico and will not grow taller than 14 inches. Like the other version, this Moses plant has little white flowers enclosed in boat-shaped beads. The flowers are nestled inside of the floppy leaves. This slow grower eventually becomes a bushy plant. The leaves of this plant will not tolerate water, but overall the plant will grow in environments with low light. Feed this plant weekly, and repot if it becomes pot bound. Propagate this plant through seed or from stem cuttings.

- **Mosaic plant** *(Fittonia vershaffltii)*: This is a nice windowsill plant, but it is not very popular. Its natural habitat is Peru, and it grows to be 2 feet tall and wide but fits well in a hanging basket. The foliage of this plant are like small mosaics, and this plant's roots like small tight spaces so it is best situated in a small container and left still until its roots begin to grow out of the drainage holes. Repot this plant if it becomes pot bound, and feed it every two to three weeks. This plant prefers light shade. Propagate by dividing the root ball. Keep the soil moist throughout the year.

N

- **New Zealand karaka nut** *(Corynocarpus Laevigatus)*: The seeds of this plant are extremely poisonous. It originated in New Zealand and thrives in sunny, humid conditions all year round. In the winter, it can be maintained at temperatures between 37 degrees and 57 degrees as long as it does not get left outdoors in temperatures below freezing. It must be kept moderately moist and fertilized and every week in the summer and also must be kept moderately moist during the winter. Propagate this plant by cutting the tips. Repotting is necessary if it overgrows the container.

P

- **Palm grass** *(Setaria palmifolia)*: This is an attractive plant that primarily grows in tropical Asia. Its flowers seldom bloom under cultivation, but this is an attractive palm with deep green long leaves. It needs to grow in light and at room temperature throughout the year. It needs little

moisture and must be fertilized every two weeks in the summer. It is recommended that the plant be repotted in the spring with soil that is rich in lime. Propagate this plant by separating the side shoots.

- **Peanut, groundnut** *(Arachis hypogae)*: A member of the bean family with a Brazilian natural habitat, the peanut plant flowers in the summer and likes sunshine and outdoor air. Keep it near a window you often leave open, or place outside a few hours a day during the summer. This plant needs a good drainage system because it does not tolerate excessive moisture. It should be potted in the early spring in temperatures that hover at or below 68 degrees. Fertilize this plant every two weeks, and propagate from seeds. Repot in the early spring.

- **Persian shield plant** *(Strobilanthes dyerianus)*: The purple-green colors of the Persian's foliage make this a unique plant that complements desks and tables. It reaches as tall as 30 inches and needs to be grown in a temperate climate with bright but indirect light. It does rest a little in the winter months but needs to remain evenly moist in the spring through autumn months. Feed this plant every two weeks lightly, and repot it in the spring if it overgrows its pot. Propagate through softwood cuttings.

- **Ponytail palm** *(Nolina recurvata)*: The "ponytail palm" is really not a palm at all. It is a member of the lily family, and is known by several names. It has earned the name "elephant's foot" because of its bulbous base. Because of its base and thin trunk, some people call it a bottle palm. It is a native of the Mexican desert, and in the wild, it

grows into a large tree. The soil mix must remain moist from spring to water, and in the winter, it only needs enough water to keep the soil from drying out. The flask-shaped trunk at the base is the plant's water storage unit so the plant copes well with occasional neglect. It grows to heights of 6 and 7 feet and needs direct sunlight with minimum winter temps of 50 degrees. Plants that grow tall and wide can always be pruned so that their leaves do not compromise the living space of its caregivers. Feed this plant lightly once a week. Repot if it becomes pot bound, and propagate from seed.

- **Purple false** or **purplespot eranthemum** (*Pseuderanthemum atroppurpureum*): This plant, originally from Polynesia, is a vertical plant that grows between 12 and 18 inches tall. Its foliage is green, purple, and white; it grows in bright light and wet soil. It is considered an aquarium plant and tolerates wet conditions. It is not recommended to buy a purple false until it has matured or reached its maximum growing heights of 12 to 18 inches because the young sprouts tend to wither and die when left to dry. This plant also needs to start in an acidic growing medium or an acidic soil. A professional nursery would best care for these plants until they are old and strong enough for novice gardeners. Fertilize lightly during the growing season. Repot this plant if it becomes pot bound, and propagate from cuttings.

R

- **Redflame** (*Hemigraphis reptans*): This member of the Acanthus family blooms tiny white flowers in the spring

and enjoys sunny living spaces. It is a long, vine-like, bushy plant with thin leaves, and it is well suited for hanging baskets. It grows in small containers, needs plenty of water, and can be grown in a watery fountain or terrarium. Feed this plant every two weeks, and repot it annually. Propagate through tip cuttings.

- **Rose of Jericho** (*Anastatica Hierochuntica*): This plant's natural habitat ranges from Morocco to southern Iran. This plant grows in water and the dry, rolled up leaves, once moistened, will open and turn green. It flowers in midsummer but should be allowed to go dormant for a period. This plant needs partial sun and should be fed lightly every other week. Repot if it becomes too large for its container, and propagate from seed.

- **Ruellia colorata** (*Acanthaceae Rellia*): This thick-leaved, grassy-looking plant grows slowly and is considered an unusual plant because its bracts produce red colorful flowers at Christmas. Its leaves are spear shaped, and the plant grows to heights of 14 inches. This is an interesting plant with deep green leaves and a grassy and bushy appearance that will produce red flowers that remain for several months from the late fall through the spring. This South American plant loves full sun and warmth but also grows in semi-shaded environments. Keep the soil moist, and repot if the plant overgrows its pot. Feed this plant every two weeks during the growing season, and propagate by dividing the root ball.

S

- **Saguaro cactus** *(Carnegiea gigantea)*: The original habitat of this cactus is Central and South America. It is a blooming, but extremely slow-growing, plant that has come to symbolize the American Southwest desert. Typically, this cactus takes more than seven years to be 2 inches tall. The large cacti found in the desert areas are plants that have been there for more than 200 years. The Saguaro cactus tolerates sunny and cool winter conditions, not below 40 degrees, needs very little water, and even less fertilizer during the summer months. It does not require water during winters. Propagate this plant from seed, and repot if it becomes too large for its container.

- **Sophronitis** *(Sophronitis floralia)*: This plant needs plenty of warmth and light during its blooming period, and when the plant is dormant, it needs to rest in dry, dark, and cool conditions, no lower than 63 degrees. Its natural habitat is Brazil, and it cannot dry out, even during its resting period. Feed this plant every two to three months, and repot it if it overgrows the container. Propagate this plant by division.

- **Spear lily** *(Doryanthes palmieri)*: A member of the agave family that has a native habitat in Australia, the spear lily likes full sun and being kept outdoors during winter. Its soil must be moistened well during the summer and fertilized every two weeks. This is a flowering plant, but like many plants removed from its natural habitat, for some unknown reason, the flowers will not grow in

cultivation. Propagate this plant using shoots, and repot the plant in the spring if it outgrows its container.

- **Sundew** *(Drosera dielsiana)*: This plant grows all over the world but primarily is found in humid and bright greenhouses or terrariums. This plant has a web-like appearance covering the leaves. The leaves are edged in brown and are green in the center. The plant is a low-growing bushy plant. This insect-devouring plant needs to be moist all of the time and prefers water free of chemicals and excess minerals. The plant does not require any fertilizer because it eats insects. Repotting is not necessary unless it overgrows its pot. Propagate by seed.

V

- **Venus flytrap** *(Dionaea muscipula)*: This carnivorous plant's natural habitat is North America, and it survives best in conditions similar to its natural habitat. It likes humid conditions, and in the summer it enjoys being outdoors in cool, shaded areas. The Venus flytrap tolerates moderate winters at temperatures that do not fall below 41 degrees. This plant requires moist soil, and you should fertilize sparingly just one time per month in the summer. Propagate by division, and repot if it outgrows its container.

- **Vase plant** *(Aechmea calyculata)*: The vase plant needs partial shade or bright, indirect light but tolerates shaded areas well. The soil should be allowed to dry between waterings. Temperatures should not fall below 50 degrees at night. Although it can tolerate cold temperatures of 40 degrees for extended periods, the plant will not grow in those

temperatures or will only grow slightly. The vase plant has long, pointed leaves that grow to be 12 inches, and bright, yellow flowers bloom from its center. Propagate this plant through offshoots, and lightly feed it every other week. Repot this plant if its soil becomes too compact with roots.

W

- **Wild petunia** *(Ruellia colorata)*: This thick-leaved, grassy-looking plant grows slowly and is considered an unusual plant because its bracts produce red colorful flowers at Christmas. Its leaves are spear shaped and the plant grows to heights of 14 inches. This is an interesting plant with deep green leaves and a grassy and bushy appearance that will produce red flowers that remain for several months from the late fall through the spring. This South American plant loves full sun and warmth but also grows in semi-shaded environments. Keep the soil moist for this plant, and feed it every month. Propagate from dividing the root ball, and repot the plant if it outgrows its container.

Z

- **ZZ plant** *(Zamioculcus zamifola)*: This East African plant is a rare find, but easy to cultivate. The plant's light green leaves extend upward in a thin, fern-like display. It likes somewhat dry soil and will survive in shaded areas. To propagate, use leaf cuttings. Feed this plant monthly, and repot if it is pot bound.

Glossary

areoles: the specialized buds where spines and new stems grow

axils: tiny folds in a leaf that hold water and aquatic life where other animals grow

cachepot: decorative pots that can hold plainer pots that allow drainage

chloroplasts: the cells found inside plant leaves that absorb and change light into energy during photosynthesis

compost: decayed material used to condition the soil

corms: similar to bulbs and tubers, they store food for the plant in order to help it grow

deep shade: lighting conditions typically associated with forest growing conditions where large foliage blocks out the sun

drenching: a watering procedure that requires gardeners to thoroughly water plants two or three times with clean, lukewarm water, allowing 30 minutes in between each watering

epiphytes: plants that live on other plants

ergonomics: the science of designing and arranging objects, such as desks and chairs, so the people who use them are as comfortable as possible

grafting: a propagation method that involves removing one part of a plant and attaching it to another plant

growth period: a time when the plant experiences a growth spurt

insectivore: a plant that eats insects

interiorscaping: the art of using plants to design aesthetically pleasing spaces

node: the place where leaves attach to the stems

offsets: new plant parts taken from an original plant that are placed into the soil for new growth

peat moss: a component of potting soil that has its pH fine tuned with ground limestone so the pH balances out at 7

photosynthesis: the process a plant uses to feed itself using the sun and water

pot bound: when a plant's roots become cramped and jammed inside of a pot

rooting mix: a soil mixture of two parts potting soil, two parts peat moss, and one part vermiculite

rooting powder: a product that accelerates root growth by stimulating plant hormones

runner: a stem that grows alongside a plant

seedlings: plants grown from a seed

spathes: tube-like growths that develop inside a flower

sphagnum: a peat moss that is compacted with stringy and fibrous content from other plant debris

systemic pesticides: pesticides that are placed into the soil and are absorbed into the plant's system

terrarium: a large glass house for a plant, similar to a fish tank

trailing plant: a plant that has vines like ivy and eventually, trails long enough to wrap around poles placed in the soil

training: using wire or another object to wrap the stem and leaves around a pole until the plant learns to grow upright without assistance

vegetative propagation: making new plants from existing plant parts

Bibliography

Accents for Home and Garden. March 28, 2011.
www.accentsforhomeandgarden.com.

Beginner Gardening. March 28, 2011.
www.beginner-gardening.com.

Eartheasy.com ~ Solutions for Sustainable Living. March 28,
2011. **http://eartheasy.com**.

The Happy Gardener — Garden Direct Sales Company.
March 28, 2011. **www.thehappygardener.info**.

Indoor Gardening Supplies. March 28, 2011.
www.indoorgardensupplies.com.

Jantra, Ingrid, and Ursula Kruger. *The Houseplant Encyclopedia*.
Richmond Hill, Ontario: Firefly, 2006.

Plant Delights Nursery Inc. March 28, 2011.
www.plantdelights.com.

Plantcontainers.com. March 28, 2011. **www.plantcontainers.com**.

Pleasant, Barbara. *The Complete Houseplant Survival Manual: Essential Know-how for Keeping (not Killing) More than 160 Indoor Plants.* North Adams, Massachusetts: Storey Publishing, 2005.

Whitman, Ann and Suzanne DeJohn. *Organic Gardening for Dummies,* Second Edition. Indianapolis, Indiana: Wiley Publishing, 2009.

Author Biography

Sandy Baker is a published author of several financial books, including, *Your Complete Guide to Early Retirement: A Step By Step Plan for Making It Happen* and *The Complete Guide to Planning Your Estate: A Step By Step Plan to Protect Your Assets, Limit Your Taxes and Ensure Your Wishes Are Fulfilled.* She also is passionate about growing, focusing most of her attention on organic lawn and houseplant care.

After years of navigating gardening in a traditional sense, Baker has created a step-by-step process used in her own lawn in Ohio. She incorporates many of the same concepts in her houseplant care. As someone who is passionate about healthy environments and taking steps to protect the Earth, Baker makes organic lawn care one of her constant studies.

Sandy Baker is a mother of three and wife to an ever-supportive husband. She has provided freelance writing for the last six years full time and writes about topics she finds fascinating.

Author Biography

Sandy Baker is a published author of several financial books, including, *Your Complete Guide to Early Retirement: A Step By Step Plan for Making It Happen* and *The Complete Guide to Planning Your Estate: A Step By Step Plan to Protect Your Assets, Limit Your Taxes and Ensure Your Wishes Are Fulfilled*. She also is passionate about growing, focusing most of her attention on organic lawn and houseplant care.

After years of navigating gardening in a traditional sense, Baker has created a step-by-step process used in her own lawn in Ohio. She incorporates many of the same concepts in her houseplant care. As someone who is passionate about healthy environments and taking steps to protect the Earth, Baker makes organic lawn care one of her constant studies.

Sandy Baker is a mother of three and wife to an ever-supportive husband. She has provided freelance writing for the last six years full time and writes about topics she finds fascinating.

Index